In 2015, more than one million refugees arrived in Europe (and at least three thousand three hundred and seventy five people died along the way).

Of that great mass of humanity, a few thousand people washed up in Calais, France, trying to attempt the dangerous crossing to England. This is a very small part of their story.

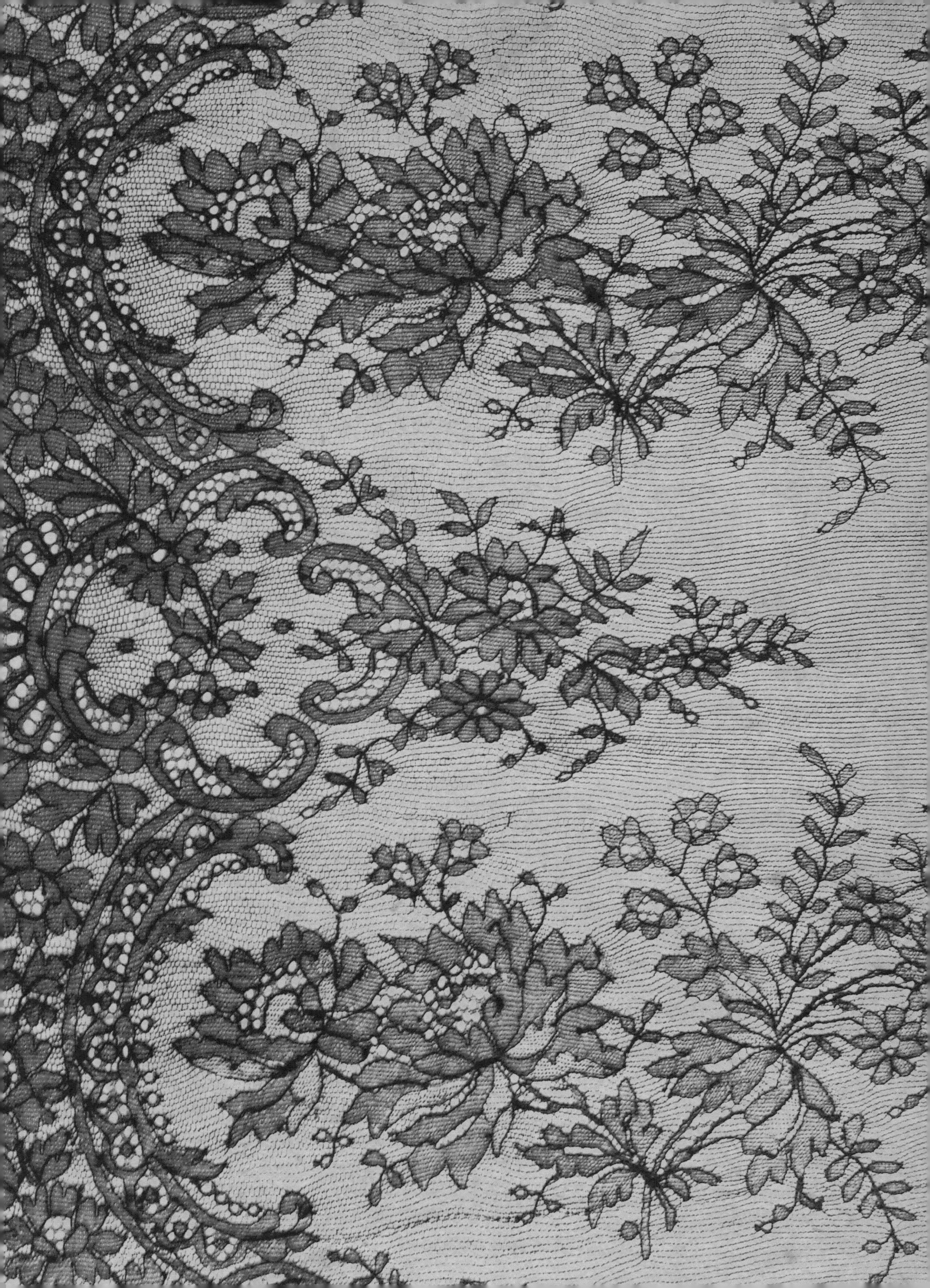

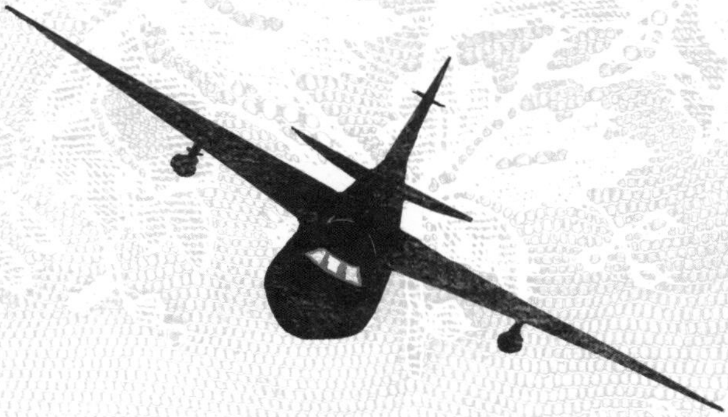

THREADS

FROM THE REFUGEE CRISIS

KATE EVANS

VERSO

Winner of the John C. Laurence Award
THE SOCIETY OF AUTHORS GRANTS
the Society of Authors' Authors' Foundation

First published by Verso 2017

1 3 5 7 9 10 8 6 4 2

Photo credits
p. 156: "Hoshyar's shelter" Pascal Rossignol
pp. 156-7: "Tear gas in street" Rowan Farrell

Verso

UK: 6 Meard Street, London W1F 0EG
US: 20 Jay Street, Suite 1010, Brooklyn, NY 11201
versobooks.com

Verso is the imprint of New Left Books

ISBN-13: 978-1-78663-173-2
eISBN-13: 978-1-78663-176-3 (US)
eISBN-13: 978-1-78663-175-6 (UK)

British Library Cataloguing in Publication Data
A catalogue record for this book is available from the British Library

Library of Congress Cataloging-in-Publication Data
A catalog record for this book is available from the Library of Congress

Printed in the UK by CPI Mackays

Thanks, and love, to Sue, Kate B., Mary, Ollie, Angie, Roo, Jo, Grainne, Hettie, Éamonn, Jape, Rowan, Hazel, Gaetan, Candida, Corinne, Linda, Lynne, Nadine, Rachel T., Andy H., Andy P., Rowan, Sarah, John, Federico, Taban, Suhan, Tom, Mipsie, Rosie, Adam, Alice, Matthew, my lovely wife Donach, and all the other people whose stories I have borrowed, but whose names I have concealed.

Contents

To protect some of the people described in this book their identities have been altered and some characters have been conflated.

But everything you are about to read really happened.

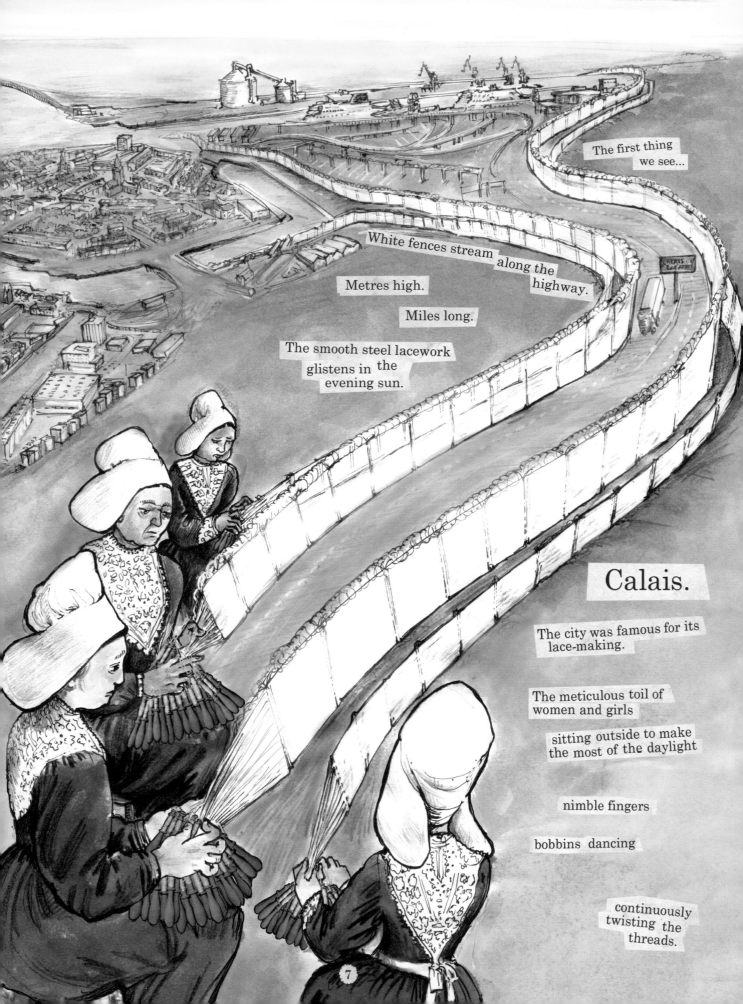

The first thing we see...

White fences stream along the highway.

Metres high.

Miles long.

The smooth steel lacework glistens in the evening sun.

Calais.

The city was famous for its lace-making.

The meticulous toil of women and girls

sitting outside to make the most of the daylight

nimble fingers

bobbins dancing

continuously twisting the threads.

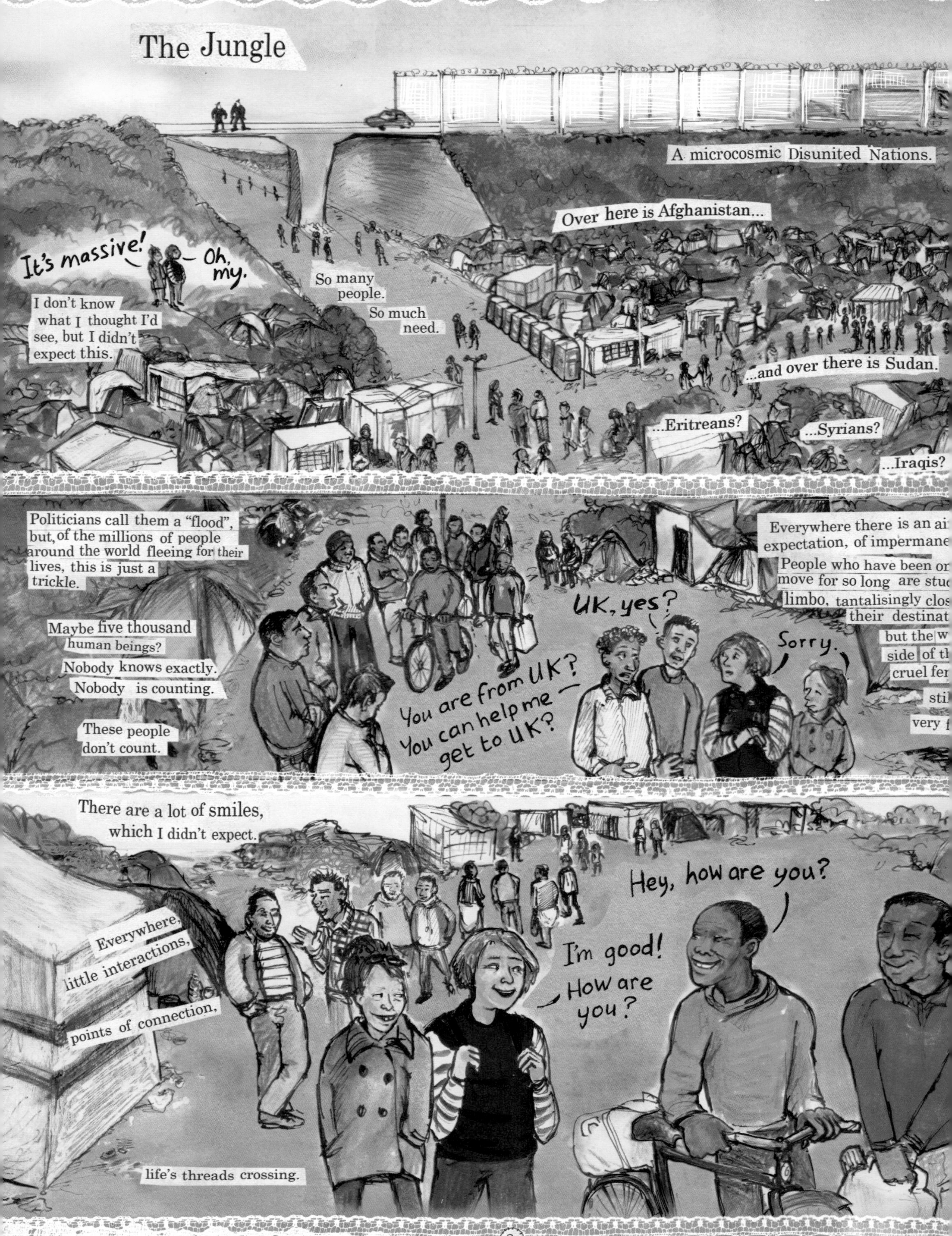

The Jungle
A microcosmic Disunited Nations.
Over here is Afghanistan...
It's massive!
Oh, my.
So many people.
So much need.
I don't know what I thought I'd see, but I didn't expect this.
...and over there is Sudan.
...Eritreans?
...Syrians?
...Iraqis?
Politicians call them a "flood", but, of the millions of people around the world fleeing for their lives, this is just a trickle.
Maybe five thousand human beings?
Nobody knows exactly.
Nobody is counting.
These people don't count.
Everywhere there is an ai
expectation, of impermane
People who have been or
move for so long are stu
limbo, tantalisingly clos
their destinat
but the w
side of th
cruel fer
sti
very
UK, yes?
Sorry.
You are from UK?
You can help me get to UK?
There are a lot of smiles, which I didn't expect.
Hey, how are you?
I'm good! How are you?
Everywhere,
little interactions,
points of connection,
life's threads crossing.

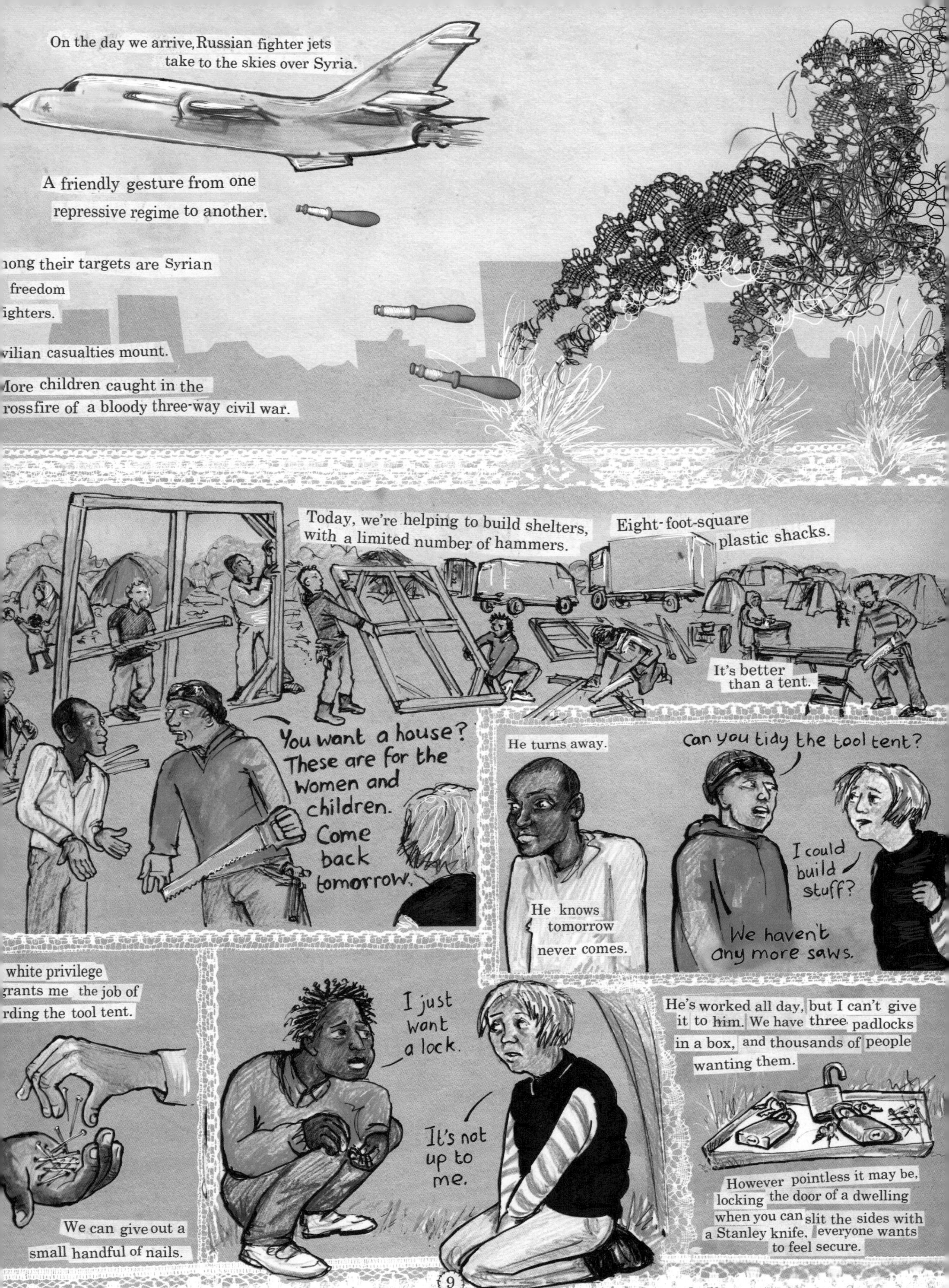
On the day we arrive, Russian fighter jets take to the skies over Syria.
A friendly gesture from one repressive regime to another.
nong their targets are Syrian freedom ighters.
vilian casualties mount.
More children caught in the rossfire of a bloody three-way civil war.
Today, we're helping to build shelters, with a limited number of hammers.
Eight-foot-square plastic shacks.
It's better than a tent.
You want a house? These are for the women and children. Come back tomorrow.
He turns away.
He knows tomorrow never comes.
Can you tidy the tool tent?
I could build stuff?
We haven't any more saws.
white privilege rants me the job of rding the tool tent.
We can give out a small handful of nails.
I just want a lock.
It's not up to me.
He's worked all day, but I can't give it to him. We have three padlocks in a box, and thousands of people wanting them.
However pointless it may be, locking the door of a dwelling when you can slit the sides with a Stanley knife, everyone wants to feel secure.

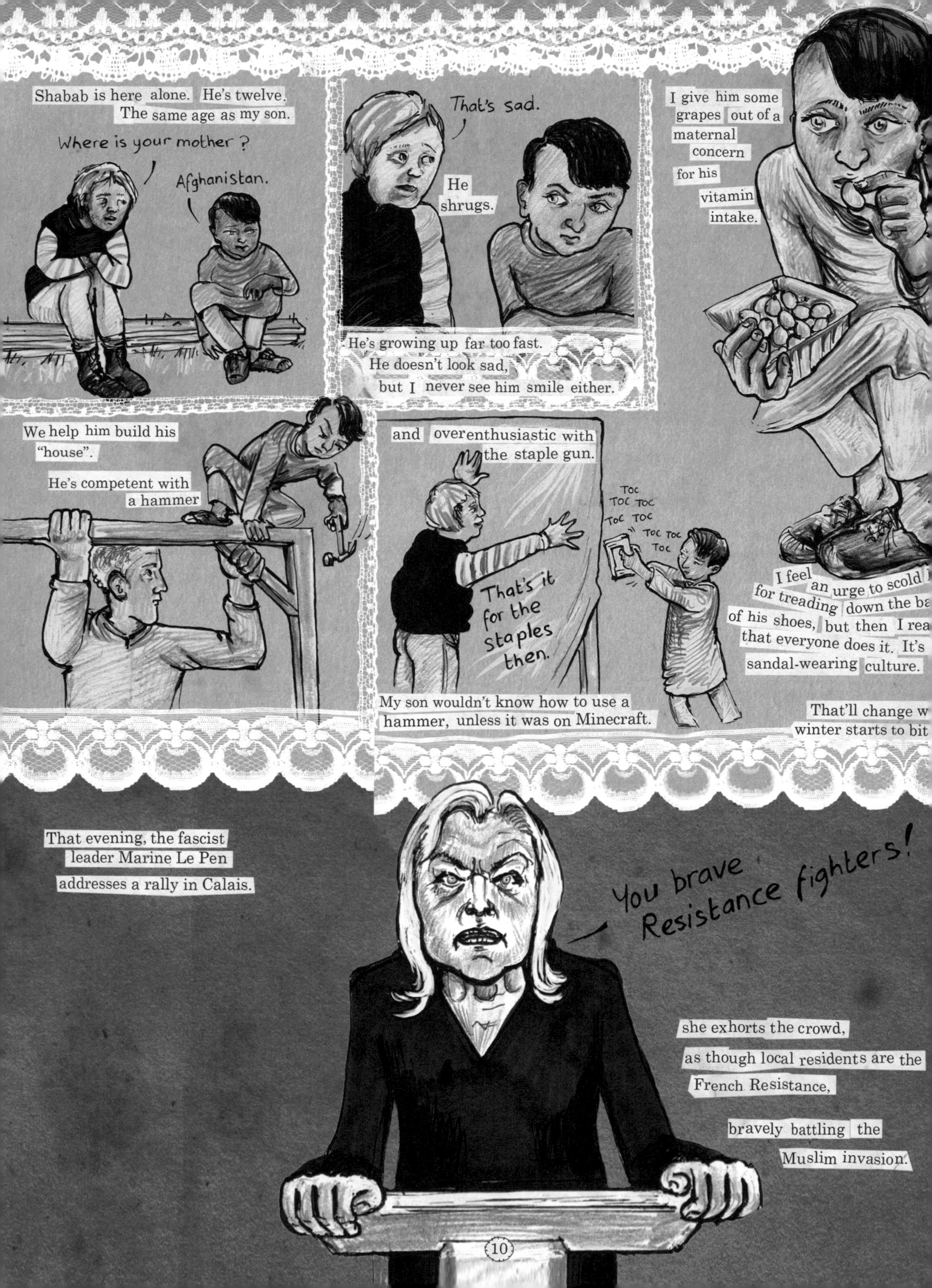

Shabab is here alone. He's twelve. The same age as my son.
Where is your mother?
Afghanistan.
That's sad.
He shrugs.
He's growing up far too fast. He doesn't look sad, but I never see him smile either.
I give him some grapes out of a maternal concern for his vitamin intake.
We help him build his "house".
He's competent with a hammer
and overenthusiastic with the staple gun.
TOC TOC TOC TOC TOC TOC TOC TOC
That's it for the staples then.
My son wouldn't know how to use a hammer, unless it was on Minecraft.
I feel an urge to scold
for treading down the ba
of his shoes, but then I rea
that everyone does it. It's
sandal-wearing culture.
That'll change w
winter starts to bit
That evening, the fascist leader Marine Le Pen addresses a rally in Calais.
You brave Resistance fighters!
she exhorts the crowd, as though local residents are the French Resistance, bravely battling the Muslim invasion.

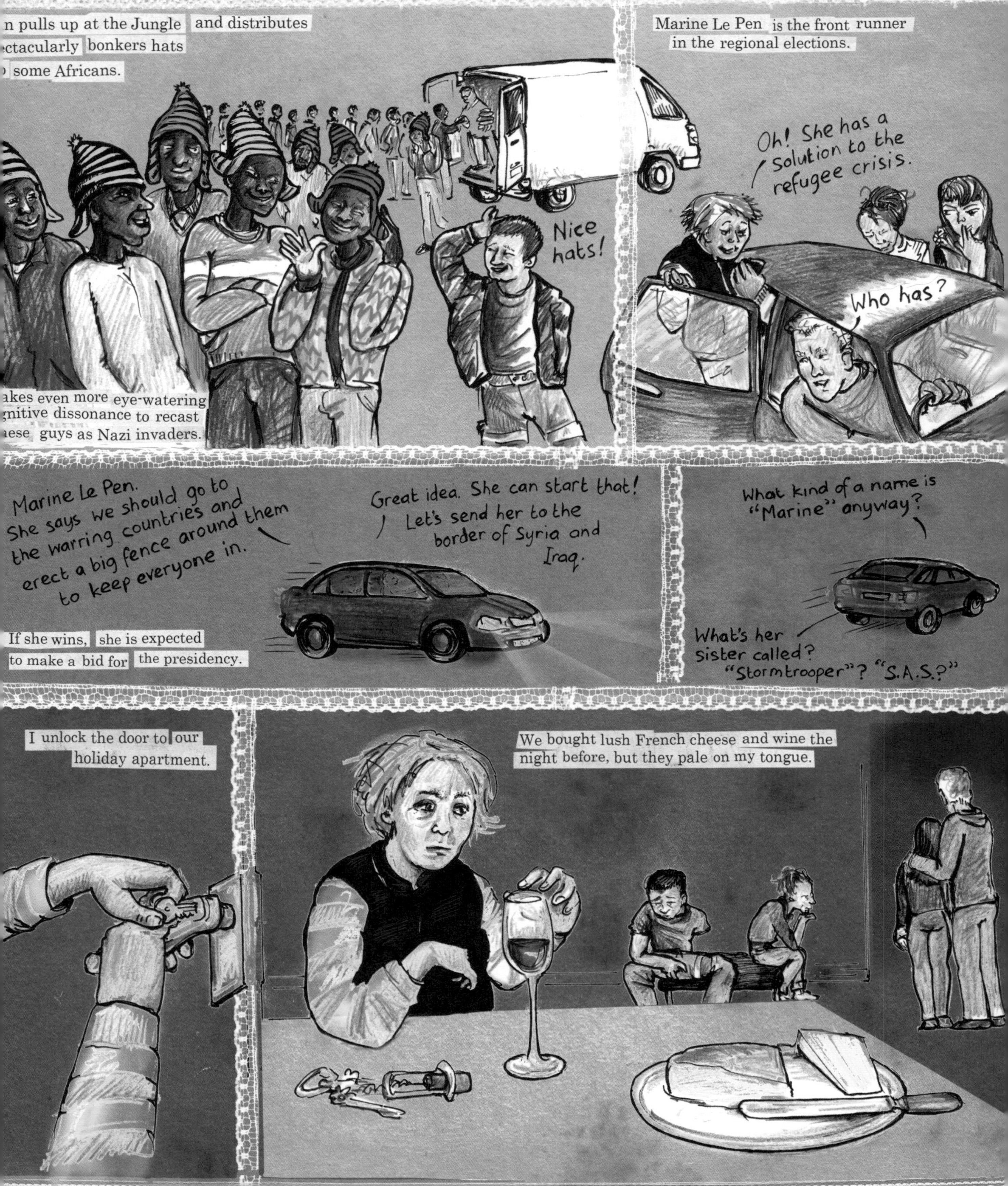

n pulls up at the Jungle and distributes
ectacularly bonkers hats
o some Africans.
Nice hats!
akes even more eye-watering
gnitive dissonance to recast
hese guys as Nazi invaders.
Marine Le Pen is the front runner
in the regional elections.
Oh! She has a solution to the refugee crisis.
Who has?
Marine Le Pen. She says we should go to the warring countries and erect a big fence around them to keep everyone in.
Great idea. She can start that! Let's send her to the border of Syria and Iraq.
If she wins, she is expected
to make a bid for the presidency.
What kind of a name is "Marine" anyway?
What's her sister called? "Stormtrooper"? "S.A.S.?"
I unlock the door to our
holiday apartment.
We bought lush French cheese and wine the
night before, but they pale on my tongue.

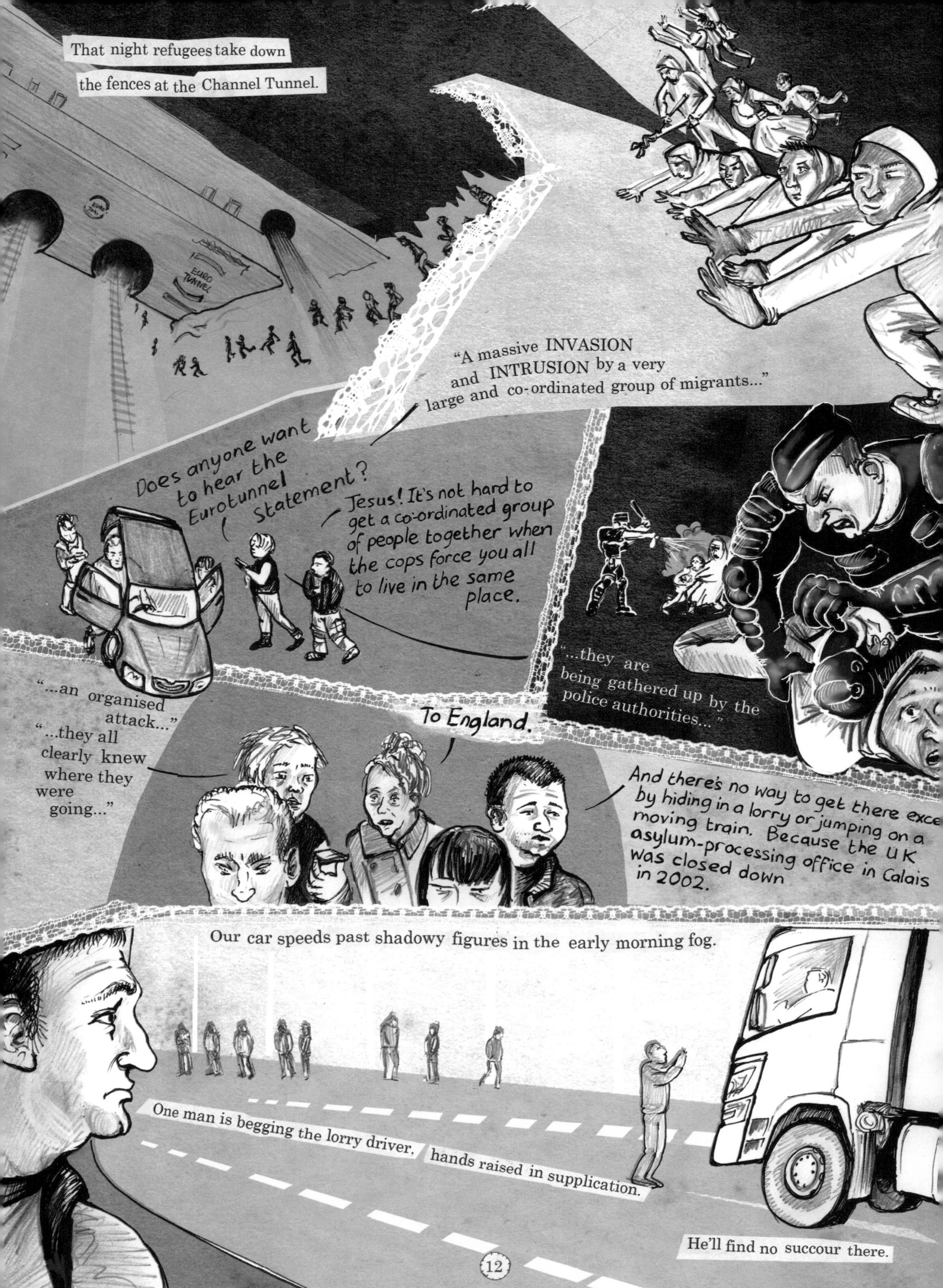
That night refugees take down the fences at the Channel Tunnel.
EURO TUNNEL
"A massive INVASION and INTRUSION by a very large and co-ordinated group of migrants..."
Does anyone want to hear the Eurotunnel Statement?
Jesus! It's not hard to get a co-ordinated group of people together when the cops force you all to live in the same place.
"...they are being gathered up by the police authorities..."
"...an organised attack..."
"...they all clearly knew where they were going..."
To England.
And there's no way to get there exce by hiding in a lorry or jumping on a moving train. Because the UK asylum-processing office in Calais was closed down in 2002.
Our car speeds past shadowy figures in the early morning fog.
One man is begging the lorry driver, hands raised in supplication.
He'll find no succour there.

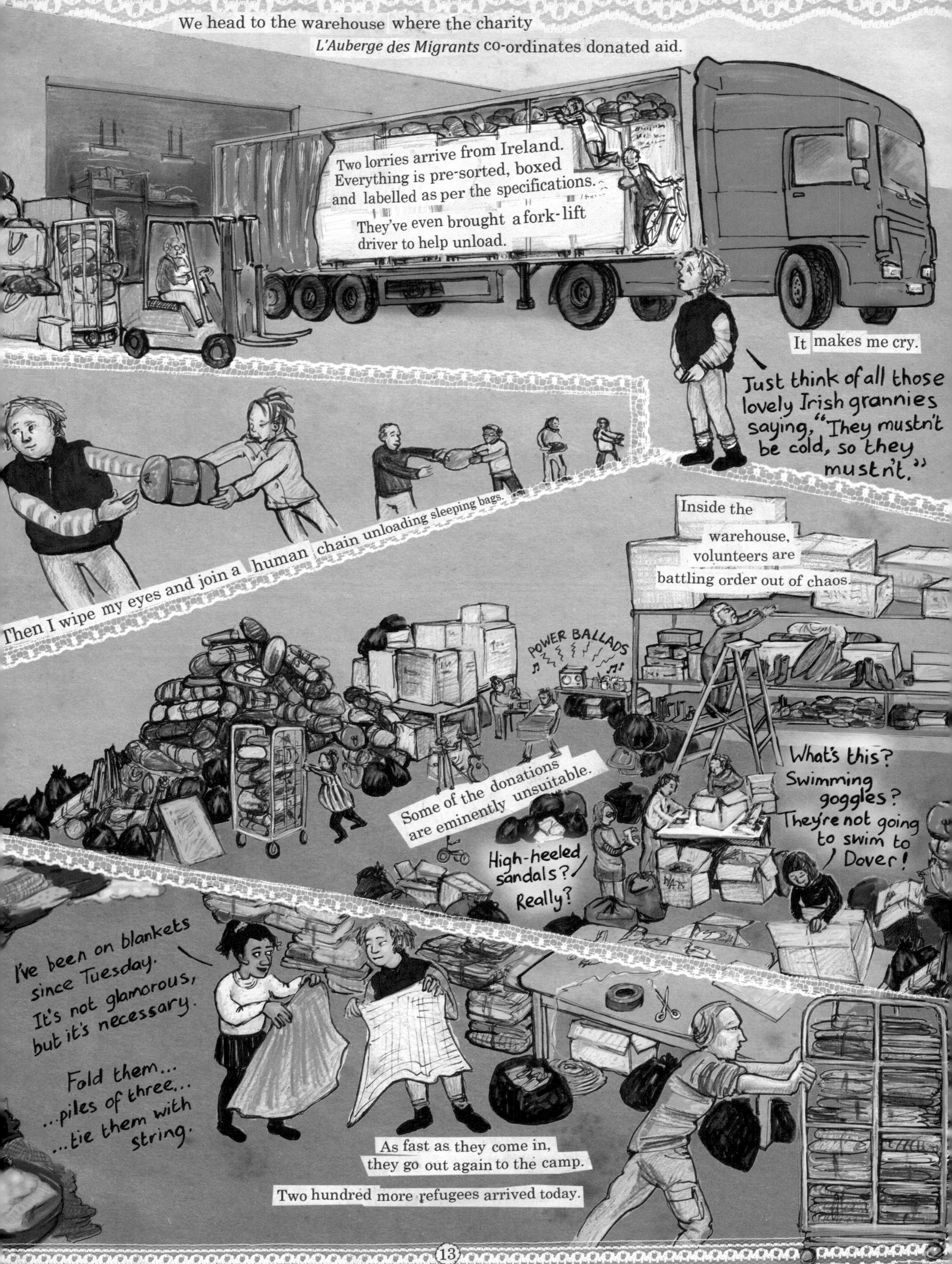

We head to the warehouse where the charity
L'Auberge des Migrants co-ordinates donated aid.
Two lorries arrive from Ireland. Everything is pre-sorted, boxed and labelled as per the specifications.
They've even brought a fork-lift driver to help unload.
It makes me cry.
Just think of all those lovely Irish grannies saying, "They mustn't be cold, so they mustn't."
Then I wipe my eyes and join a human chain unloading sleeping bags.
Inside the warehouse, volunteers are battling order out of chaos.
POWER BALLADS
Some of the donations are eminently unsuitable.
What's this? Swimming goggles? They're not going to swim to Dover!
High-heeled sandals? Really?
I've been on blankets since Tuesday. It's not glamorous, but it's necessary.
Fold them... ...piles of three... ...tie them with string.
As fast as they come in, they go out again to the camp.
Two hundred more refugees arrived today.

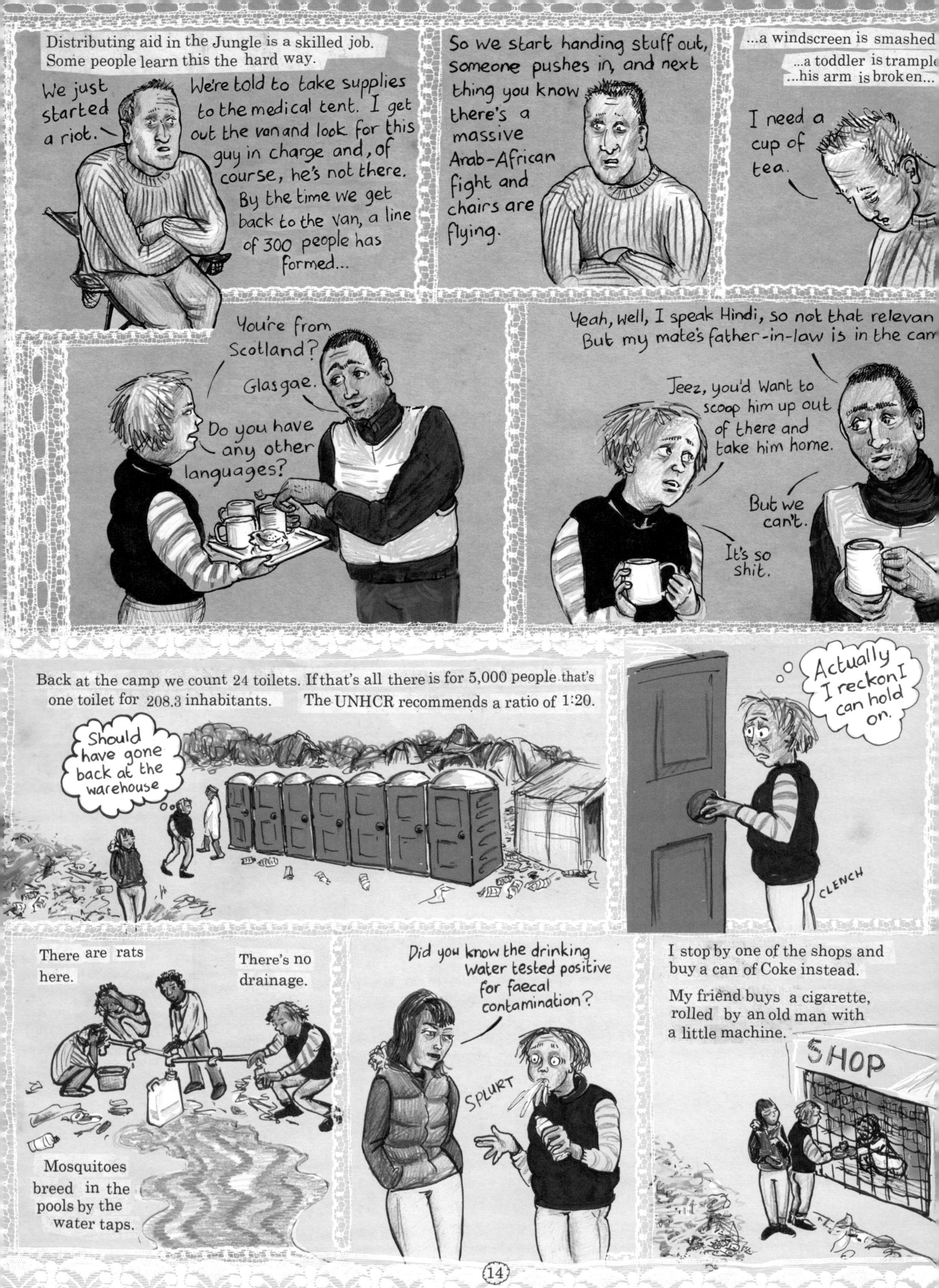

Distributing aid in the Jungle is a skilled job. Some people learn this the hard way.
We just started a riot.
We're told to take supplies to the medical tent. I get out the van and look for this guy in charge and, of course, he's not there. By the time we get back to the van, a line of 300 people has formed...
So we start handing stuff out, someone pushes in, and next thing you know there's a massive Arab-African fight and chairs are flying.
...a windscreen is smashed
...a toddler is trample
...his arm is broken...
I need a cup of tea.
You're from Scotland?
Glasgae.
Do you have any other languages?
Yeah, well, I speak Hindi, so not that relevan
But my mate's father-in-law is in the cam
Jeez, you'd want to scoop him up out of there and take him home.
But we can't.
It's so shit.
Back at the camp we count 24 toilets. If that's all there is for 5,000 people that's one toilet for 208.3 inhabitants. The UNHCR recommends a ratio of 1:20.
Should have gone back at the warehouse
Actually I reckon I can hold on.
CLENCH
There are rats here.
There's no drainage.
Mosquitoes breed in the pools by the water taps.
Did you know the drinking water tested positive for faecal contamination?
SPLURT
I stop by one of the shops and buy a can of Coke instead.
My friend buys a cigarette, rolled by an old man with a little machine.
SHOP

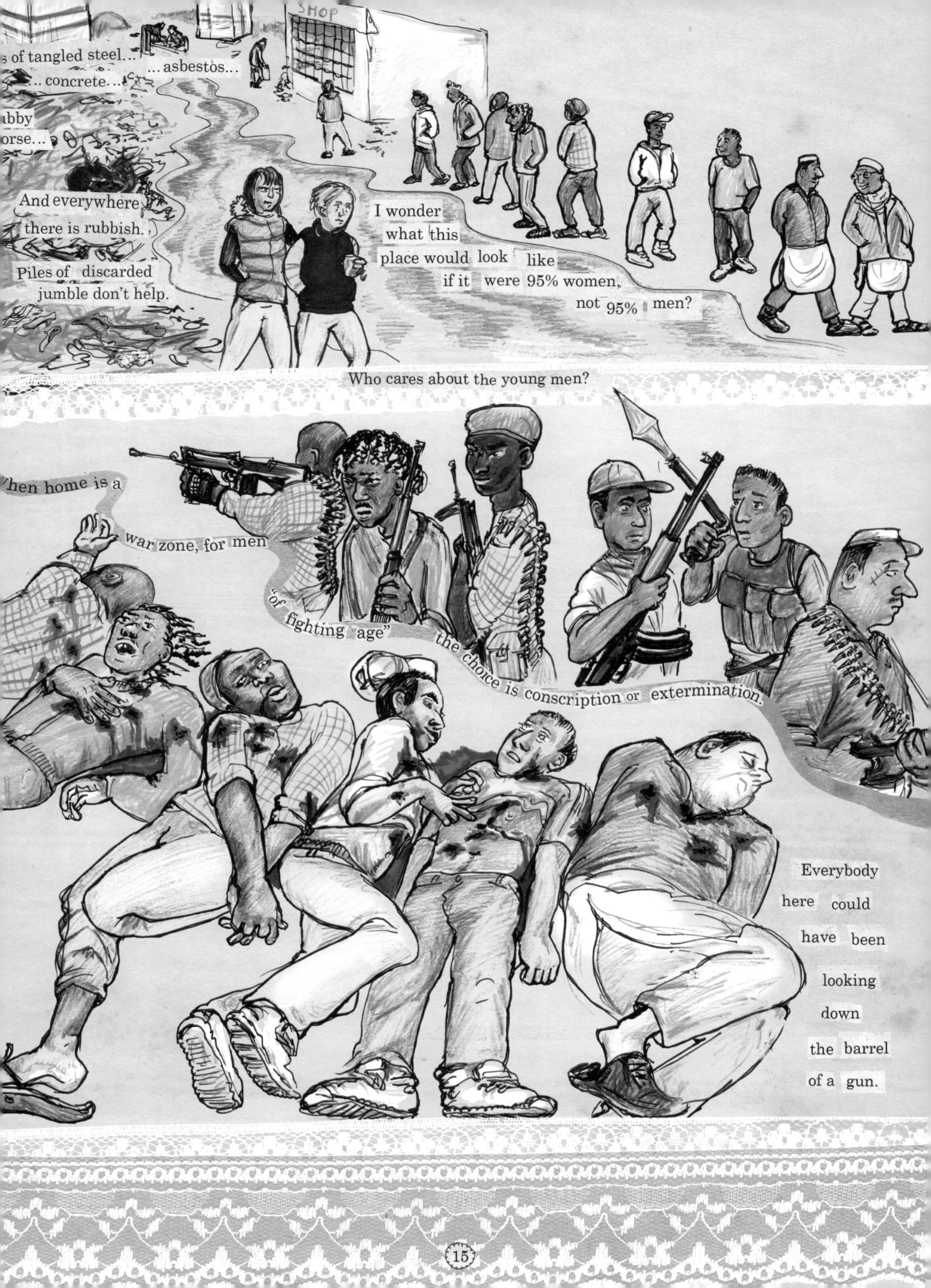

SHOP
…s of tangled steel…
… concrete…
… asbestos…
…bby
…orse…
And everywhere there is rubbish.
Piles of discarded jumble don't help.
I wonder what this place would look like if it were 95% women, not 95% men?
Who cares about the young men?
…hen home is a war zone, for men "of fighting age" the choice is conscription or extermination.
Everybody here could have been looking down the barrel of a gun.

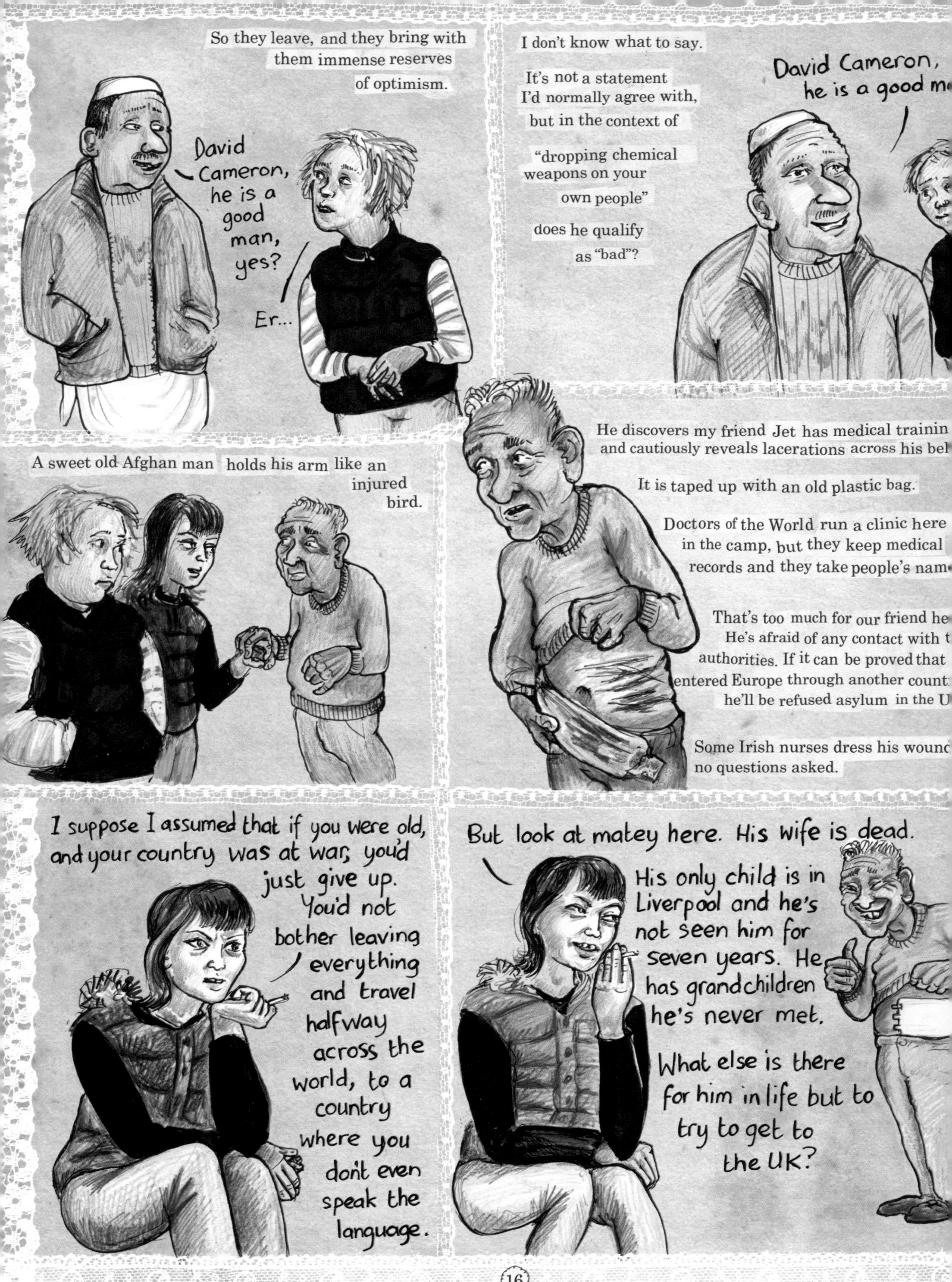
So they leave, and they bring with them immense reserves of optimism.
David Cameron, he is a good man, yes?
Er...
I don't know what to say.
It's not a statement I'd normally agree with,
but in the context of
"dropping chemical weapons on your own people"
does he qualify as "bad"?
David Cameron, he is a good m
A sweet old Afghan man holds his arm like an injured bird.
He discovers my friend Jet has medical trainin and cautiously reveals lacerations across his bel
It is taped up with an old plastic bag.
Doctors of the World run a clinic here in the camp, but they keep medical records and they take people's nam
That's too much for our friend he He's afraid of any contact with t authorities. If it can be proved that entered Europe through another count he'll be refused asylum in the U
Some Irish nurses dress his wounc no questions asked.
I suppose I assumed that if you were old, and your country was at war, you'd just give up. You'd not bother leaving everything and travel halfway across the world, to a country where you don't even speak the language.
But look at matey here. His wife is dead.
His only child is in Liverpool and he's not seen him for seven years. He has grandchildren he's never met.
What else is there for him in life but to try to get to the UK?

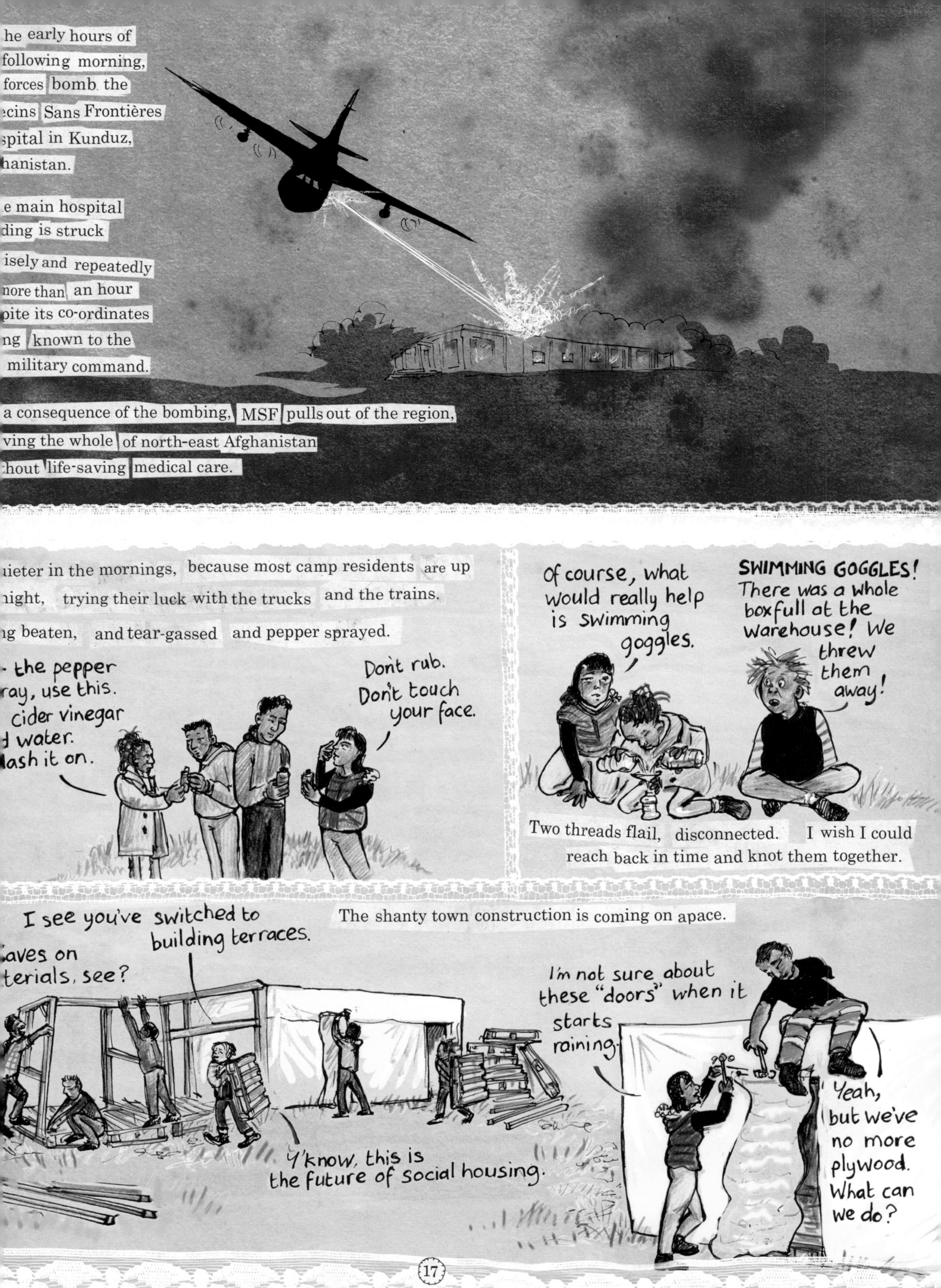

he early hours of
following morning,
forces bomb the
ecins Sans Frontières
spital in Kunduz,
hanistan.
e main hospital
ding is struck
isely and repeatedly
nore than an hour
pite its co-ordinates
ng known to the
military command.
a consequence of the bombing, MSF pulls out of the region,
ving the whole of north-east Afghanistan
hout life-saving medical care.
uieter in the mornings, because most camp residents are up
night, trying their luck with the trucks and the trains.
ng beaten, and tear-gassed and pepper sprayed.
- the pepper ray, use this. cider vinegar d water. lash it on.
Don't rub. Don't touch your face.
Of course, what would really help is swimming goggles.
SWIMMING GOGGLES! There was a whole boxfull at the warehouse! We threw them away!
Two threads flail, disconnected. I wish I could reach back in time and knot them together.
I see you've switched to building terraces.
Saves on terials, see?
The shanty town construction is coming on apace.
Y'know, this is the future of social housing.
I'm not sure about these "doors" when it starts raining.
Yeah, but we've no more plywood. What can we do?

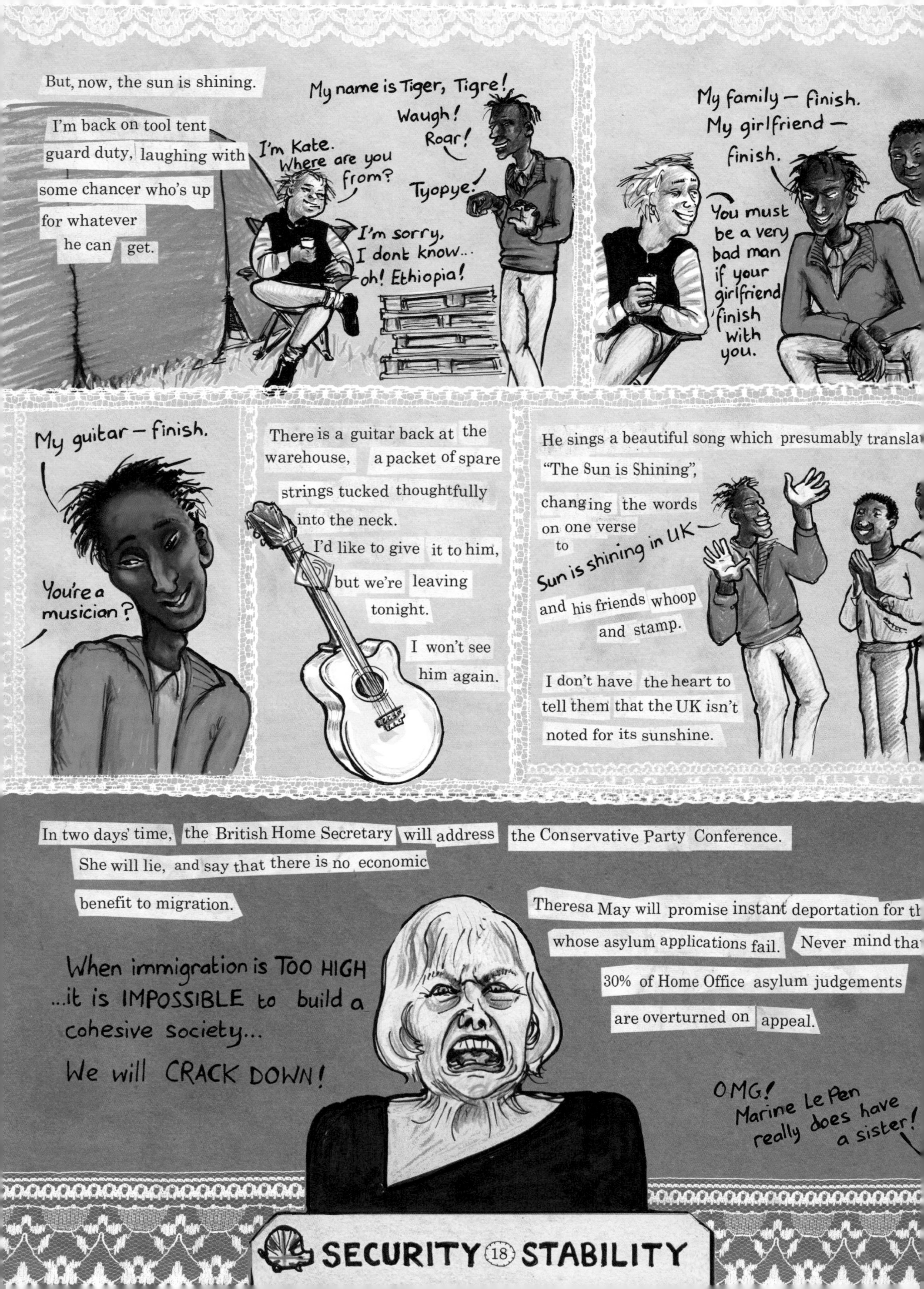

But, now, the sun is shining.
I'm back on tool tent guard duty, laughing with some chancer who's up for whatever he can get.
I'm Kate. Where are you from?
My name is Tiger, Tigre!
Waugh! Roar!
Tyopye!
I'm sorry, I dont know... oh! Ethiopia!
My family — finish. My girlfriend — finish.
You must be a very bad man if your girlfriend finish with you.
My guitar — finish.
You're a musician?
There is a guitar back at the warehouse, a packet of spare strings tucked thoughtfully into the neck.
I'd like to give it to him, but we're leaving tonight.
I won't see him again.
He sings a beautiful song which presumably translat
"The Sun is Shining",
changing the words on one verse to
Sun is shining in UK
and his friends whoop and stamp.
I don't have the heart to tell them that the UK isn't noted for its sunshine.
In two days' time, the British Home Secretary will address the Conservative Party Conference.
She will lie, and say that there is no economic benefit to migration.
Theresa May will promise instant deportation for th
whose asylum applications fail. Never mind tha
30% of Home Office asylum judgements are overturned on appeal.
When immigration is TOO HIGH ...it is IMPOSSIBLE to build a cohesive society...
We will CRACK DOWN!
OMG! Marine Le Pen really does have a sister!
SECURITY 18 STABILITY

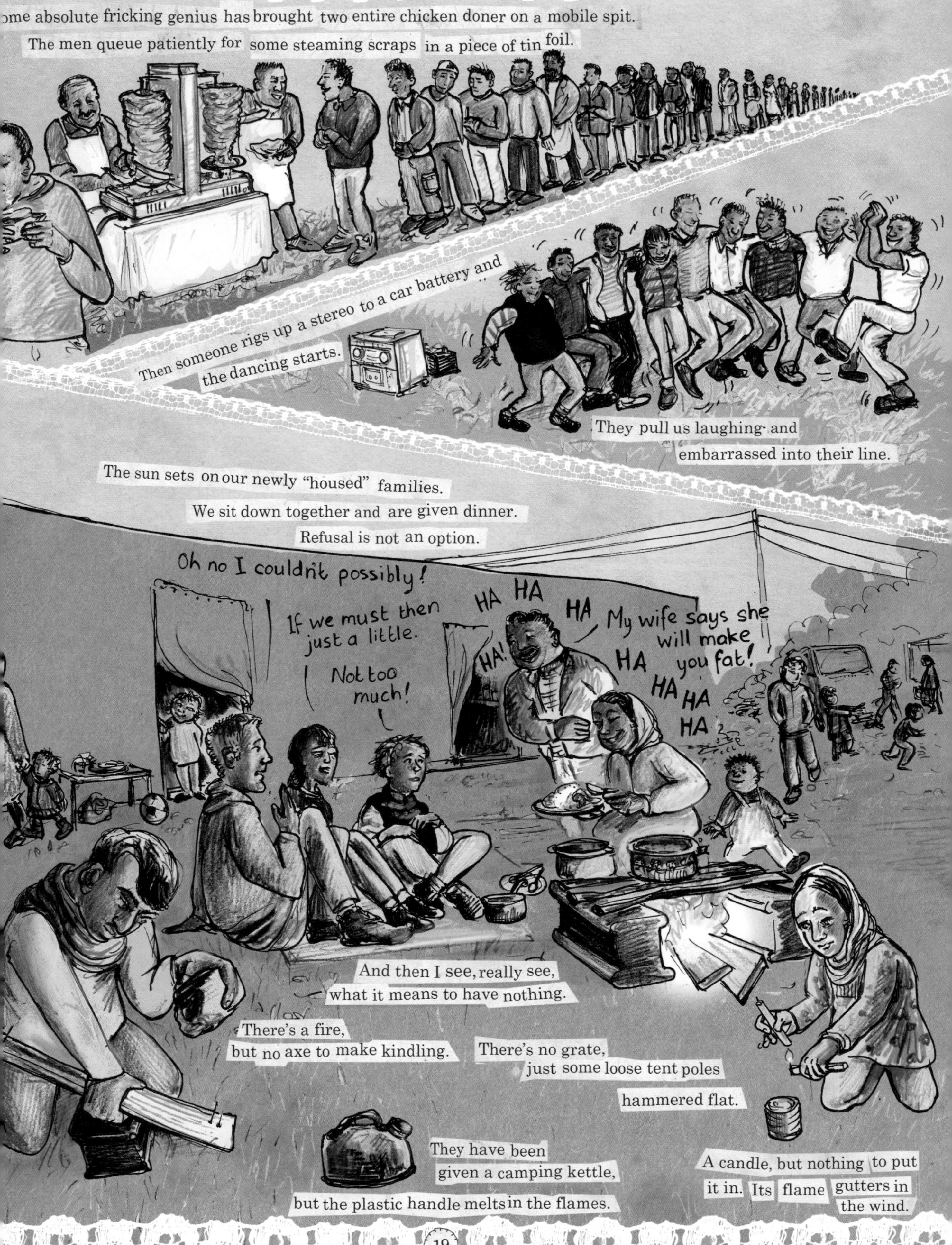

ome absolute fricking genius has brought two entire chicken doner on a mobile spit.
The men queue patiently for some steaming scraps in a piece of tin foil.
Then someone rigs up a stereo to a car battery and the dancing starts.
They pull us laughing and embarrassed into their line.
The sun sets on our newly "housed" families.
We sit down together and are given dinner.
Refusal is not an option.
Oh no I couldn't possibly!
If we must then just a little.
Not too much!
HA HA HA HA! HA HA HA HA HA
My wife says she will make you fat!
And then I see, really see, what it means to have nothing.
There's a fire, but no axe to make kindling.
There's no grate, just some loose tent poles hammered flat.
They have been given a camping kettle, but the plastic handle melts in the flames.
A candle, but nothing to put it in. Its flame gutters in the wind.

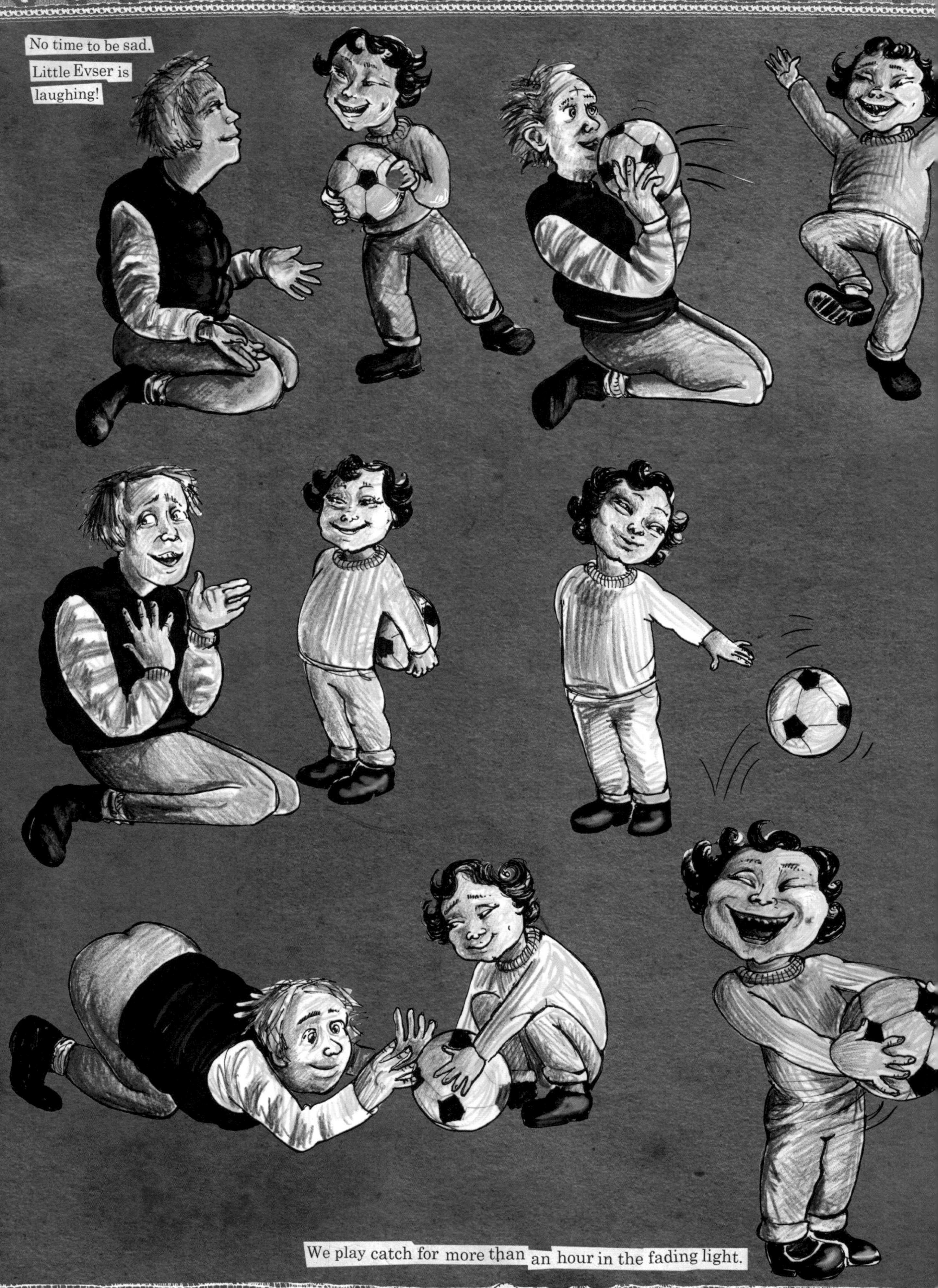
No time to be sad.
Little Evser is
laughing!
We play catch for more than an hour in the fading light.

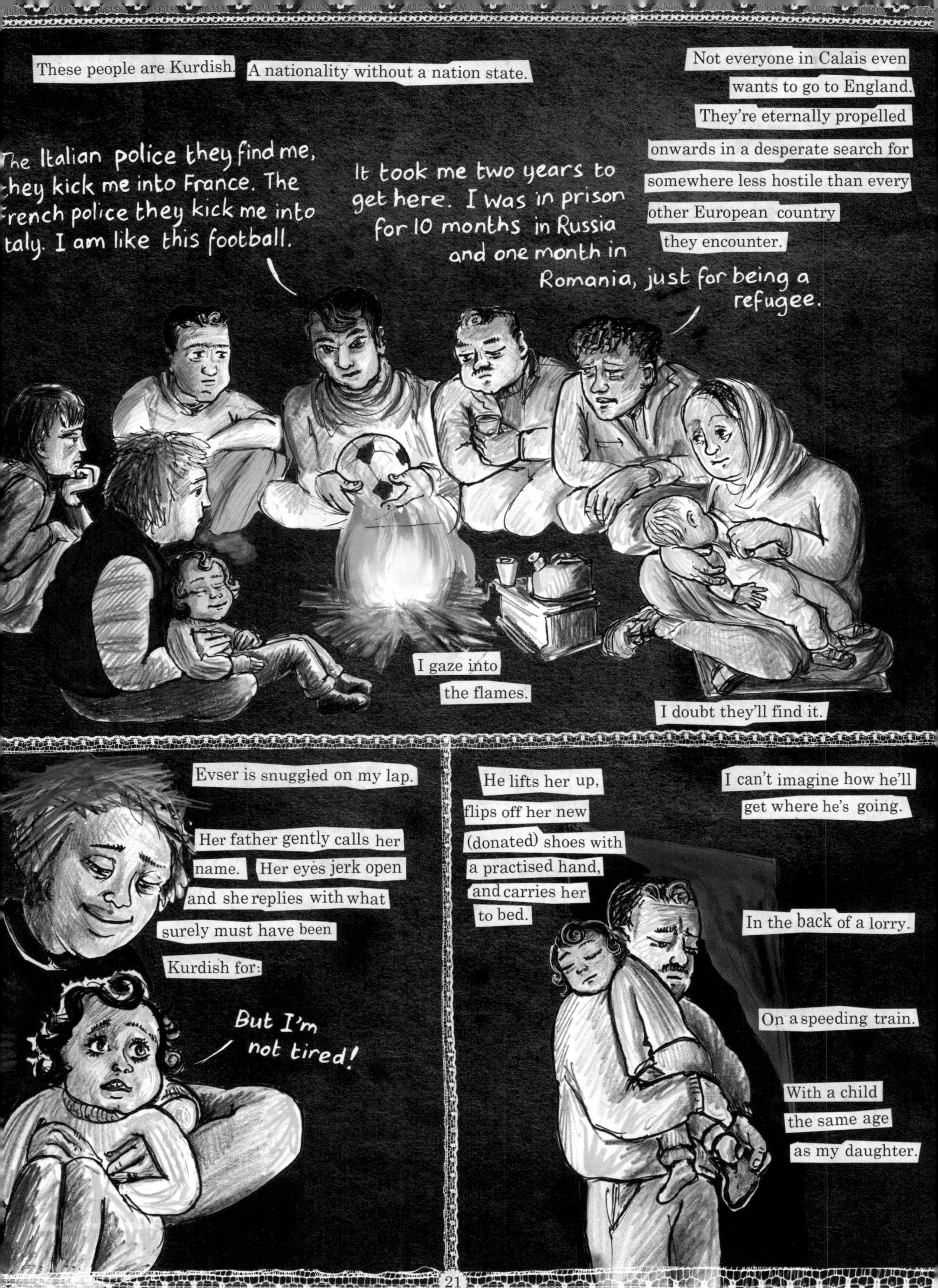
These people are Kurdish.
A nationality without a nation state.
Not everyone in Calais even wants to go to England. They're eternally propelled onwards in a desperate search for somewhere less hostile than every other European country they encounter.
The Italian police they find me, hey kick me into France. The rench police they kick me into taly. I am like this football.
It took me two years to get here. I was in prison for 10 months in Russia and one month in Romania, just for being a refugee.
I gaze into the flames.
I doubt they'll find it.
Evser is snuggled on my lap.
Her father gently calls her name.
Her eyes jerk open and she replies with what surely must have been Kurdish for:
But I'm not tired!
He lifts her up, flips off her new (donated) shoes with a practised hand, and carries her to bed.
I can't imagine how he'll get where he's going.
In the back of a lorry.
On a speeding train.
With a child the same age as my daughter.

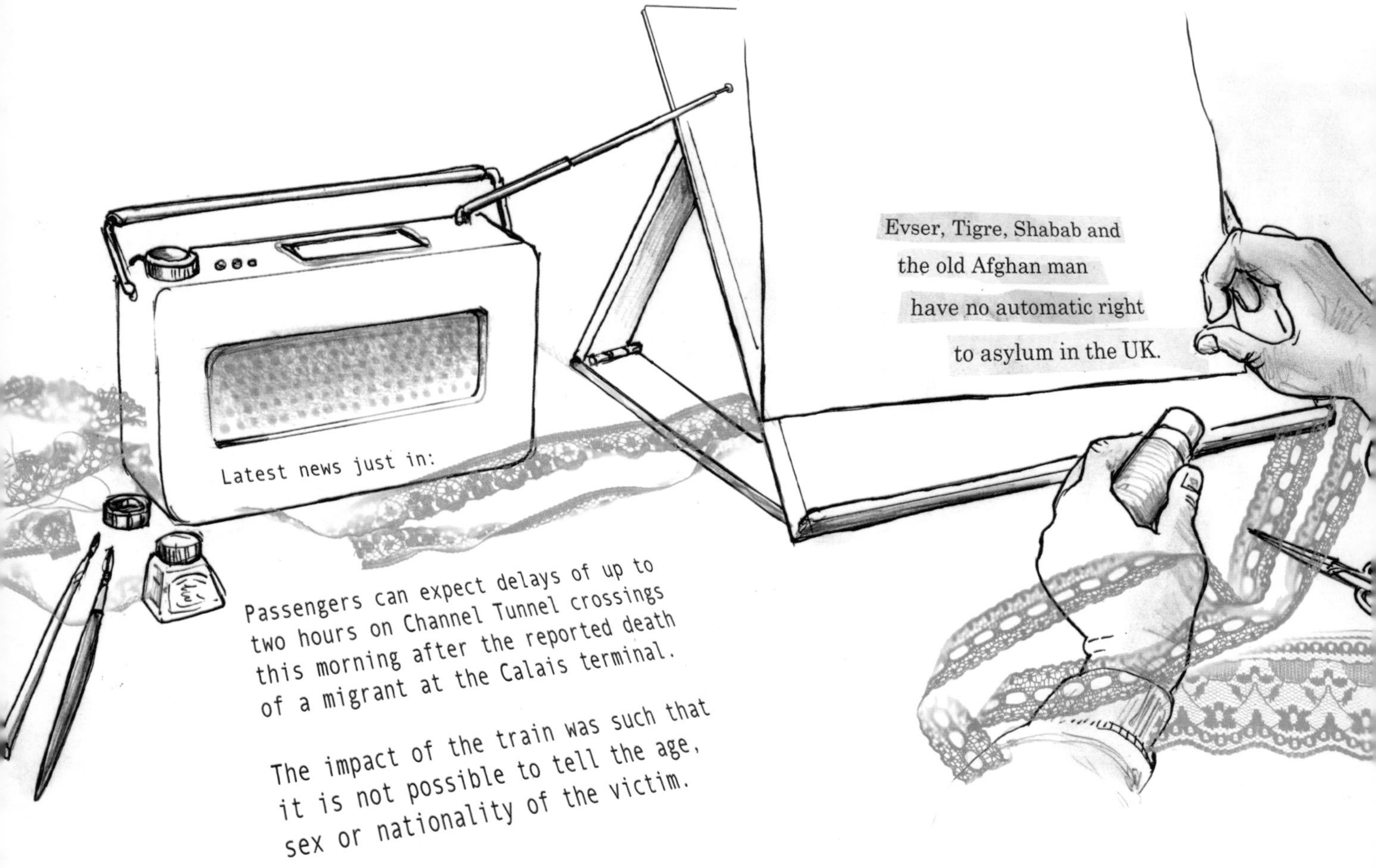
Evser, Tigre, Shabab and
the old Afghan man
have no automatic right
to asylum in the UK.
Latest news just in:
Passengers can expect delays of up to two hours on Channel Tunnel crossings this morning after the reported death of a migrant at the Calais terminal.
The impact of the train was such that it is not possible to tell the age, sex or nationality of the victim.

It could have been any of them.

My phone bleeps into life.

Connectivity.

Commentary.

Follow the threads of conversation wherever they go.

This cartoon could not be better propaganda for battlefield veteran Islamic militant males invading Northern Europe if Lenin himself produced it. The situation would not exist if they very people breaking laws in Calais did not ruin their homelands with ethnic religious hatred, intolerance, and war.
You are importing death.

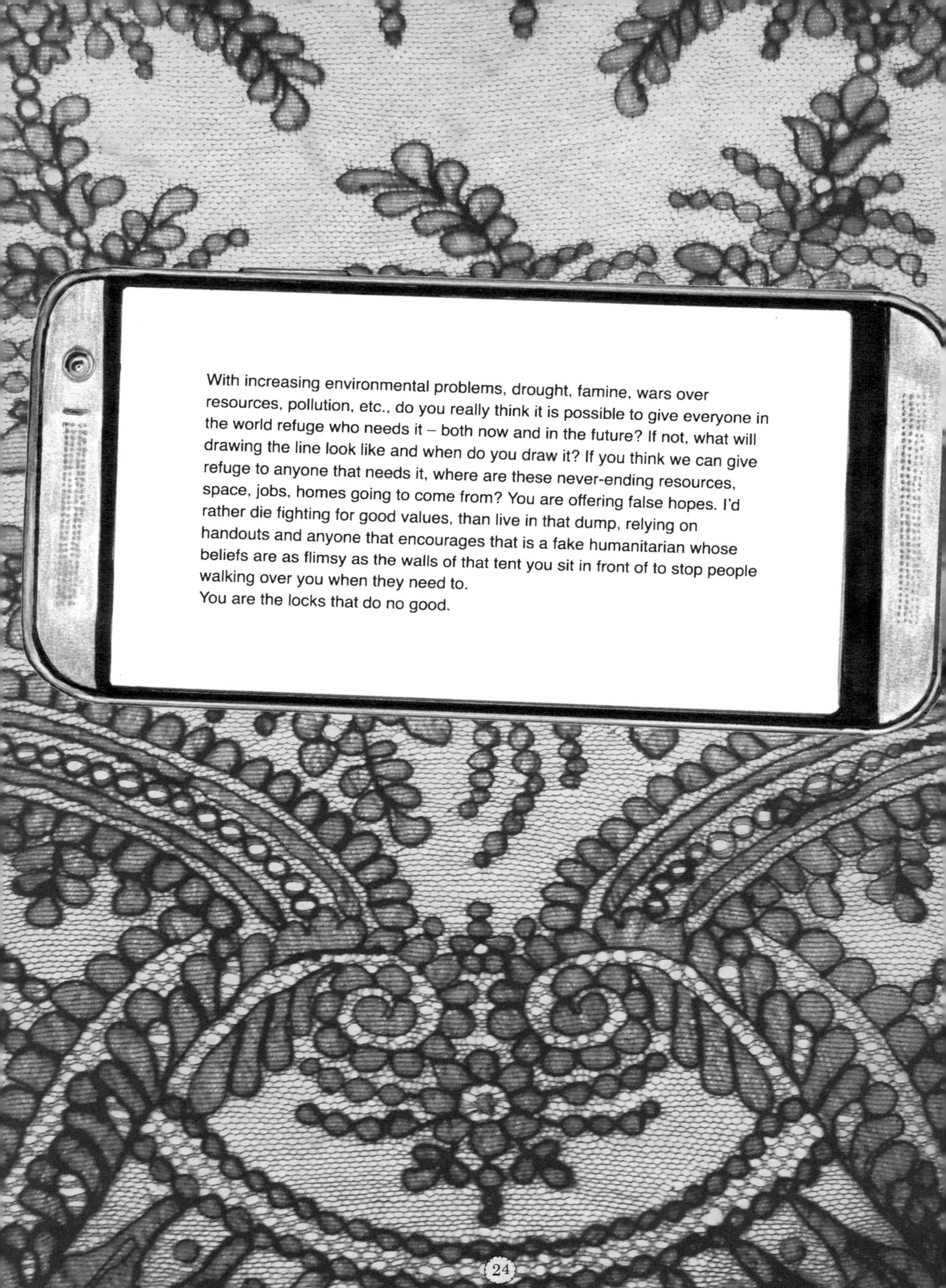
With increasing environmental problems, drought, famine, wars over resources, pollution, etc., do you really think it is possible to give everyone in the world refuge who needs it – both now and in the future? If not, what will drawing the line look like and when do you draw it? If you think we can give refuge to anyone that needs it, where are these never-ending resources, space, jobs, homes going to come from? You are offering false hopes. I'd rather die fighting for good values, than live in that dump, relying on handouts and anyone that encourages that is a fake humanitarian whose beliefs are as flimsy as the walls of that tent you sit in front of to stop people walking over you when they need to.
You are the locks that do no good.

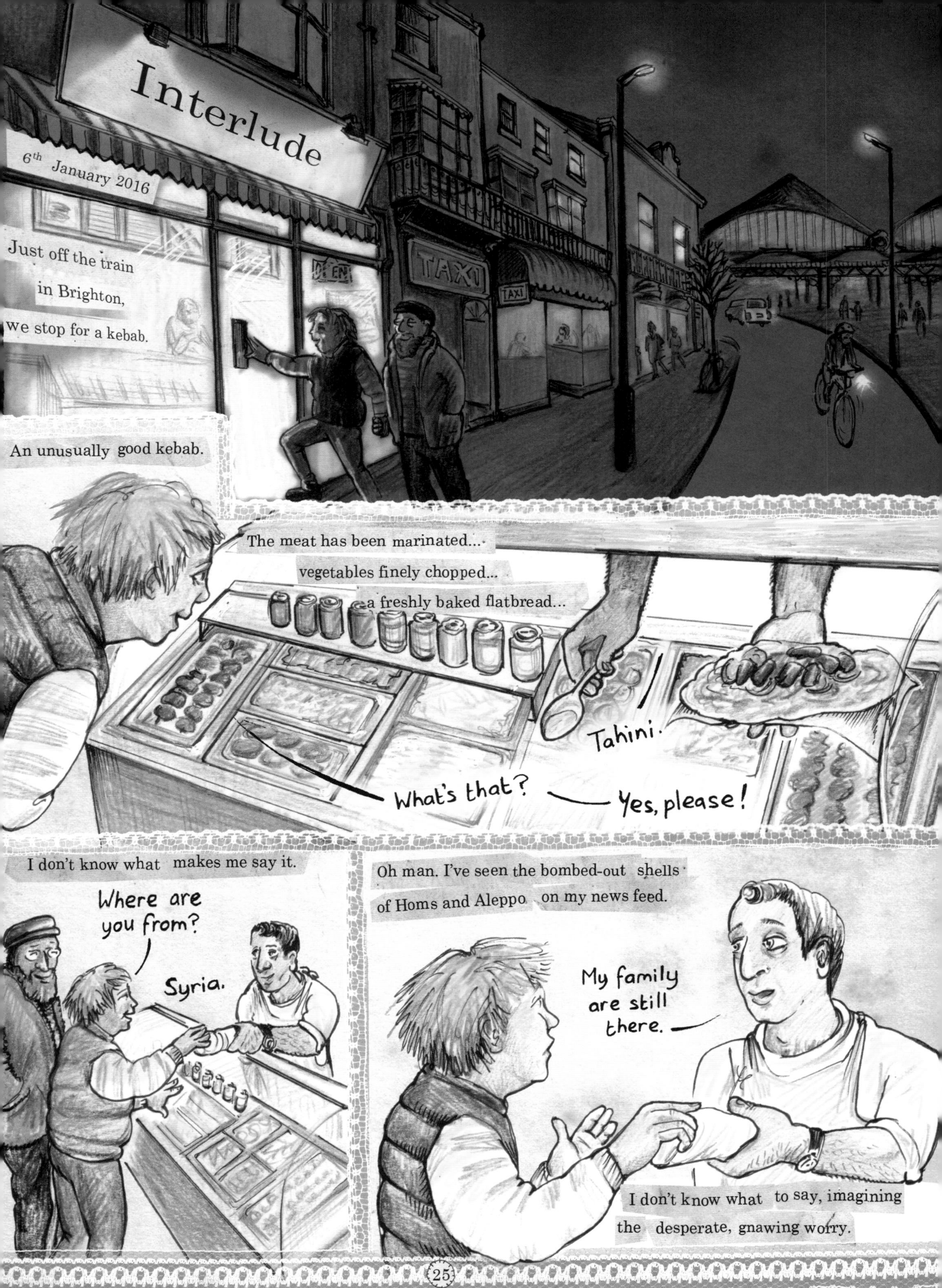

Interlude
6th January 2016
Just off the train
in Brighton,
we stop for a kebab.
OPEN
TAXI
TAXI
An unusually good kebab.
The meat has been marinated...
vegetables finely chopped...
a freshly baked flatbread...
Tahini.
What's that?
Yes, please!
I don't know what makes me say it.
Where are you from?
Syria.
Oh man. I've seen the bombed-out shells
of Homs and Aleppo on my news feed.
My family are still there.
I don't know what to say, imagining
the desperate, gnawing worry.

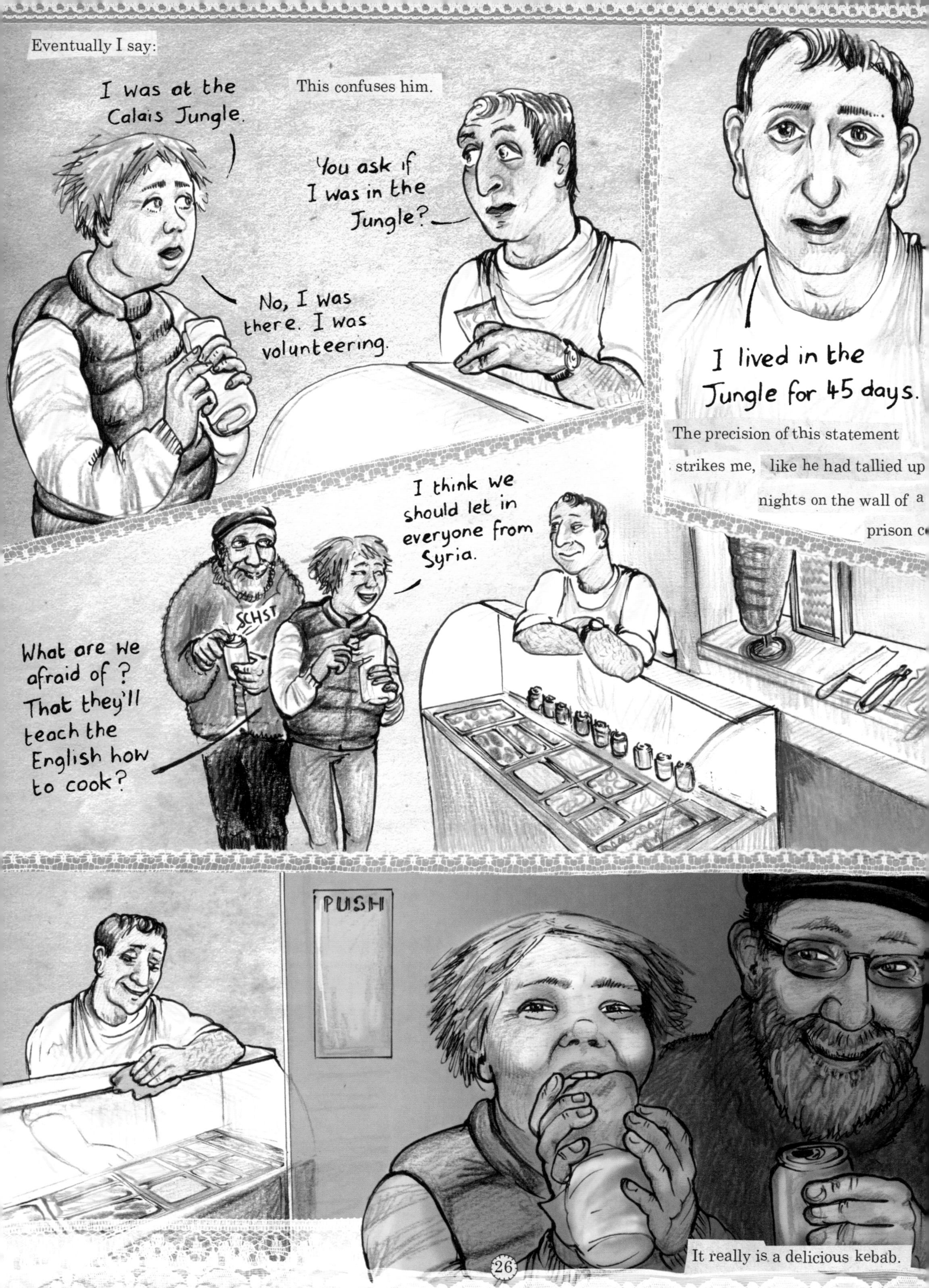
Eventually I say:
I was at the Calais Jungle.
This confuses him.
You ask if I was in the Jungle?
No, I was there. I was volunteering.
I lived in the Jungle for 45 days.
The precision of this statement strikes me, like he had tallied up nights on the wall of a prison c
I think we should let in everyone from Syria.
SCHST
What are we afraid of? That they'll teach the English how to cook?
PUSH
It really is a delicious kebab.

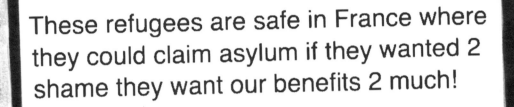

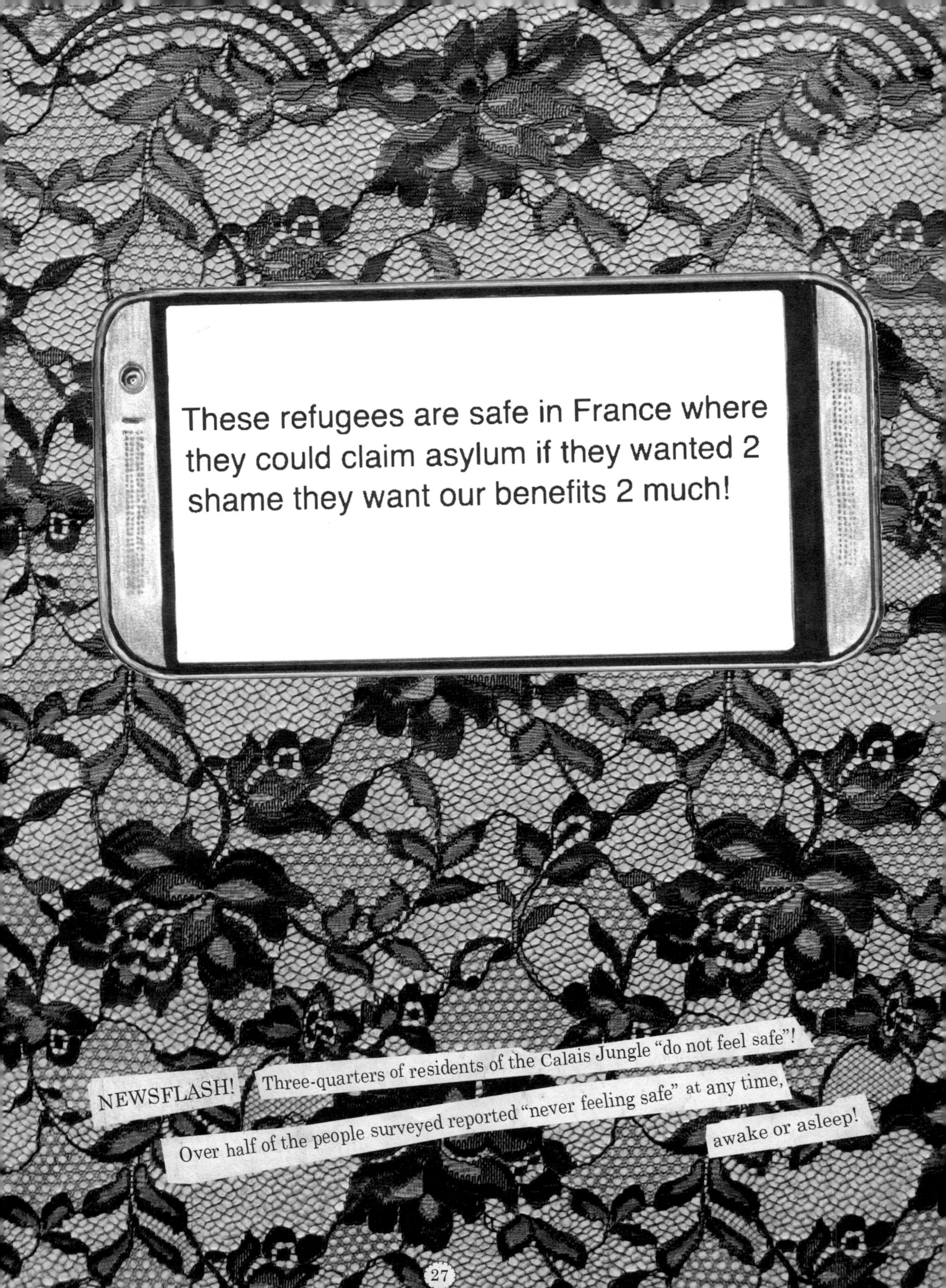

These refugees are safe in France where they could claim asylum if they wanted 2 shame they want our benefits 2 much!

NEWSFLASH! Three-quarters of residents of the Calais Jungle "do not feel safe"! Over half of the people surveyed reported "never feeling safe" at any time, awake or asleep!

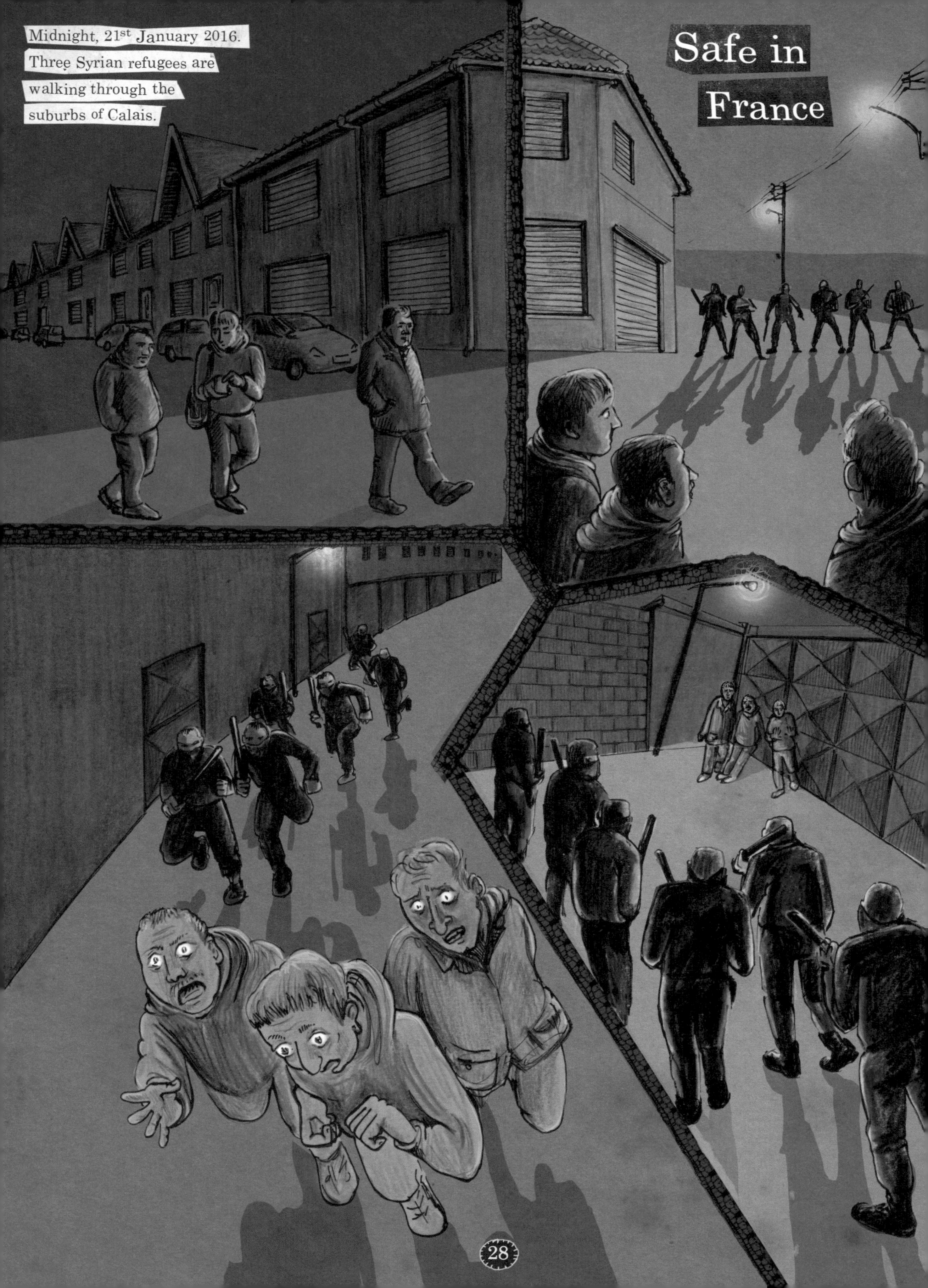
Safe in France
Midnight, 21st January 2016. Three Syrian refugees are walking through the suburbs of Calais.

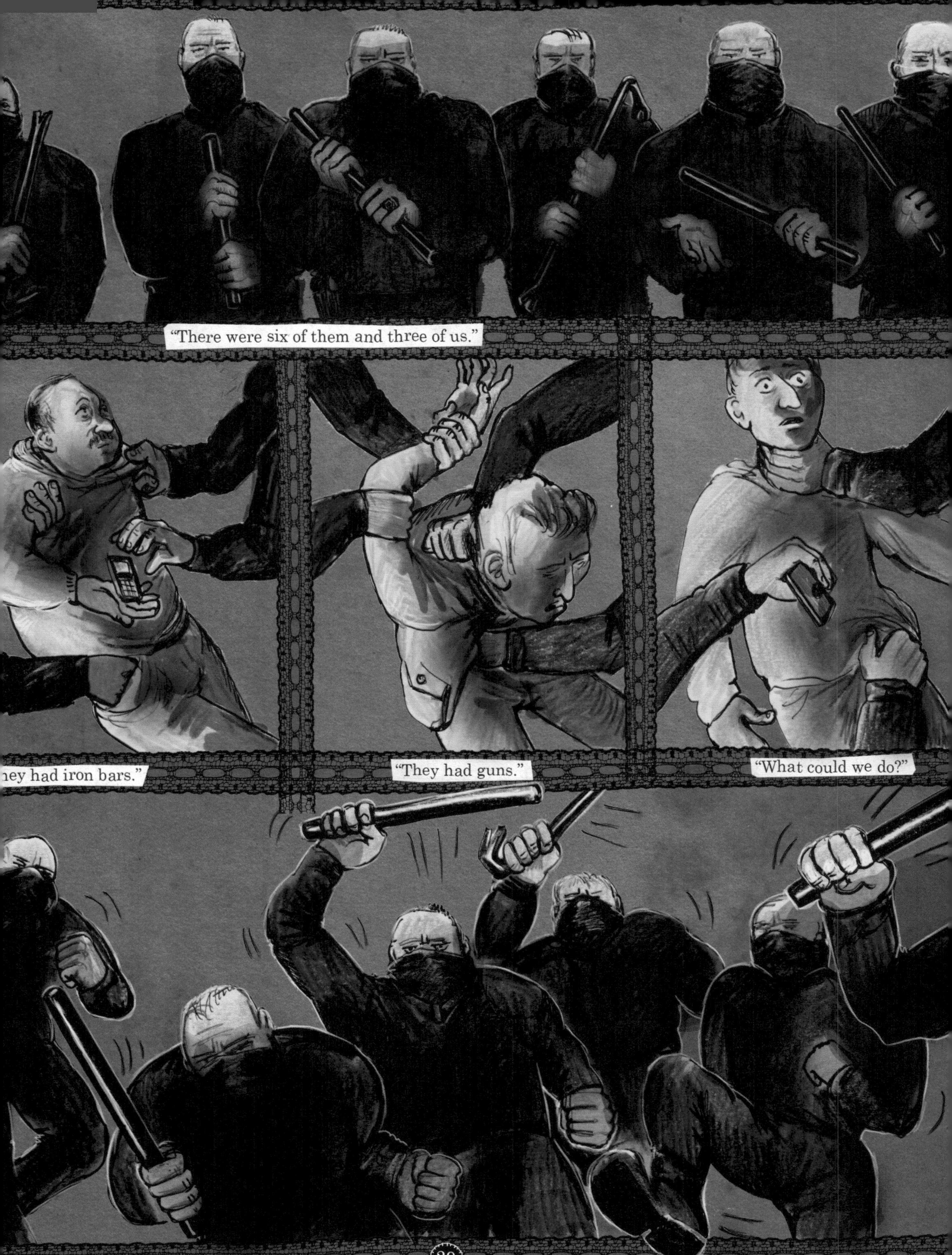
"There were six of them and three of us."
hey had iron bars."
"They had guns."
"What could we do?"

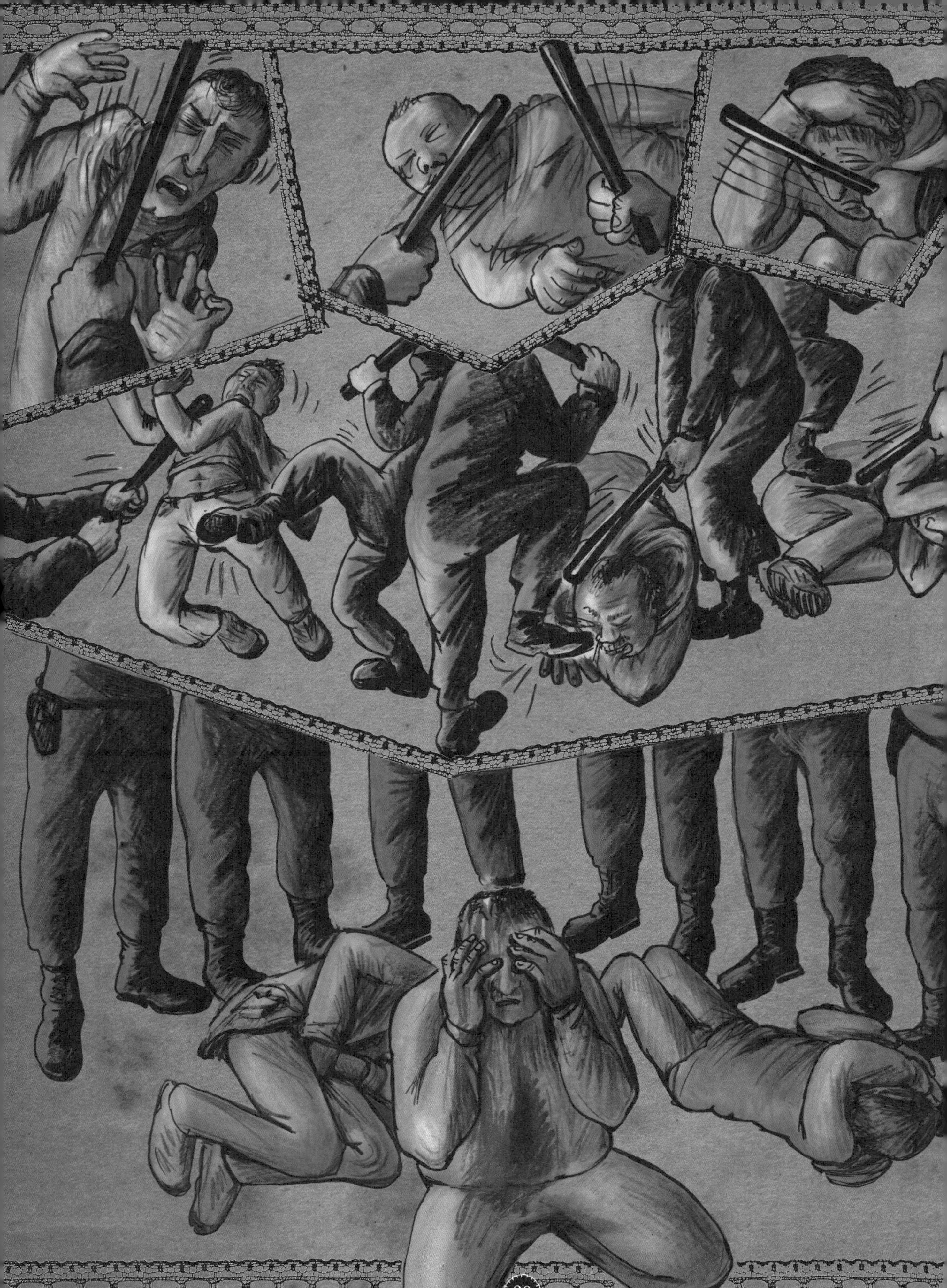

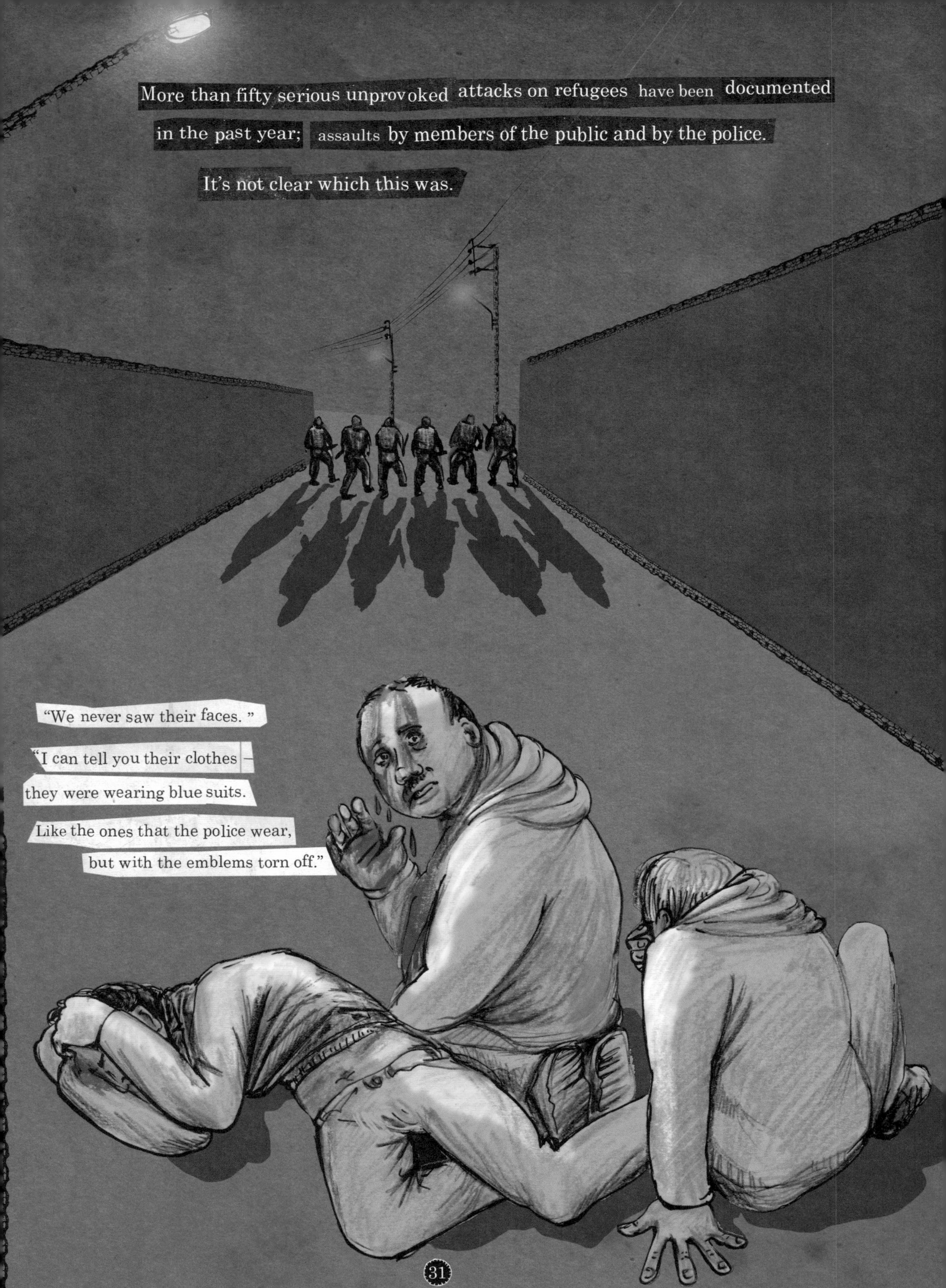
More than fifty serious unprovoked attacks on refugees have been documented
in the past year; assaults by members of the public and by the police.
It's not clear which this was.
"We never saw their faces. "
"I can tell you their clothes –
they were wearing blue suits.
Like the ones that the police wear,
but with the emblems torn off."

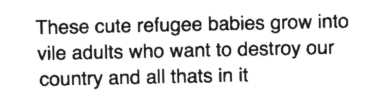

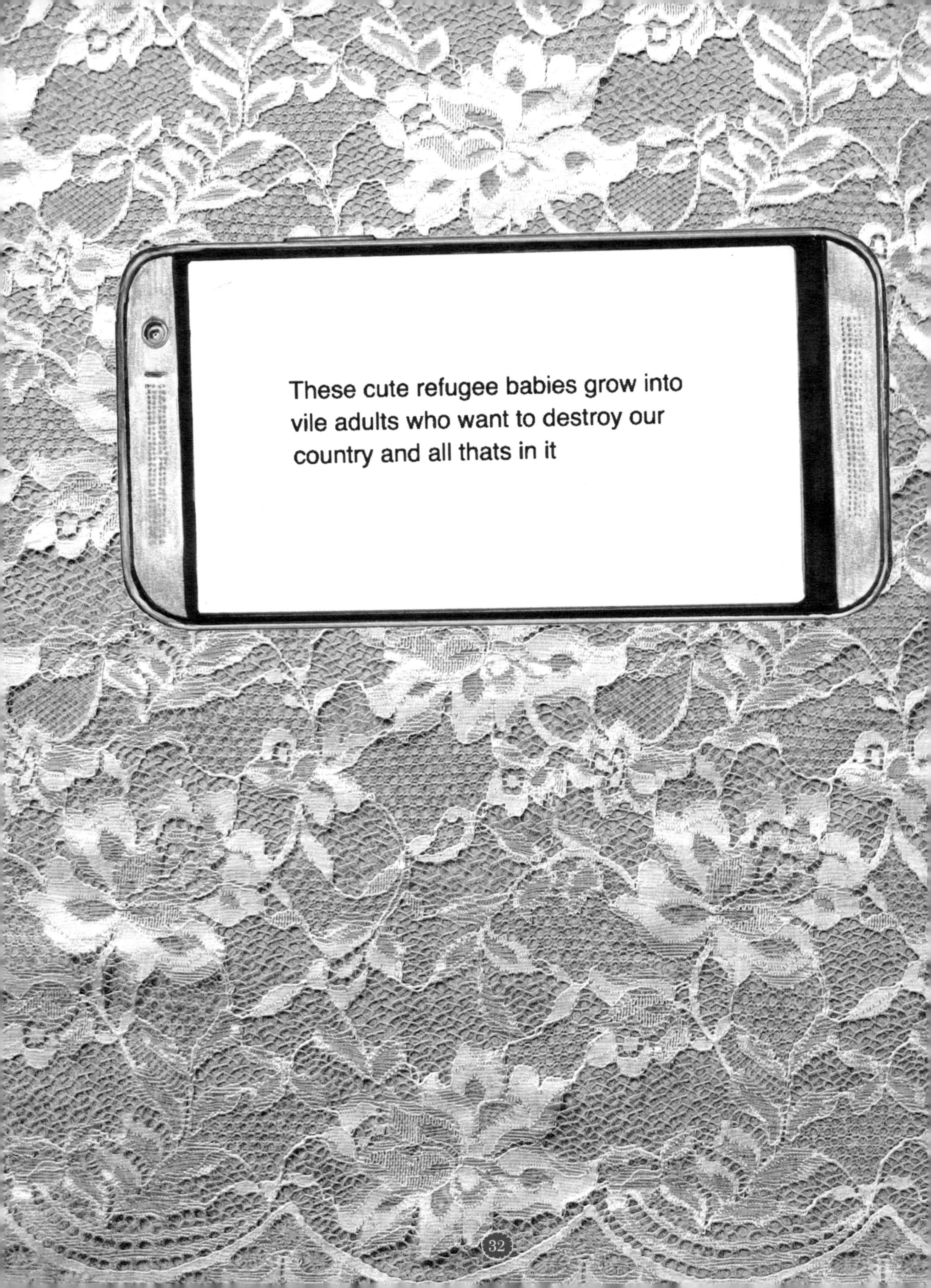

These cute refugee babies grow into vile adults who want to destroy our country and all thats in it

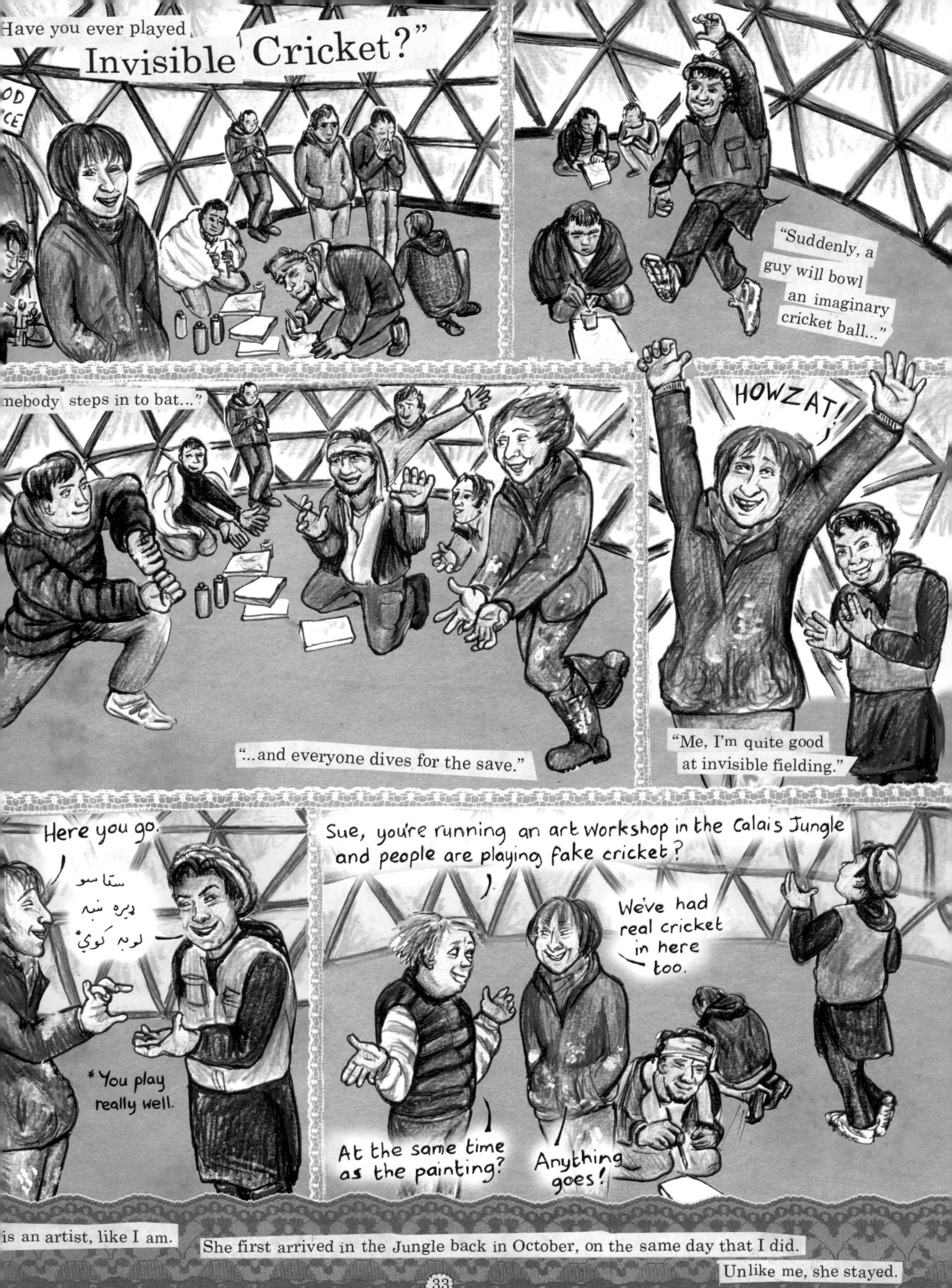
Have you ever played Invisible Cricket?"
"Suddenly, a guy will bowl an imaginary cricket ball..."
mebody steps in to bat..."
HOWZAT!
"...and everyone dives for the save."
"Me, I'm quite good at invisible fielding."
Here you go.
ستاسو ډیره ښه لوبه کوي*
*You play really well.
Sue, you're running an art workshop in the Calais Jungle and people are playing fake cricket?
We've had real cricket in here too.
At the same time as the painting?
Anything goes!
is an artist, like I am.
She first arrived in the Jungle back in October, on the same day that I did.
Unlike me, she stayed.

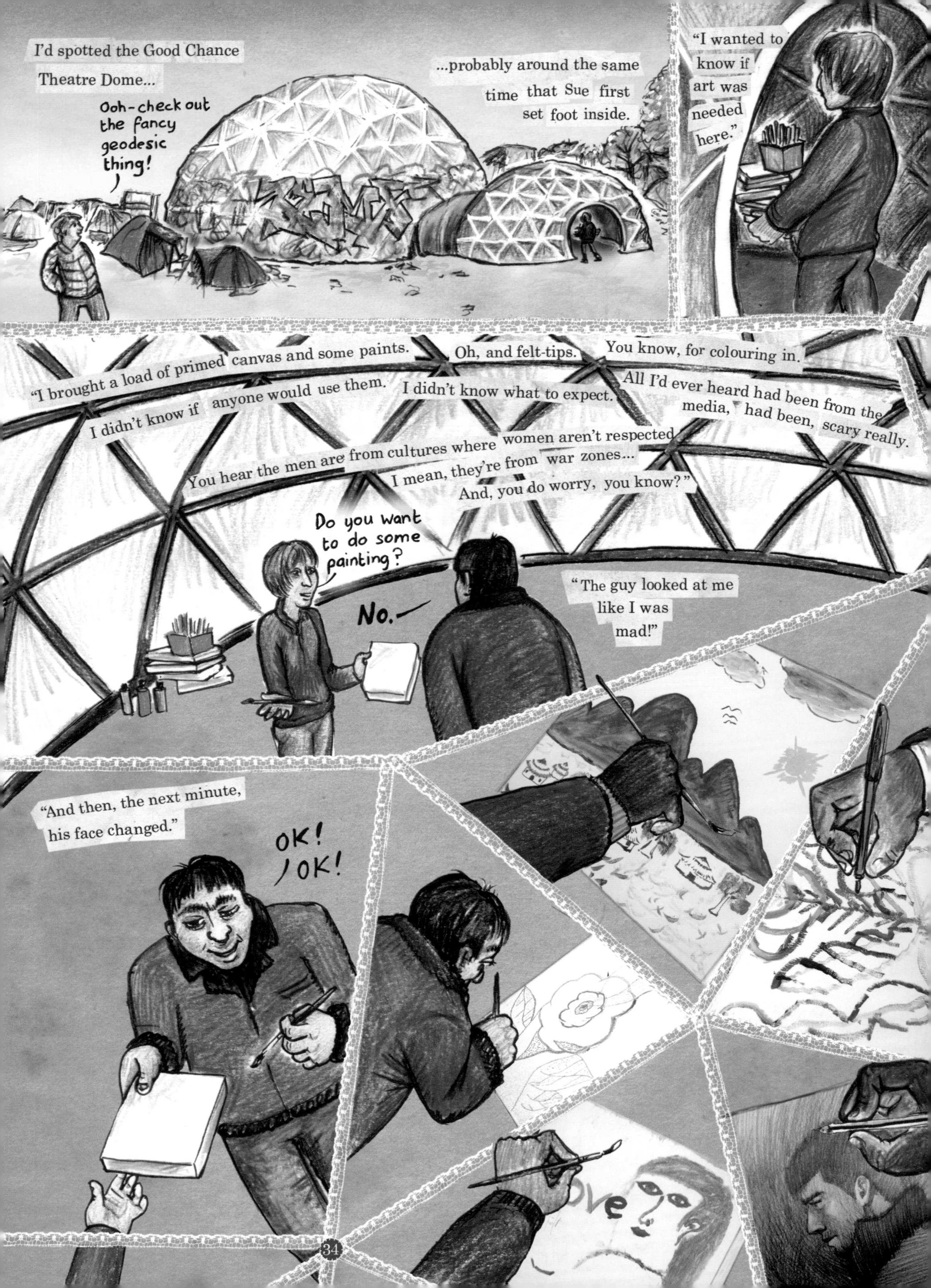

I'd spotted the Good Chance Theatre Dome...
Ooh-check out the fancy geodesic thing!
...probably around the same time that Sue first set foot inside.
"I wanted to know if art was needed here."
"I brought a load of primed canvas and some paints. Oh, and felt-tips. You know, for colouring in.
I didn't know if anyone would use them. I didn't know what to expect. All I'd ever heard had been from the media, had been, scary really.
You hear the men are from cultures where women aren't respected I mean, they're from war zones...
And, you do worry, you know?"
Do you want to do some painting?
No.
"The guy looked at me like I was mad!"
"And then, the next minute, his face changed."
OK! OK!

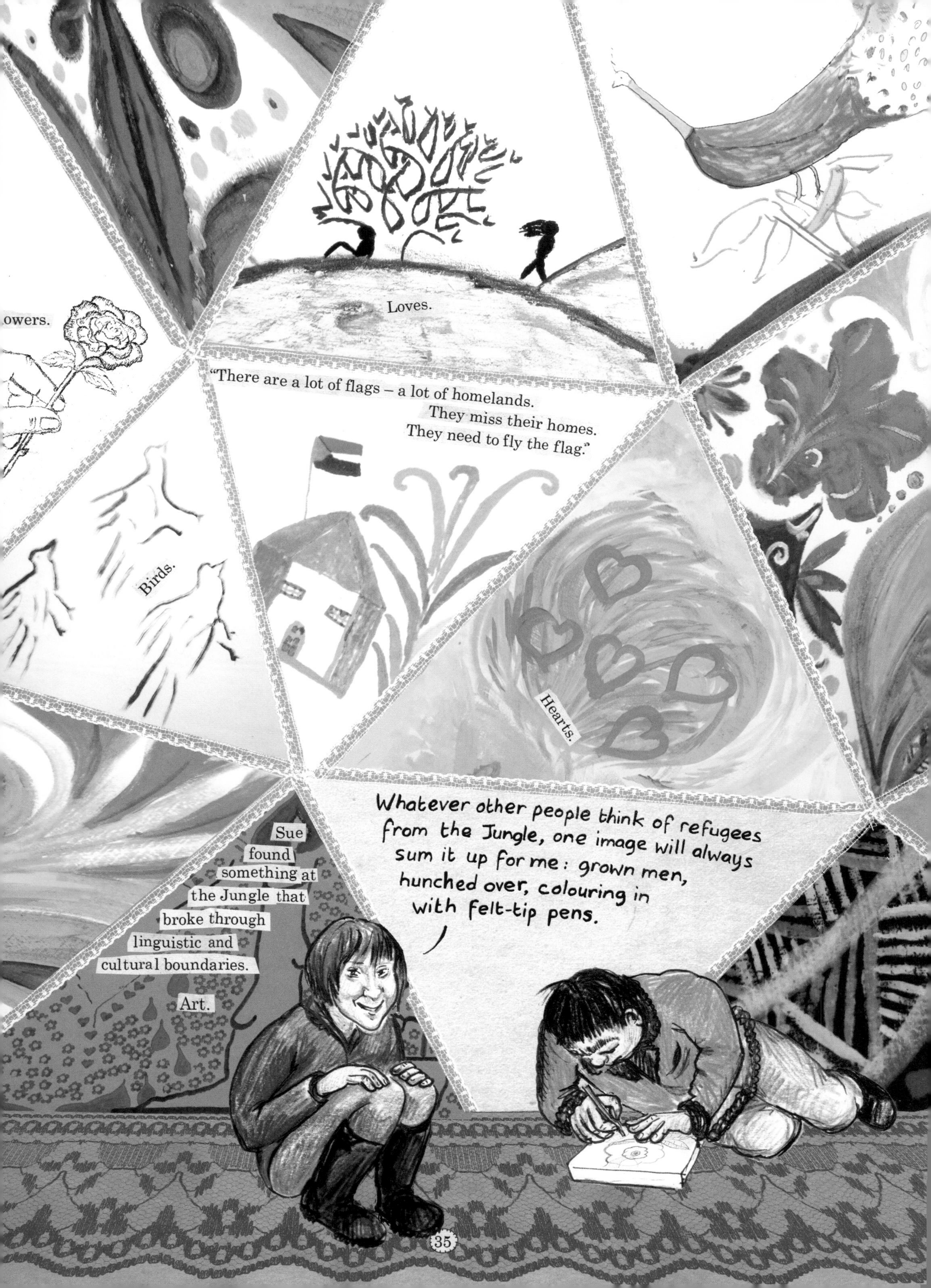
owers.
Loves.
"There are a lot of flags – a lot of homelands.
They miss their homes.
They need to fly the flag."
Birds.
Hearts.
Sue found something at the Jungle that broke through linguistic and cultural boundaries.
Art.
Whatever other people think of refugees from the Jungle, one image will always sum it up for me: grown men, hunched over, colouring in with felt-tip pens.

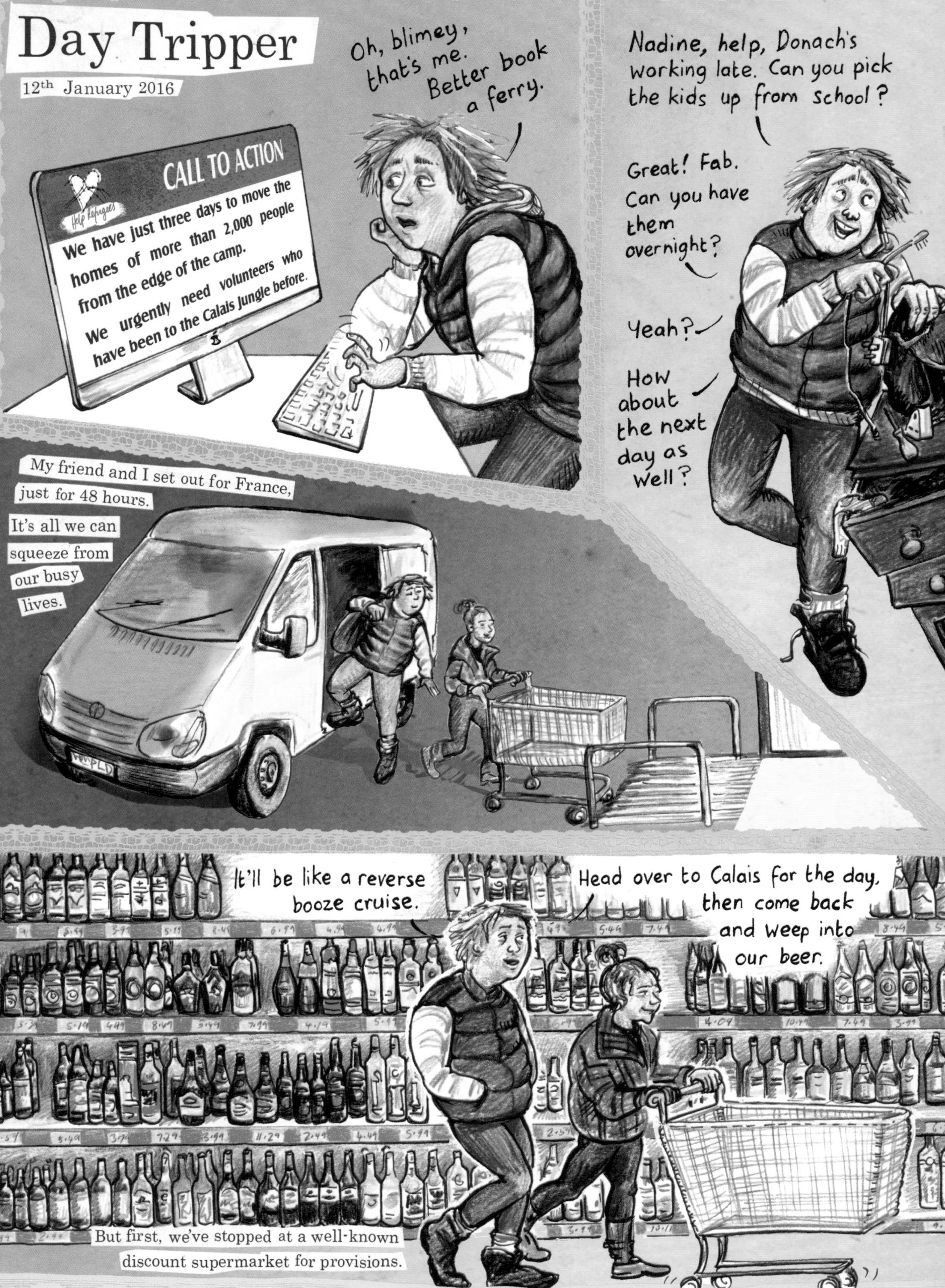

Day Tripper
12th January 2016
CALL TO ACTION
Help Refugees
We have just three days to move the homes of more than 2,000 people from the edge of the camp.
We urgently need volunteers who have been to the Calais Jungle before.
Oh, blimey, that's me. Better book a ferry.
Nadine, help, Donach's working late. Can you pick the kids up from school?
Great! Fab. Can you have them overnight?
Yeah?
How about the next day as well?
My friend and I set out for France, just for 48 hours.
It's all we can squeeze from our busy lives.
It'll be like a reverse booze cruise.
Head over to Calais for the day, then come back and weep into our beer.
But first, we've stopped at a well-known discount supermarket for provisions.

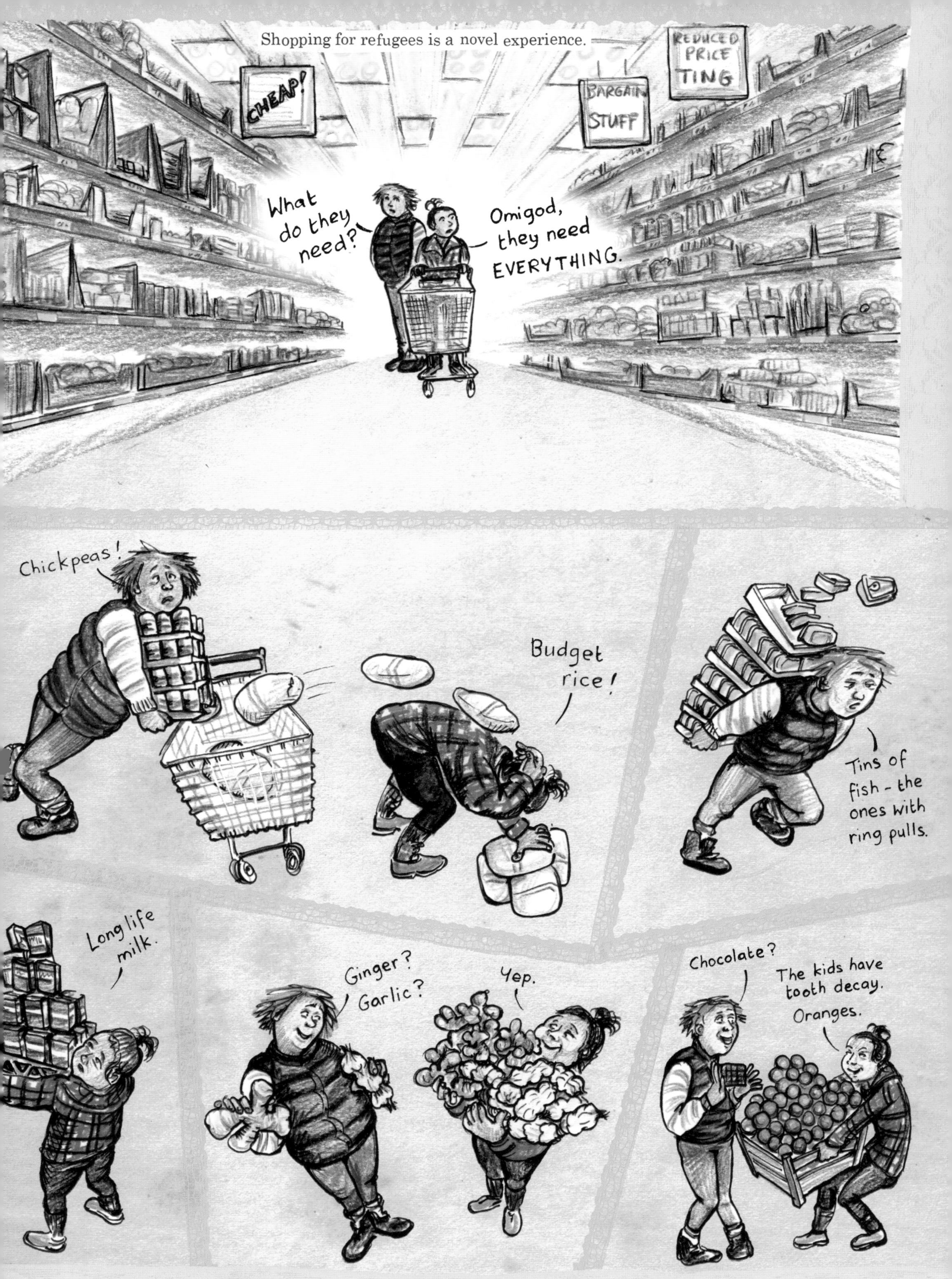
Shopping for refugees is a novel experience.
CHEAP!
BARGAIN STUFF
REDUCED PRICE TING
What do they need?
Omigod, they need EVERYTHING.
Chickpeas!
Budget rice!
Tins of fish - the ones with ring pulls.
Long life milk.
Ginger? Garlic?
Yep.
Chocolate?
The kids have tooth decay. Oranges.

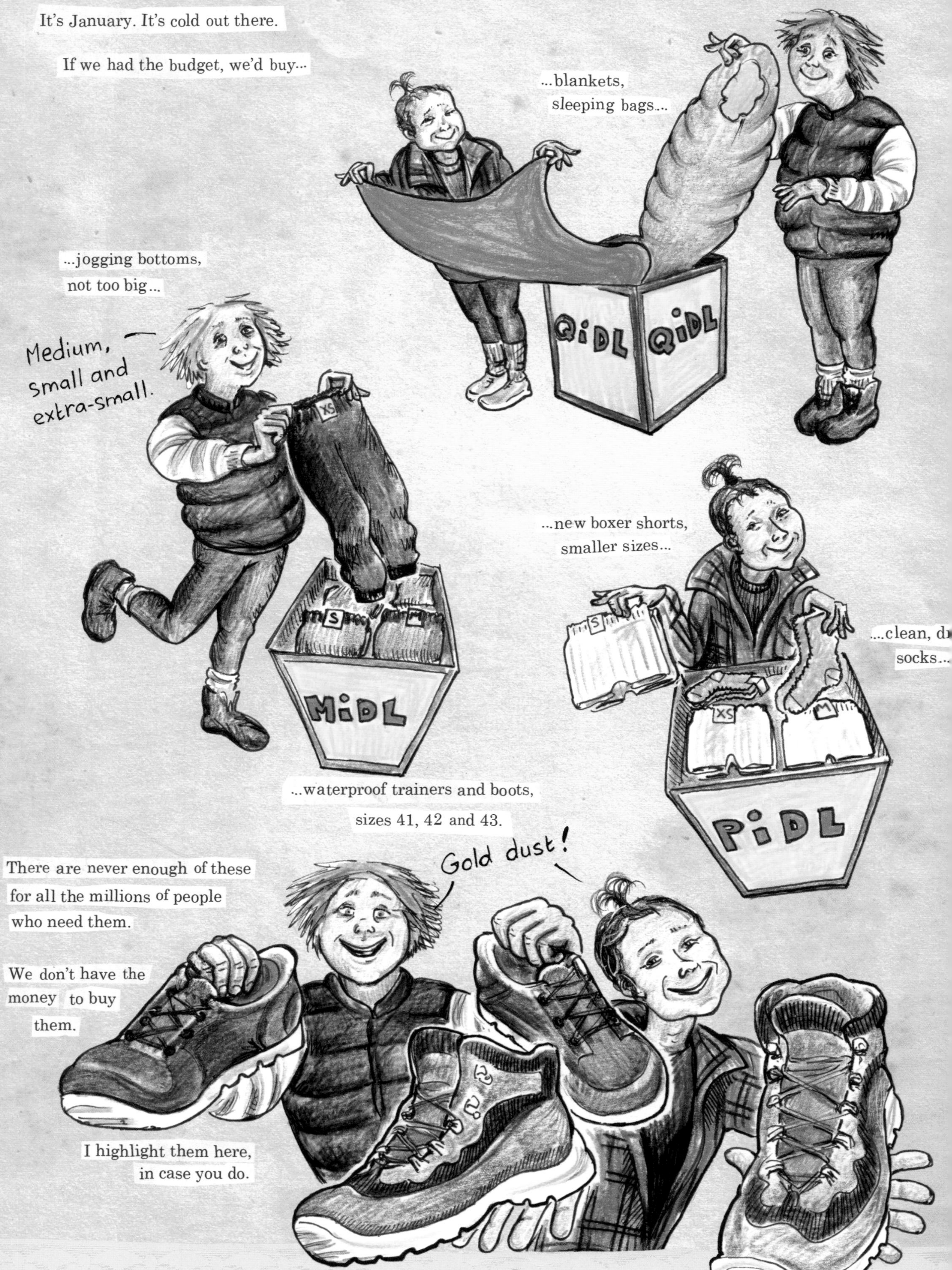
It's January. It's cold out there.
If we had the budget, we'd buy...
...blankets,
sleeping bags...
QiDL QiDL
...jogging bottoms,
not too big...
Medium, small and extra-small.
XS
S
MiDL
...new boxer shorts,
smaller sizes...
....clean, dr
socks...
S
XS
PiDL
...waterproof trainers and boots,
sizes 41, 42 and 43.
There are never enough of these
for all the millions of people
who need them.
Gold dust!
We don't have the
money to buy
them.
I highlight them here,
in case you do.

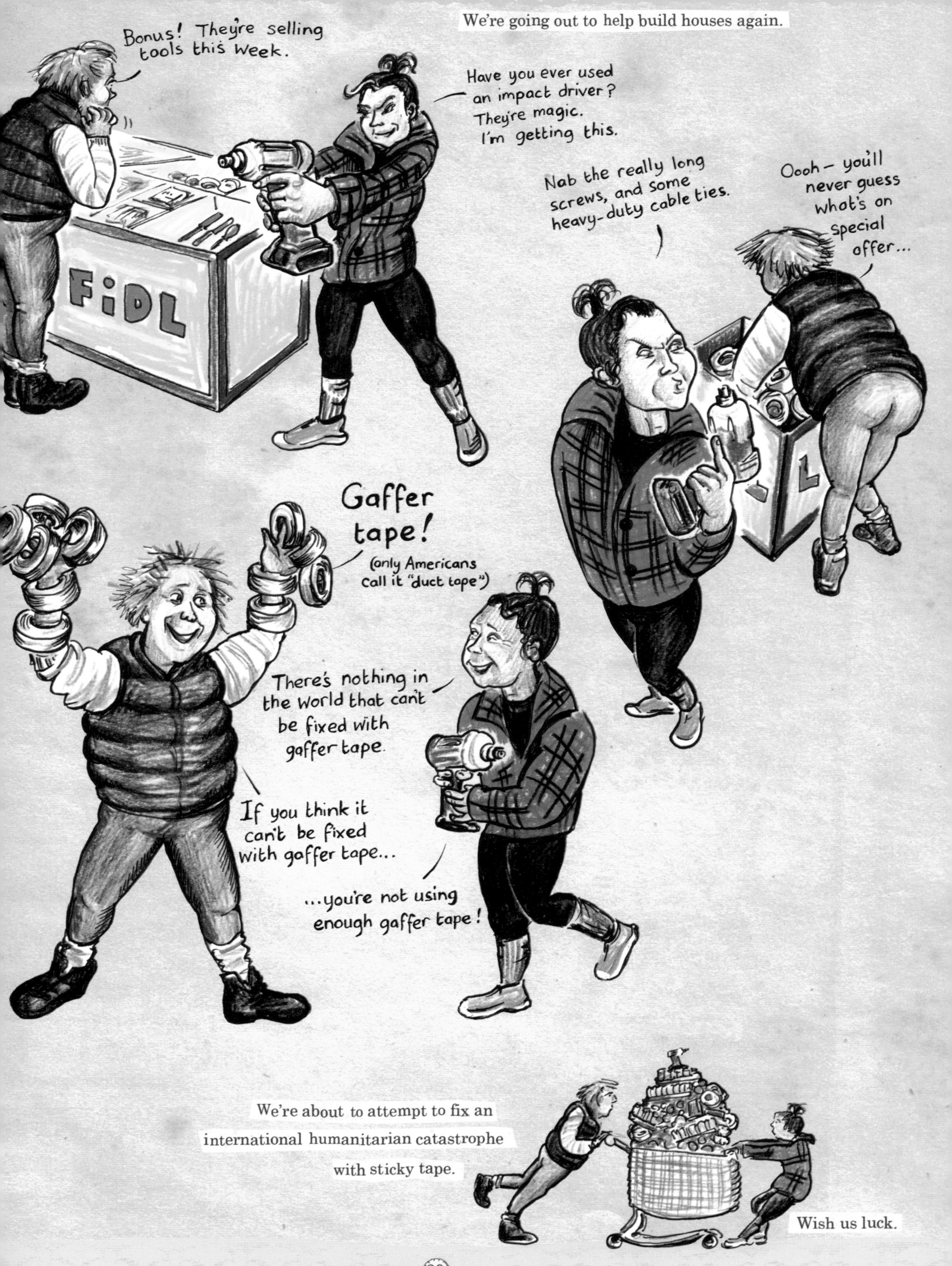
We're going out to help build houses again.
Bonus! They're selling tools this week.
Have you ever used an impact driver? They're magic. I'm getting this.
FiDL
Nab the really long screws, and some heavy-duty cable ties.
Oooh – you'll never guess what's on special offer...
Gaffer tape!
(only Americans call it "duct tape")
There's nothing in the world that can't be fixed with gaffer tape.
If you think it can't be fixed with gaffer tape...
...you're not using enough gaffer tape!
We're about to attempt to fix an international humanitarian catastrophe with sticky tape.
Wish us luck.

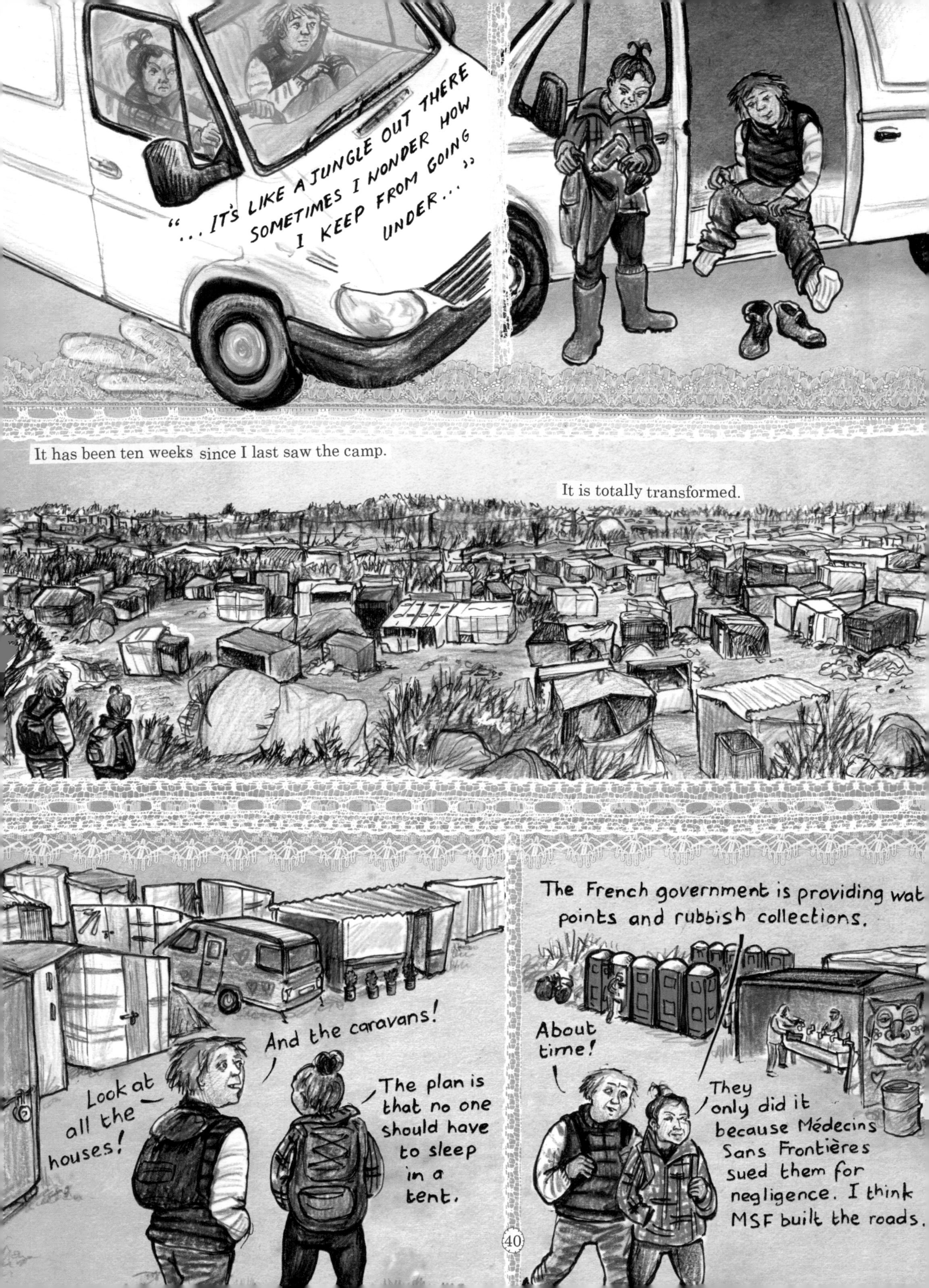

"... IT'S LIKE A JUNGLE OUT THERE
SOMETIMES I WONDER HOW
I KEEP FROM GOING
UNDER..."
It has been ten weeks since I last saw the camp.
It is totally transformed.
Look at all the houses!
And the caravans!
The plan is that no one should have to sleep in a tent.
The French government is providing wat points and rubbish collections.
About time!
They only did it because Médecins Sans Frontières sued them for negligence. I think MSF built the roads.

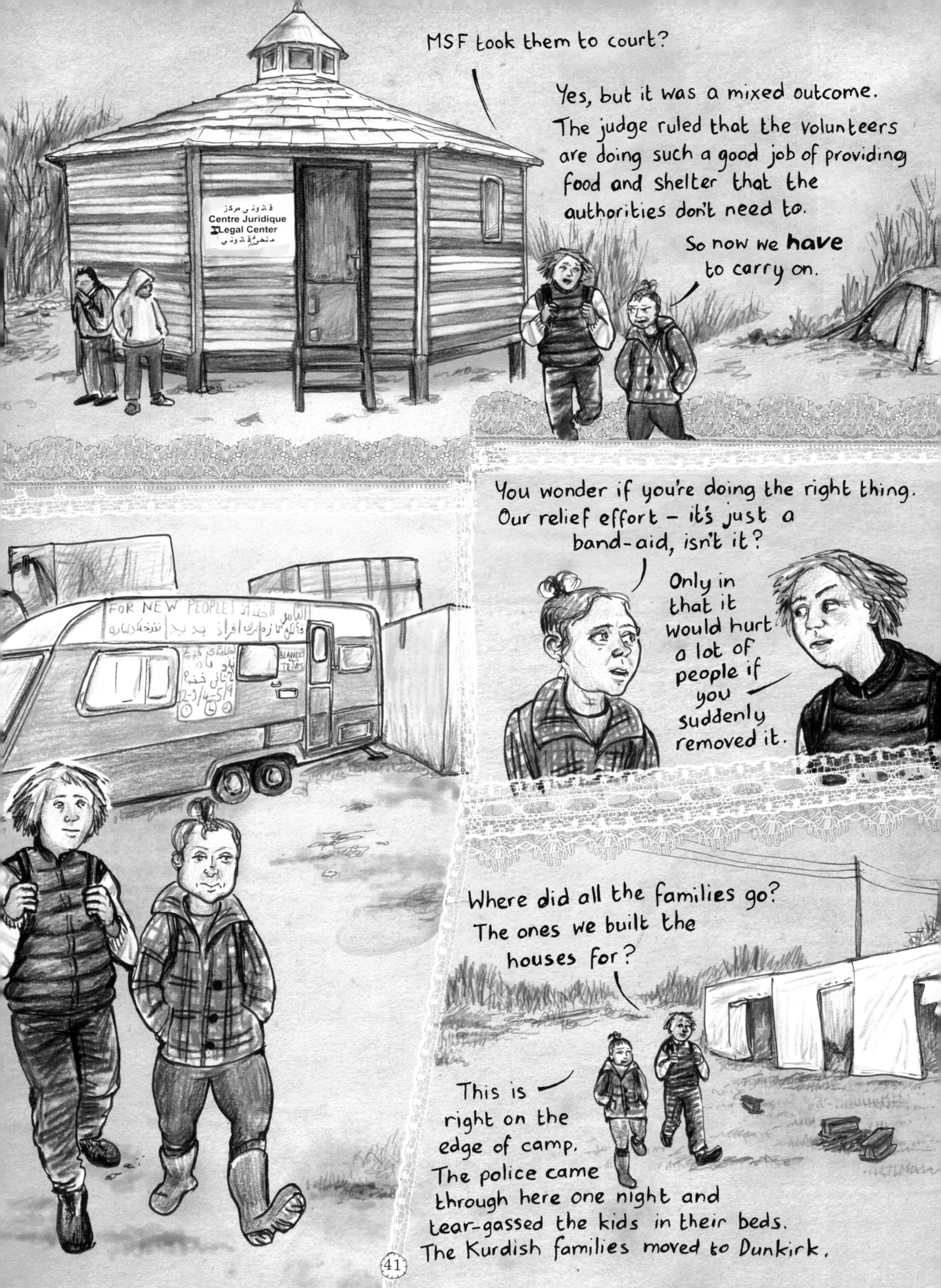
Centre Juridique
Legal Center
MSF took them to court?
Yes, but it was a mixed outcome.
The judge ruled that the volunteers are doing such a good job of providing food and shelter that the authorities don't need to.
So now we **have** to carry on.
FOR NEW PEOPLE!
You wonder if you're doing the right thing. Our relief effort – it's just a band-aid, isn't it?
Only in that it would hurt a lot of people if you suddenly removed it.
Where did all the families go? The ones we built the houses for?
This is right on the edge of camp. The police came through here one night and tear-gassed the kids in their beds. The Kurdish families moved to Dunkirk.

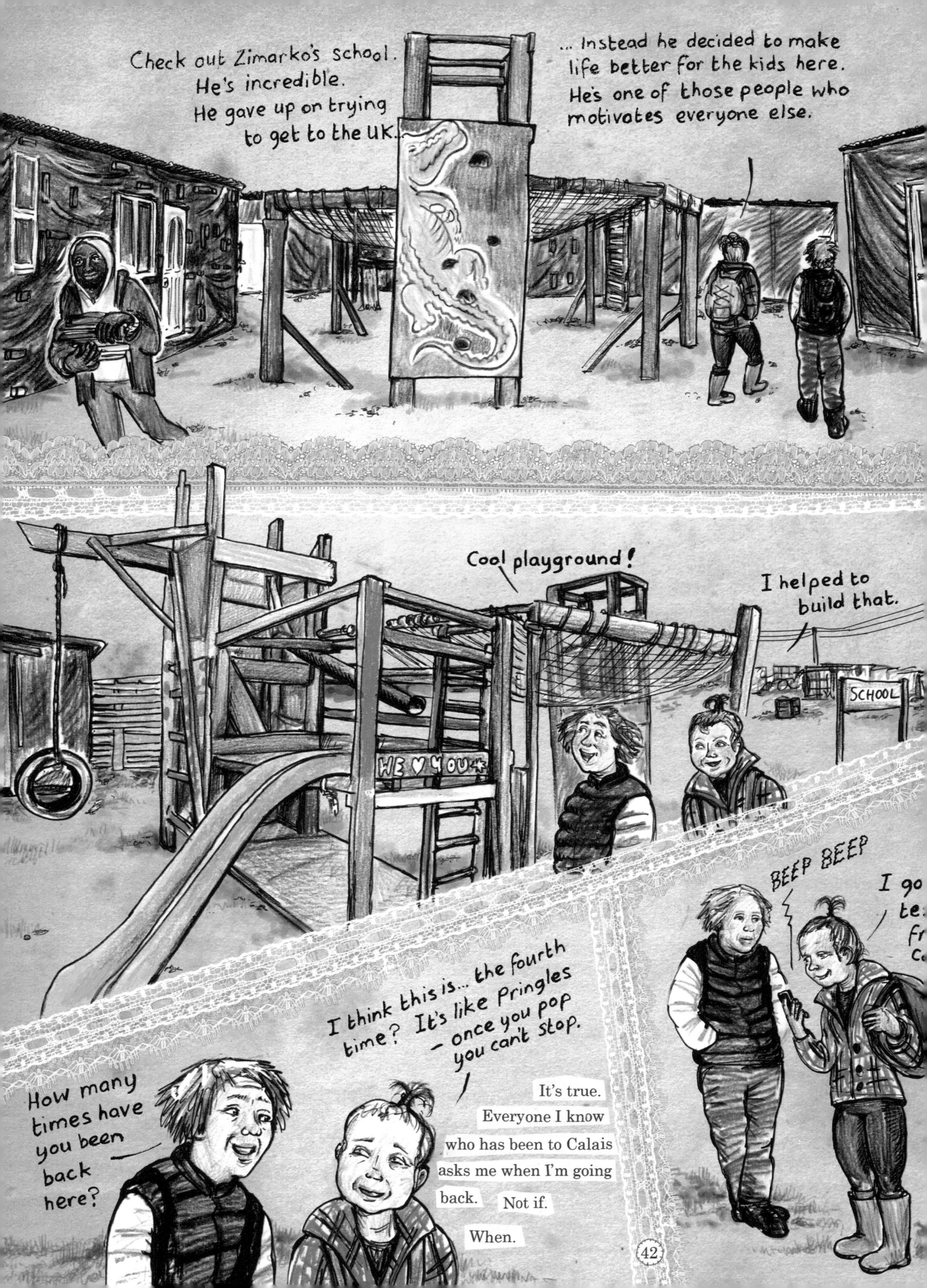
Check out Zimarko's school. He's incredible. He gave up on trying to get to the UK...
... Instead he decided to make life better for the kids here. He's one of those people who motivates everyone else.
Cool playground!
I helped to build that.
WE ♥ YOU
SCHOOL
How many times have you been back here?
I think this is... the fourth time? It's like Pringles – once you pop you can't stop.
It's true.
Everyone I know
who has been to Calais
asks me when I'm going
back.
Not if.
When.
BEEP BEEP
I go

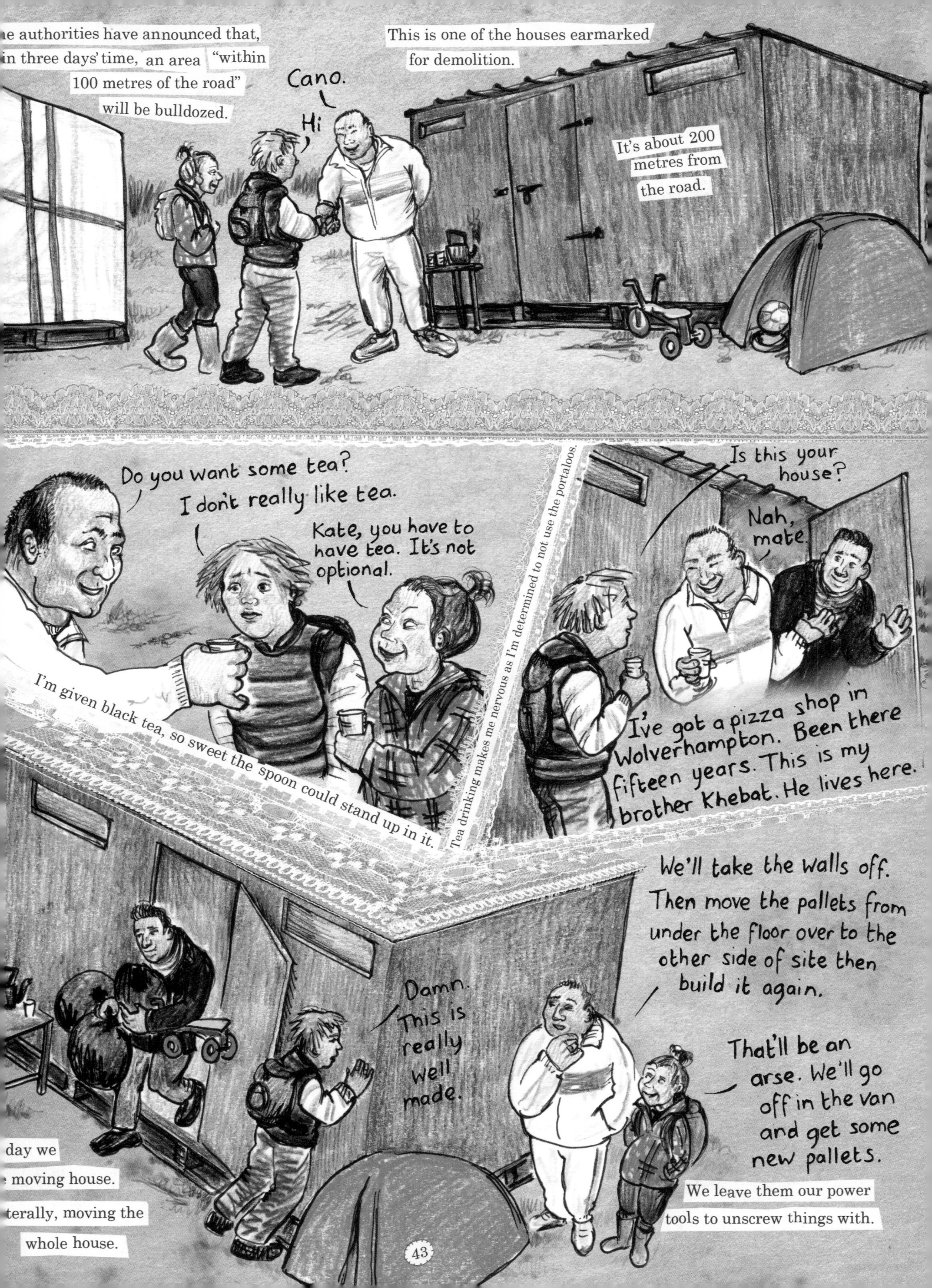

e authorities have announced that, in three days' time, an area "within 100 metres of the road" will be bulldozed.
This is one of the houses earmarked for demolition.
Cano.
Hi
It's about 200 metres from the road.
Do you want some tea?
I don't really like tea.
Kate, you have to have tea. It's not optional.
I'm given black tea, so sweet the spoon could stand up in it.
Tea drinking makes me nervous as I'm determined to not use the portaloos.
Is this your house?
Nah, mate.
I've got a pizza shop in Wolverhampton. Been there fifteen years. This is my brother Khebat. He lives here.
We'll take the walls off. Then move the pallets from under the floor over to the other side of site then build it again.
Damn. This is really well made.
That'll be an arse. We'll go off in the van and get some new pallets.
day we moving house. terally, moving the whole house.
We leave them our power tools to unscrew things with.

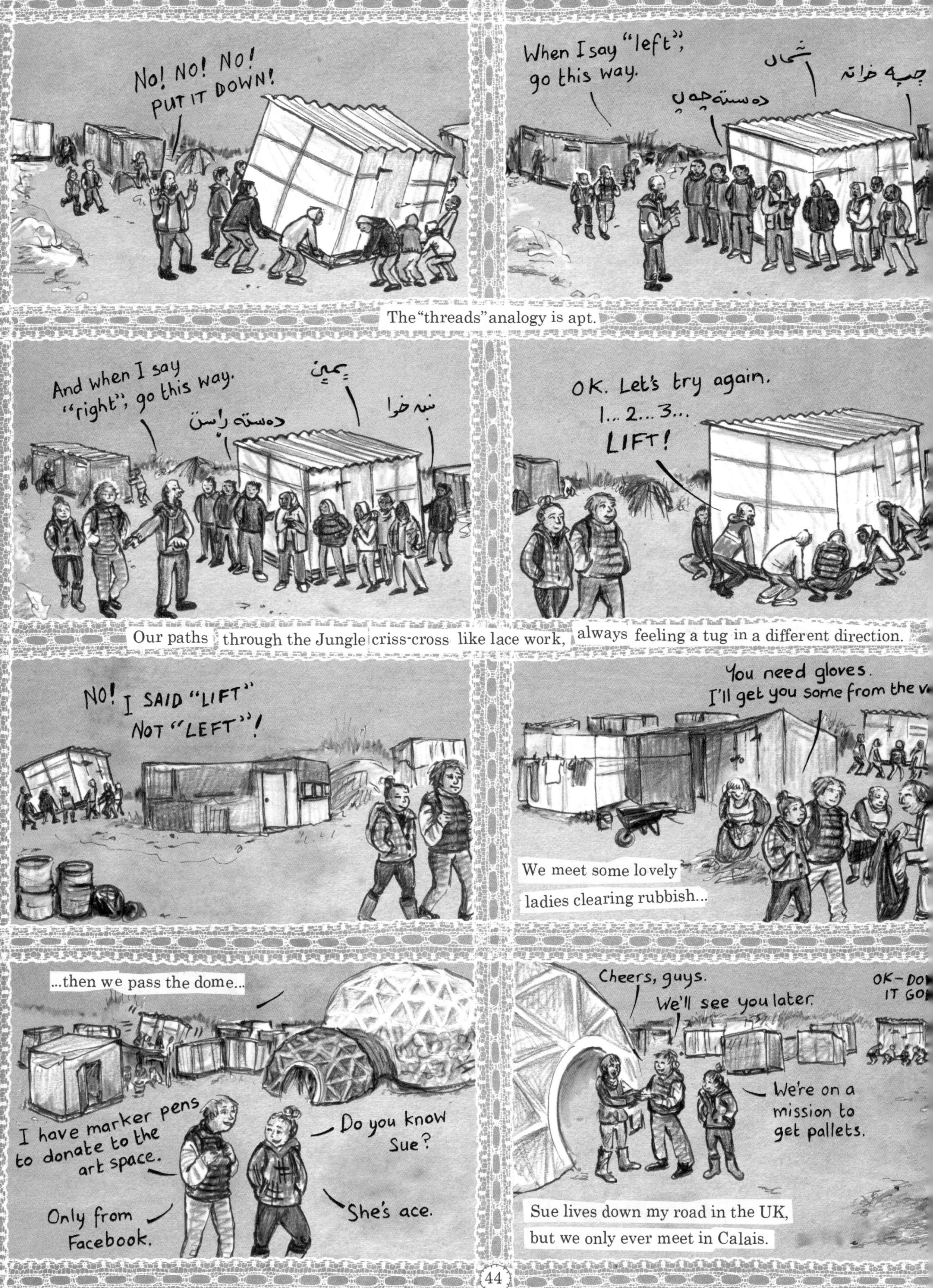
No! NO! NO! PUT IT DOWN!
When I say "left", go this way.
شمال
دەستەچەپ
چپه خواته
The "threads" analogy is apt.
And when I say "right", go this way.
يمين
دەستە راست
ښه خوا
OK. Let's try again. 1... 2... 3... LIFT!
Our paths through the Jungle criss-cross like lace work, always feeling a tug in a different direction.
NO! I SAID "LIFT" NOT "LEFT"!
You need gloves. I'll get you some from the v
We meet some lovely ladies clearing rubbish...
...then we pass the dome...
I have marker pens to donate to the art space.
Do you know Sue?
Only from Facebook.
She's ace.
Cheers, guys.
We'll see you later.
OK-DO IT GO
We're on a mission to get pallets.
Sue lives down my road in the UK, but we only ever meet in Calais.

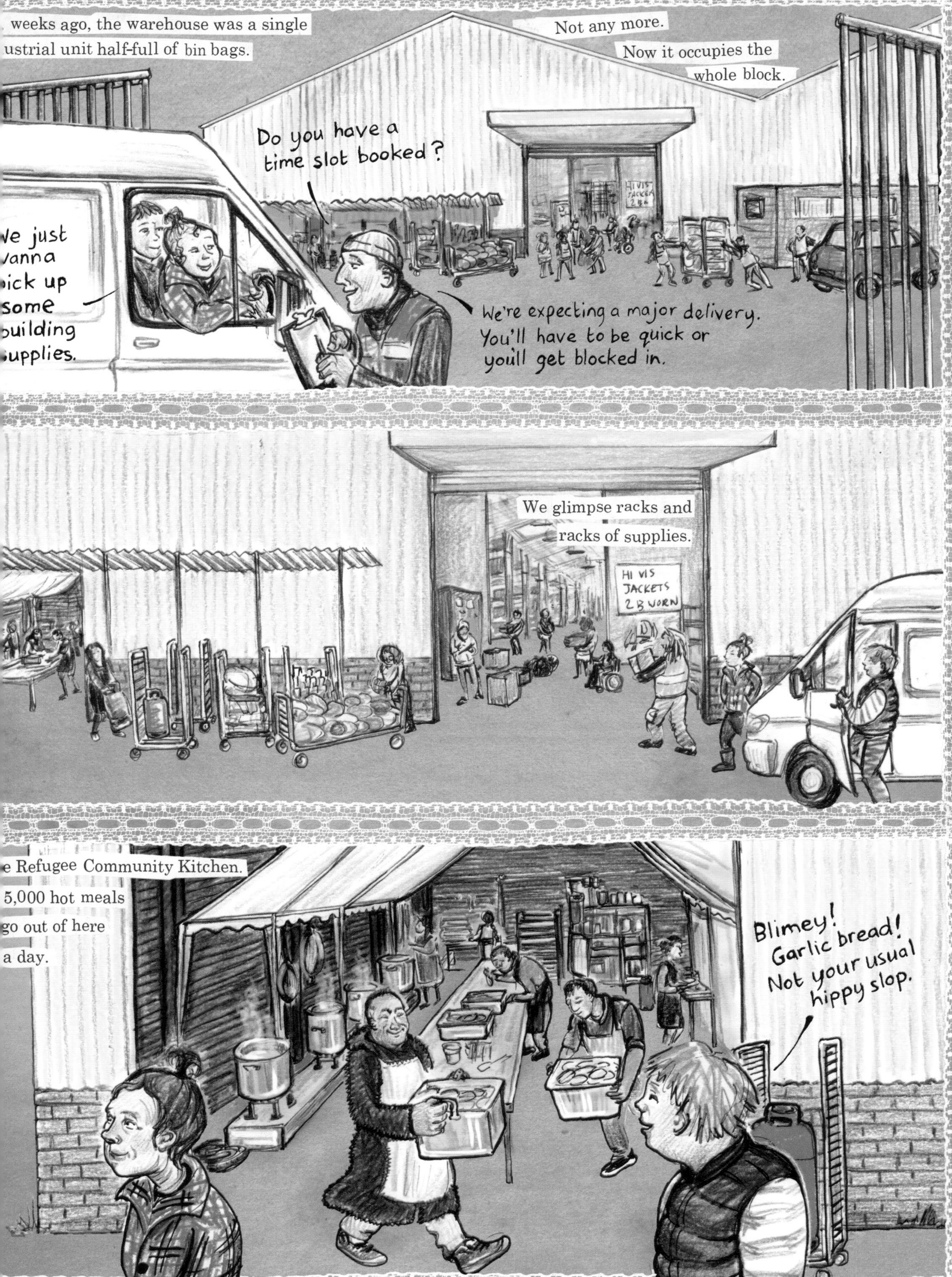
weeks ago, the warehouse was a single
ustrial unit half-full of bin bags.
Not any more.
Now it occupies the
whole block.
Do you have a time slot booked?
We just wanna pick up some building supplies.
We're expecting a major delivery. You'll have to be quick or you'll get blocked in.
We glimpse racks and
racks of supplies.
HI VIS JACKETS 2B WORN
e Refugee Community Kitchen.
5,000 hot meals
go out of here
a day.
Blimey! Garlic bread! Not your usual hippy slop.

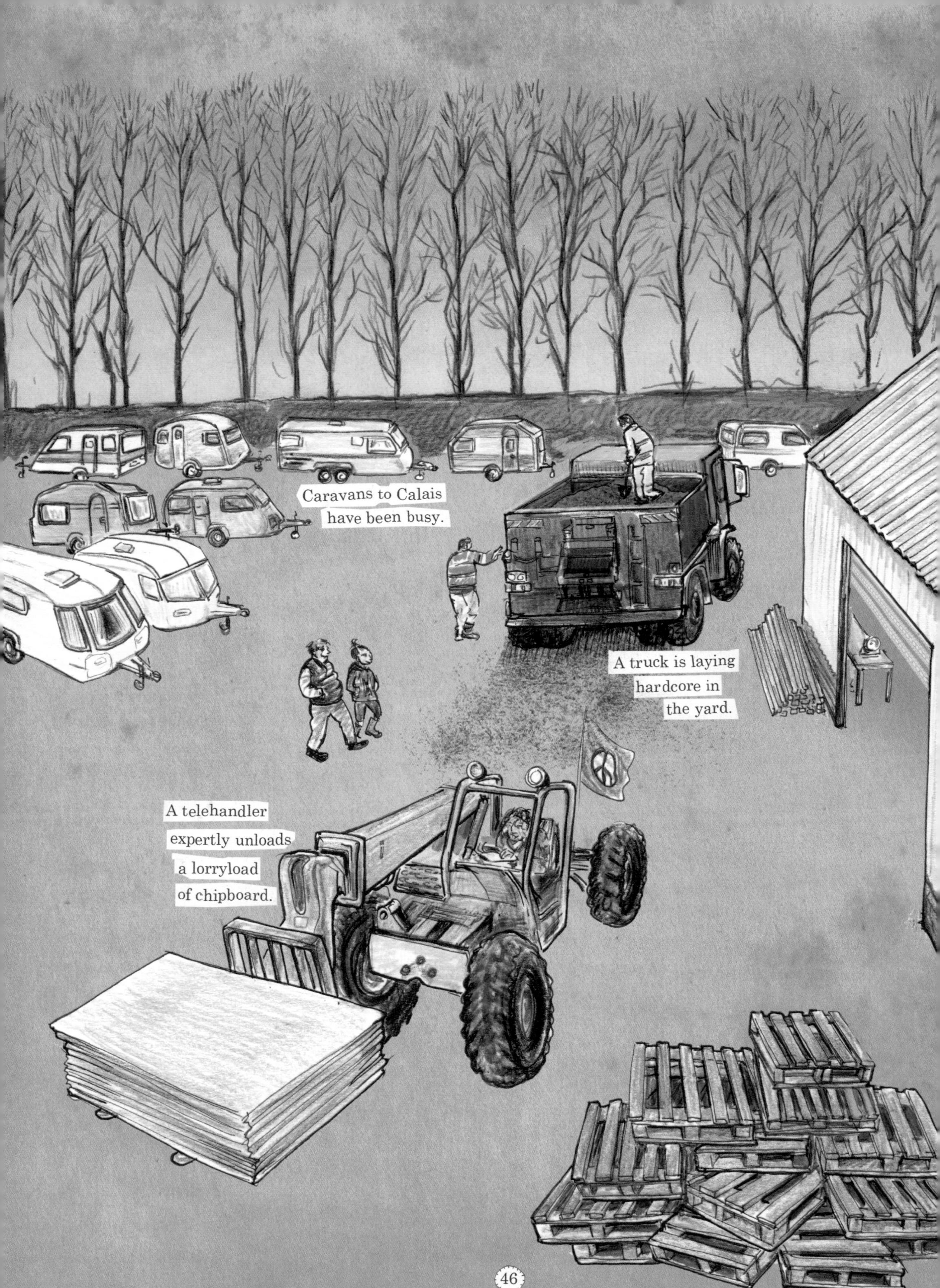
Caravans to Calais have been busy.
A truck is laying hardcore in the yard.
A telehandler expertly unloads a lorryload of chipboard.

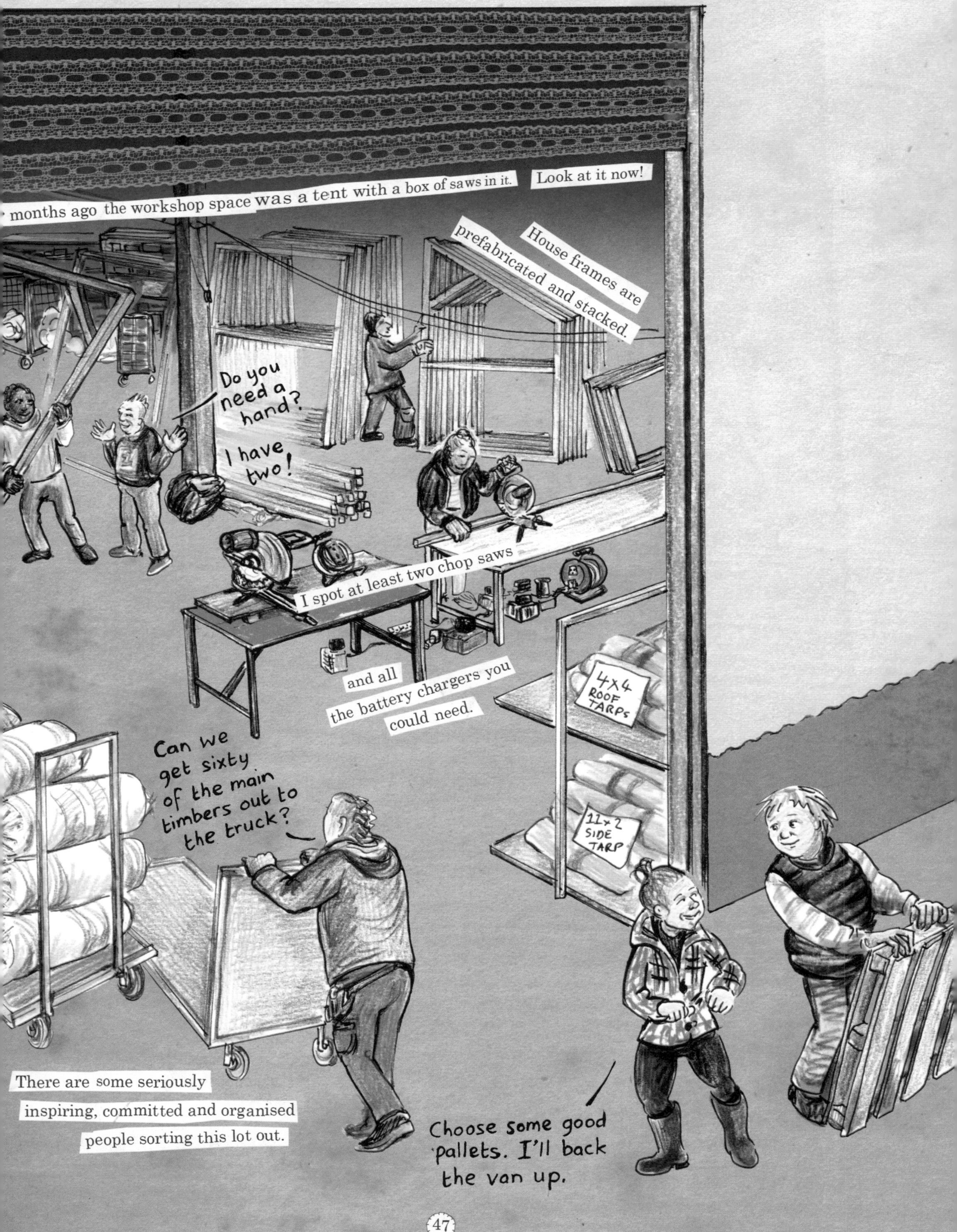
months ago the workshop space was a tent with a box of saws in it.
Look at it now!
House frames are prefabricated and stacked.
Do you need a hand?
I have two!
I spot at least two chop saws
and all the battery chargers you could need.
4x4 ROOF TARPS
11x2 SIDE TARP
Can we get sixty of the main timbers out to the truck?
There are some seriously inspiring, committed and organised people sorting this lot out.
Choose some good pallets. I'll back the van up.

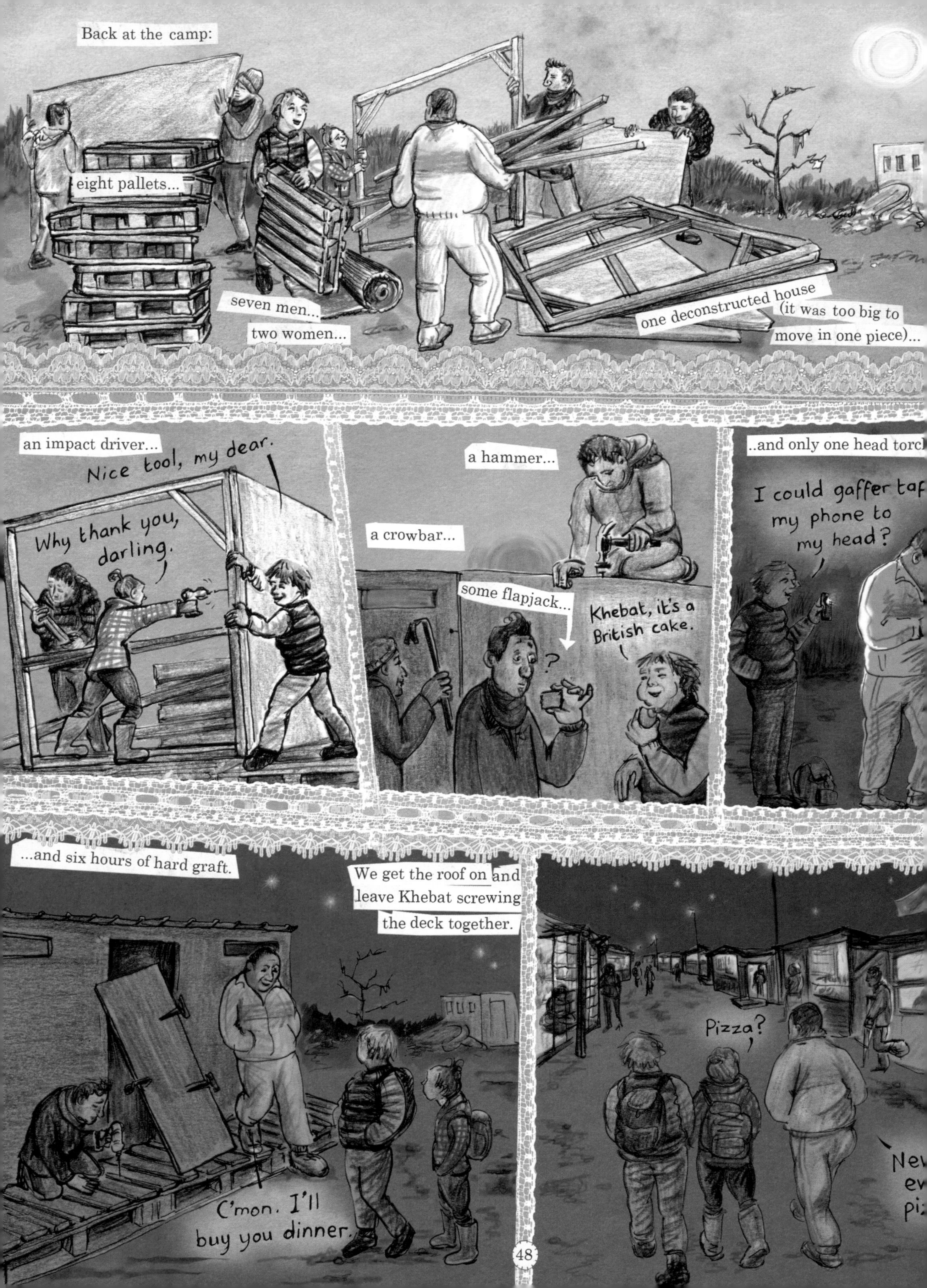

Back at the camp:
eight pallets...
seven men...
two women...
one deconstructed house (it was too big to move in one piece)...
an impact driver...
Nice tool, my dear.
Why thank you, darling.
a hammer...
a crowbar...
some flapjack...
?
Khebat, it's a British cake.
..and only one head torc
I could gaffer ta
my phone to
my head?
...and six hours of hard graft.
We get the roof on and leave Khebat screwing the deck together.
C'mon. I'll buy you dinner.
Pizza?

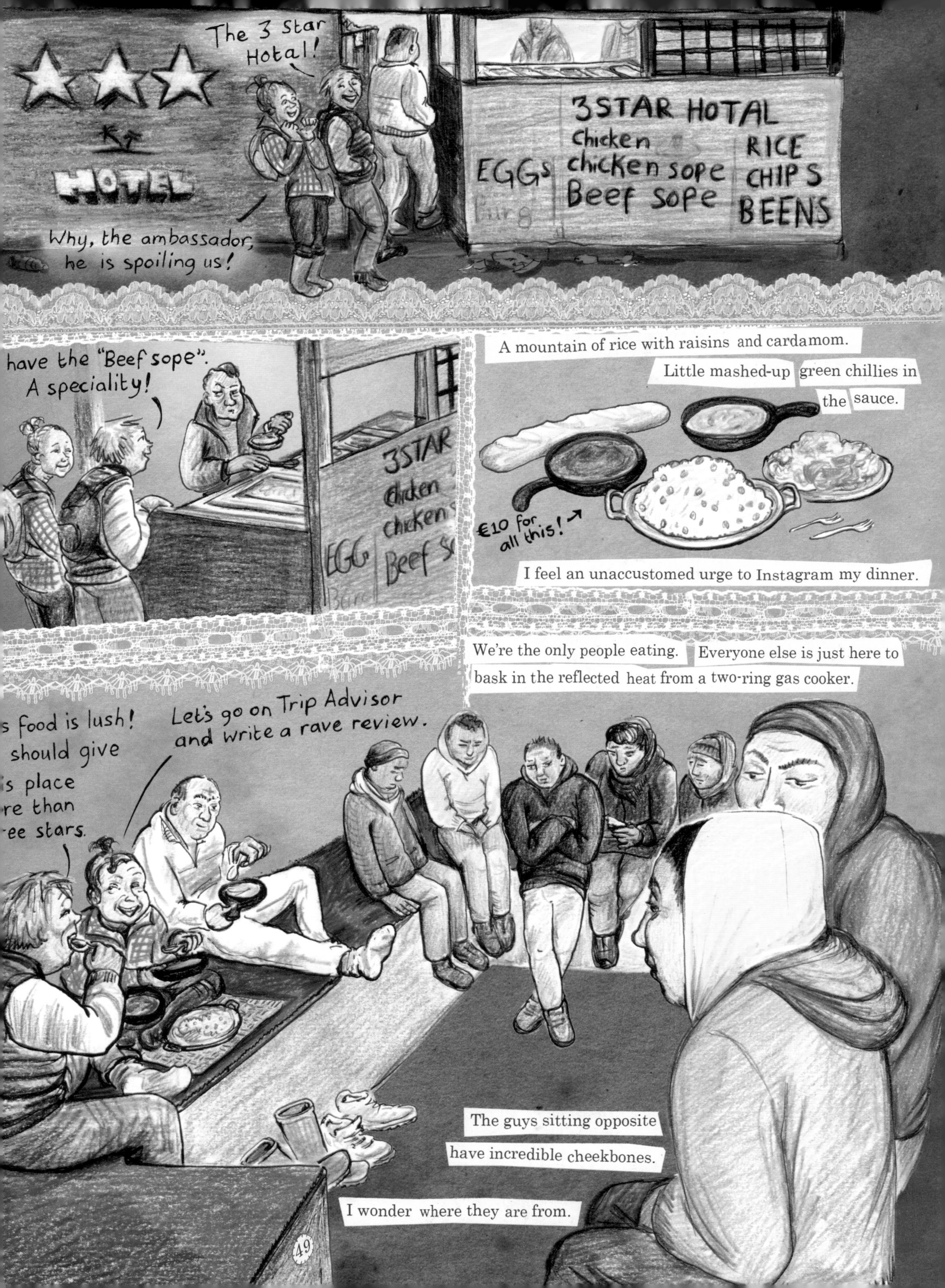

The 3 Star Hotal!
HOTEL
Why, the ambassador, he is spoiling us!
3STAR HOTAL
EGGs
Chicken
chicken sope
Beef sope
RICE
CHIPS
BEENS
have the "Beef sope". A speciality!
3STAR
Chicken
chicken
EGG
Beef S
A mountain of rice with raisins and cardamom.
Little mashed-up green chillies in the sauce.
€10 for all this!
I feel an unaccustomed urge to Instagram my dinner.
We're the only people eating. Everyone else is just here to bask in the reflected heat from a two-ring gas cooker.
s food is lush! should give s place re than ee stars.
Let's go on Trip Advisor and write a rave review.
The guys sitting opposite have incredible cheekbones.
I wonder where they are from.

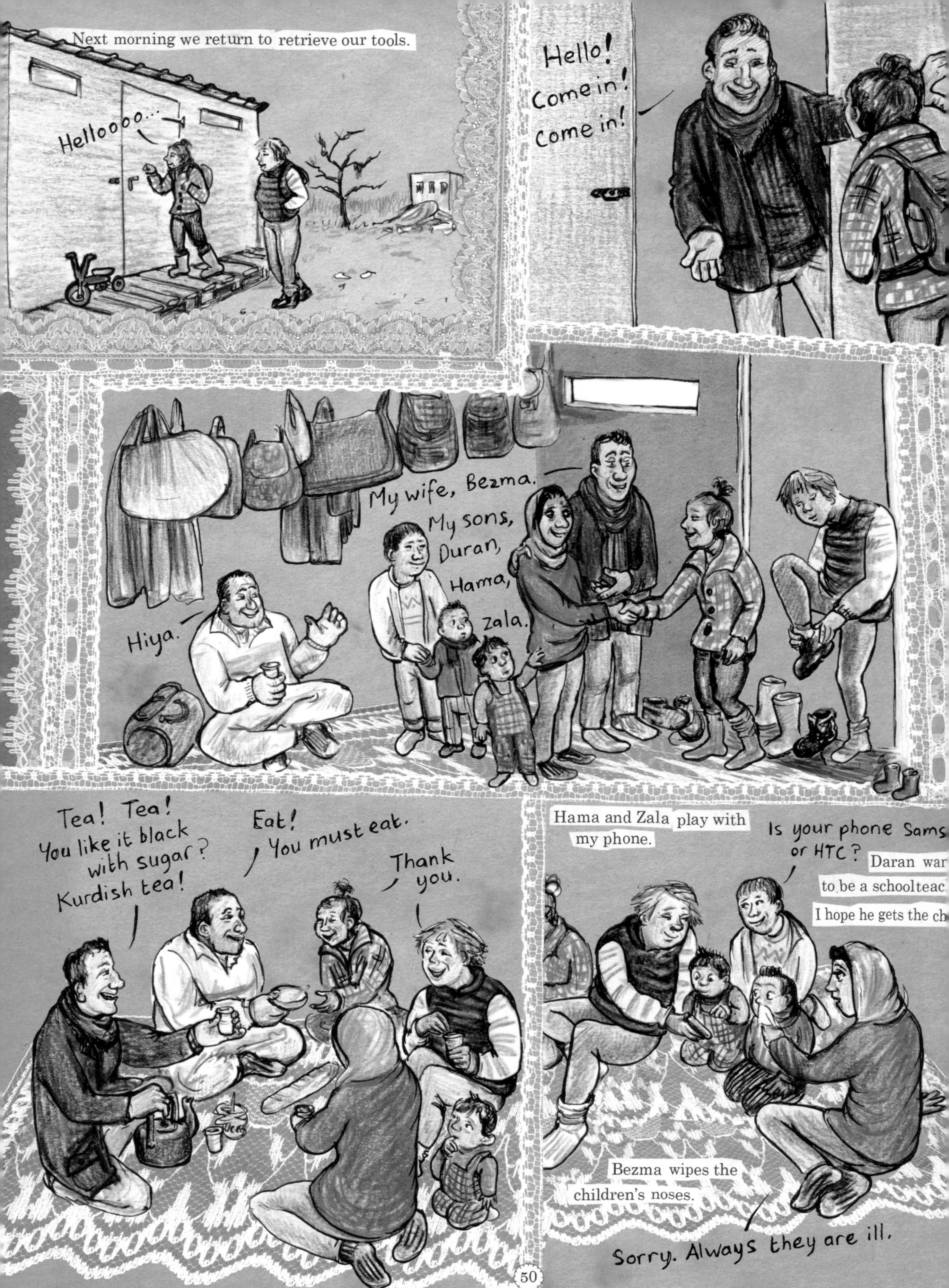
Next morning we return to retrieve our tools.
Helloooo...
Hello! Come in! Come in!
My wife, Bezma.
My sons, Duran, Hama, Zala.
Hiya.
Tea! Tea! You like it black with sugar? Kurdish tea!
Eat! You must eat.
Thank you.
Hama and Zala play with my phone.
Is your phone Sams or HTC?
Daran war to be a schoolteac
I hope he gets the ch
Bezma wipes the children's noses.
Sorry. Always they are ill.

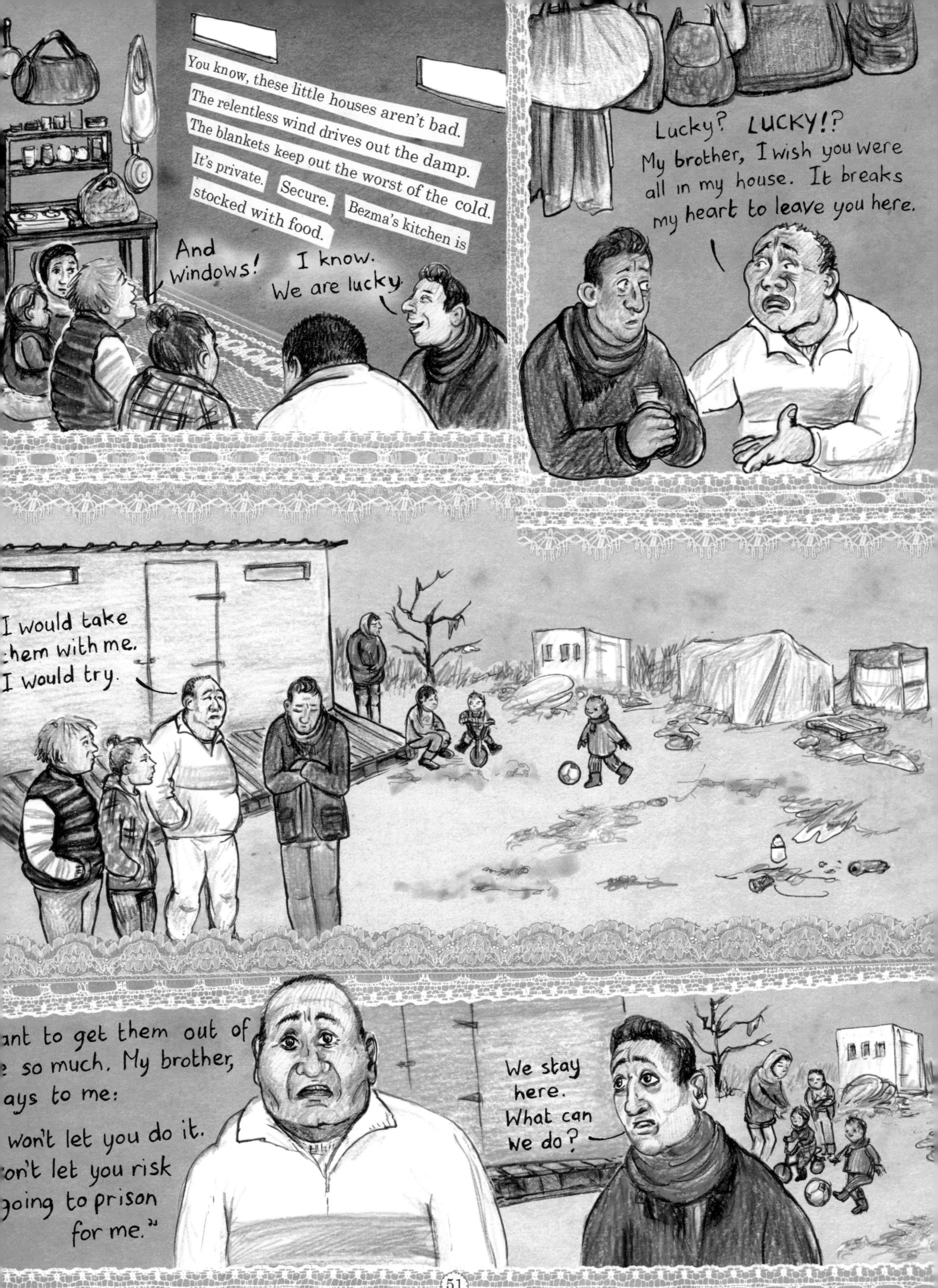
You know, these little houses aren't bad.
The relentless wind drives out the damp.
The blankets keep out the worst of the cold.
It's private.
Secure.
Bezma's kitchen is stocked with food.
And windows!
I know. We are lucky.
Lucky? LUCKY!?
My brother, I wish you were all in my house. It breaks my heart to leave you here.
I would take
hem with me.
I would try.
ant to get them out of
e so much. My brother,
ays to me:
won't let you do it.
on't let you risk
going to prison
for me."
We stay here. What can we do?

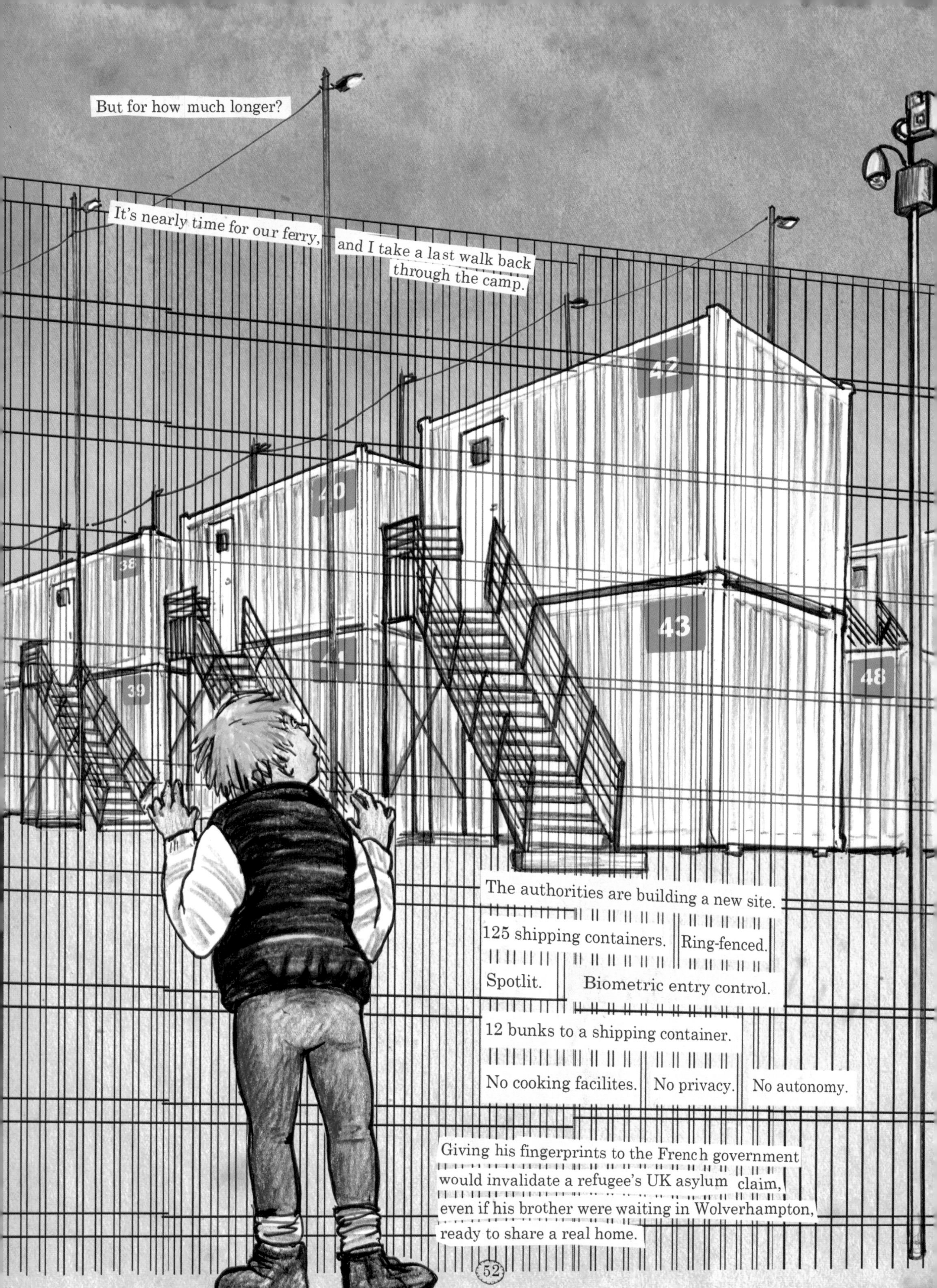
But for how much longer?
It's nearly time for our ferry,
and I take a last walk back through the camp.
The authorities are building a new site.
125 shipping containers.
Ring-fenced.
Spotlit.
Biometric entry control.
12 bunks to a shipping container.
No cooking facilites.
No privacy.
No autonomy.
Giving his fingerprints to the French government would invalidate a refugee's UK asylum claim, even if his brother were waiting in Wolverhampton, ready to share a real home.

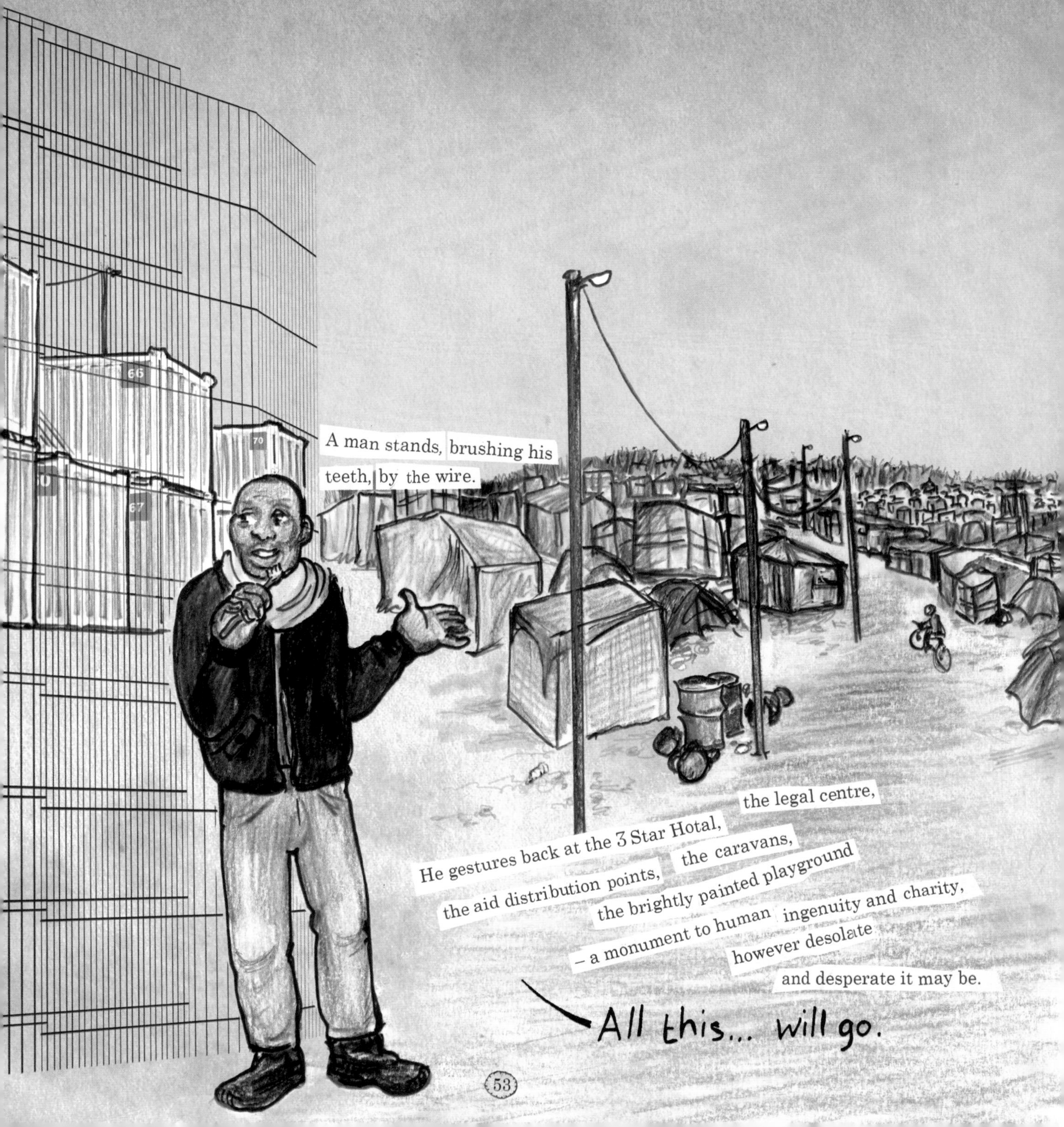
A man stands, brushing his teeth, by the wire.
He gestures back at the 3 Star Hotal, the legal centre,
the aid distribution points, the caravans,
the brightly painted playground
– a monument to human ingenuity and charity,
however desolate
and desperate it may be.
All this... will go.

Oh, you're volunteering in Calais?
That's, like, the ultimate fashion statement these days...

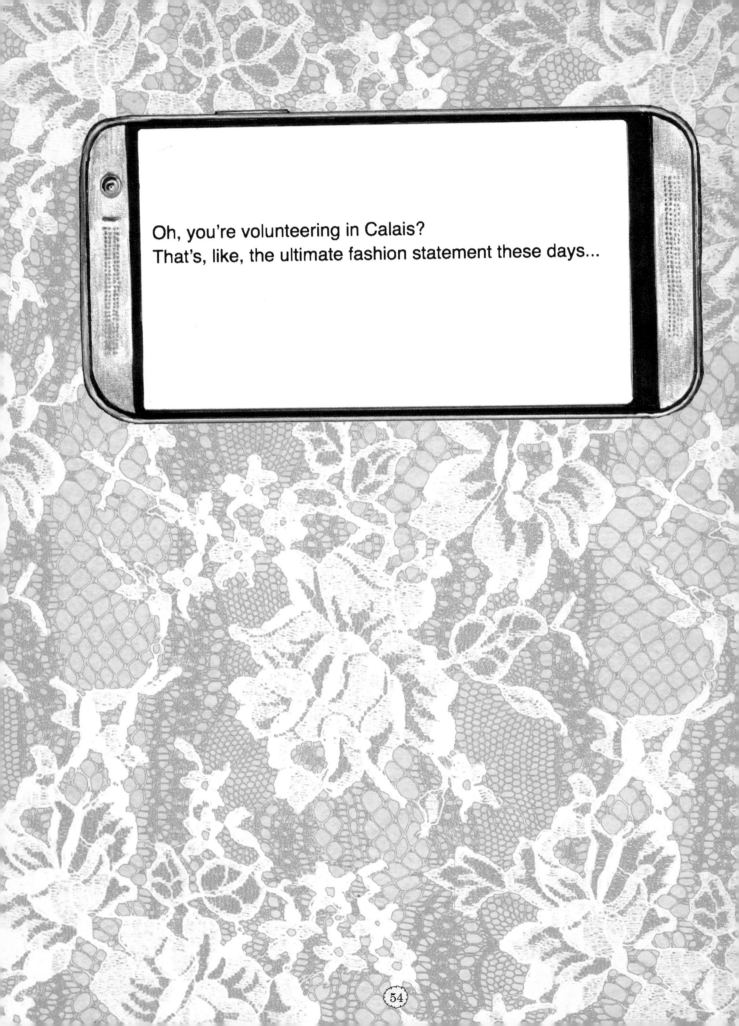

It's Not a Fucking Day Trip

Fuck misery tourism.

What are we doing, swanning about Calais, congratulating ourselves on our fabulous relief effort?

It's not about a bunch of white, middle-class do-gooders off on a charity holiday.

Let me tell you about Hoshyar.

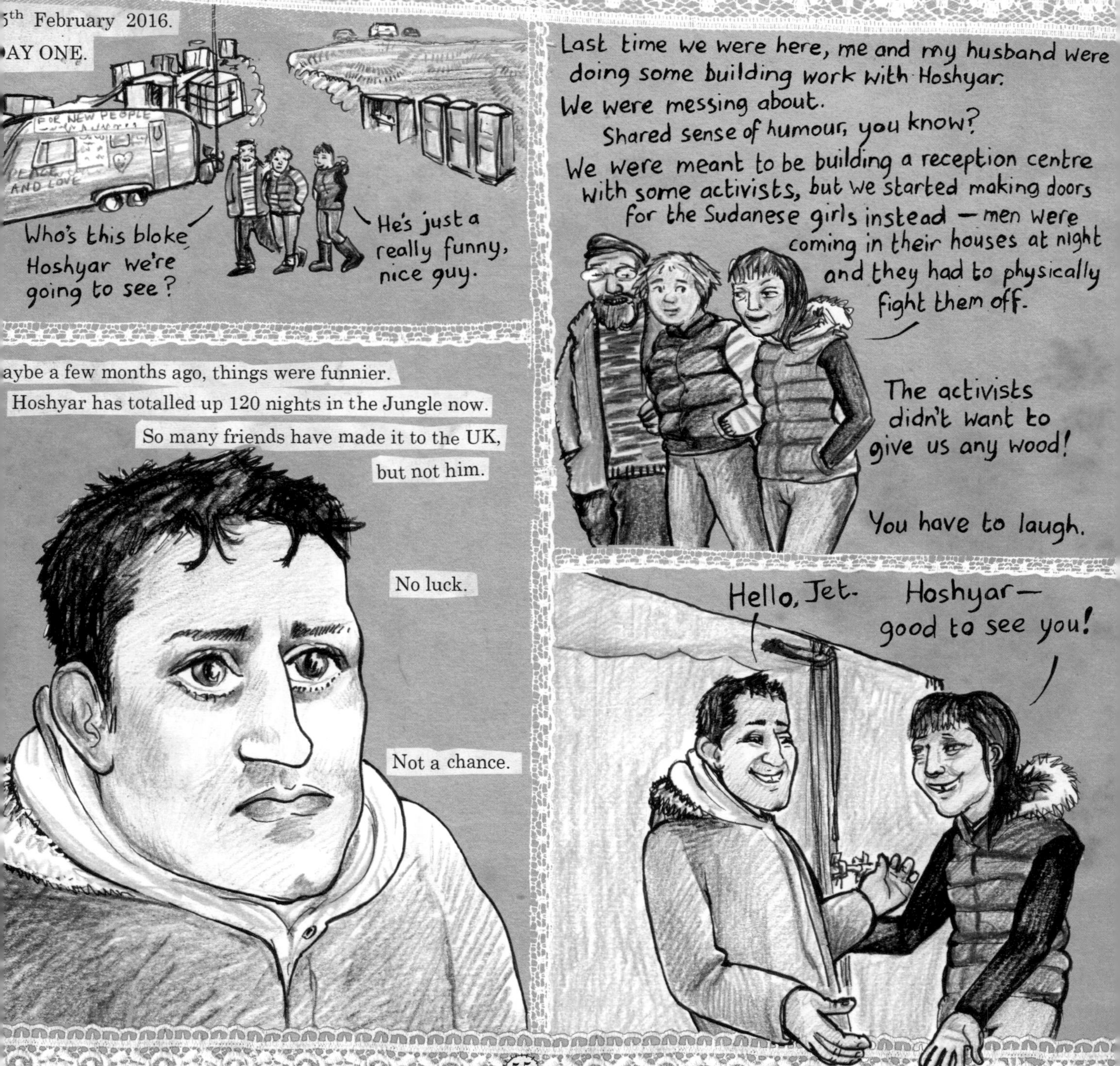

5th February 2016.
AY ONE.
FOR NEW PEOPLE
PEACE AND LOVE
Who's this bloke Hoshyar we're going to see?
He's just a really funny, nice guy.
Last time we were here, me and my husband were doing some building work with Hoshyar.
We were messing about.
Shared sense of humour, you know?
We were meant to be building a reception centre with some activists, but we started making doors for the Sudanese girls instead — men were coming in their houses at night and they had to physically fight them off.
The activists didn't want to give us any wood!
You have to laugh.
aybe a few months ago, things were funnier.
Hoshyar has totalled up 120 nights in the Jungle now.
So many friends have made it to the UK,
but not him.
No luck.
Not a chance.
Hello, Jet.
Hoshyar — good to see you!

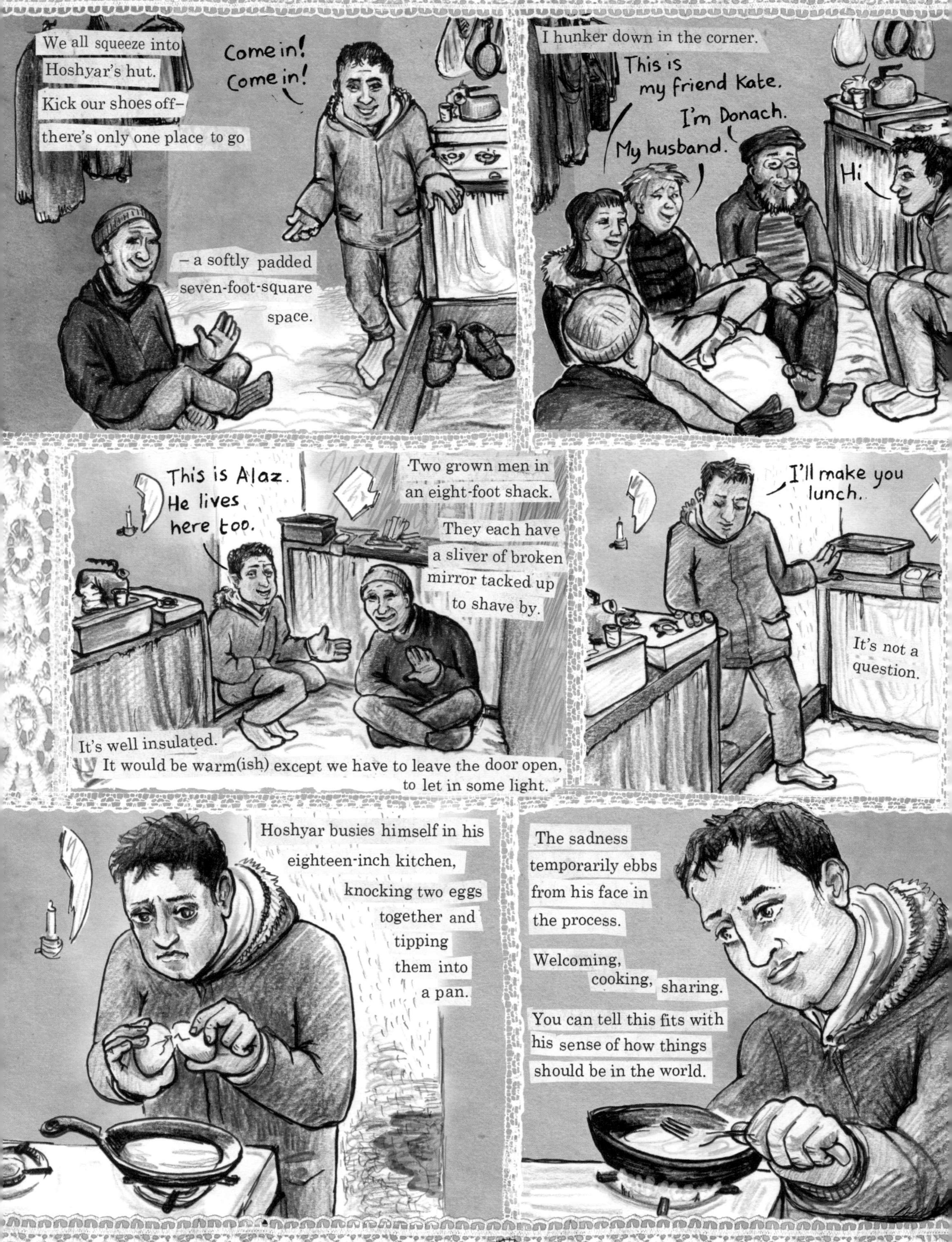

We all squeeze into
Hoshyar's hut.
Kick our shoes off–
there's only one place to go
Come in! Come in!
– a softly padded
seven-foot-square
space.
I hunker down in the corner.
This is my friend Kate.
My husband.
I'm Donach.
Hi
This is Alaz. He lives here too.
Two grown men in
an eight-foot shack.
They each have
a sliver of broken
mirror tacked up
to shave by.
It's well insulated.
It would be warm(ish) except we have to leave the door open,
to let in some light.
I'll make you lunch.
It's not a
question.
Hoshyar busies himself in his
eighteen-inch kitchen,
knocking two eggs
together and
tipping
them into
a pan.
The sadness
temporarily ebbs
from his face in
the process.
Welcoming,
cooking,
sharing.
You can tell this fits with
his sense of how things
should be in the world.

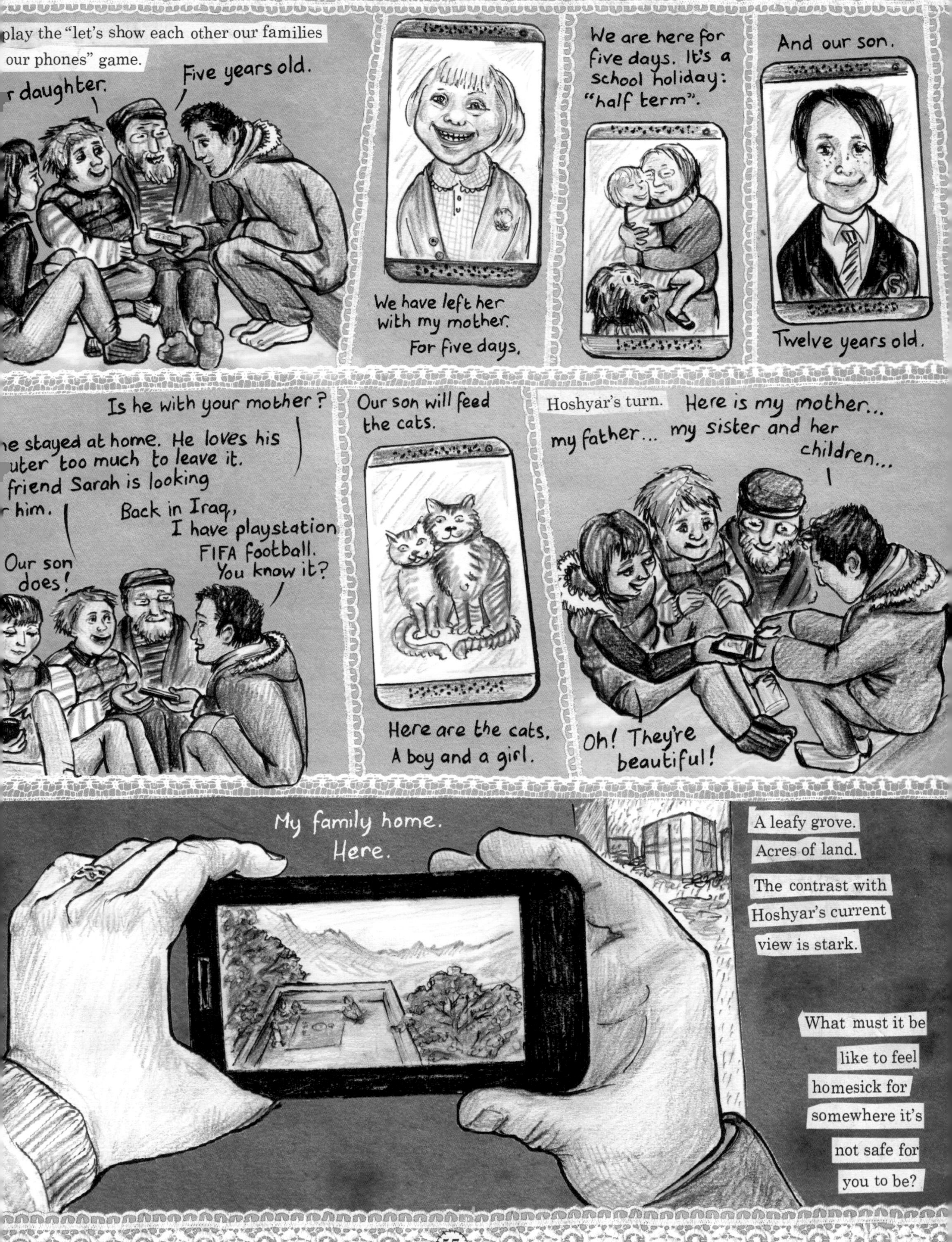

play the "let's show each other our families
our phones" game.
r daughter.
Five years old.
We have left her with my mother.
For five days.
We are here for five days. It's a school holiday: "half term".
And our son.
Twelve years old.
Is he with your mother?
he stayed at home. He loves his
uter too much to leave it.
friend Sarah is looking
r him.
Our son does!
Back in Iraq, I have playstation FIFA football. You know it?
Our son will feed the cats.
Here are the cats. A boy and a girl.
Hoshyar's turn.
Here is my mother... my father... my sister and her children...
Oh! They're beautiful!
My family home. Here.
A leafy grove.
Acres of land.
The contrast with Hoshyar's current view is stark.
What must it be like to feel homesick for somewhere it's not safe for you to be?

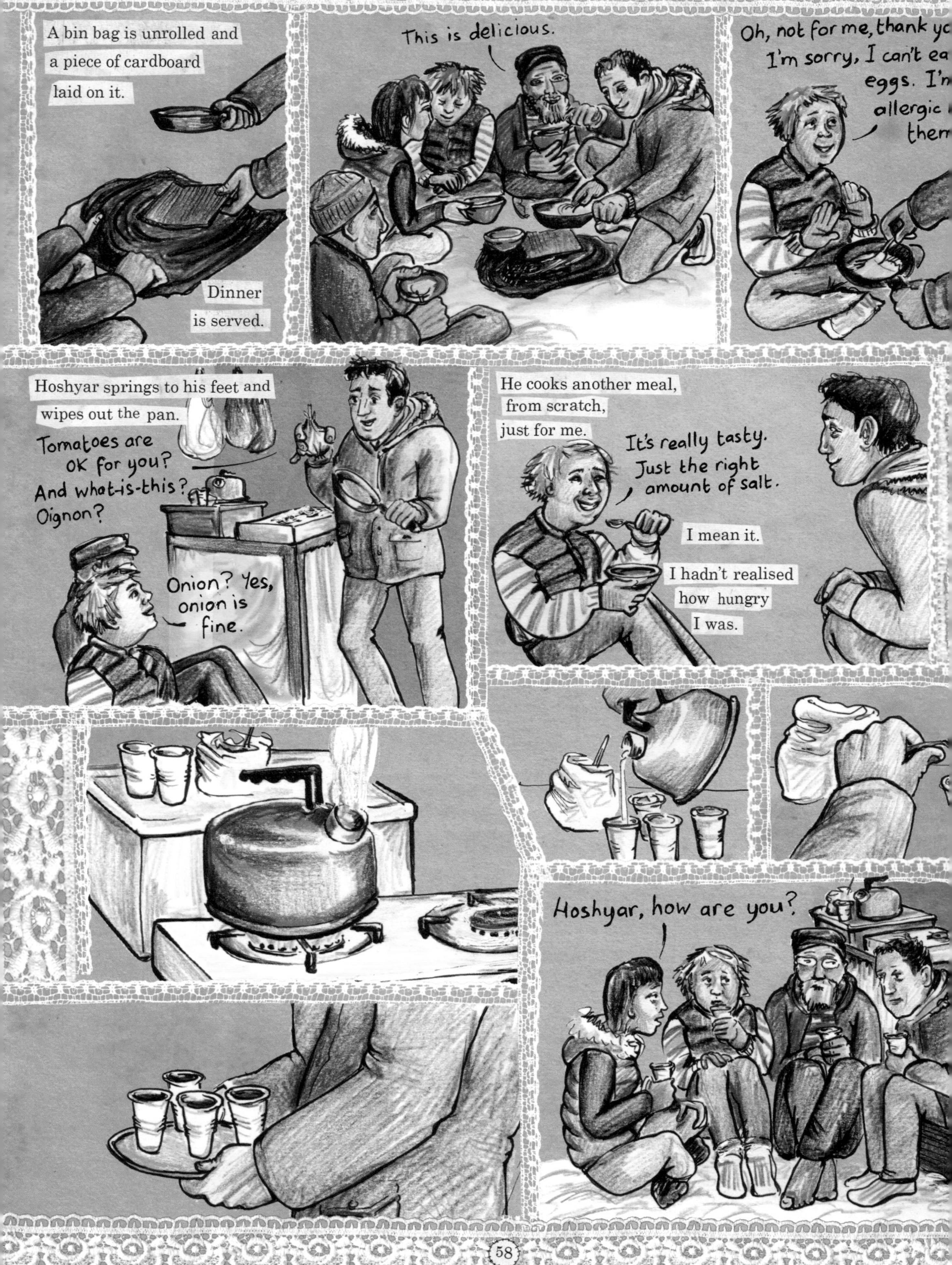
A bin bag is unrolled and a piece of cardboard laid on it.
Dinner is served.
This is delicious.
Oh, not for me, thank yo
I'm sorry, I can't ea
eggs. I'r
allergic
them
Hoshyar springs to his feet and wipes out the pan.
Tomatoes are OK for you? And what-is-this? Oignon?
Onion? Yes, onion is fine.
He cooks another meal, from scratch, just for me.
It's really tasty. Just the right amount of salt.
I mean it.
I hadn't realised how hungry I was.
Hoshyar, how are you?

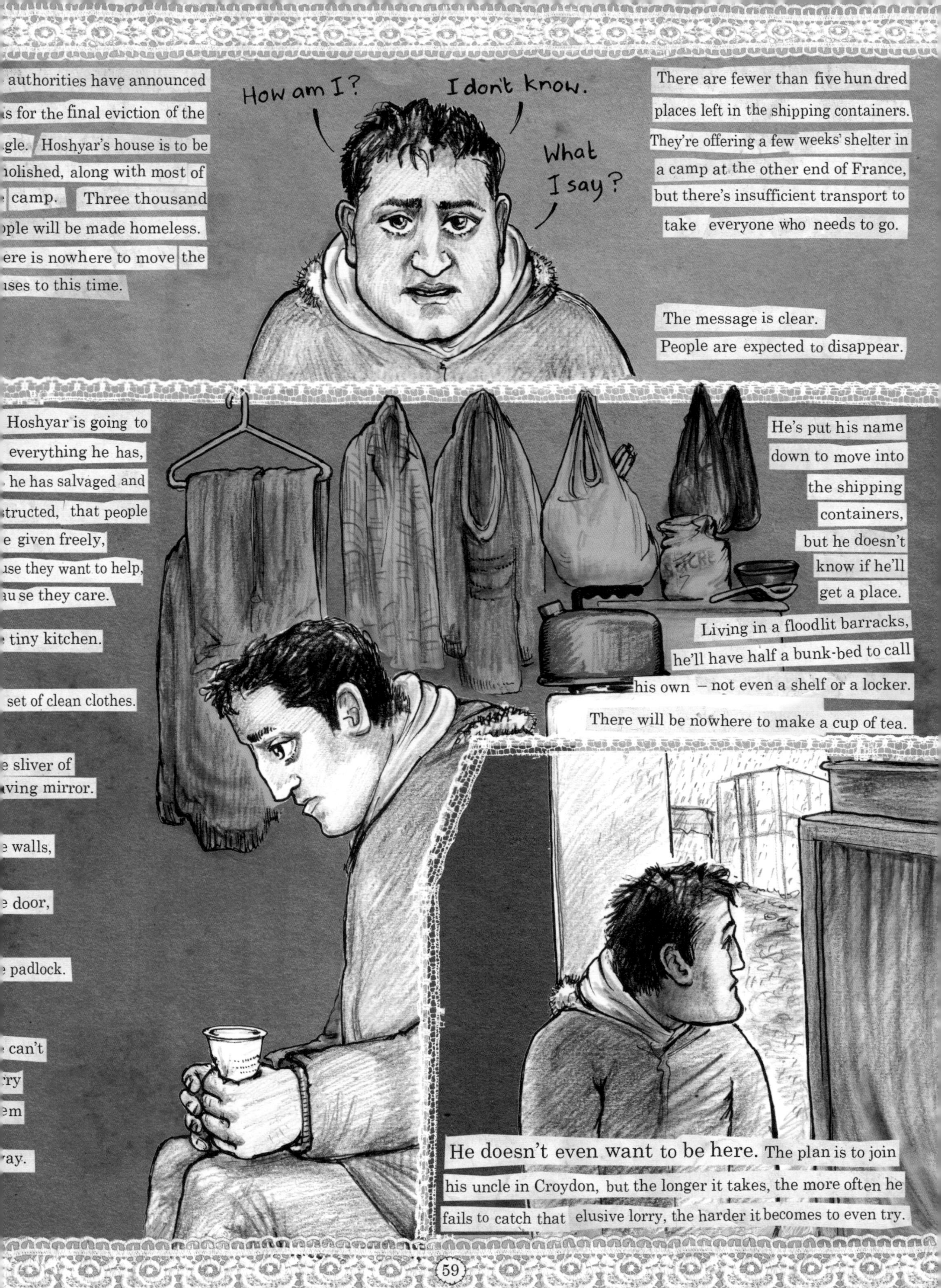
authorities have announced
is for the final eviction of the
gle. Hoshyar's house is to be
nolished, along with most of
camp. Three thousand
ople will be made homeless.
ere is nowhere to move the
uses to this time.
How am I?
I don't know.
What I say?
There are fewer than five hundred places left in the shipping containers. They're offering a few weeks' shelter in a camp at the other end of France, but there's insufficient transport to take everyone who needs to go.
The message is clear.
People are expected to disappear.
Hoshyar is going to
everything he has,
he has salvaged and
tructed, that people
e given freely,
use they want to help,
ause they care.
tiny kitchen.
set of clean clothes.
sliver of
ving mirror.
walls,
door,
padlock.
can't
rry
em
ay.
He's put his name down to move into the shipping containers, but he doesn't know if he'll get a place.
Living in a floodlit barracks, he'll have half a bunk-bed to call his own – not even a shelf or a locker.
There will be nowhere to make a cup of tea.
He doesn't even want to be here. The plan is to join his uncle in Croydon, but the longer it takes, the more often he fails to catch that elusive lorry, the harder it becomes to even try.

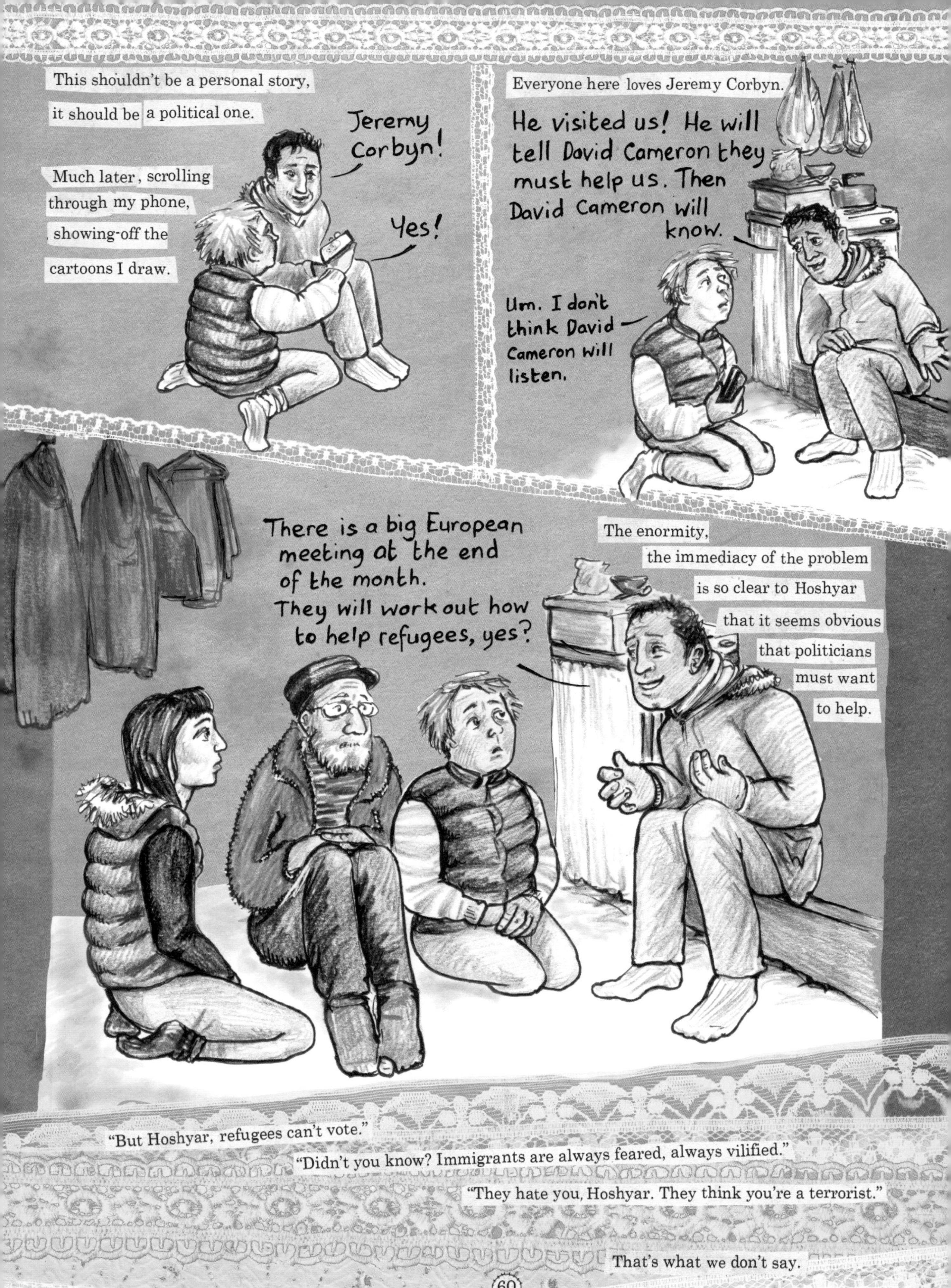
This shouldn't be a personal story,
it should be a political one.
Jeremy Corbyn!
Much later, scrolling through my phone, showing-off the cartoons I draw.
Yes!
Everyone here loves Jeremy Corbyn.
He visited us! He will tell David Cameron they must help us. Then David Cameron will know.
Um. I don't think David Cameron will listen.
There is a big European meeting at the end of the month. They will work out how to help refugees, yes?
The enormity, the immediacy of the problem is so clear to Hoshyar that it seems obvious that politicians must want to help.
"But Hoshyar, refugees can't vote."
"Didn't you know? Immigrants are always feared, always vilified."
"They hate you, Hoshyar. They think you're a terrorist."
That's what we don't say.

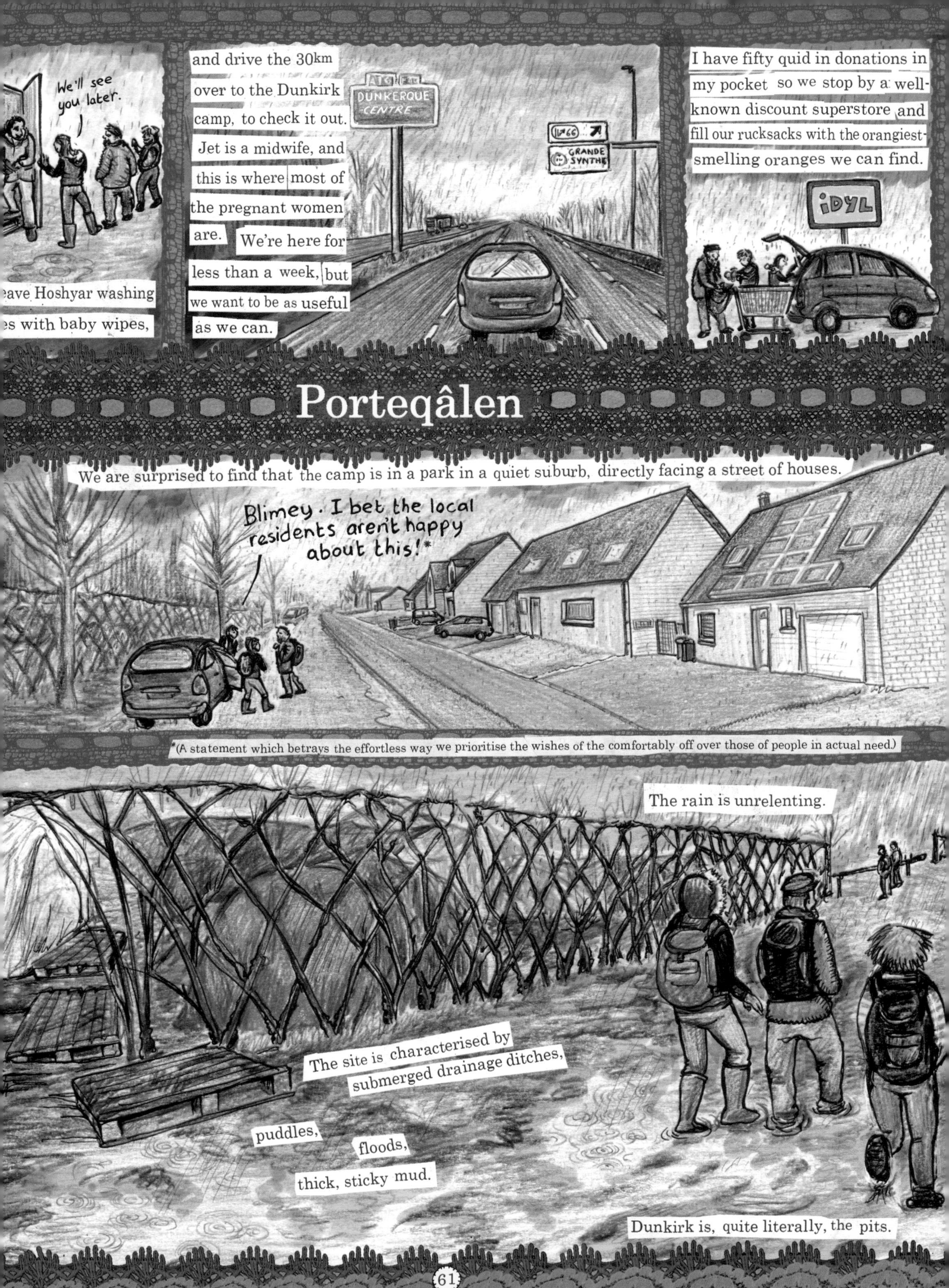
We'll see you later.
eave Hoshyar washing
es with baby wipes,
and drive the 30km over to the Dunkirk camp, to check it out.
DUNKERQUE CENTRE
GRANDE SYNTHE
Jet is a midwife, and this is where most of the pregnant women are.
We're here for less than a week, but we want to be as useful as we can.
I have fifty quid in donations in my pocket so we stop by a well-known discount superstore and fill our rucksacks with the orangiest-smelling oranges we can find.
IDYL
Porteqâlen
We are surprised to find that the camp is in a park in a quiet suburb, directly facing a street of houses.
Blimey. I bet the local residents aren't happy about this!*
*(A statement which betrays the effortless way we prioritise the wishes of the comfortably off over those of people in actual need.)
The rain is unrelenting.
The site is characterised by submerged drainage ditches,
puddles,
floods,
thick, sticky mud.
Dunkirk is, quite literally, the pits.

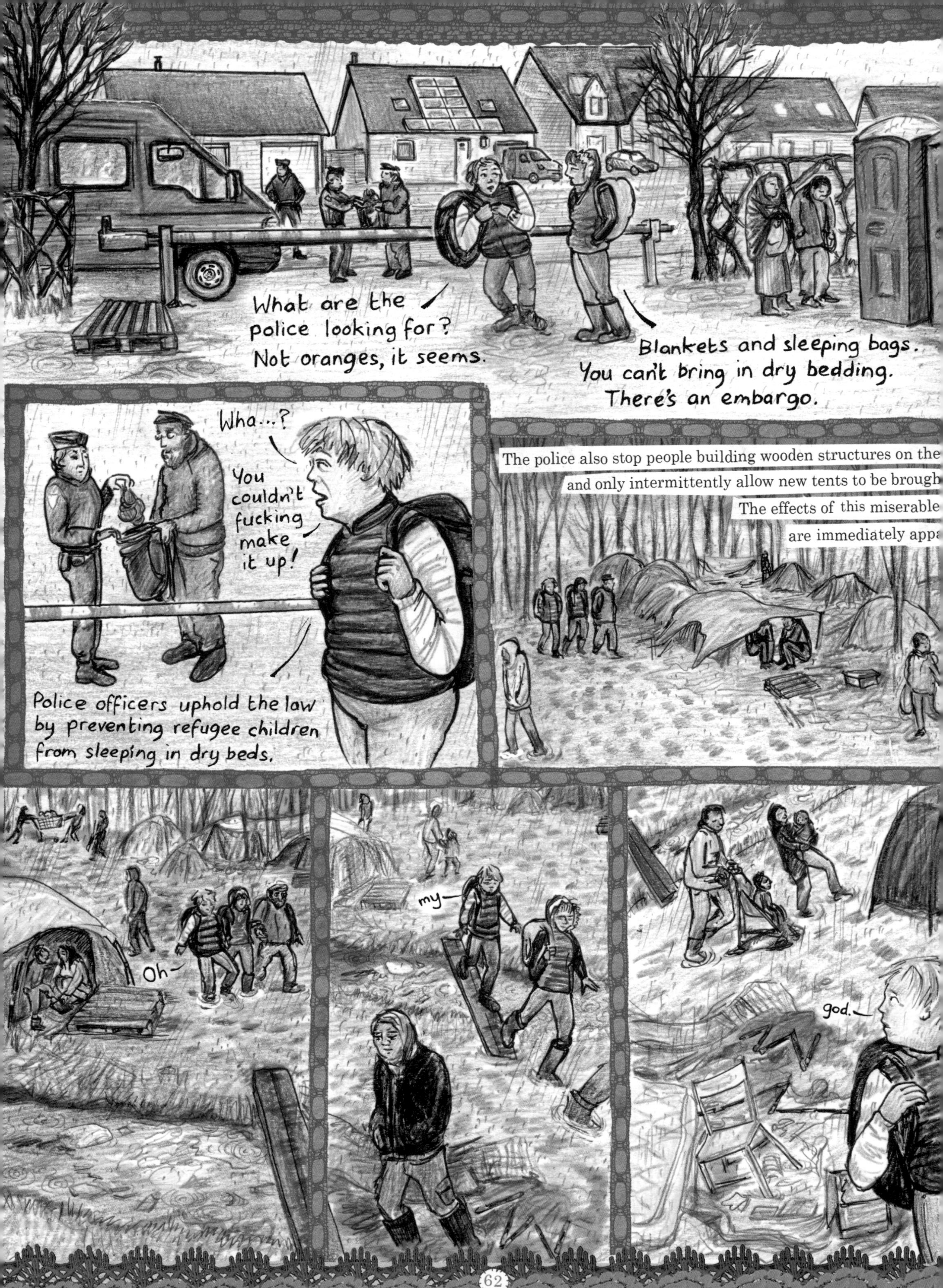
What are the police looking for? Not oranges, it seems.
Blankets and sleeping bags. You can't bring in dry bedding. There's an embargo.
Wha...?
You couldn't fucking make it up!
Police officers uphold the law by preventing refugee children from sleeping in dry beds.
The police also stop people building wooden structures on the
and only intermittently allow new tents to be brough
The effects of this miserable
are immediately appa
Oh-
my-
god.-

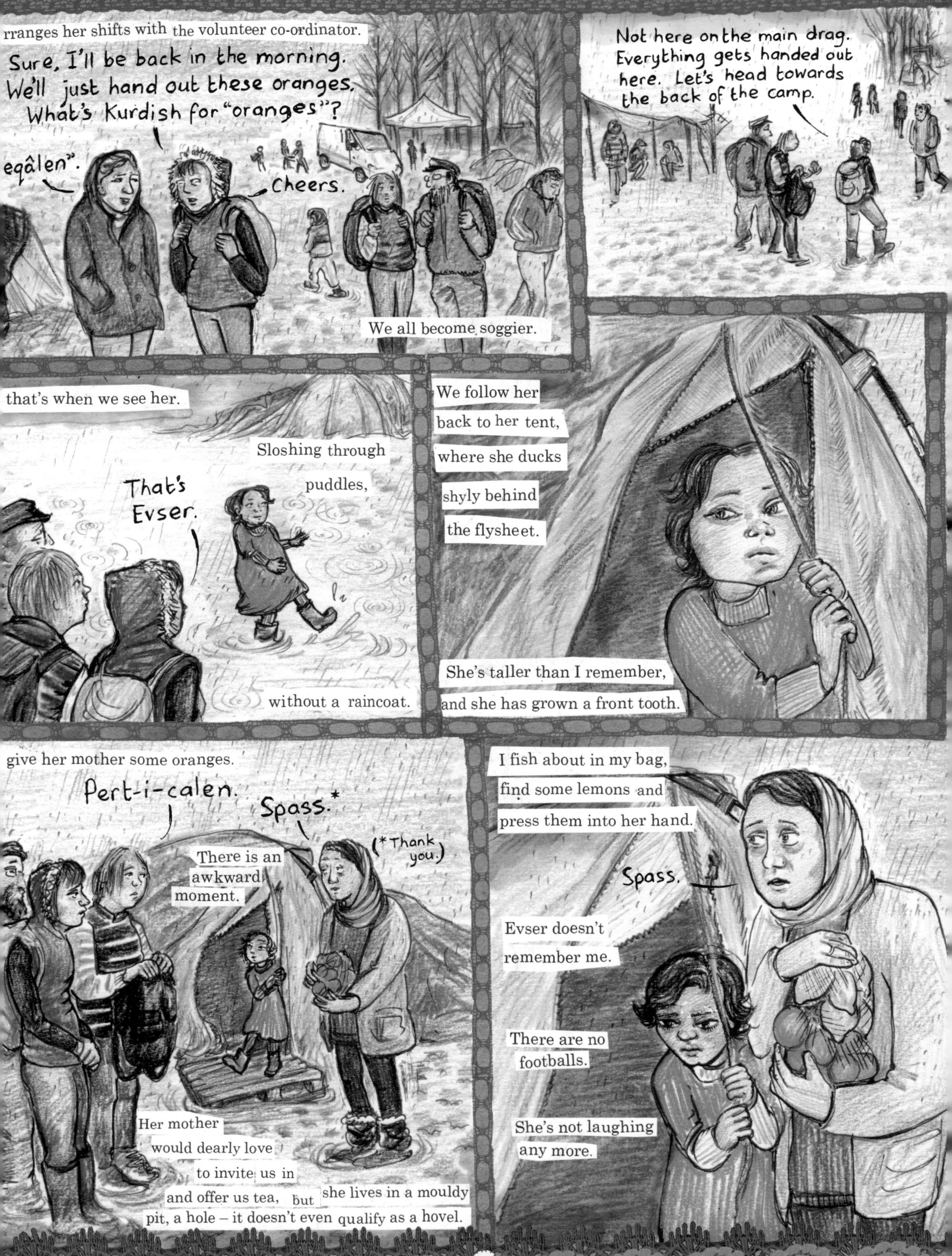
rranges her shifts with the volunteer co-ordinator.
Sure, I'll be back in the morning. We'll just hand out these oranges. What's Kurdish for "oranges"?
eqâlen".
Cheers.
We all become soggier.
Not here on the main drag. Everything gets handed out here. Let's head towards the back of the camp.
that's when we see her.
Sloshing through
puddles,
That's Evser.
without a raincoat.
We follow her
back to her tent,
where she ducks
shyly behind
the flysheet.
She's taller than I remember,
and she has grown a front tooth.
give her mother some oranges.
Pert-i-calen.
Spass.*
(*Thank you.)
There is an awkward moment.
Her mother
would dearly love
to invite us in
and offer us tea, but she lives in a mouldy
pit, a hole – it doesn't even qualify as a hovel.
I fish about in my bag,
find some lemons and
press them into her hand.
Spass.
Evser doesn't
remember me.
There are no footballs.
She's not laughing
any more.

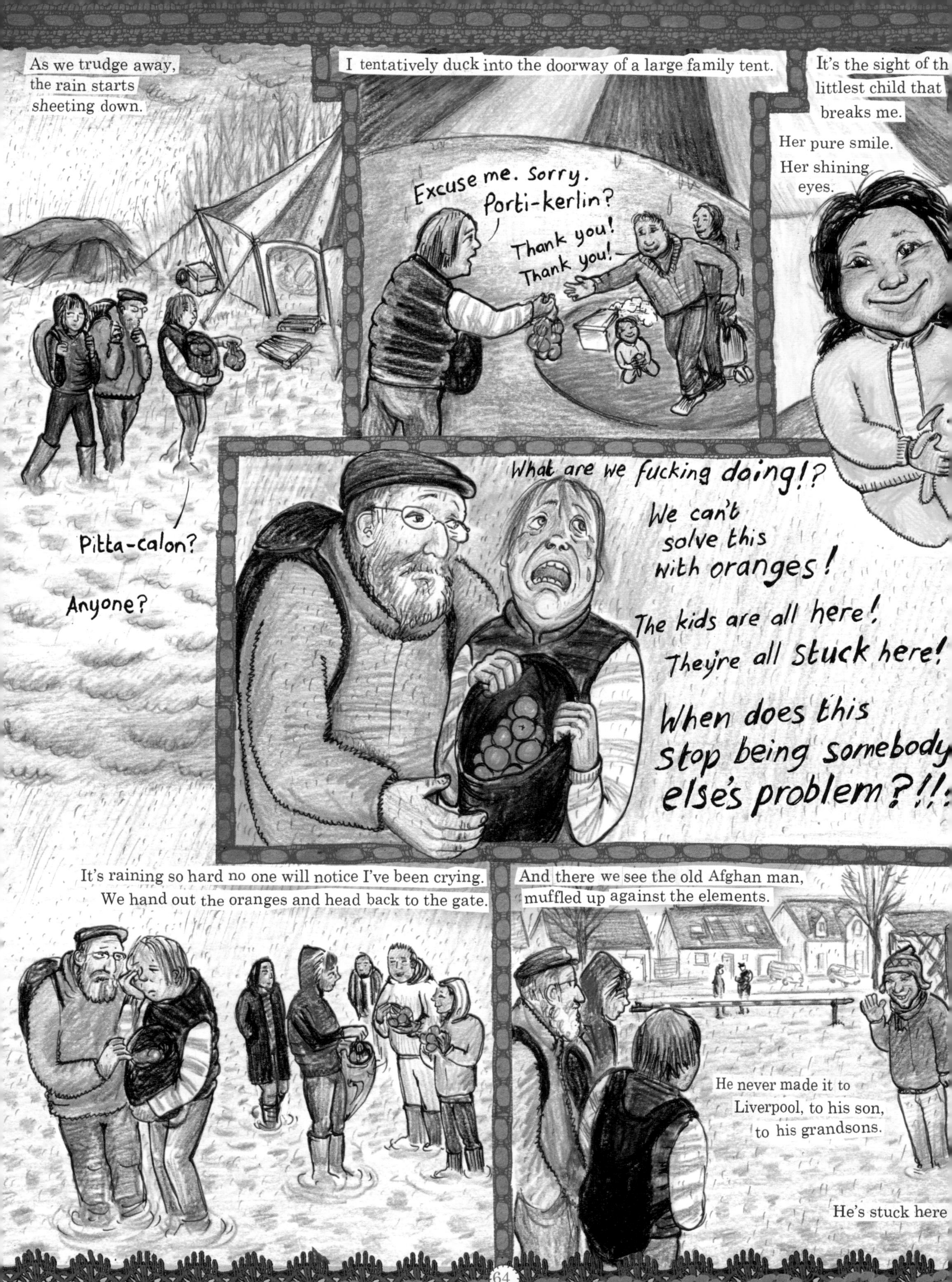
As we trudge away, the rain starts sheeting down.
Pitta-calon?
Anyone?
I tentatively duck into the doorway of a large family tent.
Excuse me. Sorry. Porti-kerlin?
Thank you! Thank you!
It's the sight of th littlest child that breaks me.
Her pure smile.
Her shining eyes.
What are we fucking doing!?
We can't solve this with oranges!
The kids are all here!
They're all stuck here!
When does this stop being somebody else's problem?!!
It's raining so hard no one will notice I've been crying.
We hand out the oranges and head back to the gate.
And there we see the old Afghan man, muffled up against the elements.
He never made it to Liverpool, to his son, to his grandsons.
He's stuck here

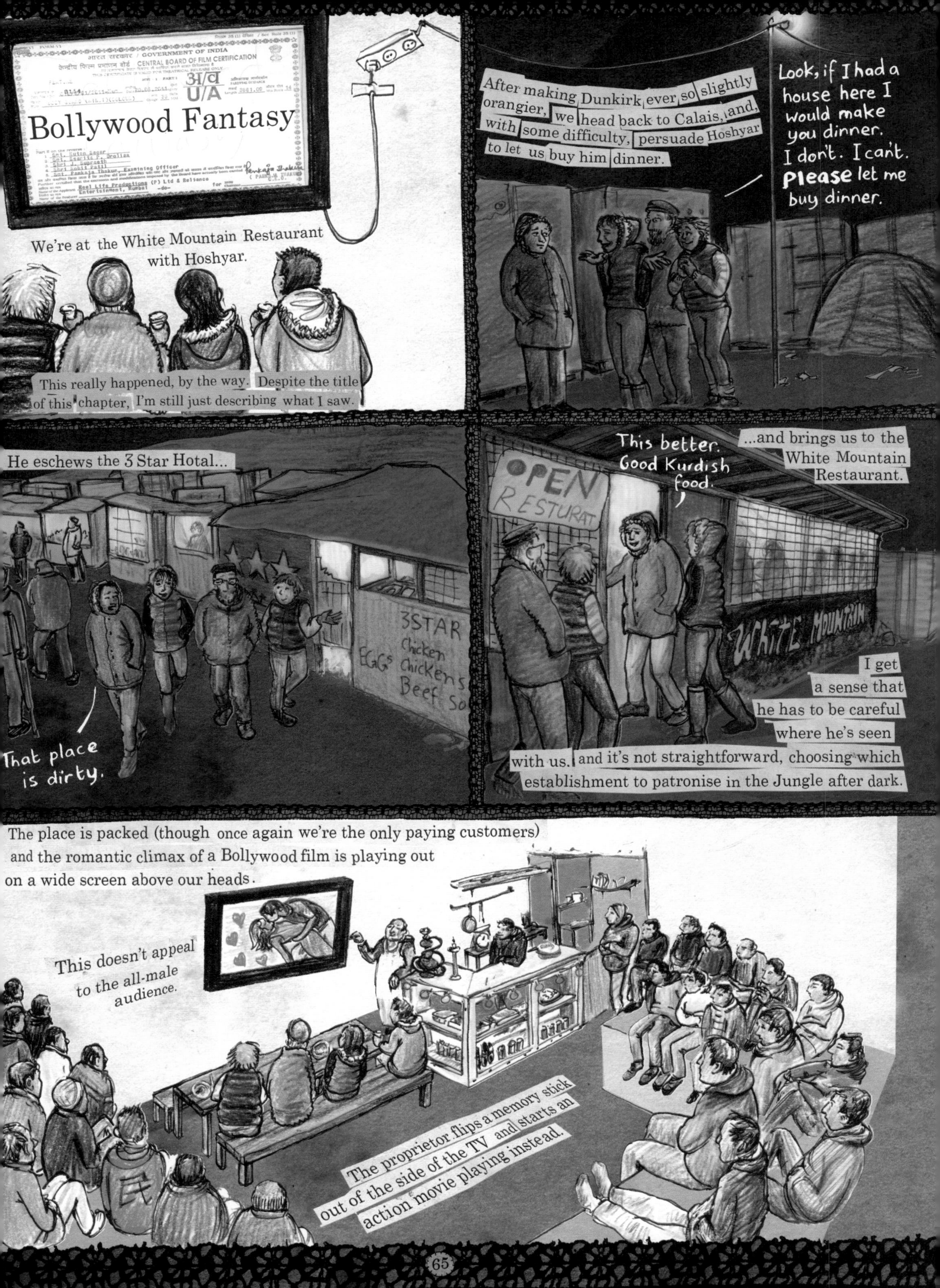

GOVERNMENT OF INDIA
CENTRAL BOARD OF FILM CERTIFICATION
अ/व
U/A
Bollywood Fantasy
We're at the White Mountain Restaurant with Hoshyar.
This really happened, by the way. Despite the title of this chapter, I'm still just describing what I saw.
After making Dunkirk ever so slightly orangier, we head back to Calais, and, with some difficulty, persuade Hoshyar to let us buy him dinner.
Look, if I had a house here I would make you dinner. I don't. I can't. PLEASE let me buy dinner.
He eschews the 3 Star Hotal...
3STAR
Chicken
EGGs Chickens
Beef So
That place is dirty.
This better. Good Kurdish food.
...and brings us to the White Mountain Restaurant.
OPEN
RESTURAT
WHITE MOUNTAIN
I get a sense that he has to be careful where he's seen with us, and it's not straightforward, choosing which establishment to patronise in the Jungle after dark.
The place is packed (though once again we're the only paying customers) and the romantic climax of a Bollywood film is playing out on a wide screen above our heads.
This doesn't appeal to the all-male audience.
The proprietor flips a memory stick out of the side of the TV and starts an action movie playing instead.

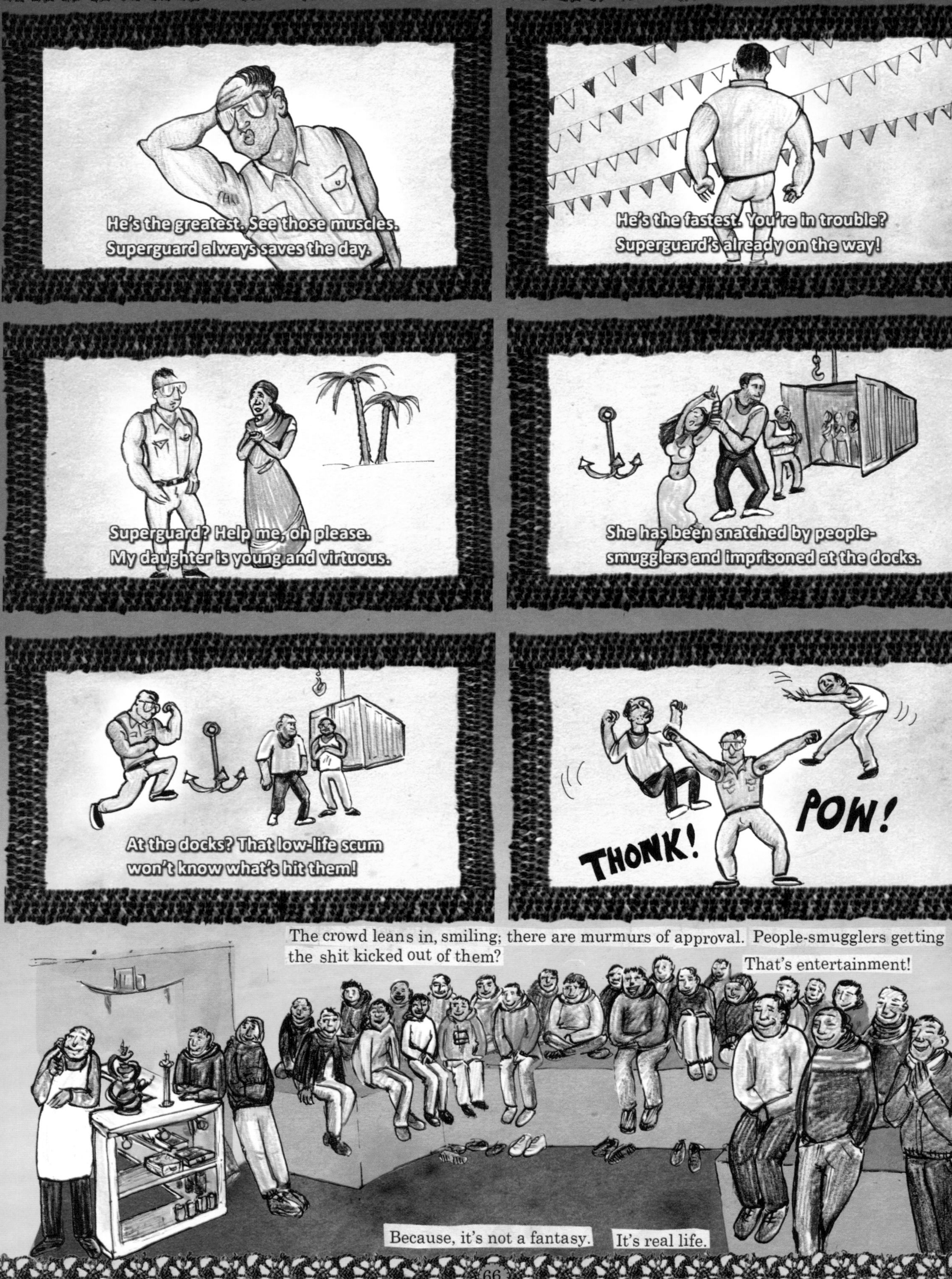
He's the greatest. See those muscles.
Superguard always saves the day.
He's the fastest. You're in trouble?
Superguard's already on the way!
Superguard? Help me, oh please.
My daughter is young and virtuous.
She has been snatched by people-smugglers and imprisoned at the docks.
At the docks? That low-life scum won't know what's hit them!
THONK!
POW!
The crowd leans in, smiling; there are murmurs of approval. People-smugglers getting the shit kicked out of them?
That's entertainment!
Because, it's not a fantasy.
It's real life.

Let's talk about people-smugglers.

For now, we'll resort to that dubious metaphor, of refugees as a flood.
And so, spending millions upon millions of pounds of public money on fencing and policing to seal the porous border at Calais can be likened to putting a plug in a sink.

But
the
water
still
flows.

Towards England, why? Perhaps because people around the world speak our language, and also because our country is (perhaps wrongly) perceived as fair and tolerant. And also because, having watched their families die, people are desperate for reunion with relatives in the UK.

What turned on the tap?

The bombs and the guns: the ones that we drop and we sell and we profit from.

The marauding psychotic death cults of Daesh (ISIS) and the Taliban, which rose from the ashes of the countries we invaded.

Just imagine that you have a young child – half the world's refugees are children. Imagine your country is at war, that your government is dropping bombs on your city, that the terror troops are a day away from your town.

What kind of a parent would you be if you stayed?

Putting
the
plug in that
sink
forces the
water to
rise up
and
spill over
the sides.

If the only way to the UK is via people-smugglers, that's what people will resort to.

We have created a market run by unscrupulous crooks preying on the vulnerable. Gangsters with no incentive to tell their victims the truth.

Any driver stopped at the UK border with an "illegal migrant" on board their vehicle faces a mandatory £2,000 fine.

Look, we even set the minimum price.

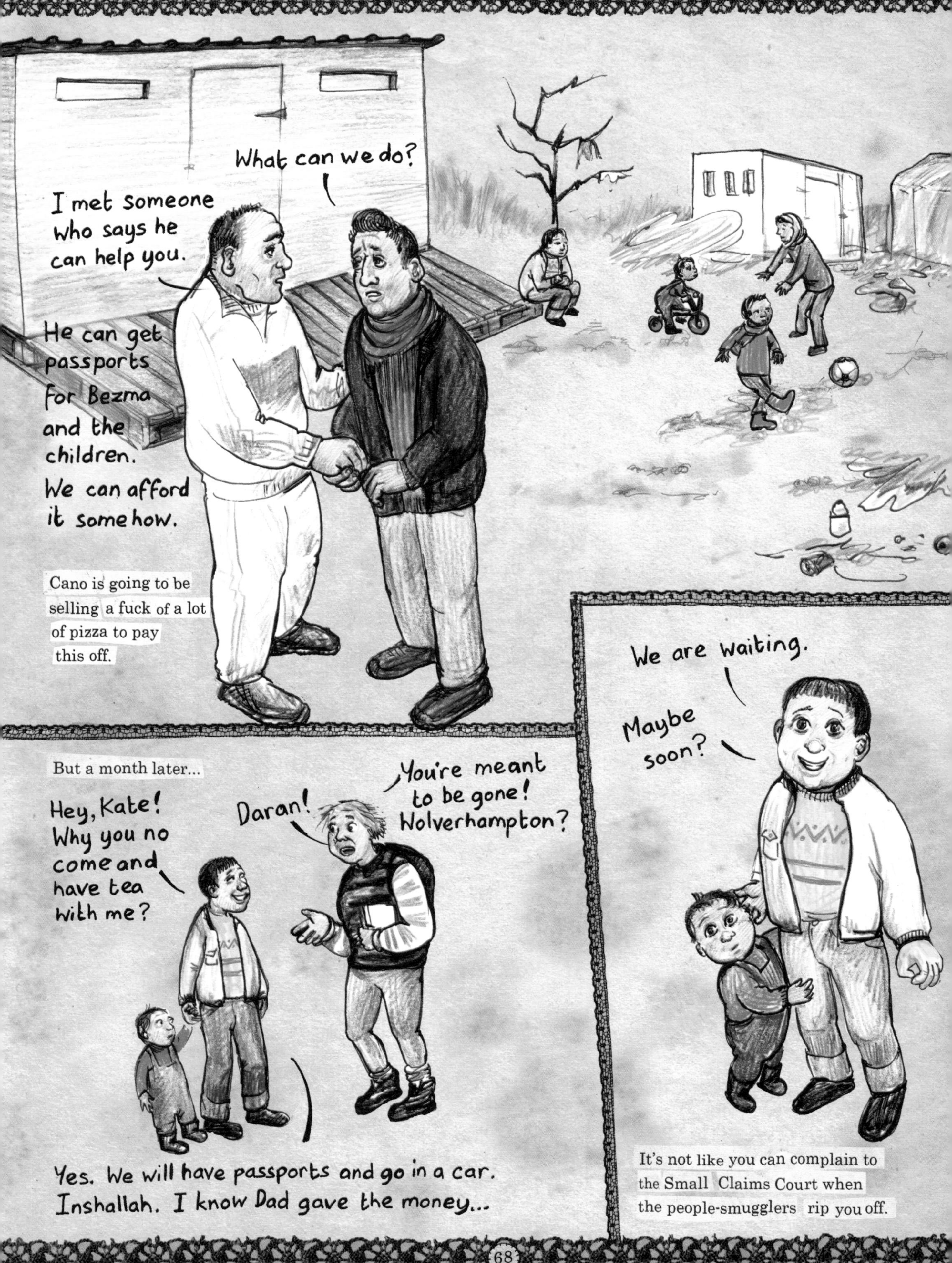
What can we do?
I met someone who says he can help you.
He can get passports for Bezma and the children.
We can afford it somehow.
Cano is going to be selling a fuck of a lot of pizza to pay this off.
But a month later...
Hey, Kate! Why you no come and have tea with me?
Daran!
You're meant to be gone! Wolverhampton?
Yes. We will have passports and go in a car. Inshallah. I know Dad gave the money...
We are waiting.
Maybe soon?
It's not like you can complain to the Small Claims Court when the people-smugglers rip you off.

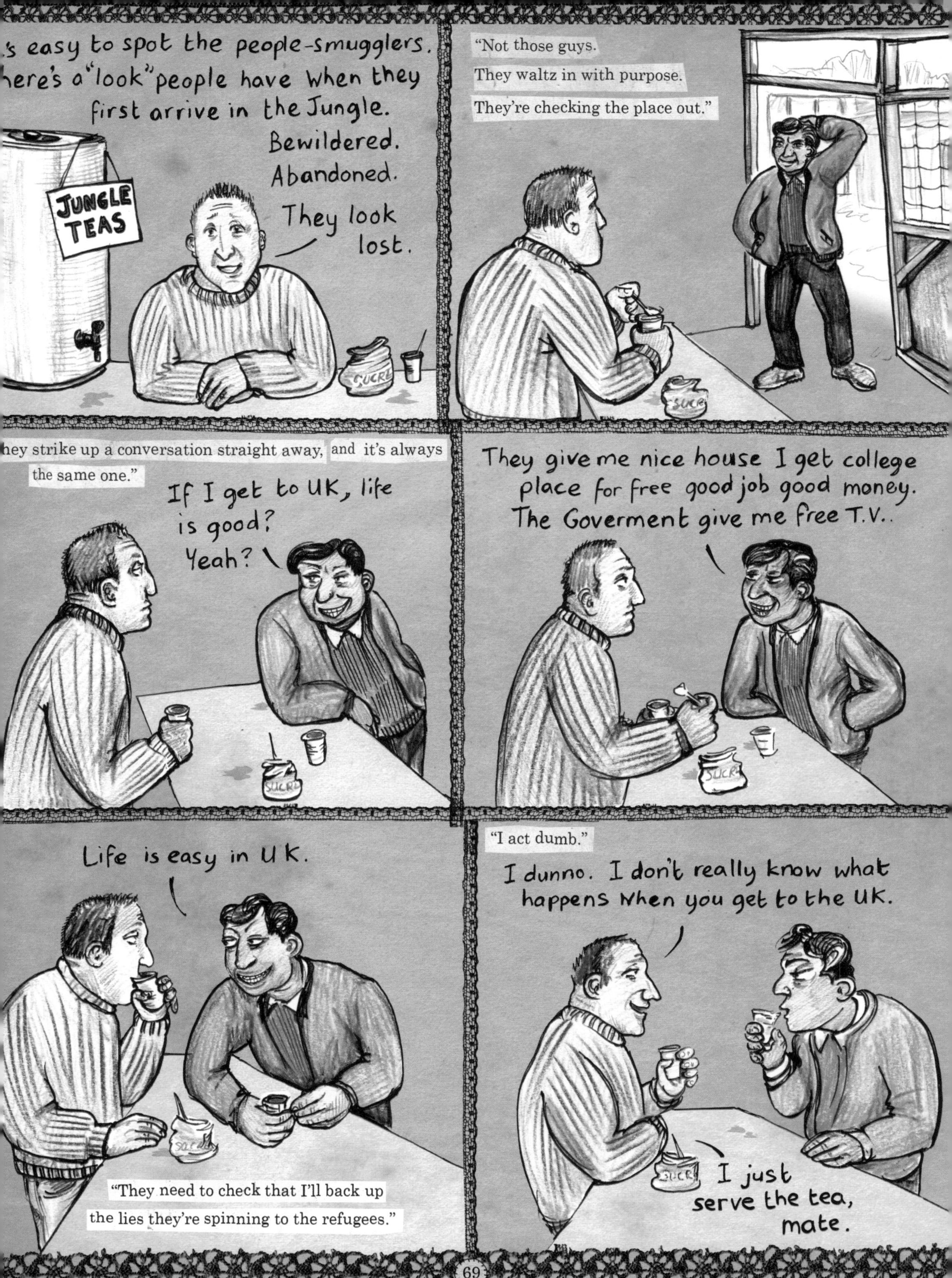
s easy to spot the people-smugglers.
here's a "look" people have when they first arrive in the Jungle.
Bewildered.
Abandoned.
They look lost.
JUNGLE TEAS
SUCRE
"Not those guys.
They waltz in with purpose.
They're checking the place out."
SUCRE
hey strike up a conversation straight away, and it's always the same one."
If I get to UK, life is good? Yeah?
SUCRE
They give me nice house I get college place for free good job good money. The Goverment give me free T.V..
SUCRE
Life is easy in UK.
SUCRE
"They need to check that I'll back up the lies they're spinning to the refugees."
"I act dumb."
I dunno. I don't really know what happens when you get to the UK.
I just serve the tea, mate.
SUCRE

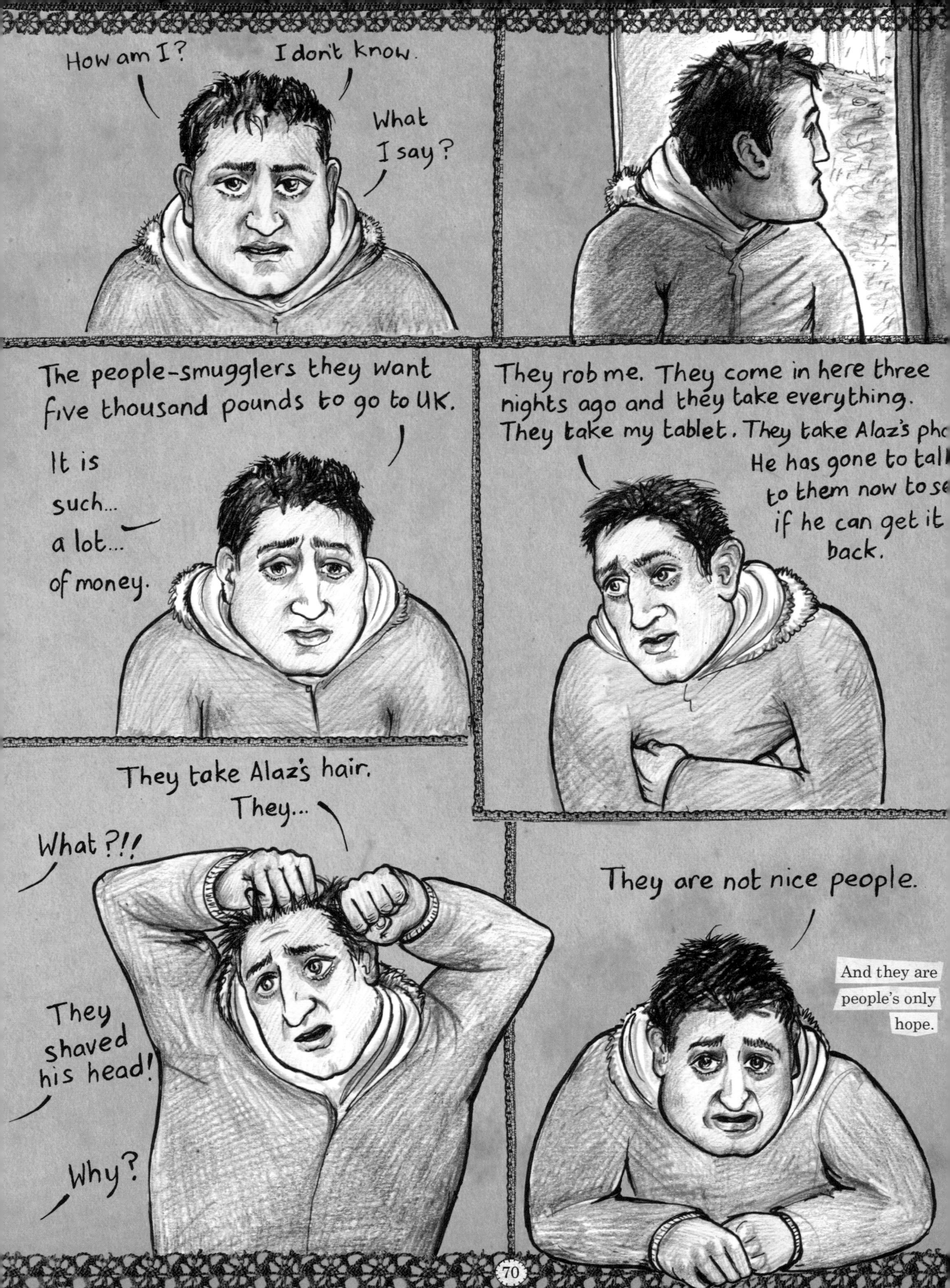
How am I?
I don't know.
What I say?
The people-smugglers they want five thousand pounds to go to UK.
It is such... a lot... of money.
They rob me. They come in here three nights ago and they take everything. They take my tablet. They take Alaz's pho
He has gone to tal to them now to se if he can get it back.
They take Alaz's hair. They...
What?!!
They shaved his head!
Why?
They are not nice people.
And they are people's only hope.

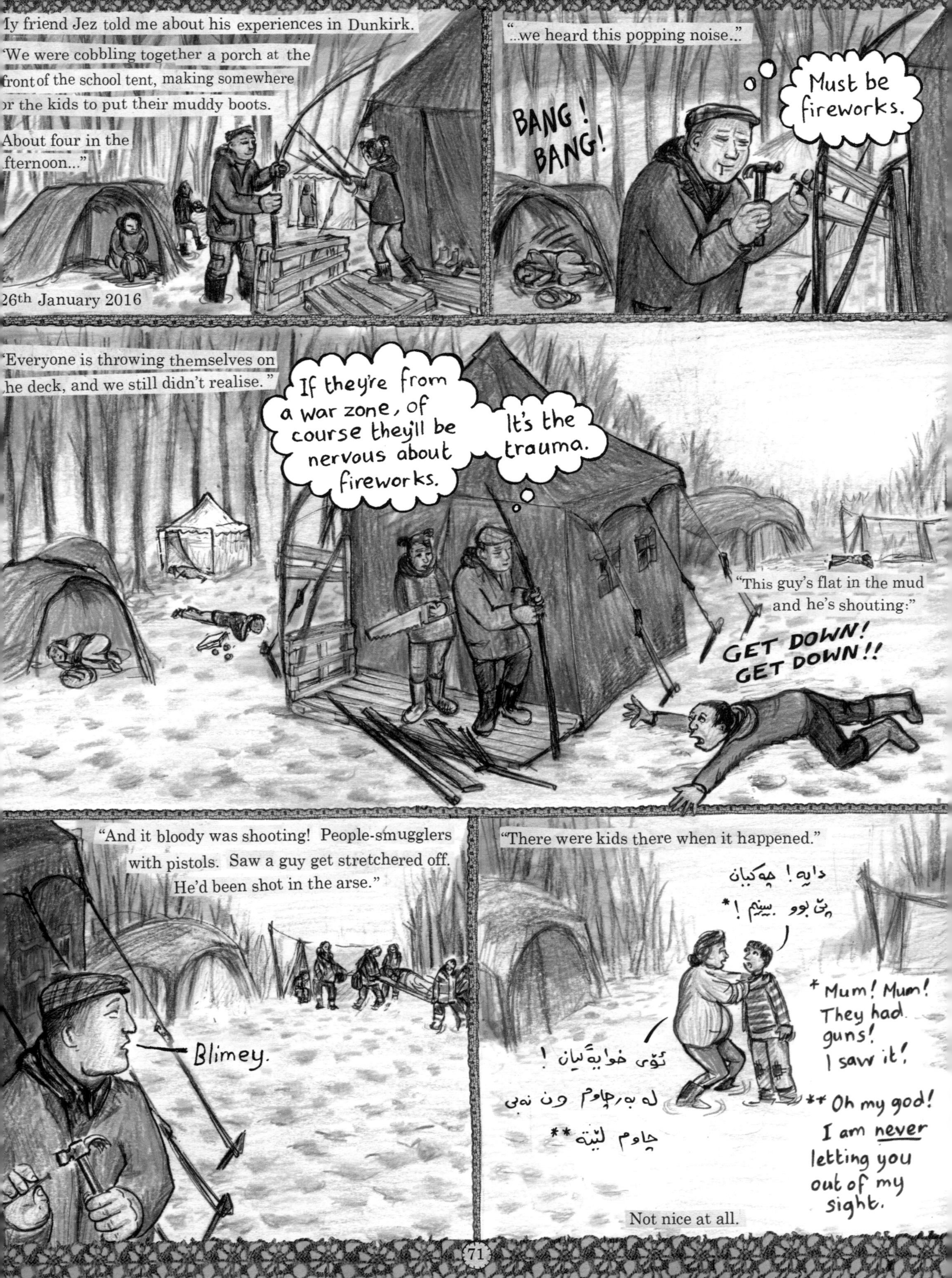

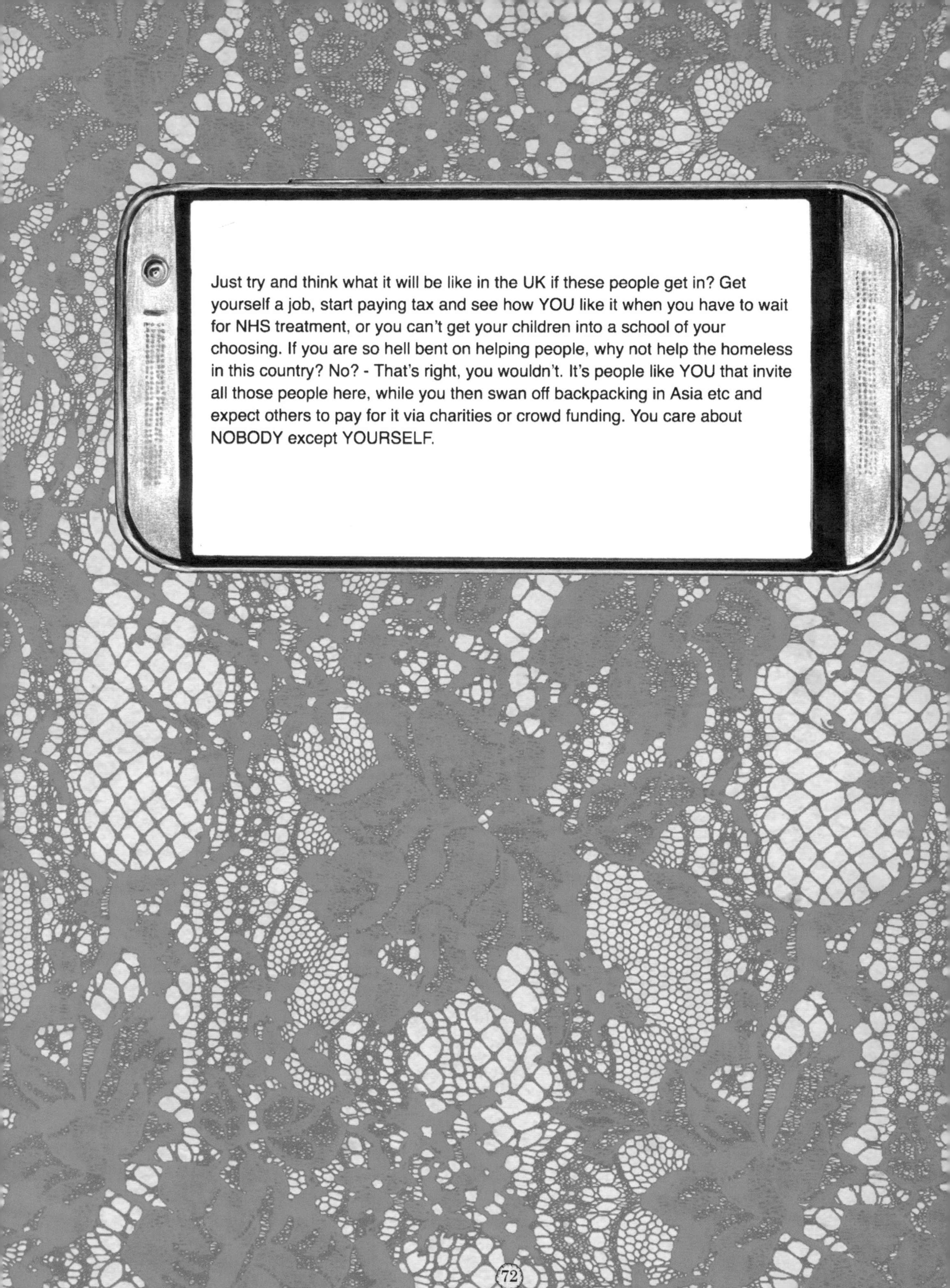
Just try and think what it will be like in the UK if these people get in? Get yourself a job, start paying tax and see how YOU like it when you have to wait for NHS treatment, or you can't get your children into a school of your choosing. If you are so hell bent on helping people, why not help the homeless in this country? No? - That's right, you wouldn't. It's people like YOU that invite all those people here, while you then swan off backpacking in Asia etc and expect others to pay for it via charities or crowd funding. You care about NOBODY except YOURSELF.

th February 2016

Triple Three-in-One Action (Part I)

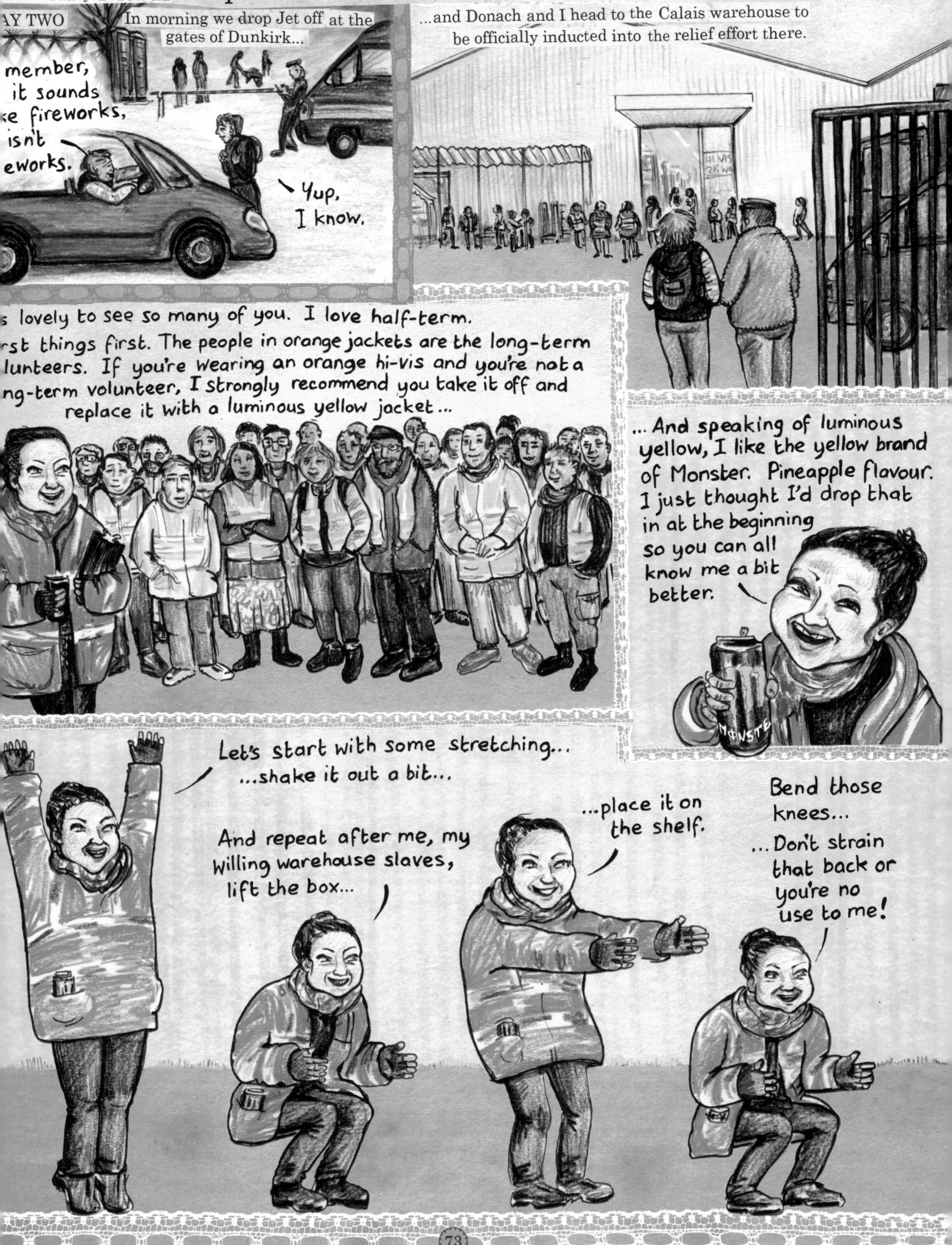
AY TWO
In morning we drop Jet off at the gates of Dunkirk...
member, it sounds ke fireworks, isn't eworks.
Yup, I know.
...and Donach and I head to the Calais warehouse to be officially inducted into the relief effort there.
s lovely to see so many of you. I love half-term.
rst things first. The people in orange jackets are the long-term lunteers. If you're wearing an orange hi-vis and you're not a ng-term volunteer, I strongly recommend you take it off and replace it with a luminous yellow jacket...
... And speaking of luminous yellow, I like the yellow brand of Monster. Pineapple flavour. I just thought I'd drop that in at the beginning so you can all know me a bit better.
Let's start with some stretching... ...shake it out a bit...
And repeat after me, my willing warehouse slaves, lift the box...
...place it on the shelf.
Bend those knees...
...Don't strain that back or you're no use to me!

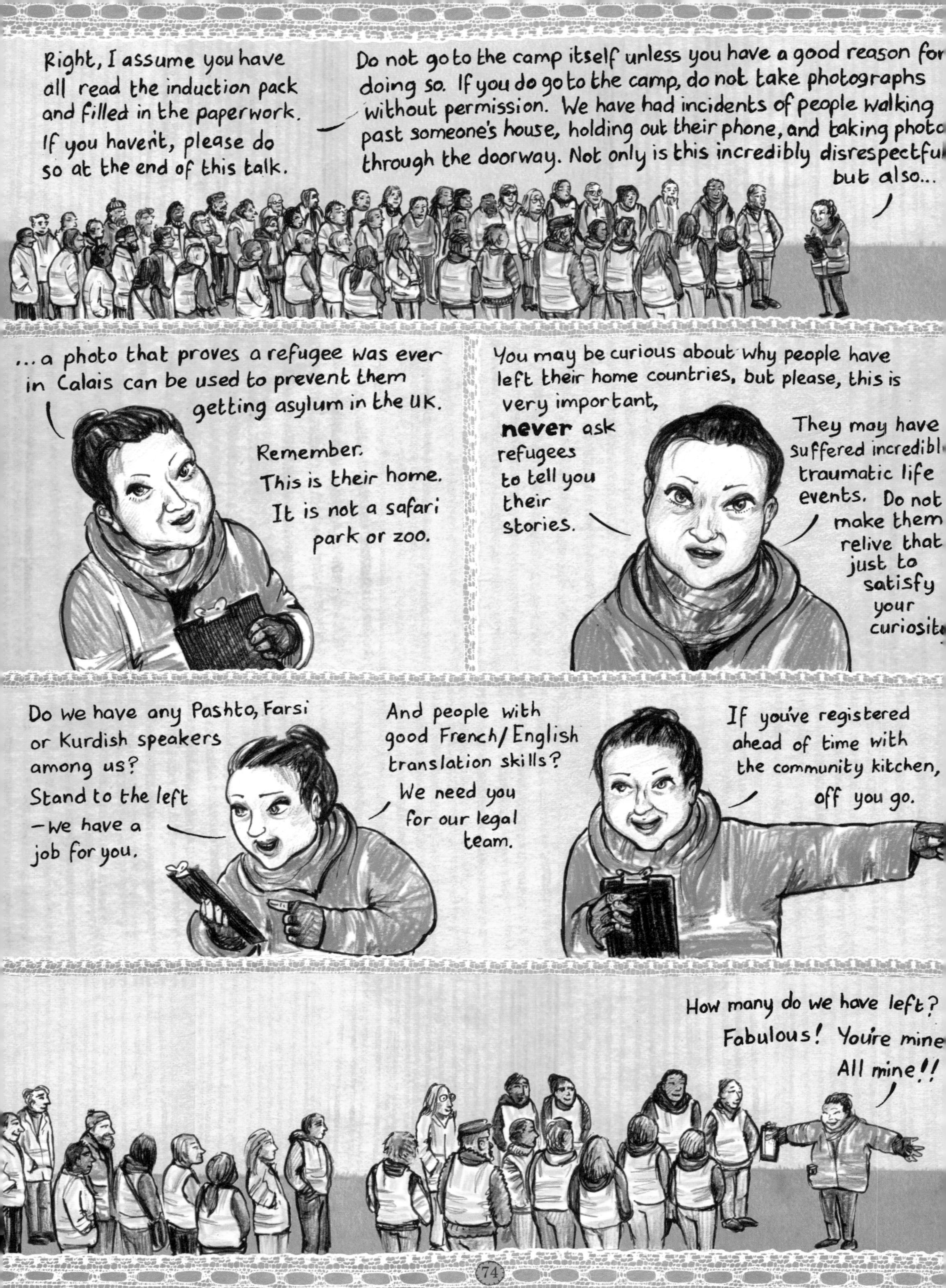
Right, I assume you have all read the induction pack and filled in the paperwork. If you haven't, please do so at the end of this talk.
Do not go to the camp itself unless you have a good reason for doing so. If you do go to the camp, do not take photographs without permission. We have had incidents of people walking past someone's house, holding out their phone, and taking photo through the doorway. Not only is this incredibly disrespectful but also...
...a photo that proves a refugee was ever in Calais can be used to prevent them getting asylum in the UK.
Remember. This is their home. It is not a safari park or zoo.
You may be curious about why people have left their home countries, but please, this is very important,
never ask refugees to tell you their stories.
They may have suffered incredibl traumatic life events. Do not make them relive that just to satisfy your curiosit
Do we have any Pashto, Farsi or Kurdish speakers among us? Stand to the left —we have a job for you.
And people with good French/English translation skills?
We need you for our legal team.
If you've registered ahead of time with the community kitchen, off you go.
How many do we have left?
Fabulous! You're mine
All mine!!

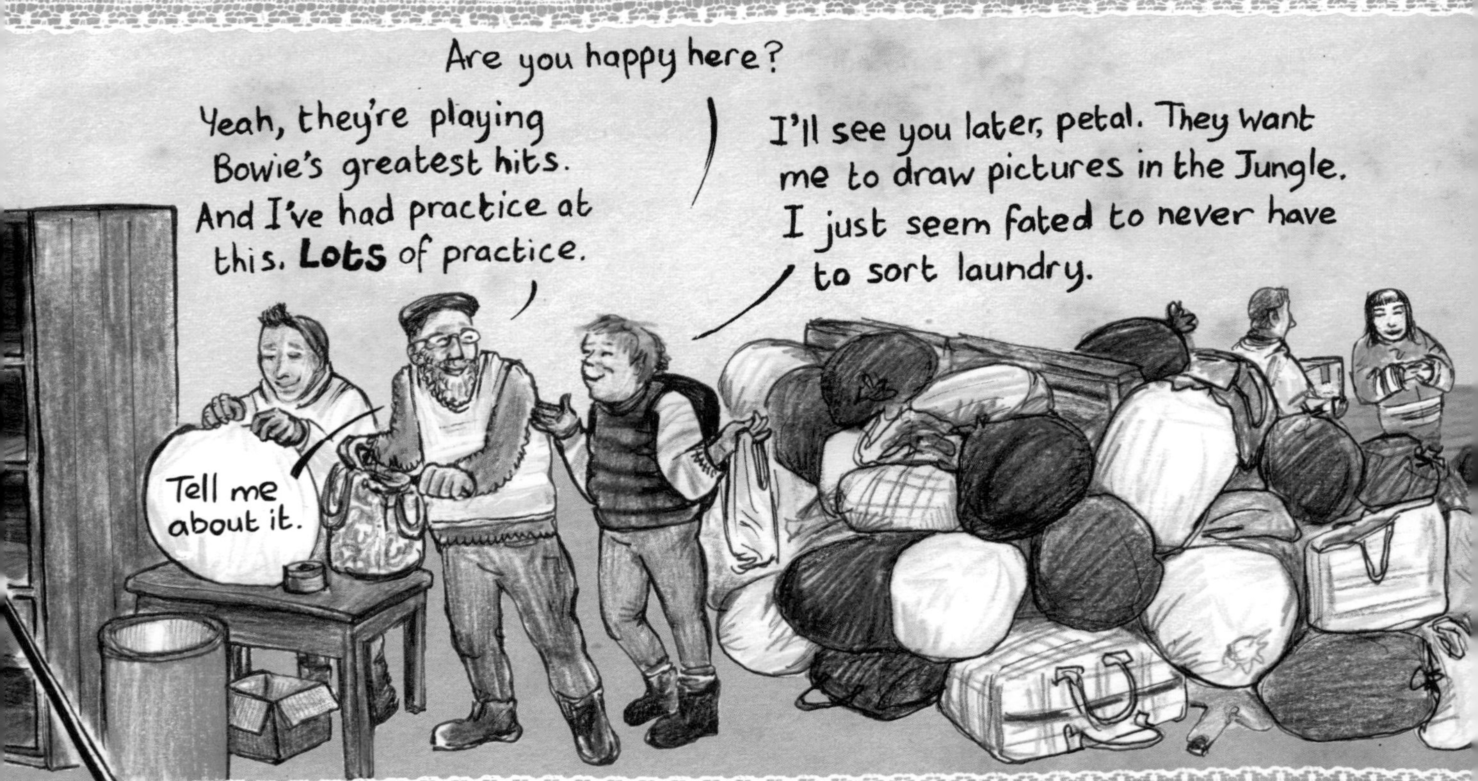
Are you happy here?
Yeah, they're playing Bowie's greatest hits. And I've had practice at this. **Lots** of practice.
Tell me about it.
I'll see you later, petal. They want me to draw pictures in the Jungle. I just seem fated to never have to sort laundry.

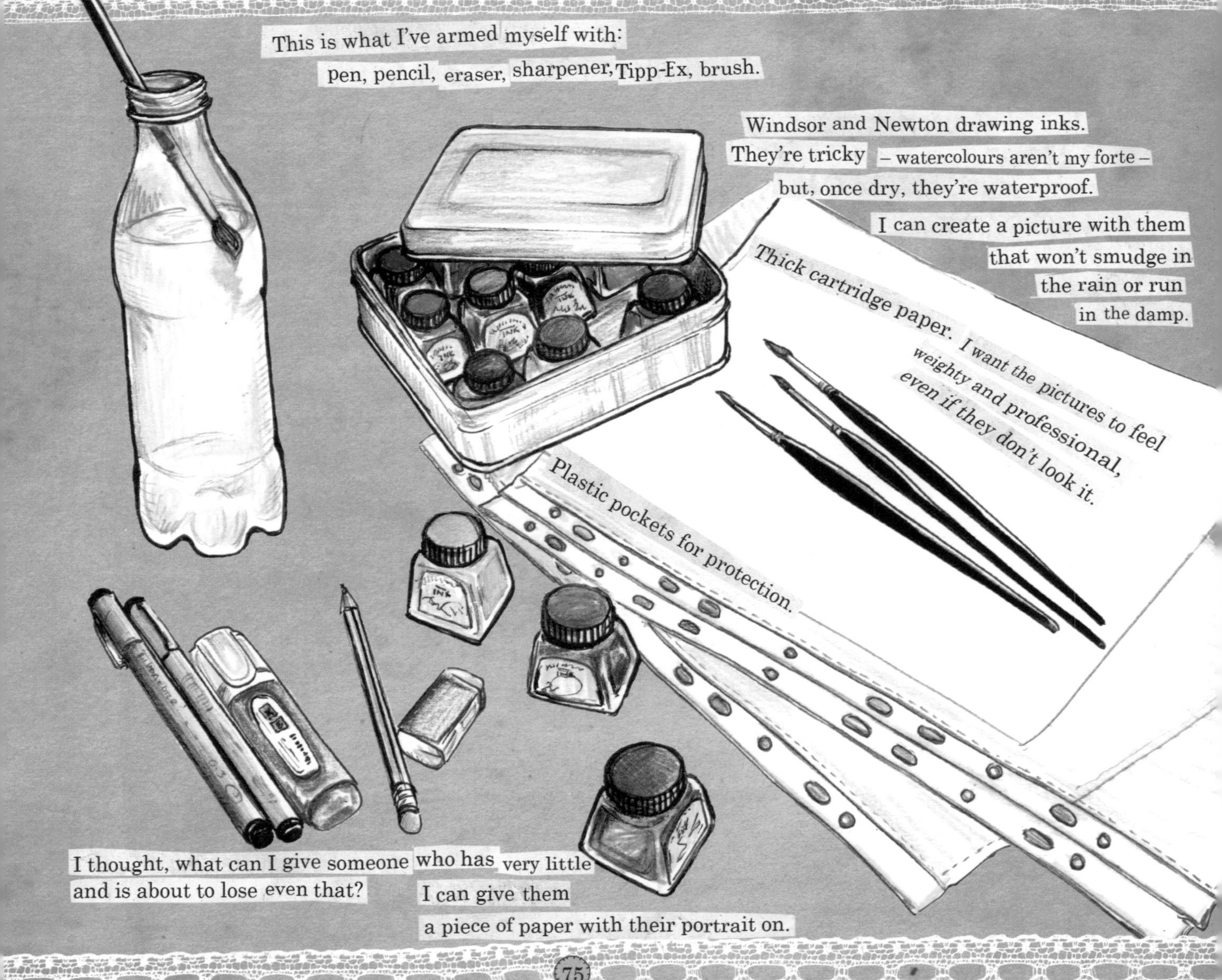
This is what I've armed myself with:
pen, pencil, eraser, sharpener, Tipp-Ex, brush.
Windsor and Newton drawing inks.
They're tricky – watercolours aren't my forte – but, once dry, they're waterproof.
I can create a picture with them that won't smudge in the rain or run in the damp.
Thick cartridge paper. I want the pictures to feel weighty and professional, even if they don't look it.
Plastic pockets for protection.
I thought, what can I give someone who has very little and is about to lose even that? I can give them a piece of paper with their portrait on.

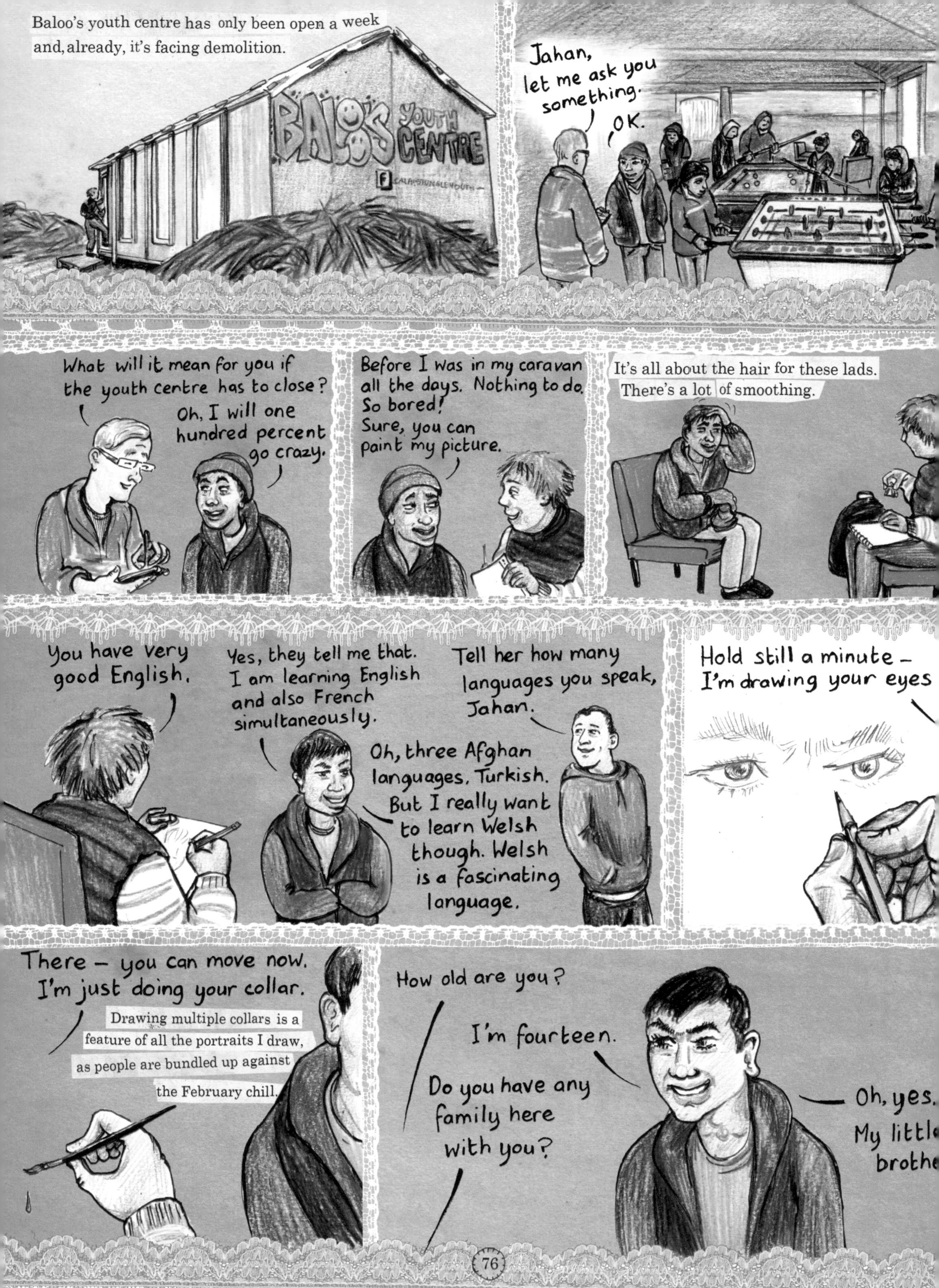

Baloo's youth centre has only been open a week and, already, it's facing demolition.
BALOO'S YOUTH CENTRE
Jahan, let me ask you something.
OK.
What will it mean for you if the youth centre has to close?
Oh, I will one hundred percent go crazy.
Before I was in my caravan all the days. Nothing to do. So bored!
Sure, you can paint my picture.
It's all about the hair for these lads. There's a lot of smoothing.
You have very good English.
Yes, they tell me that. I am learning English and also French simultaneously.
Tell her how many languages you speak, Jahan.
Oh, three Afghan languages, Turkish. But I really want to learn Welsh though. Welsh is a fascinating language.
Hold still a minute – I'm drawing your eyes
There – you can move now. I'm just doing your collar.
Drawing multiple collars is a feature of all the portraits I draw, as people are bundled up against the February chill.
How old are you?
I'm fourteen.
Do you have any family here with you?
Oh, yes.

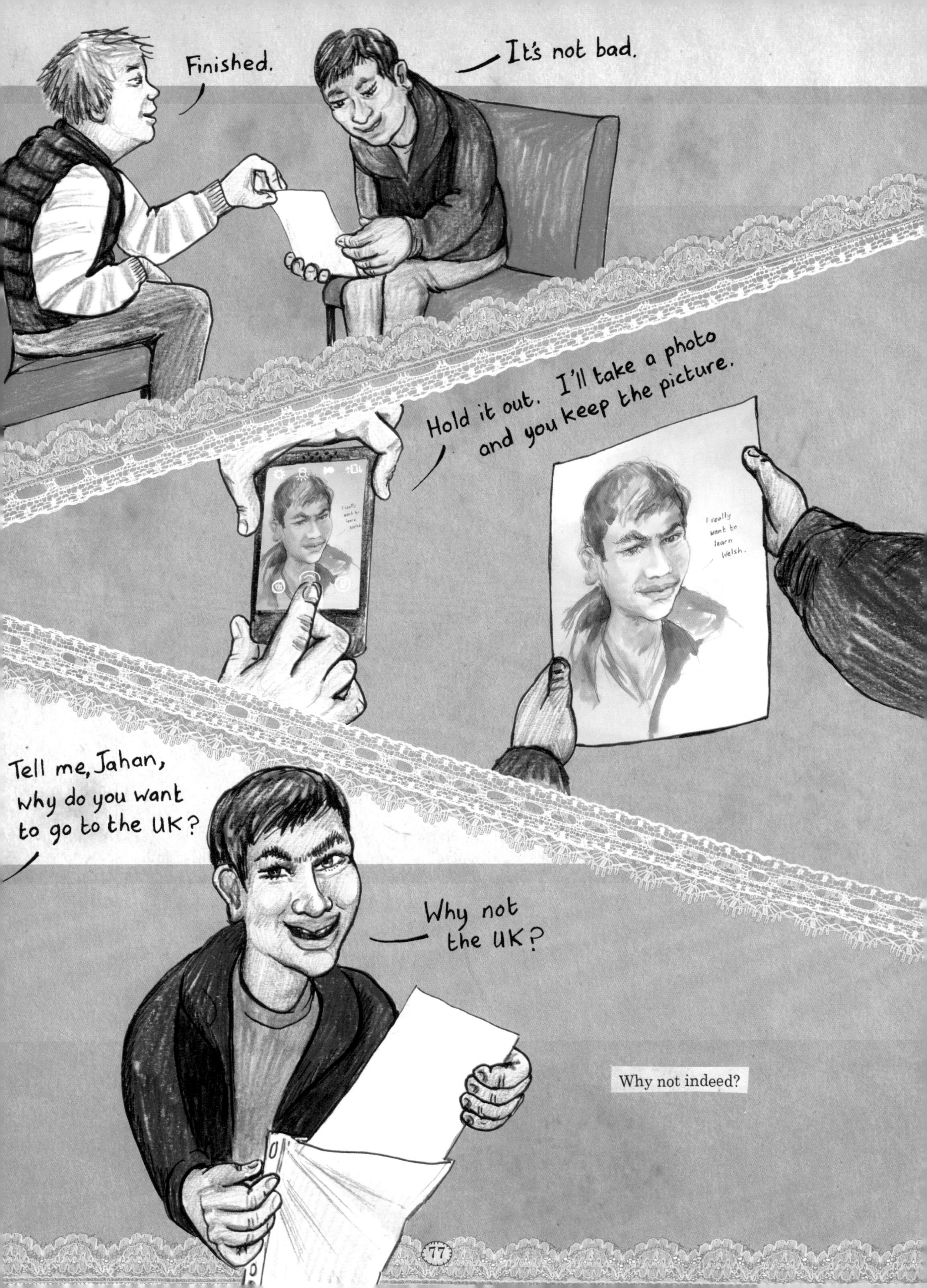

Finished.
It's not bad.
Hold it out. I'll take a photo and you keep the picture.
I really want to learn Welsh.
Tell me, Jahan, why do you want to go to the UK?
Why not the UK?
Why not indeed?

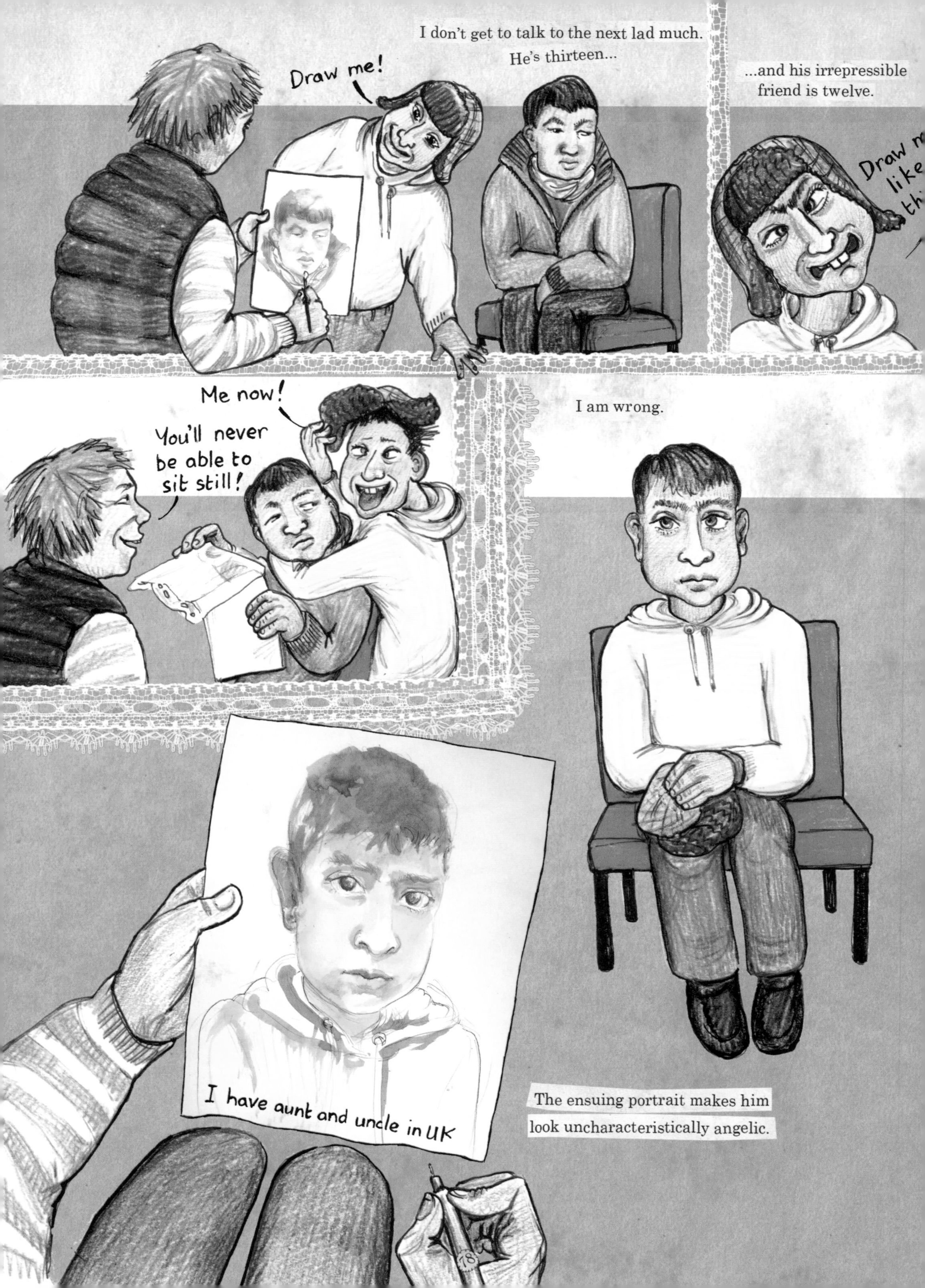

Draw me!
I don't get to talk to the next lad much.
He's thirteen...
...and his irrepressible friend is twelve.
Draw m
like
th
Me now!
You'll never be able to sit still!
I am wrong.
I have aunt and uncle in UK
The ensuing portrait makes him look uncharacteristically angelic.

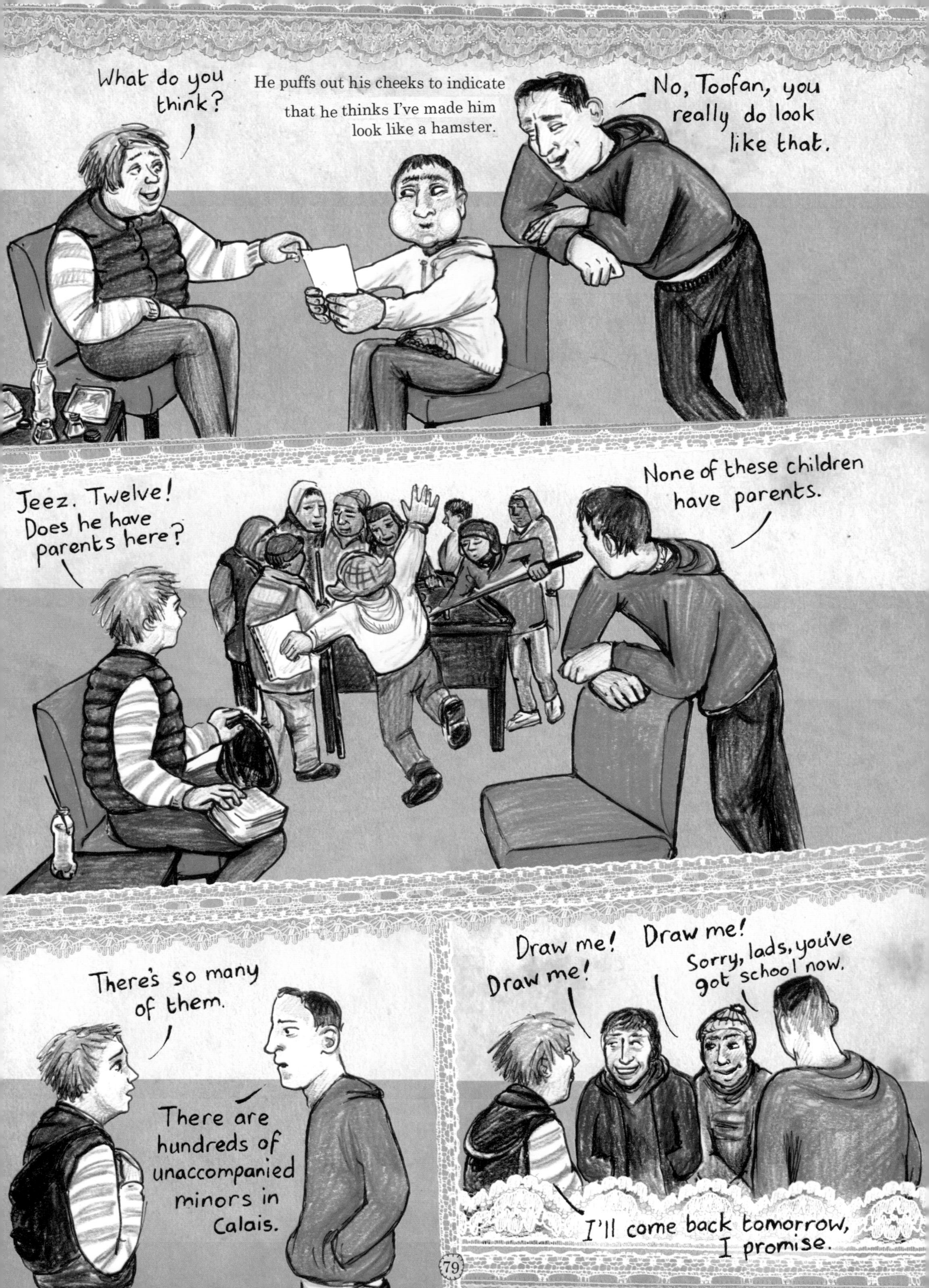
What do you think?
He puffs out his cheeks to indicate that he thinks I've made him look like a hamster.
No, Toofan, you really do look like that.
Jeez. Twelve! Does he have parents here?
None of these children have parents.
There's so many of them.
There are hundreds of unaccompanied minors in Calais.
Draw me!
Draw me!
Draw me!
Sorry, lads, you've got school now.
I'll come back tomorrow, I promise.

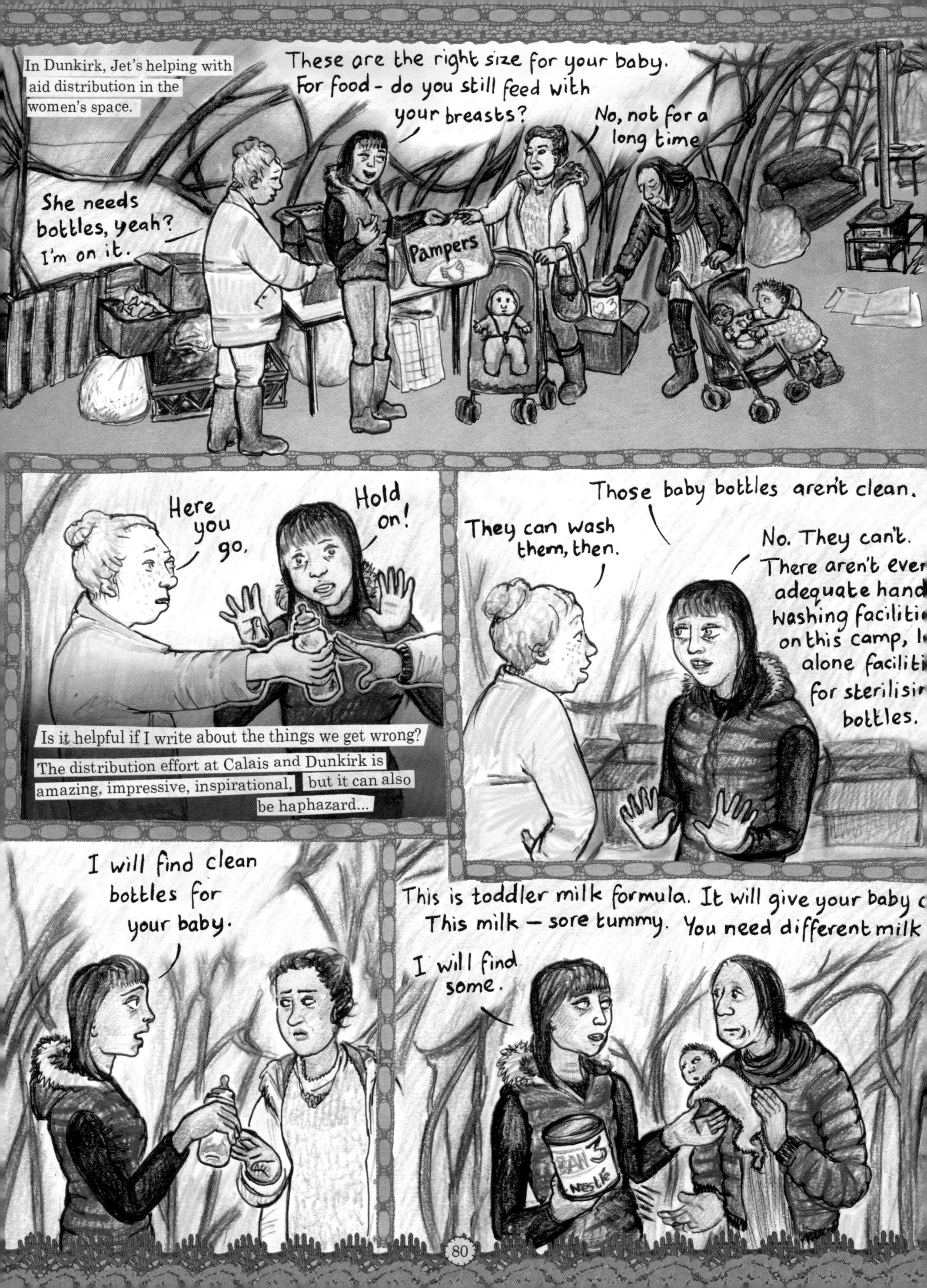
In Dunkirk, Jet's helping with aid distribution in the women's space.
These are the right size for your baby. For food - do you still feed with your breasts?
No, not for a long time
She needs bottles, yeah? I'm on it.
Pampers
Here you go.
Hold on!
Is it helpful if I write about the things we get wrong?
The distribution effort at Calais and Dunkirk is amazing, impressive, inspirational, but it can also be haphazard...
Those baby bottles aren't clean.
They can wash them, then.
No. They can't. There aren't eve adequate hand washing faciliti on this camp, l alone faciliti for sterilisi bottles.
I will find clean bottles for your baby.
This is toddler milk formula. It will give your baby This milk – sore tummy. You need different milk
I will find some.
BAN 3 Nestlé

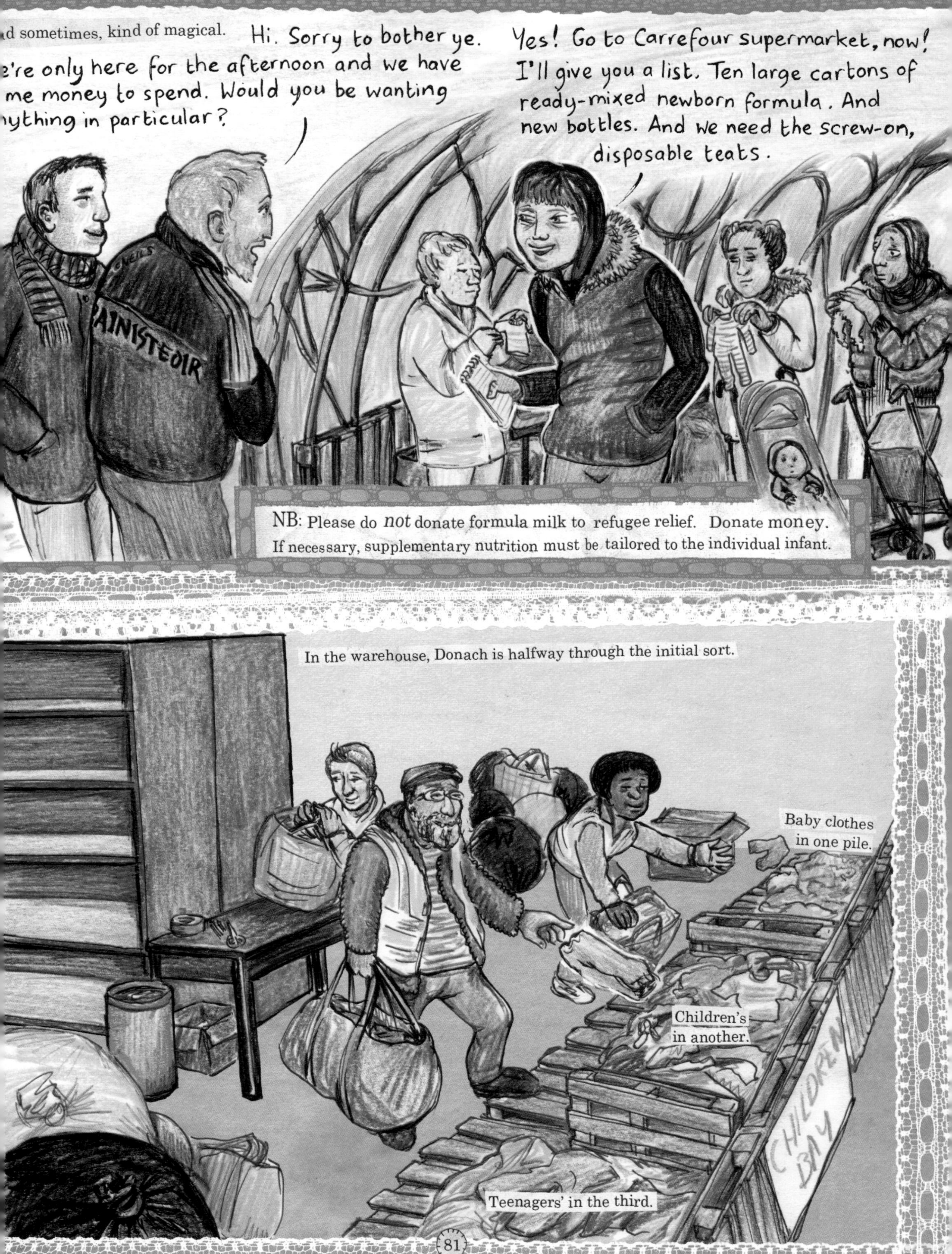
nd sometimes, kind of magical.
Hi. Sorry to bother ye.
e're only here for the afternoon and we have me money to spend. Would you be wanting nything in particular?
Yes! Go to Carrefour supermarket, now! I'll give you a list. Ten large cartons of ready-mixed newborn formula. And new bottles. And we need the screw-on, disposable teats.
AINISTEOIR
NB: Please do *not* donate formula milk to refugee relief. Donate money.
If necessary, supplementary nutrition must be tailored to the individual infant.
In the warehouse, Donach is halfway through the initial sort.
Baby clothes in one pile.
Children's in another.
Teenagers' in the third.
CHILDREN BAY

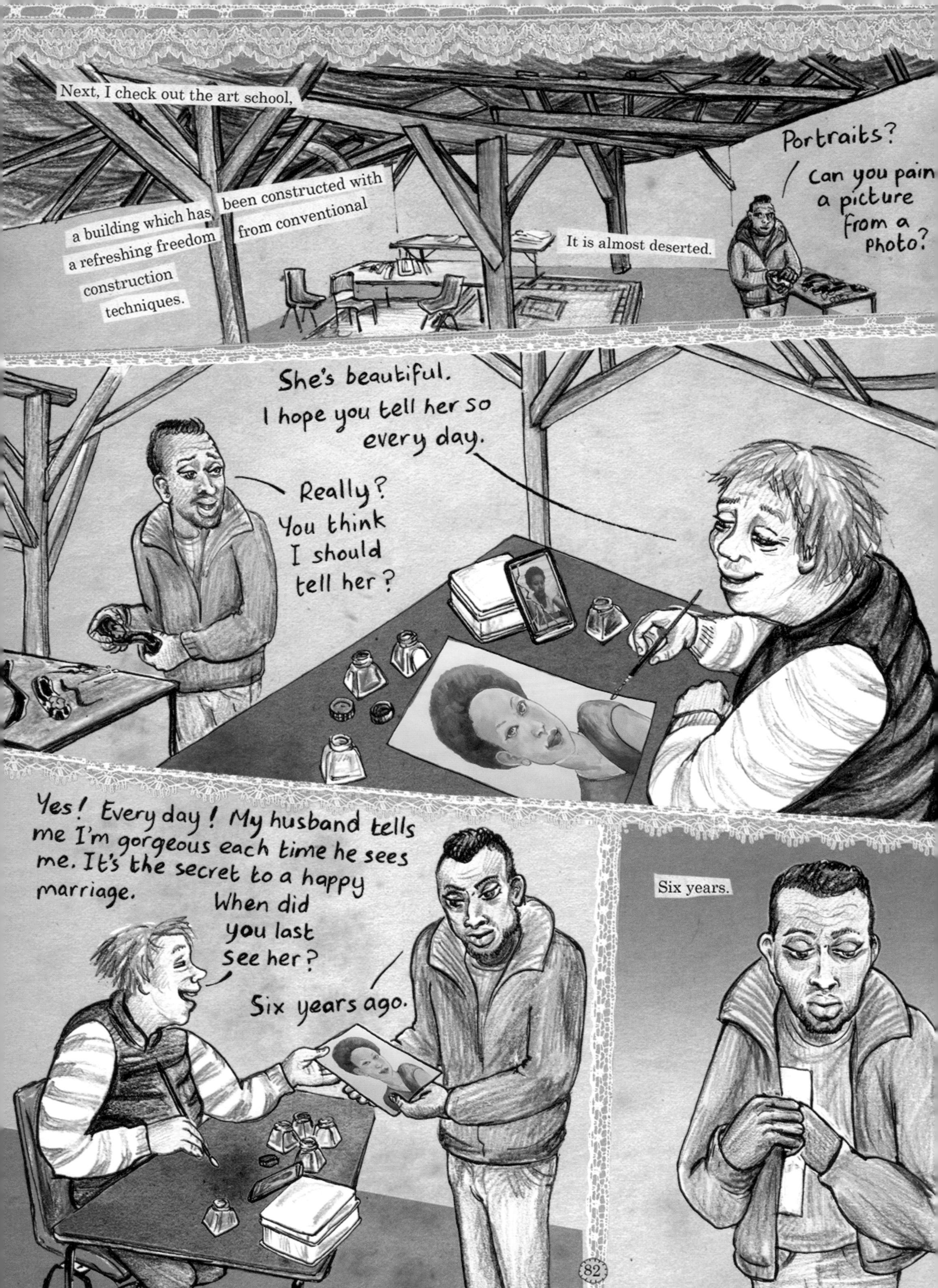

Next, I check out the art school,
a building which has been constructed with a refreshing freedom from conventional construction techniques.
It is almost deserted.
Portraits?
Can you pain a picture from a photo?
She's beautiful.
I hope you tell her so every day.
Really? You think I should tell her?
Yes! Every day! My husband tells me I'm gorgeous each time he sees me. It's the secret to a happy marriage.
When did you last see her?
Six years ago.
Six years.

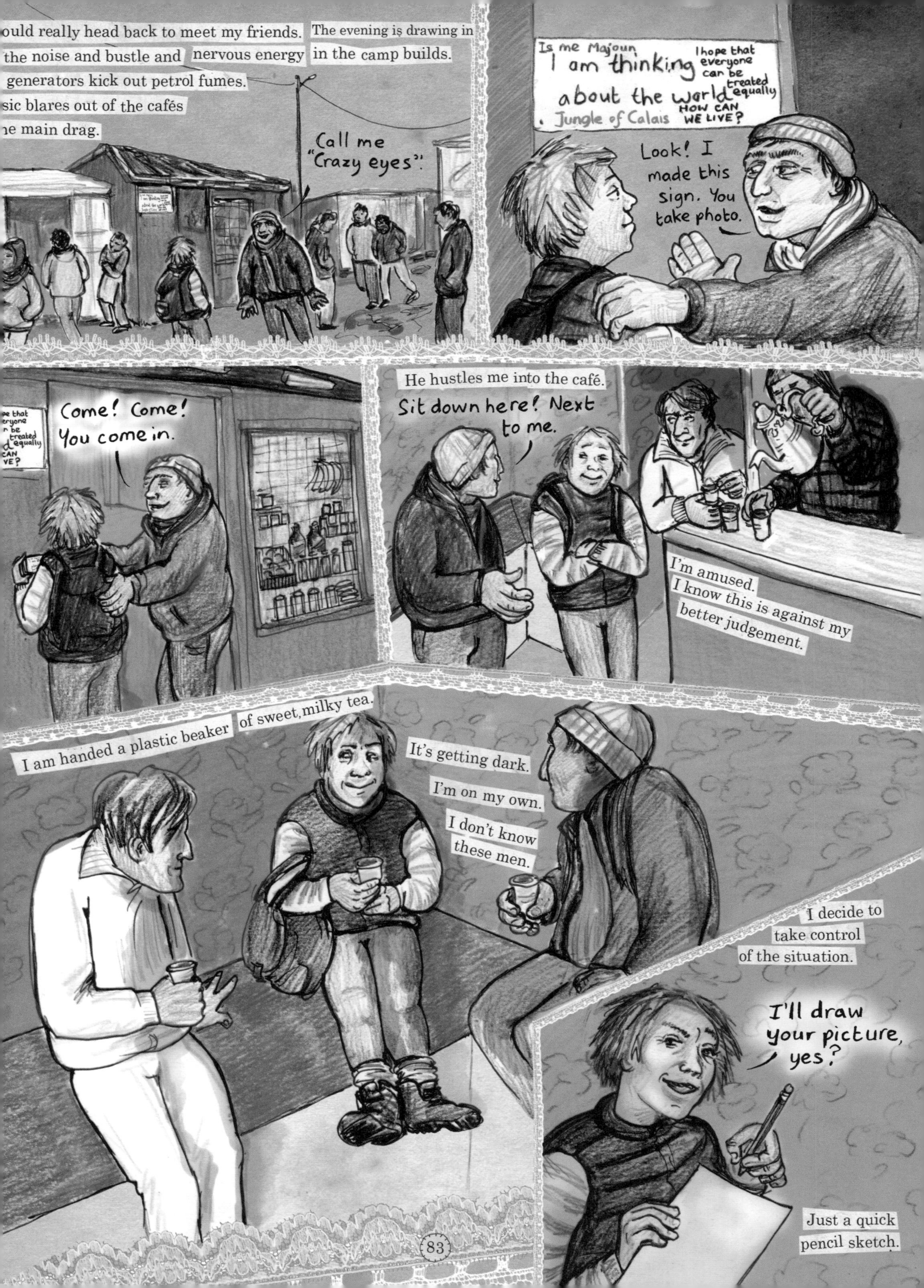

ould really head back to meet my friends.
The evening is drawing in
the noise and bustle and
nervous energy
in the camp builds.
generators kick out petrol fumes.
sic blares out of the cafés
ne main drag.
Call me "Crazy eyes".
Is me Majoun
I am thinking about the world
I hope that everyone can be treated equally
Jungle of Calais
HOW CAN WE LIVE?
Look! I made this sign. You take photo.
Come! Come! You come in.
He hustles me into the café.
Sit down here! Next to me.
I'm amused.
I know this is against my better judgement.
I am handed a plastic beaker
of sweet, milky tea.
It's getting dark.
I'm on my own.
I don't know these men.
I decide to take control of the situation.
I'll draw your picture, yes?
Just a quick pencil sketch.

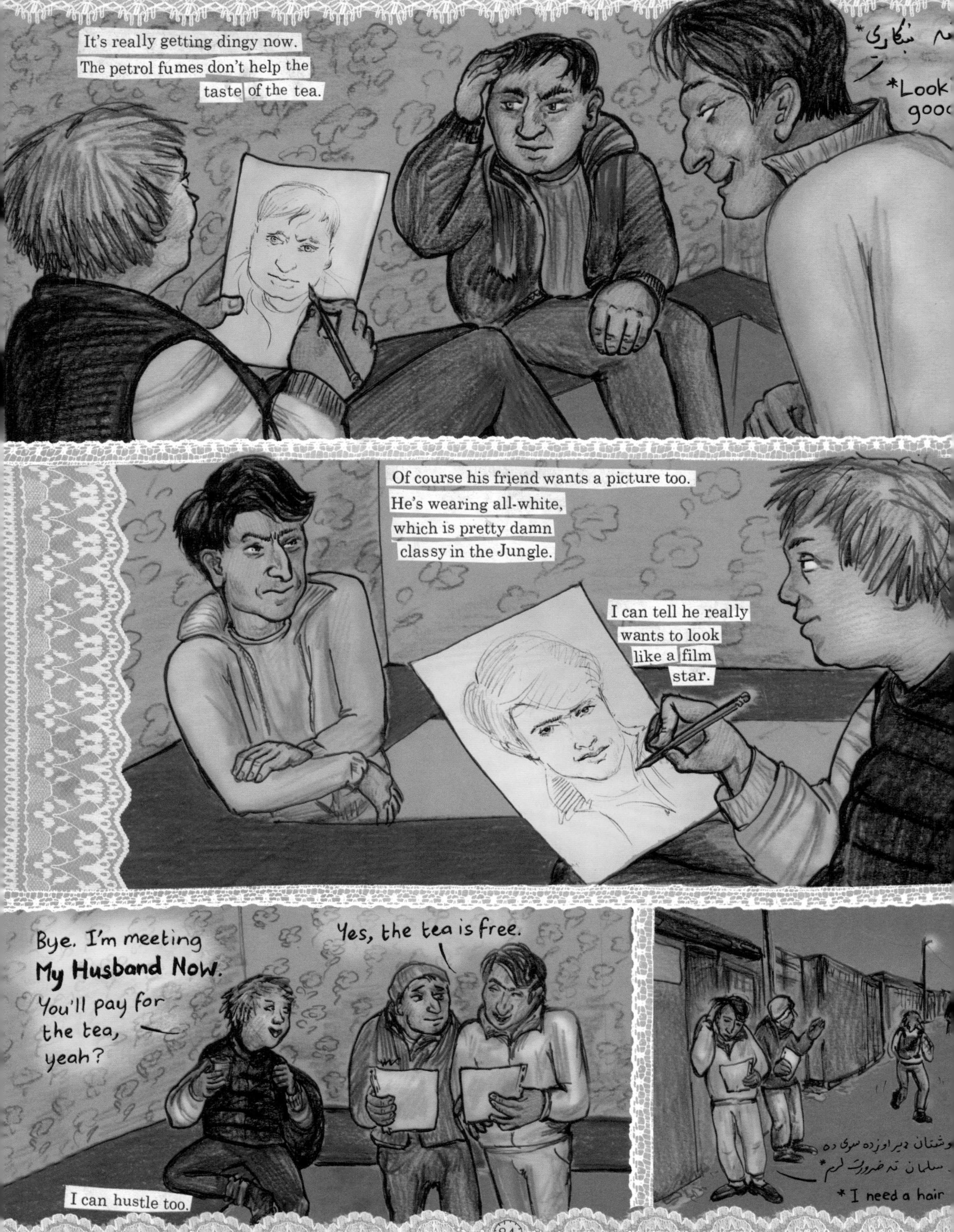

It's really getting dingy now.
The petrol fumes don't help the taste of the tea.
*Look goo
Of course his friend wants a picture too.
He's wearing all-white, which is pretty damn classy in the Jungle.
I can tell he really wants to look like a film star.
Bye. I'm meeting My Husband Now.
You'll pay for the tea, yeah?
Yes, the tea is free.
I can hustle too.
*I need a hair

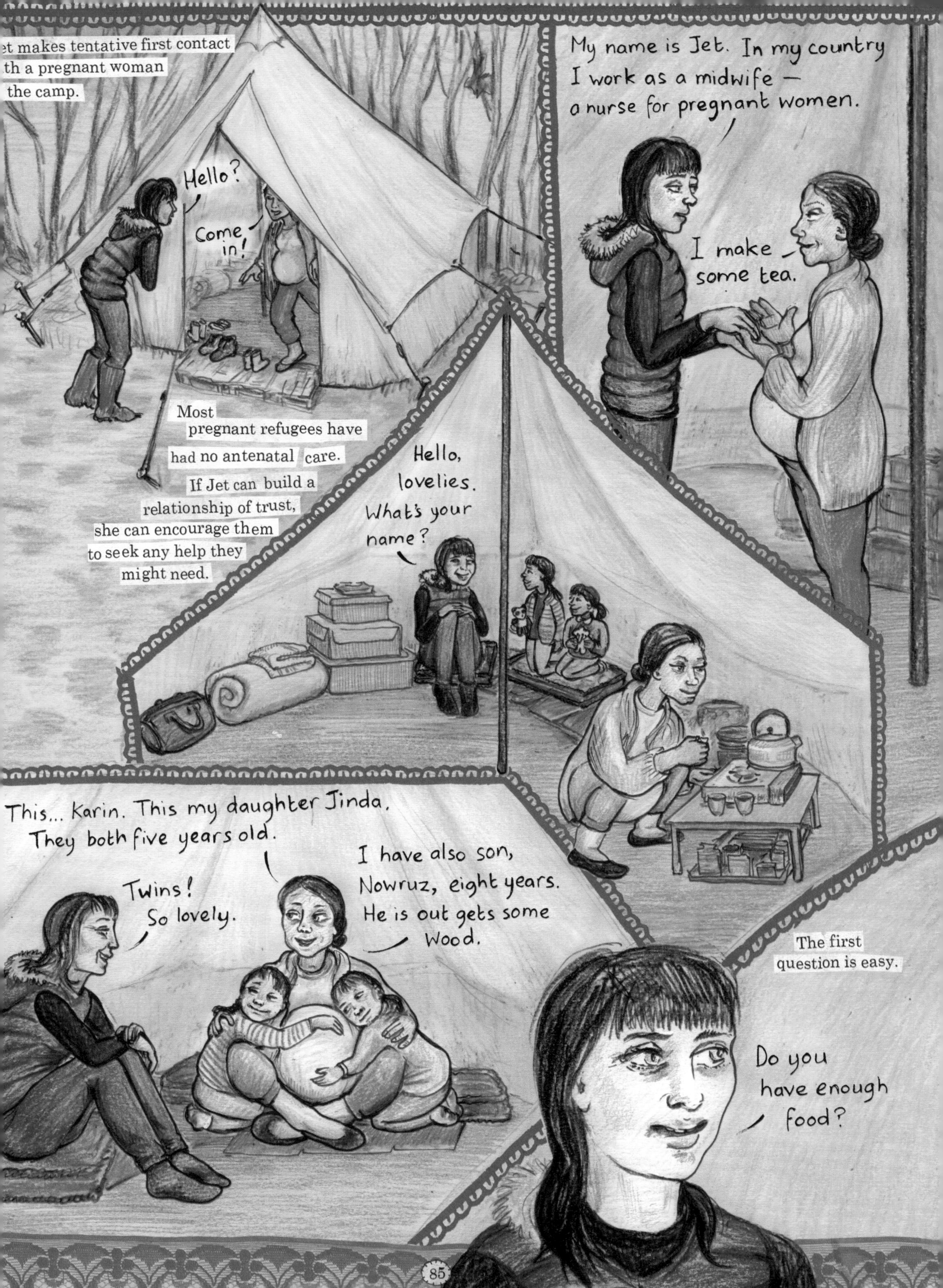

et makes tentative first contact
th a pregnant woman
the camp.
Hello?
Come in!
My name is Jet. In my country I work as a midwife — a nurse for pregnant women.
I make some tea.
Most pregnant refugees have had no antenatal care. If Jet can build a relationship of trust, she can encourage them to seek any help they might need.
Hello, lovelies. What's your name?
This... Karin. This my daughter Jinda. They both five years old.
Twins! So lovely.
I have also son, Nowruz, eight years. He is out gets some wood.
The first question is easy.
Do you have enough food?

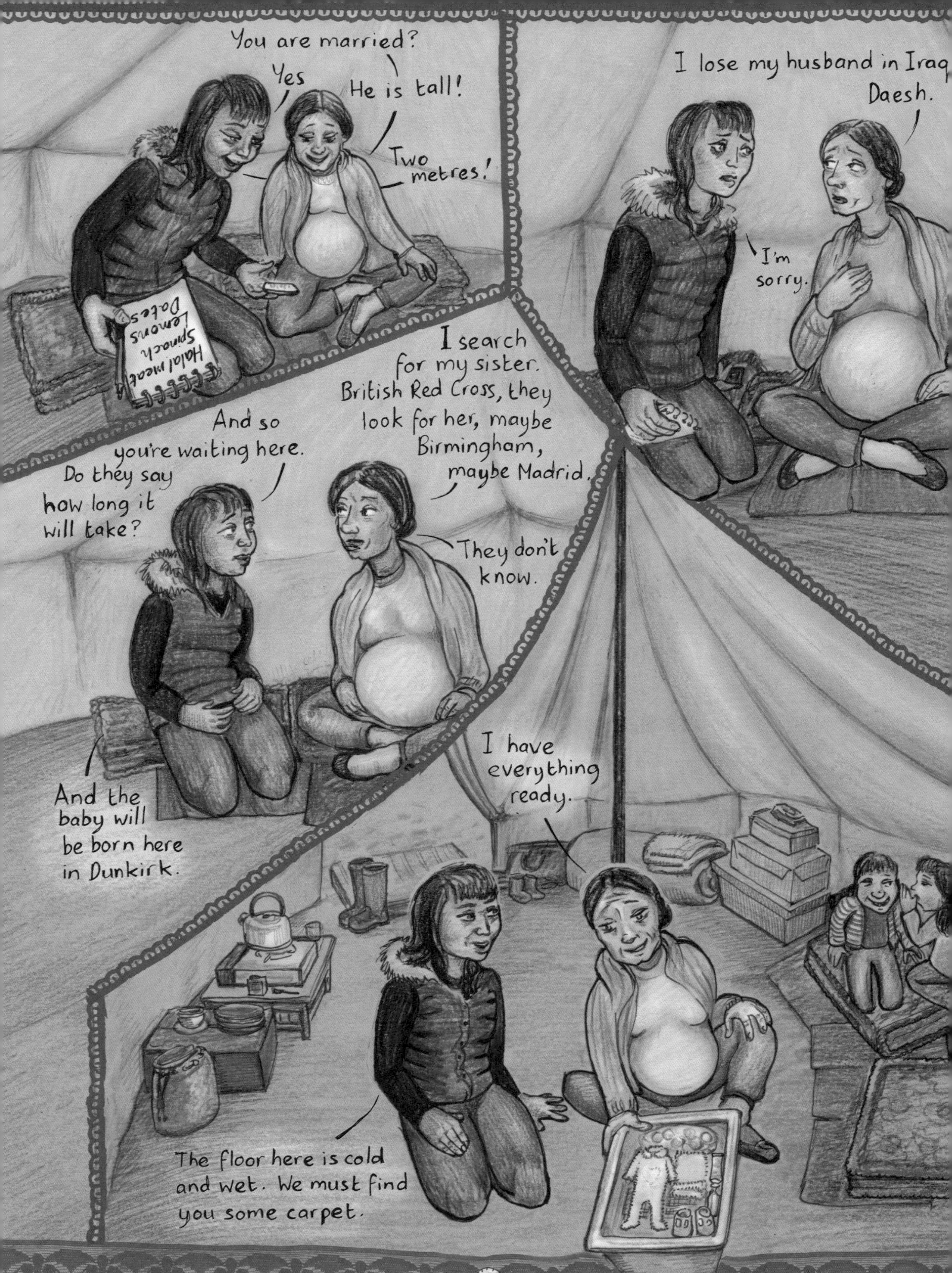
You are married?
Yes
He is tall!
Two metres!
Halal meat
Spinach
Lemons
Dates
I lose my husband in Iraq
Daesh.
I'm sorry.
I search for my sister. British Red Cross, they look for her, maybe Birmingham, maybe Madrid.
And so you're waiting here. Do they say how long it will take?
They don't know.
And the baby will be born here in Dunkirk.
I have everything ready.
The floor here is cold and wet. We must find you some carpet.

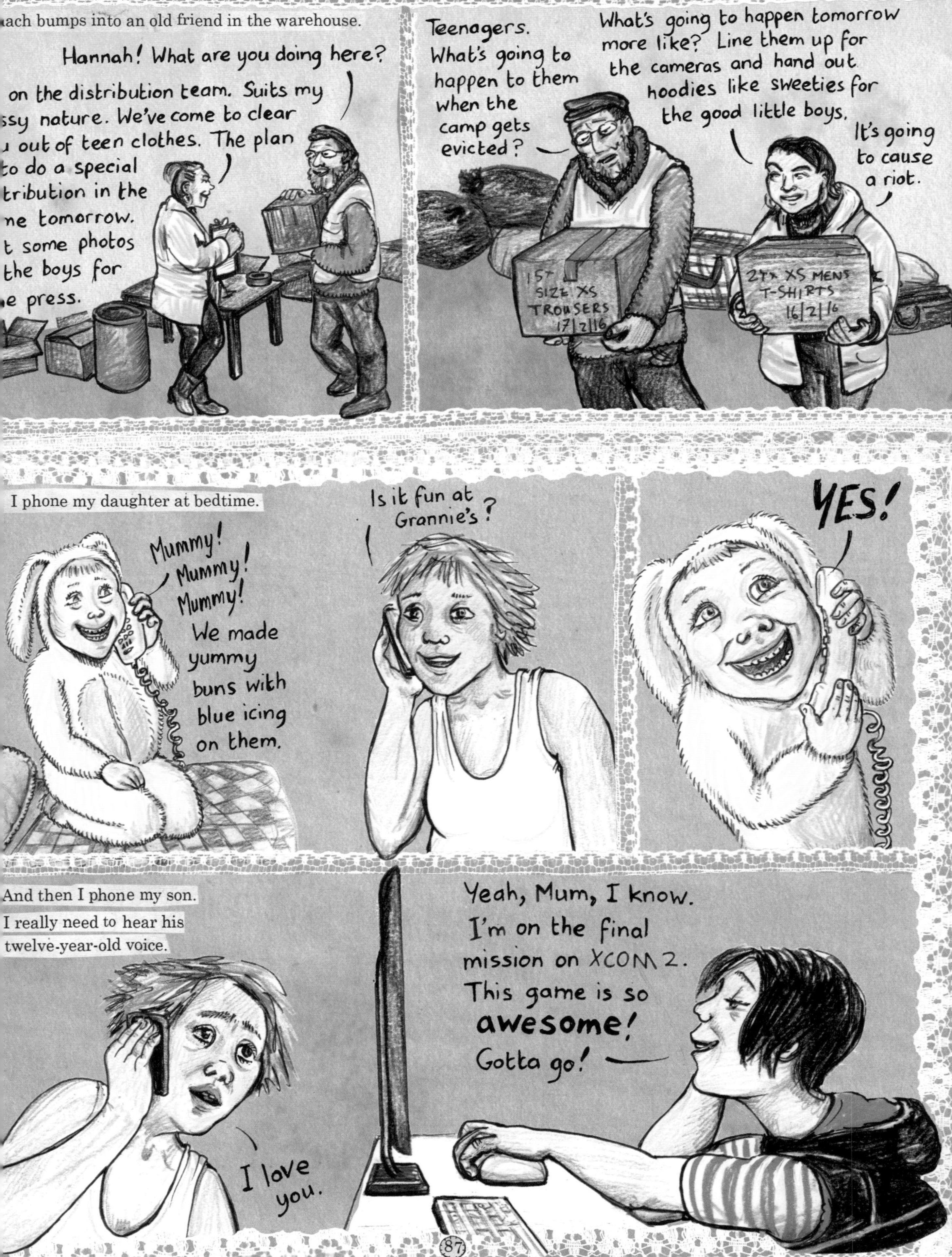

ach bumps into an old friend in the warehouse.
Hannah! What are you doing here?
on the distribution team. Suits my
ssy nature. We've come to clear
u out of teen clothes. The plan
to do a special
tribution in the
ne tomorrow.
t some photos
the boys for
e press.
Teenagers. What's going to happen to them when the camp gets evicted?
What's going to happen tomorrow more like? Line them up for the cameras and hand out hoodies like sweeties for the good little boys.
It's going to cause a riot.
15 x SIZE XS TROUSERS 17/2/16
27 x XS MENS T-SHIRTS 16/2/16
I phone my daughter at bedtime.
Mummy! Mummy! Mummy! We made yummy buns with blue icing on them.
Is it fun at Grannie's?
YES!
And then I phone my son.
I really need to hear his
twelve-year-old voice.
Yeah, Mum, I know. I'm on the final mission on XCOM 2. This game is so **awesome**! Gotta go!
I love you.

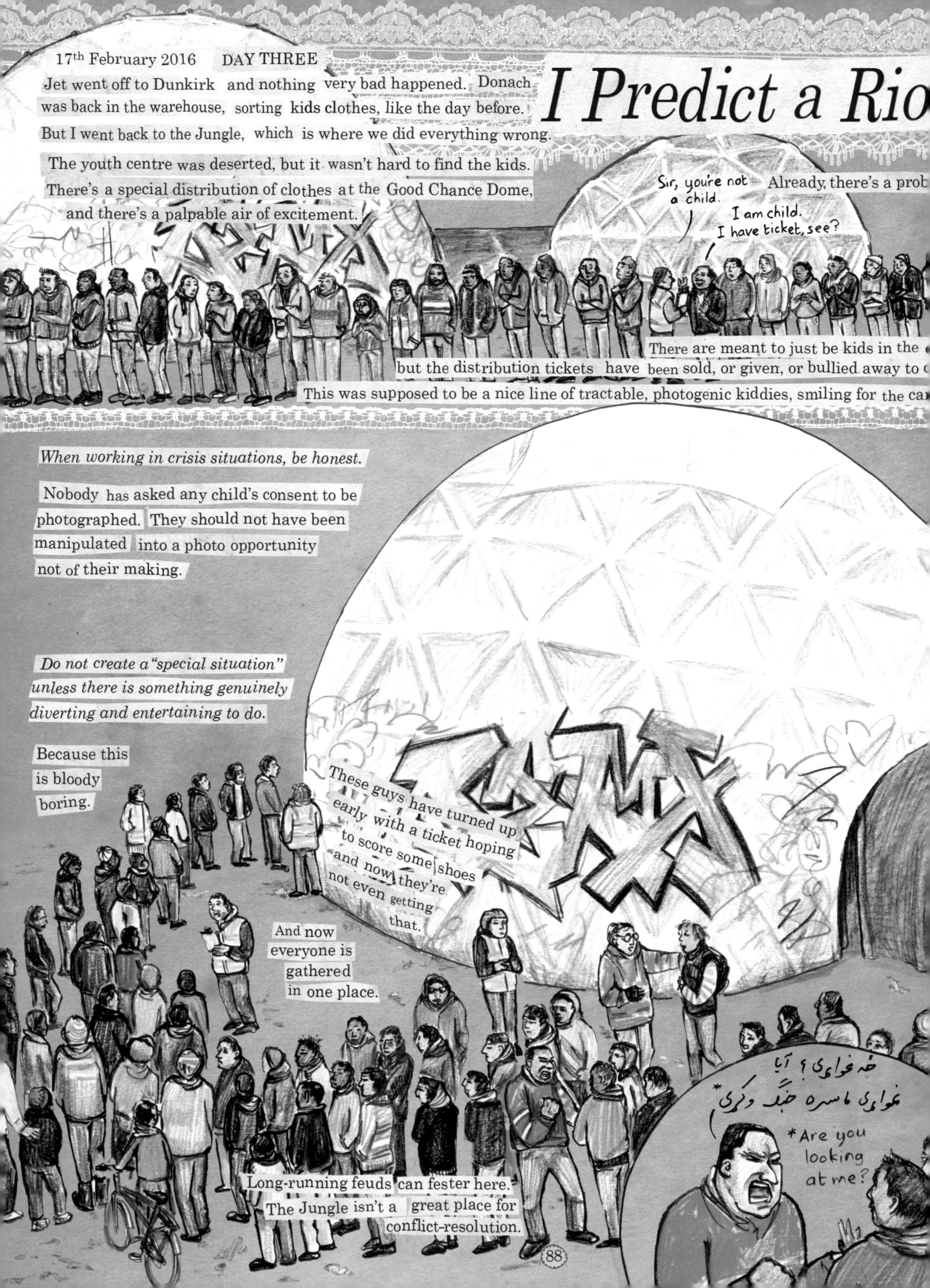

17th February 2016 DAY THREE
I Predict a Rio
Jet went off to Dunkirk and nothing very bad happened. Donach was back in the warehouse, sorting kids clothes, like the day before. But I went back to the Jungle, which is where we did everything wrong.
The youth centre was deserted, but it wasn't hard to find the kids. There's a special distribution of clothes at the Good Chance Dome, and there's a palpable air of excitement.
Already, there's a prob
Sir, you're not a child.
I am child. I have ticket, see?
There are meant to just be kids in the
but the distribution tickets have been sold, or given, or bullied away to
This was supposed to be a nice line of tractable, photogenic kiddies, smiling for the ca
When working in crisis situations, be honest.
Nobody has asked any child's consent to be photographed. They should not have been manipulated into a photo opportunity not of their making.
Do not create a "special situation" unless there is something genuinely diverting and entertaining to do.
Because this is bloody boring.
These guys have turned up early with a ticket hoping to score some shoes and now they're not even getting that.
And now everyone is gathered in one place.
خه نخوای؟ آیا
نخوای ما سره جنگ وکنی*
*Are you looking at me?
Long-running feuds can fester here. The Jungle isn't a great place for conflict-resolution.

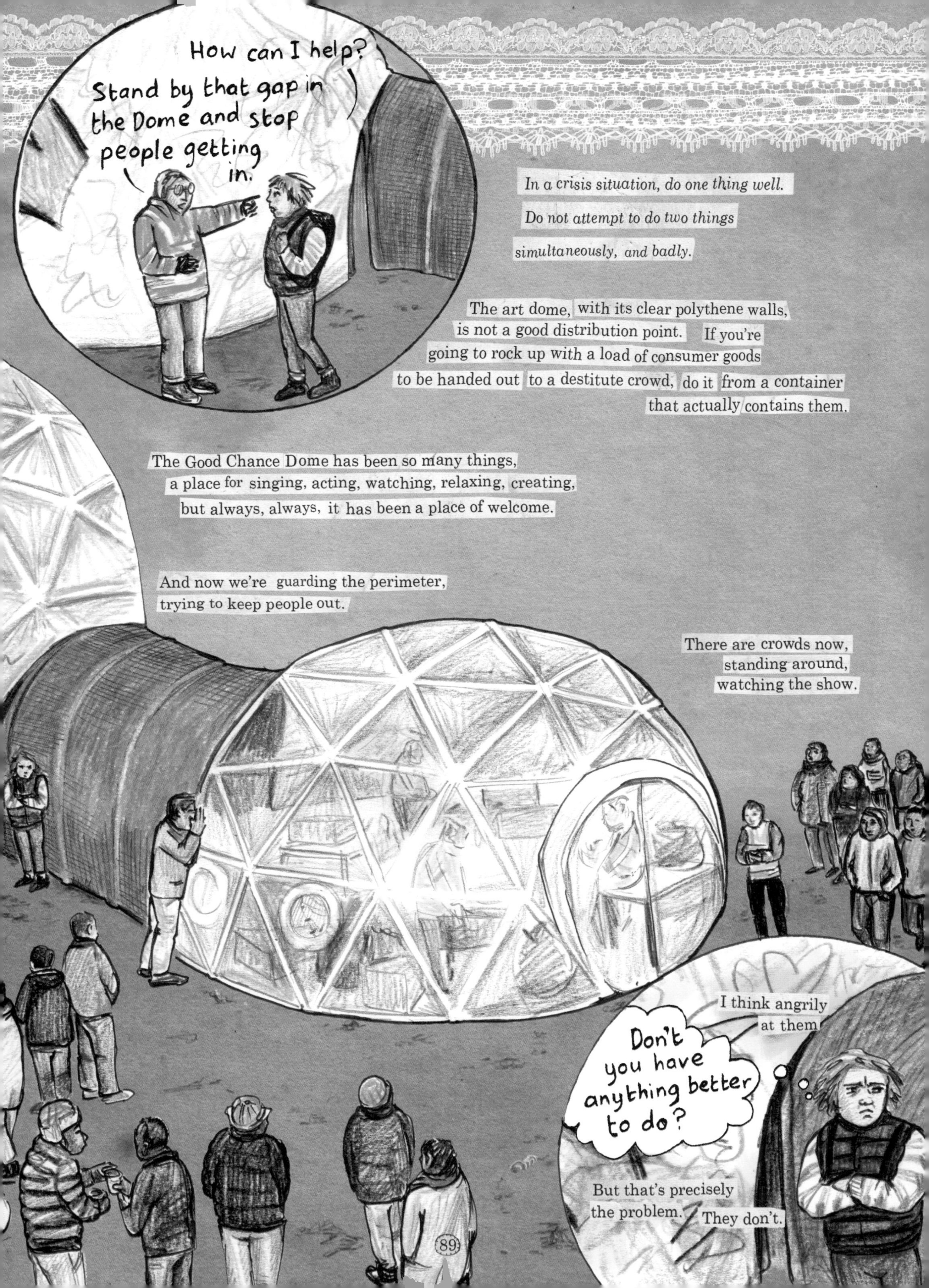

How can I help?
Stand by that gap in the Dome and stop people getting in.
In a crisis situation, do one thing well.
Do not attempt to do two things simultaneously, and badly.
The art dome, with its clear polythene walls, is not a good distribution point. If you're going to rock up with a load of consumer goods to be handed out to a destitute crowd, do it from a container that actually contains them.
The Good Chance Dome has been so many things, a place for singing, acting, watching, relaxing, creating, but always, always, it has been a place of welcome.
And now we're guarding the perimeter, trying to keep people out.
There are crowds now, standing around, watching the show.
I think angrily at them
Don't you have anything better to do?
But that's precisely the problem. They don't.

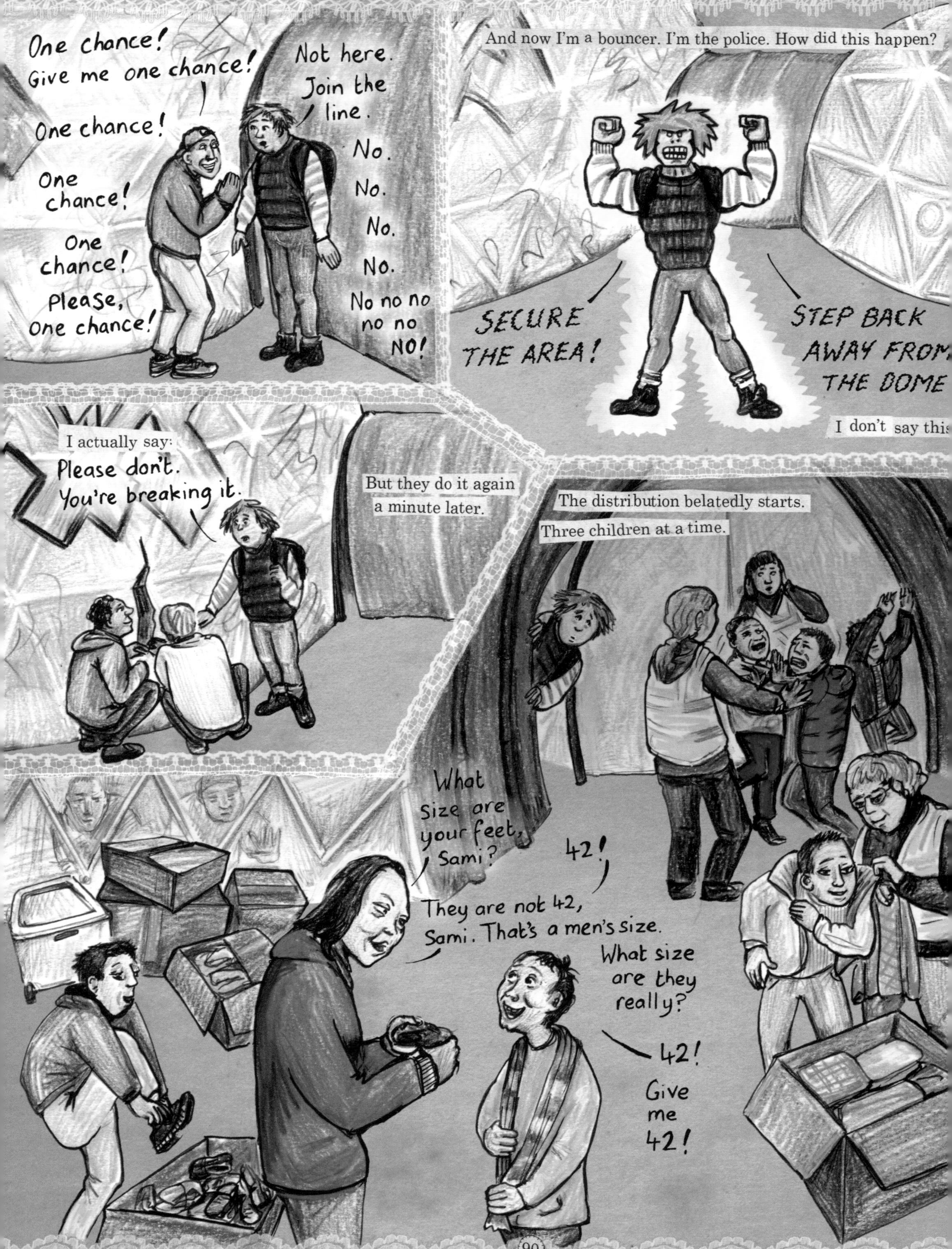
One chance!
Give me one chance!
One chance!
One chance!
One chance!
Please, one chance!
Not here. Join the line.
No.
No.
No.
No.
No no no no no NO!
And now I'm a bouncer. I'm the police. How did this happen?
SECURE THE AREA!
STEP BACK AWAY FROM THE DOME
I don't say this
I actually say:
Please don't. You're breaking it.
But they do it again a minute later.
The distribution belatedly starts.
Three children at a time.
What size are your feet, Sami?
42!
They are not 42, Sami. That's a men's size.
What size are they really?
42!
Give me 42!

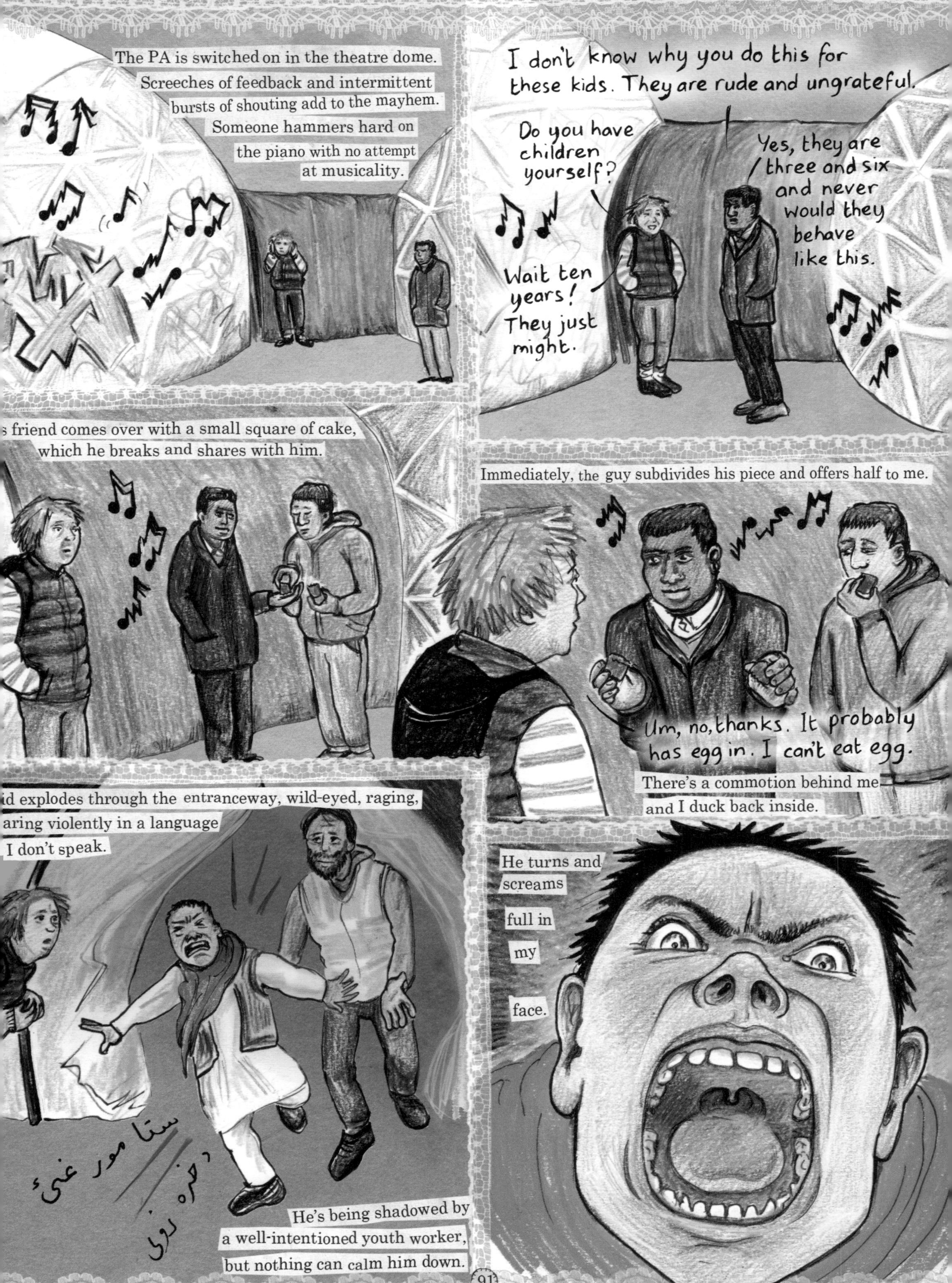

The PA is switched on in the theatre dome.
Screeches of feedback and intermittent bursts of shouting add to the mayhem.
Someone hammers hard on the piano with no attempt at musicality.
I don't know why you do this for these kids. They are rude and ungrateful.
Do you have children yourself?
Yes, they are three and six and never would they behave like this.
Wait ten years! They just might.
s friend comes over with a small square of cake, which he breaks and shares with him.
Immediately, the guy subdivides his piece and offers half to me.
Um, no, thanks. It probably has egg in. I can't eat egg.
There's a commotion behind me and I duck back inside.
id explodes through the entranceway, wild-eyed, raging,
aring violently in a language I don't speak.
He's being shadowed by a well-intentioned youth worker, but nothing can calm him down.
He turns and screams full in my face.

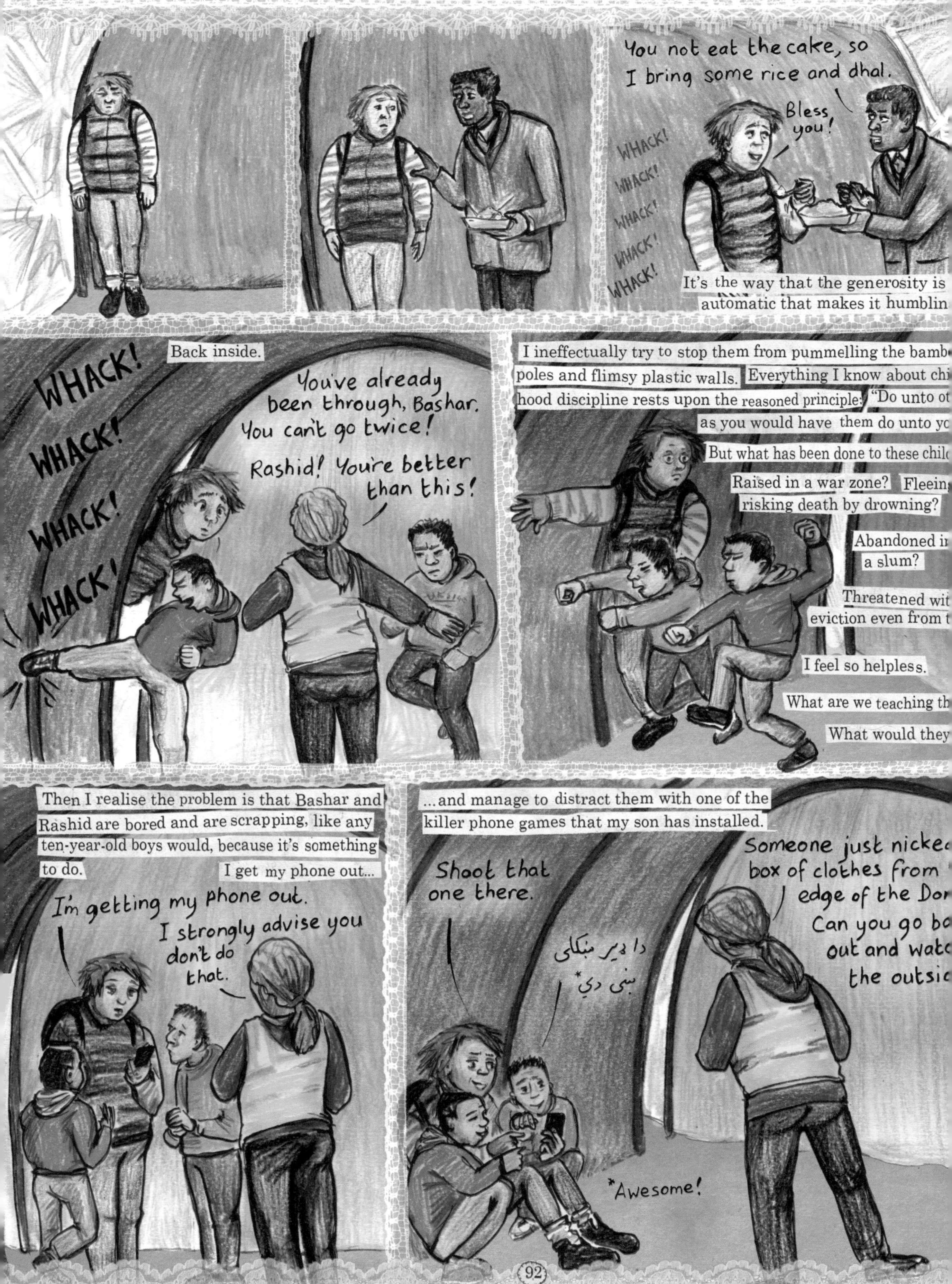

You not eat the cake, so I bring some rice and dhal.
Bless you!
WHACK!
WHACK!
WHACK!
WHACK!
WHACK!
It's the way that the generosity is automatic that makes it humblin
Back inside.
WHACK!
WHACK!
WHACK!
WHACK!
You've already been through, Bashar. You can't go twice!
Rashid! You're better than this!
I ineffectually try to stop them from pummelling the bamb poles and flimsy plastic walls.
Everything I know about chi hood discipline rests upon the reasoned principle: "Do unto ot as you would have them do unto yo
But what has been done to these chil
Raised in a war zone?
Fleein risking death by drowning?
Abandoned i a slum?
Threatened wit eviction even from t
I feel so helpless.
What are we teaching th
What would they
Then I realise the problem is that Bashar and Rashid are bored and are scrapping, like any ten-year-old boys would, because it's something to do.
I get my phone out...
I'm getting my phone out.
I strongly advise you don't do that.
...and manage to distract them with one of the killer phone games that my son has installed.
Shoot that one there.
دا ډیر ښکلی
ښې دي*
*Awesome!
Someone just nicke box of clothes from edge of the Do Can you go b out and wat the outsi

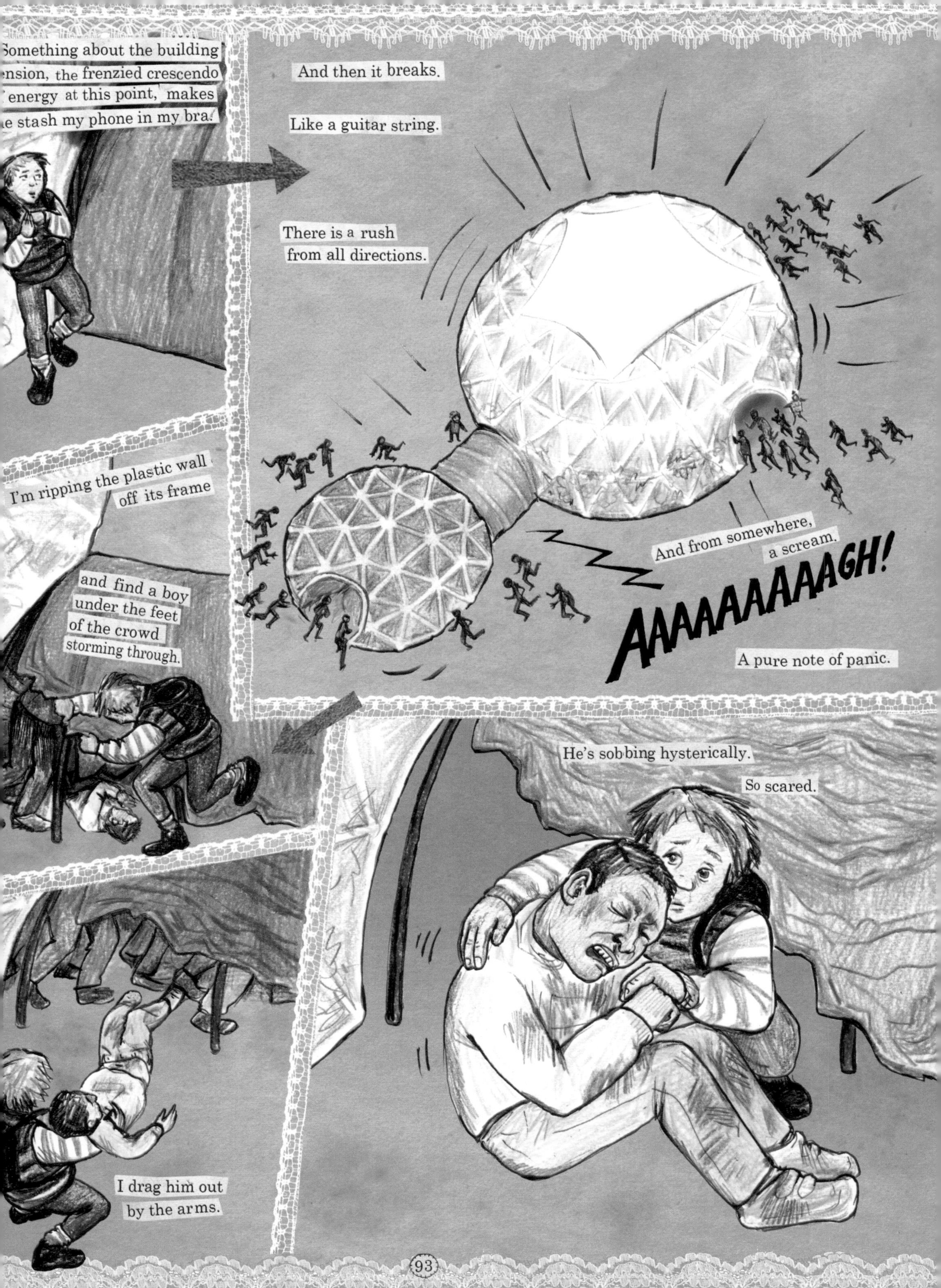

Something about the building
ension, the frenzied crescendo
' energy at this point, makes
ie stash my phone in my bra.
And then it breaks.
Like a guitar string.
There is a rush
from all directions.
And from somewhere,
a scream.
AAAAAAAAAGH!
A pure note of panic.
I'm ripping the plastic wall
off its frame
and find a boy
under the feet
of the crowd
storming through.
I drag him out
by the arms.
He's sobbing hysterically.
So scared.

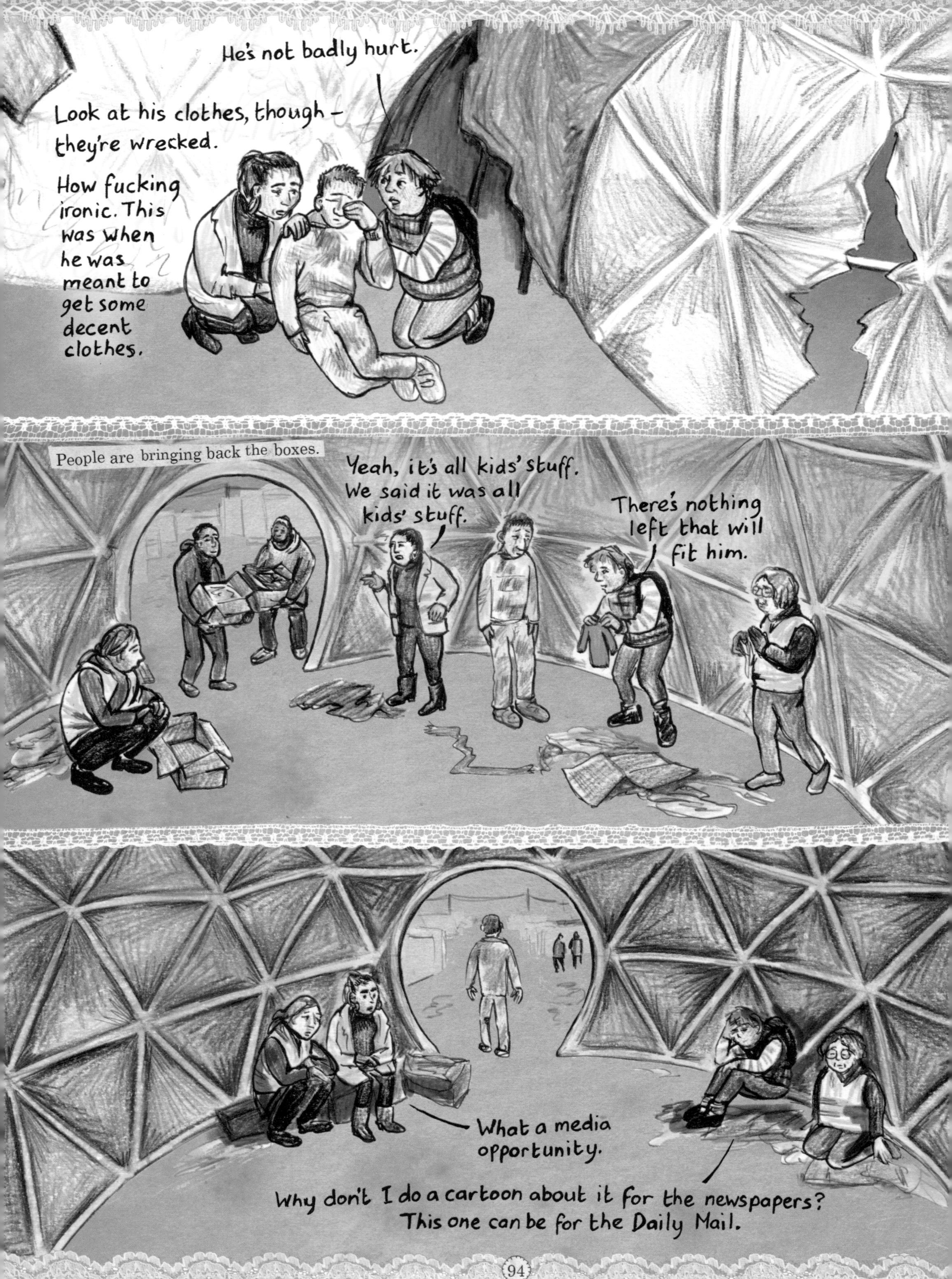
He's not badly hurt.
Look at his clothes, though – they're wrecked.
How fucking ironic. This was when he was meant to get some decent clothes.
People are bringing back the boxes.
Yeah, it's all kids' stuff. We said it was all kids' stuff.
There's nothing left that will fit him.
What a media opportunity.
Why don't I do a cartoon about it for the newspapers? This one can be for the Daily Mail.

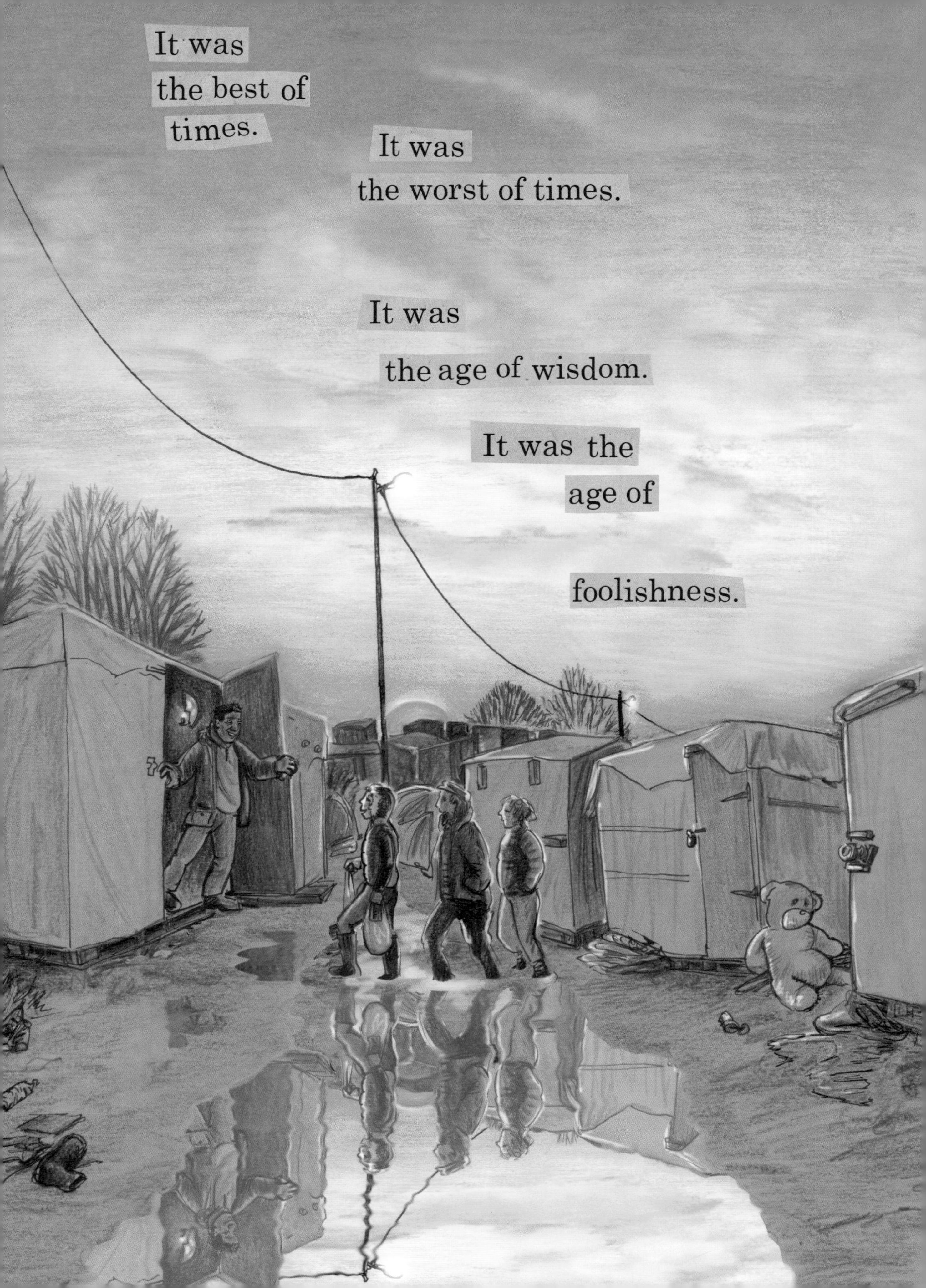
It was
the best of
times.
It was
the worst of times.
It was
the age of wisdom.
It was the
age of
foolishness.

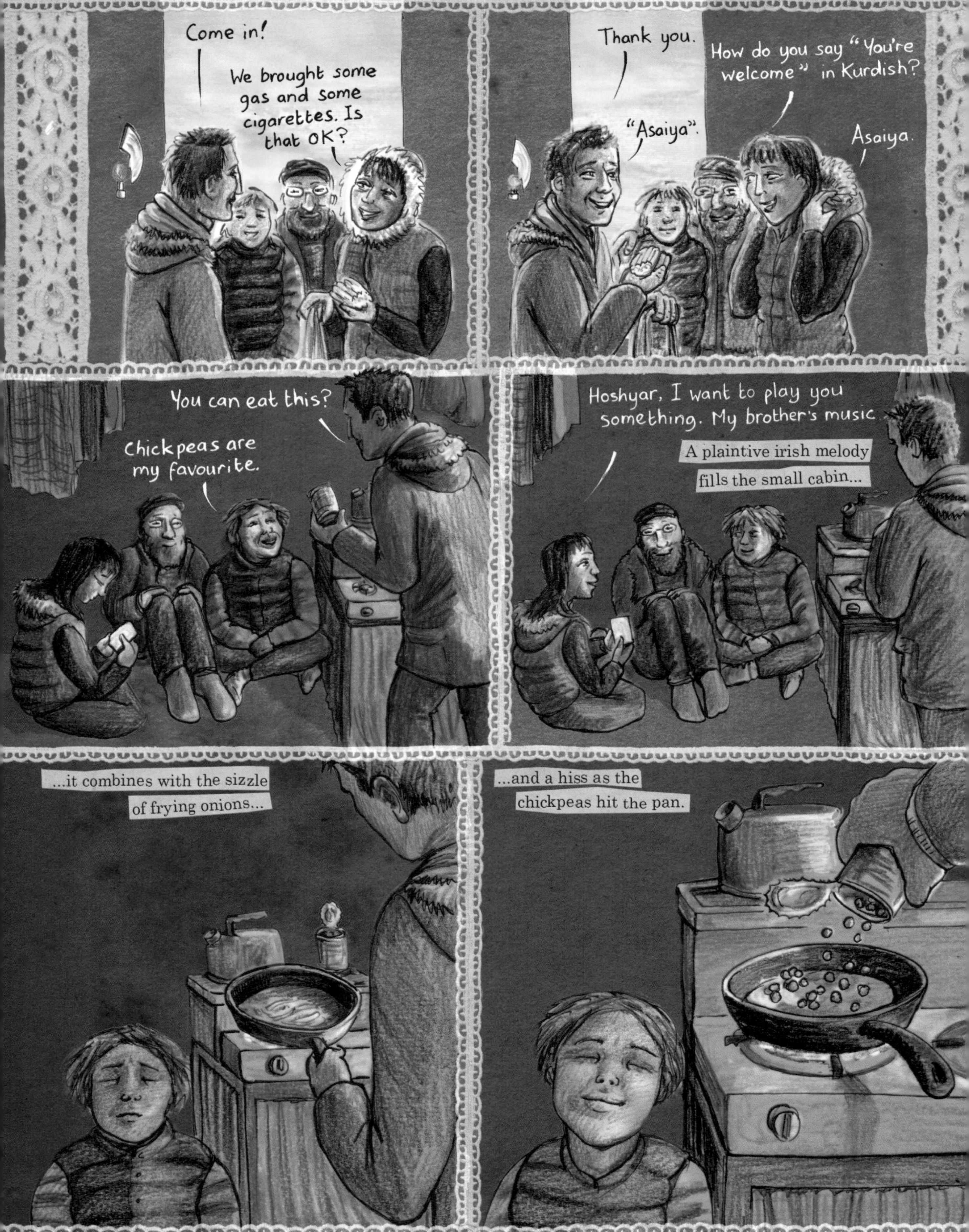
Come in!
We brought some gas and some cigarettes. Is that OK?
Thank you.
"Asaiya".
How do you say "You're welcome" in Kurdish?
Asaiya.
You can eat this?
Chickpeas are my favourite.
Hoshyar, I want to play you something. My brother's music.
A plaintive irish melody fills the small cabin...
...it combines with the sizzle of frying onions...
...and a hiss as the chickpeas hit the pan.

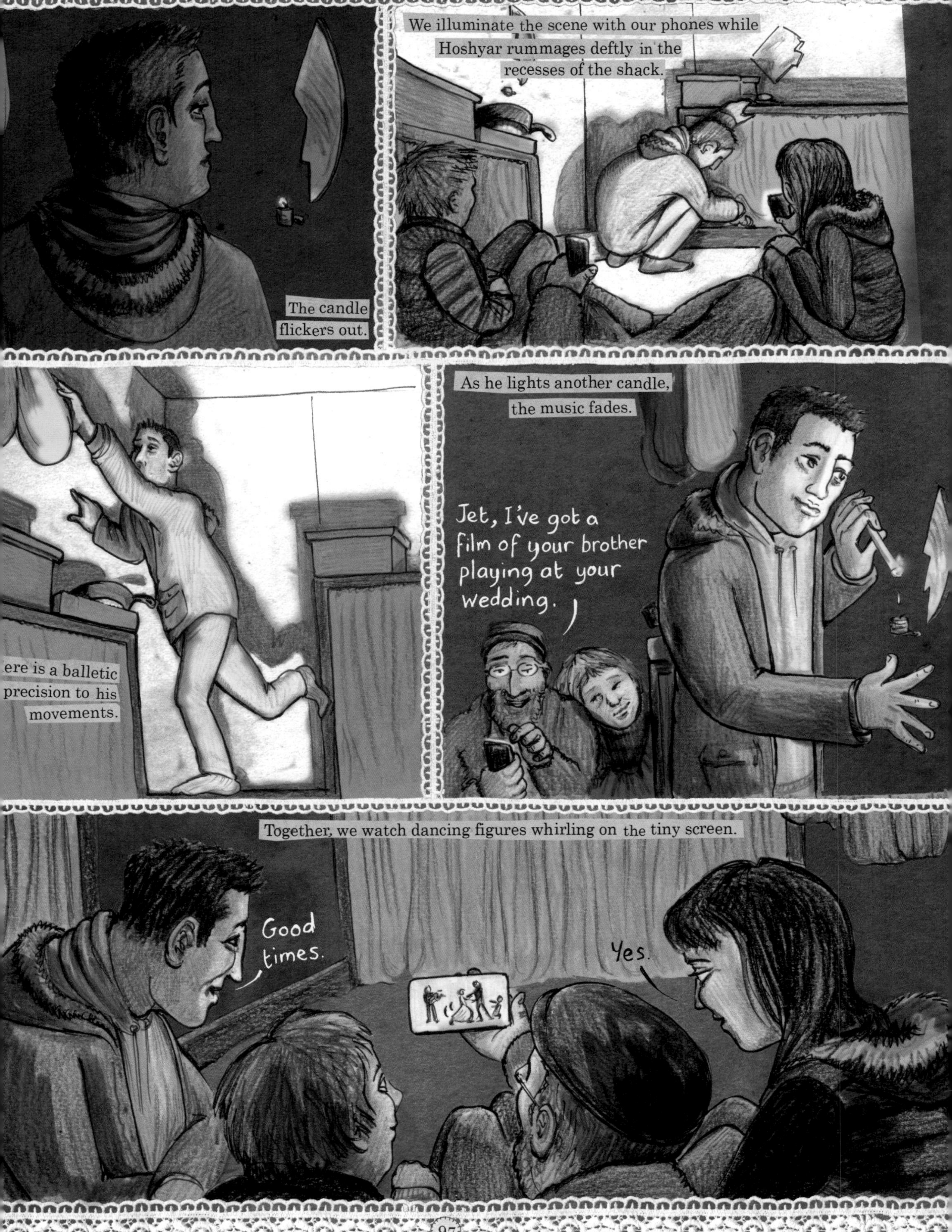
The candle flickers out.
We illuminate the scene with our phones while Hoshyar rummages deftly in the recesses of the shack.
ere is a balletic precision to his movements.
As he lights another candle, the music fades.
Jet, I've got a film of your brother playing at your wedding.
Together, we watch dancing figures whirling on the tiny screen.
Good times.
Yes.

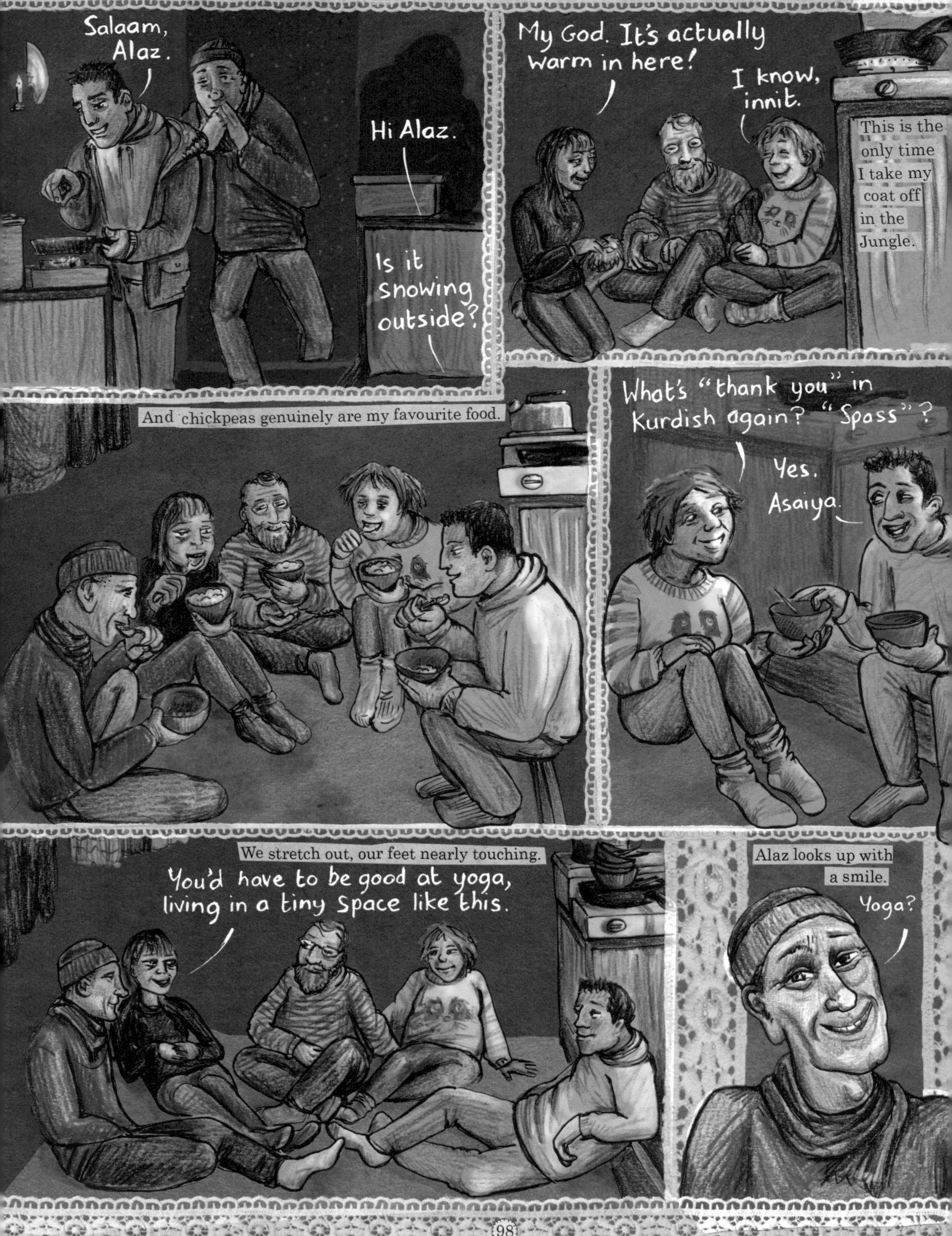

Salaam, Alaz.
Hi Alaz.
Is it snowing outside?
My God. It's actually warm in here!
I know, innit.
This is the only time I take my coat off in the Jungle.
And chickpeas genuinely are my favourite food.
What's "thank you" in Kurdish again? "Spass"?
Yes. Asaiya.
We stretch out, our feet nearly touching.
You'd have to be good at yoga, living in a tiny space like this.
Alaz looks up with a smile.
Yoga?

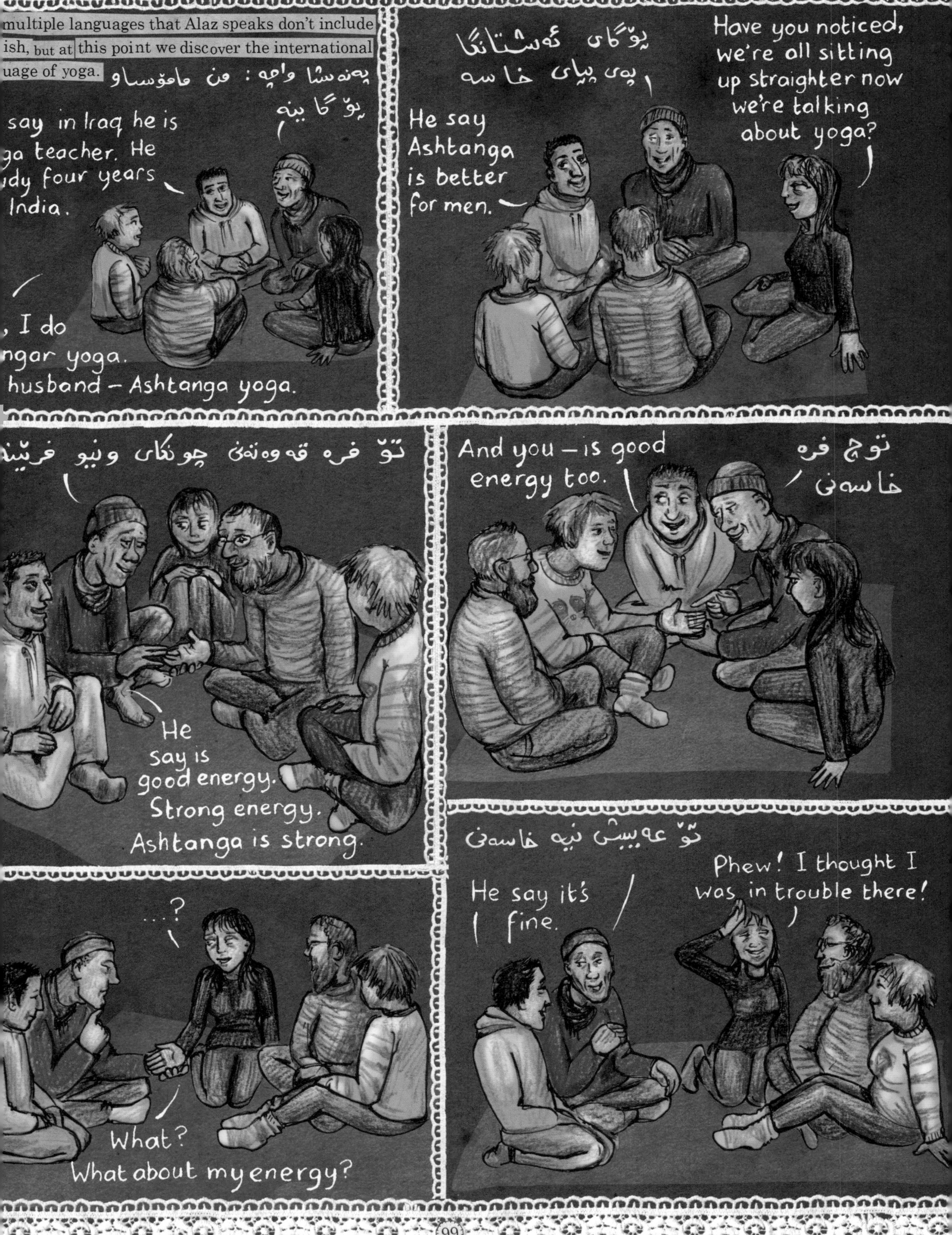
multiple languages that Alaz speaks don't include
ish, but at this point we discover the international
uage of yoga.
پەنەشا واچە: من ماموّساو یوّگا بنە
say in Iraq he is
ga teacher. He
idy four years
India.
, I do
ngar yoga.
husband – Ashtanga yoga.
یوّگای ئەشتانگا پەی پیای خاسە
He say Ashtanga is better for men.
Have you noticed, we're all sitting up straighter now we're talking about yoga?
توّ فرە قەوەتەی چونکای ونیو فرێنە
He say is good energy. Strong energy. Ashtanga is strong.
And you – is good energy too.
توج فرە خاسەنی
...?
What? What about my energy?
توّ عەیبش نیە خاسەنی
He say it's fine.
Phew! I thought I was in trouble there!

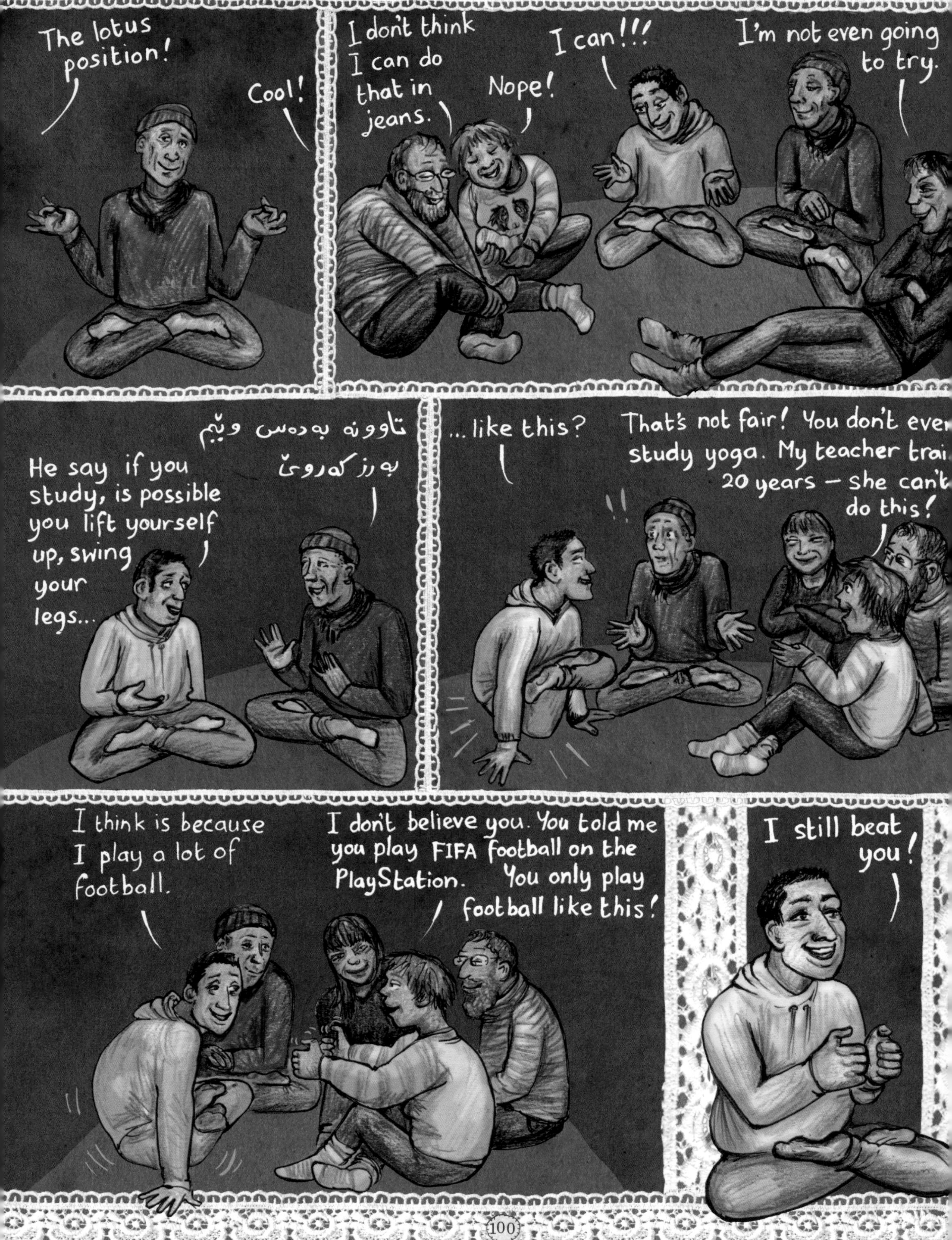
The lotus position!
Cool!
I don't think I can do that in jeans.
Nope!
I can!!!
I'm not even going to try.
تاوونە بەدەس وێم
بەرز کەروێ
He say if you study, is possible you lift yourself up, swing your legs...
... like this?
!!
That's not fair! You don't even study yoga. My teacher trai 20 years – she can't do this!
I think is because I play a lot of football.
I don't believe you. You told me you play FIFA football on the PlayStation. You only play football like this!
I still beat you!

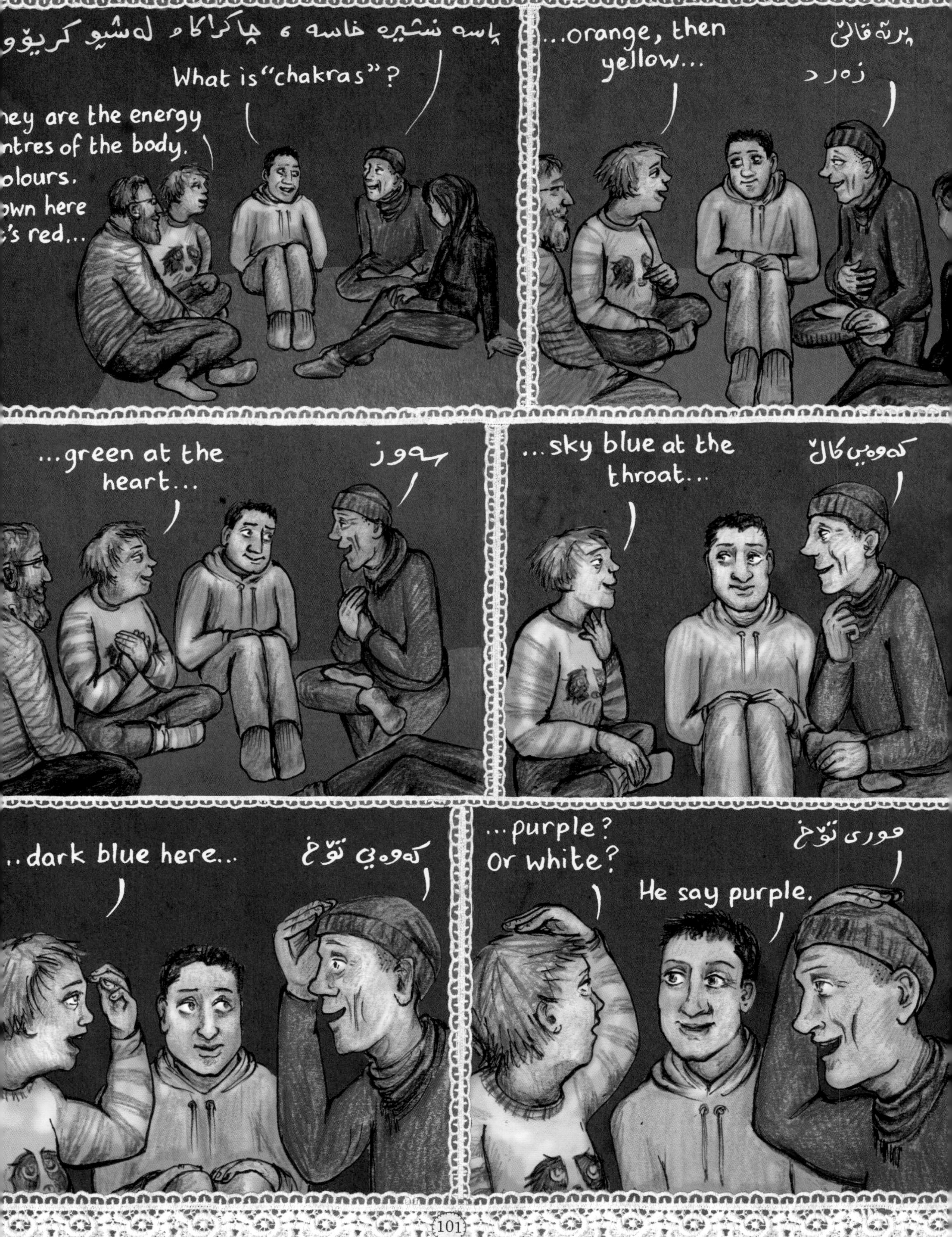

What is "chakras"?
پاسە نشیرە خاسە و چاکراکام لەشیو کریۆو
ney are the energy
ntres of the body.
olours.
own here
t's red...
...orange, then
yellow...
پرتەقاڵی
زەرد
...green at the
heart...
سەوز
...sky blue at the
throat...
کەوەیی کاڵ
..dark blue here...
کەوەیی تۆخ
...purple?
Or white?
He say purple.
موری تۆخ

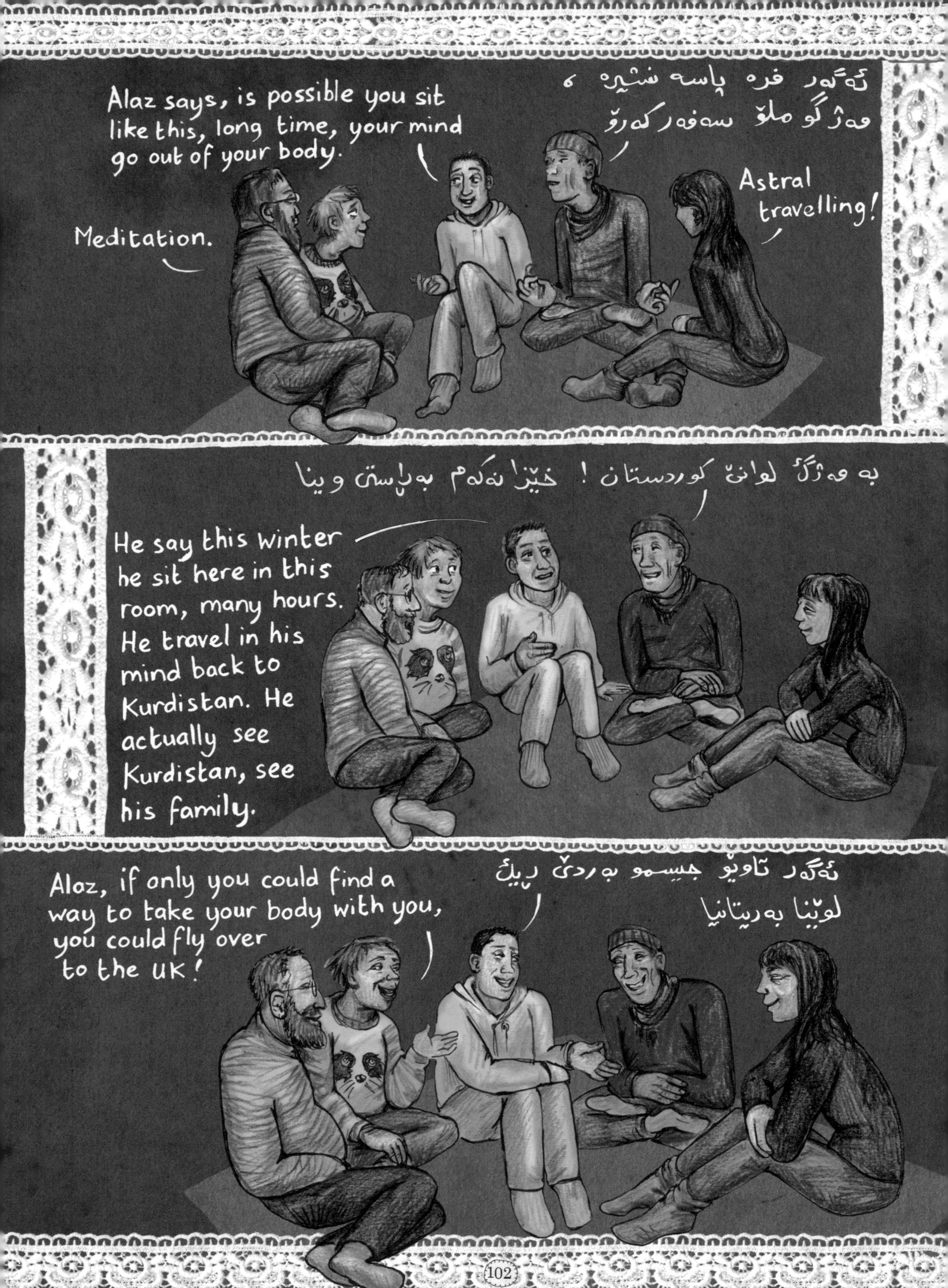
Alaz says, is possible you sit like this, long time, your mind go out of your body.
ئەگەر فرە پاسە نشیرە ە
مەژگو ملۆ سەفەرکەرۆ
Meditation.
Astral travelling!
بە مەژگێ لوانێ کوردستان ! خێزانەکەم بەراستی وینا
He say this winter he sit here in this room, many hours. He travel in his mind back to Kurdistan. He actually see Kurdistan, see his family.
Aloz, if only you could find a way to take your body with you, you could fly over to the UK!
ئەگەر تاویۆ جیسمو بەردێ دیێ
لوێنا بەریتانیا

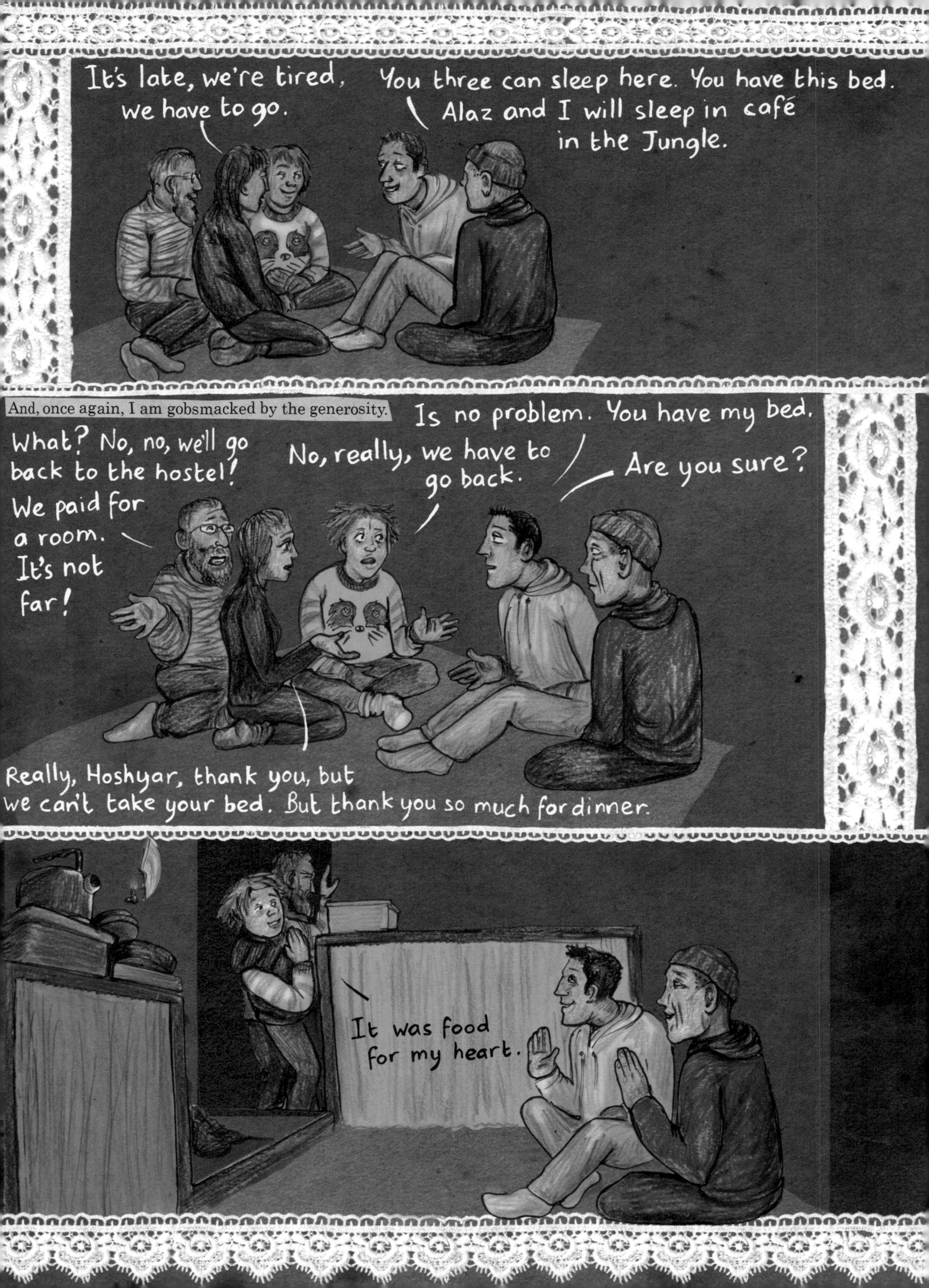

It's late, we're tired, we have to go.
You three can sleep here. You have this bed. Alaz and I will sleep in café in the Jungle.
And, once again, I am gobsmacked by the generosity.
What? No, no, we'll go back to the hostel! We paid for a room. It's not far!
No, really, we have to go back.
Is no problem. You have my bed.
Are you sure?
Really, Hoshyar, thank you, but we can't take your bed. But thank you so much for dinner.
It was food for my heart.

18th February 2016

Triple Three-in-One Action (Part II)

DAY FOUR

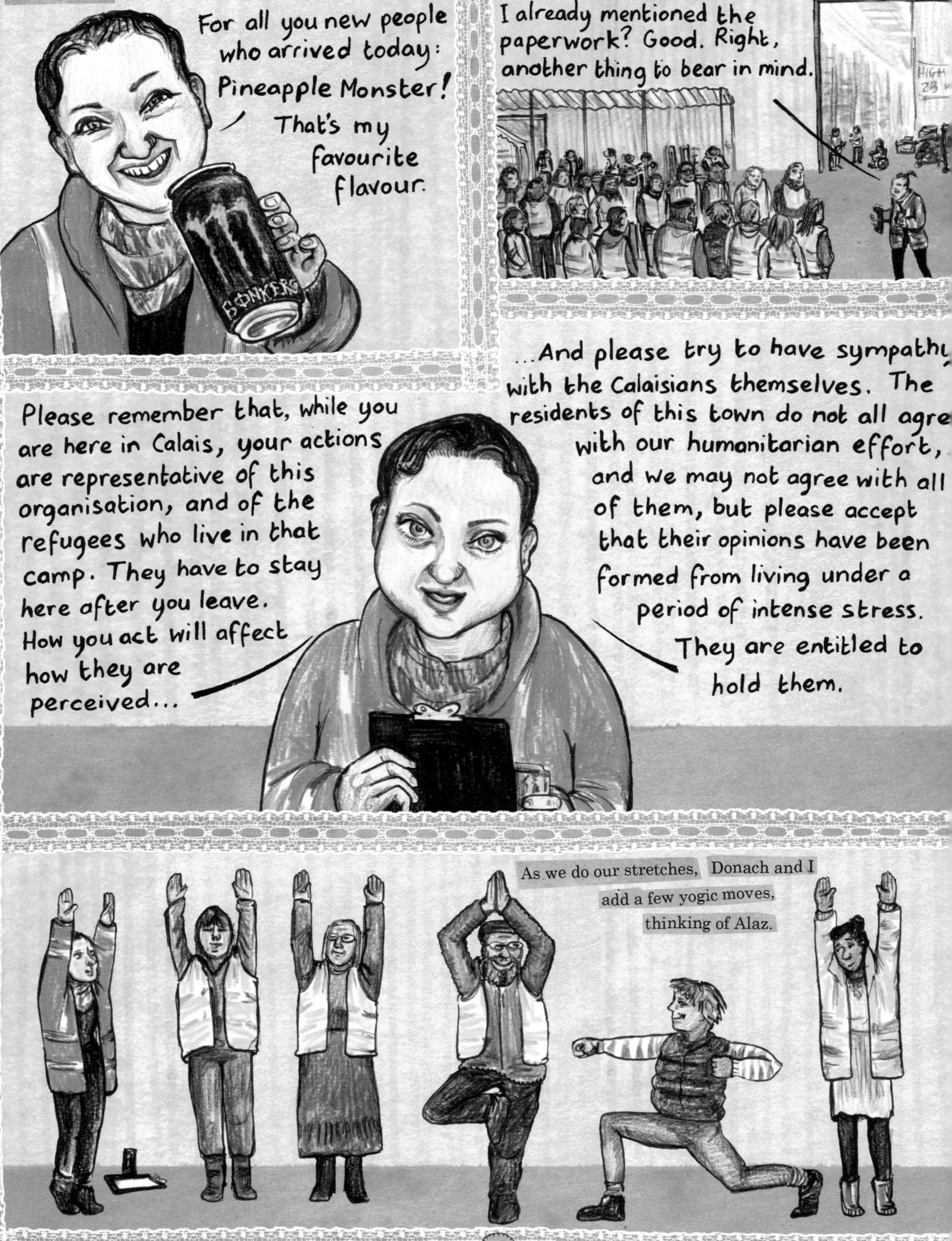

For all you new people who arrived today: Pineapple Monster!
That's my favourite flavour.
I already mentioned the paperwork? Good. Right, another thing to bear in mind.
Please remember that, while you are here in Calais, your actions are representative of this organisation, and of the refugees who live in that camp. They have to stay here after you leave. How you act will affect how they are perceived...
...And please try to have sympathy with the Calaisians themselves. The residents of this town do not all agre with our humanitarian effort, and we may not agree with all of them, but please accept that their opinions have been formed from living under a period of intense stress.
They are entitled to hold them.
As we do our stretches, Donach and I add a few yogic moves, thinking of Alaz.

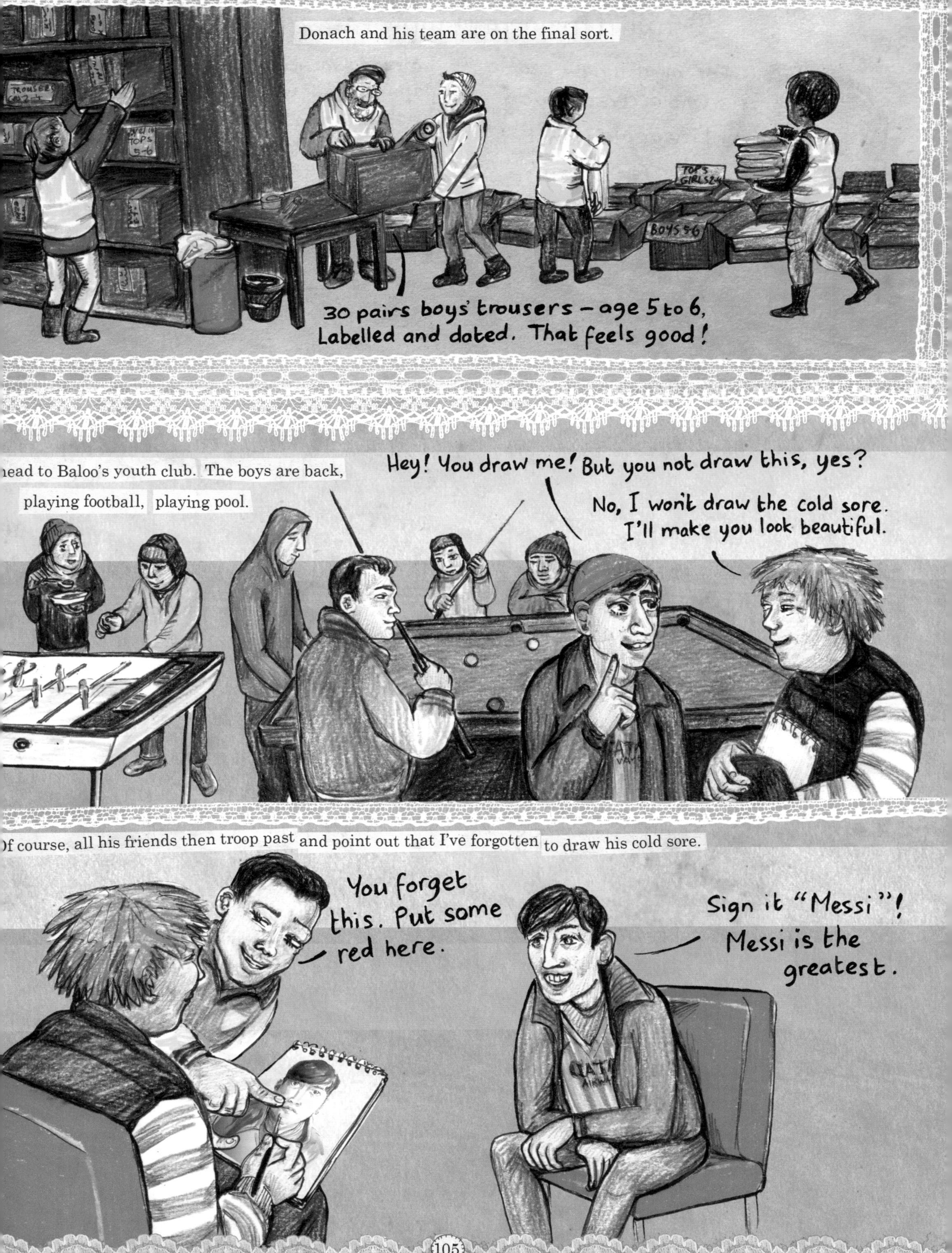

Donach and his team are on the final sort.
BOYS 5-6
30 pairs boys' trousers – age 5 to 6,
Labelled and dated. That feels good!
ead to Baloo's youth club. The boys are back,
playing football, playing pool.
Hey! You draw me! But you not draw this, yes?
No, I won't draw the cold sore.
I'll make you look beautiful.
f course, all his friends then troop past and point out that I've forgotten to draw his cold sore.
You forget this. Put some red here.
Sign it "Messi"!
Messi is the greatest.

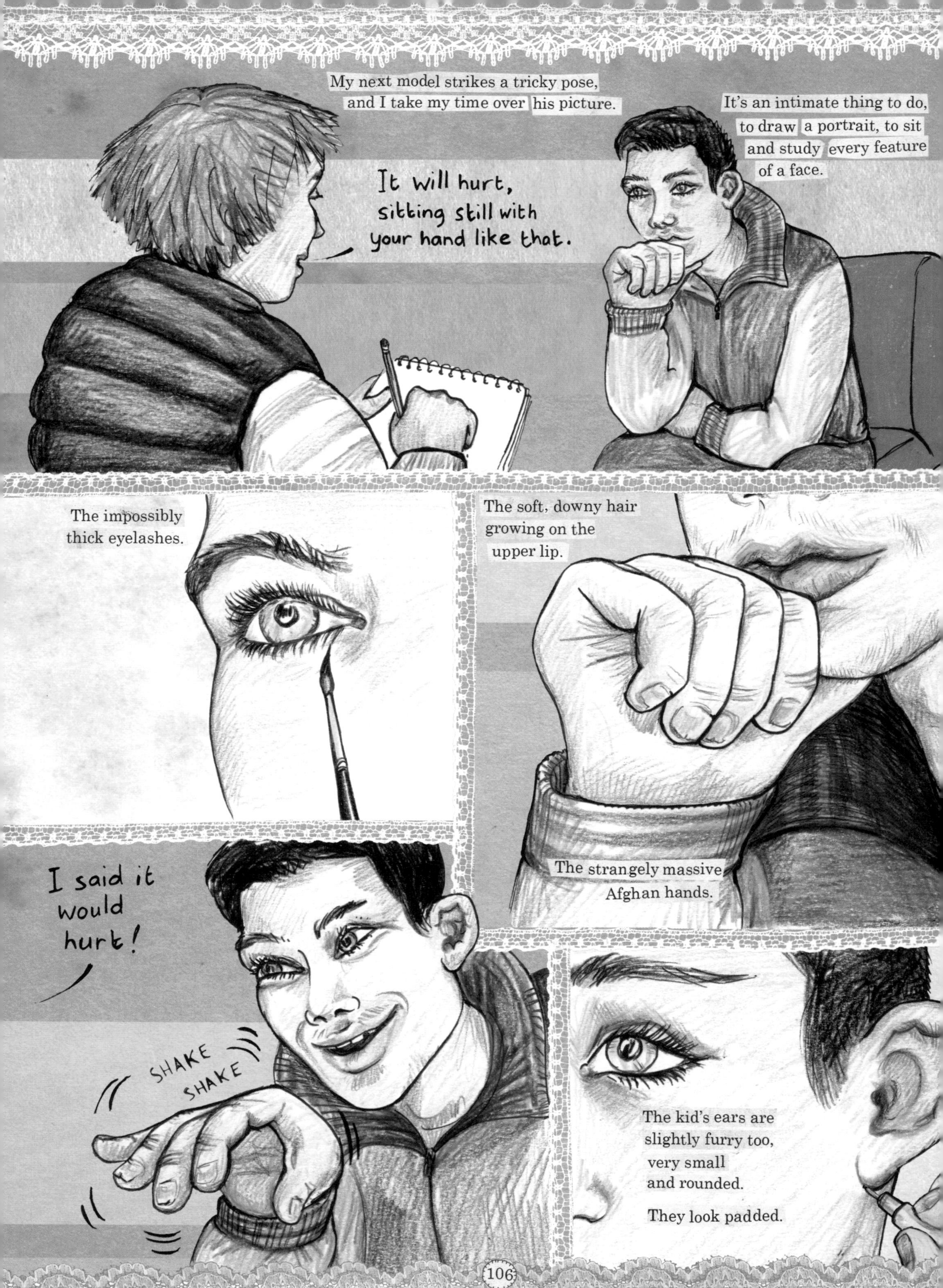
My next model strikes a tricky pose, and I take my time over his picture.
It will hurt, sitting still with your hand like that.
It's an intimate thing to do, to draw a portrait, to sit and study every feature of a face.
The impossibly thick eyelashes.
The soft, downy hair growing on the upper lip.
The strangely massive Afghan hands.
I said it would hurt!
SHAKE SHAKE
The kid's ears are slightly furry too, very small and rounded.
They look padded.

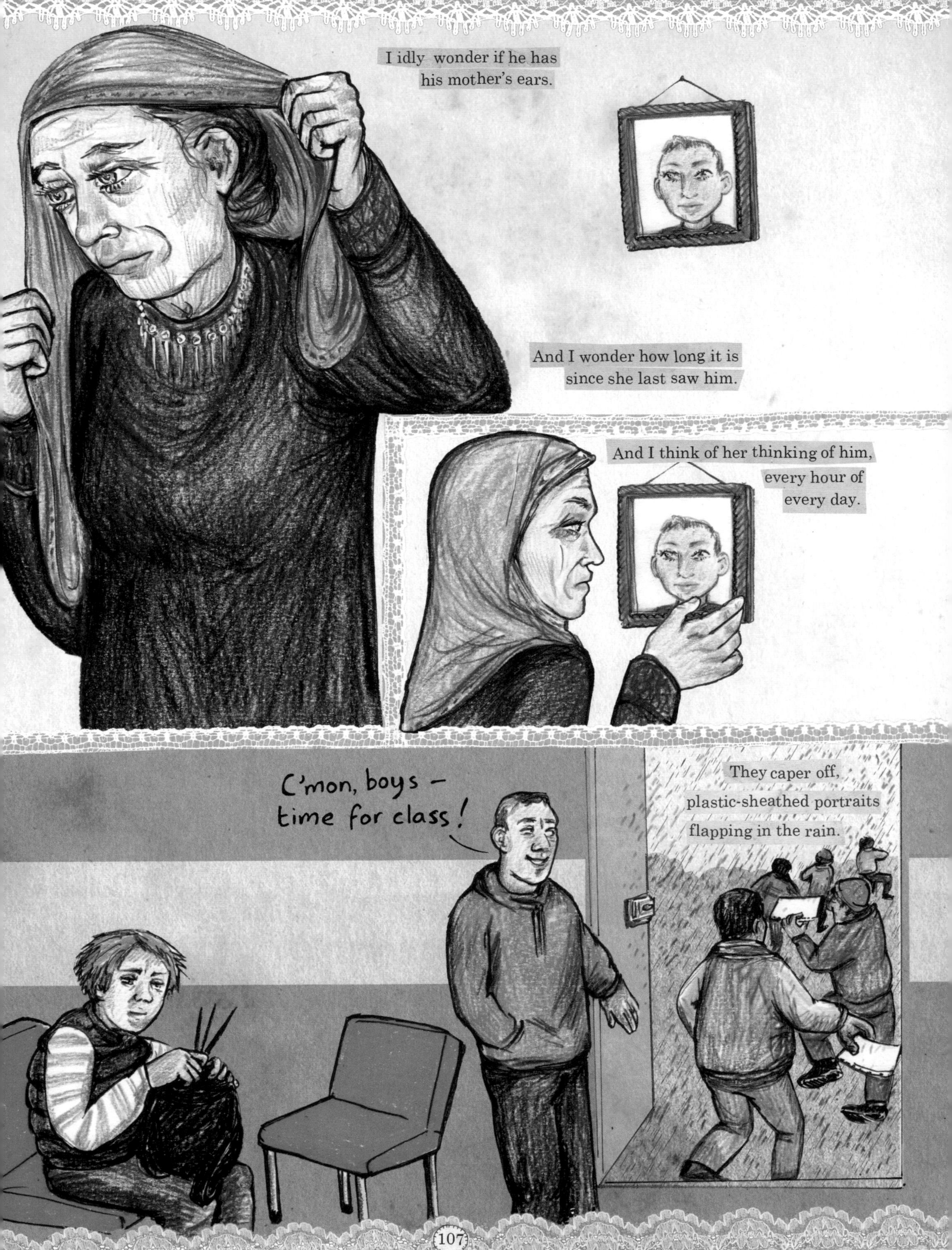
I idly wonder if he has his mother's ears.
And I wonder how long it is since she last saw him.
And I think of her thinking of him, every hour of every day.
C'mon, boys – time for class!
They caper off, plastic-sheathed portraits flapping in the rain.

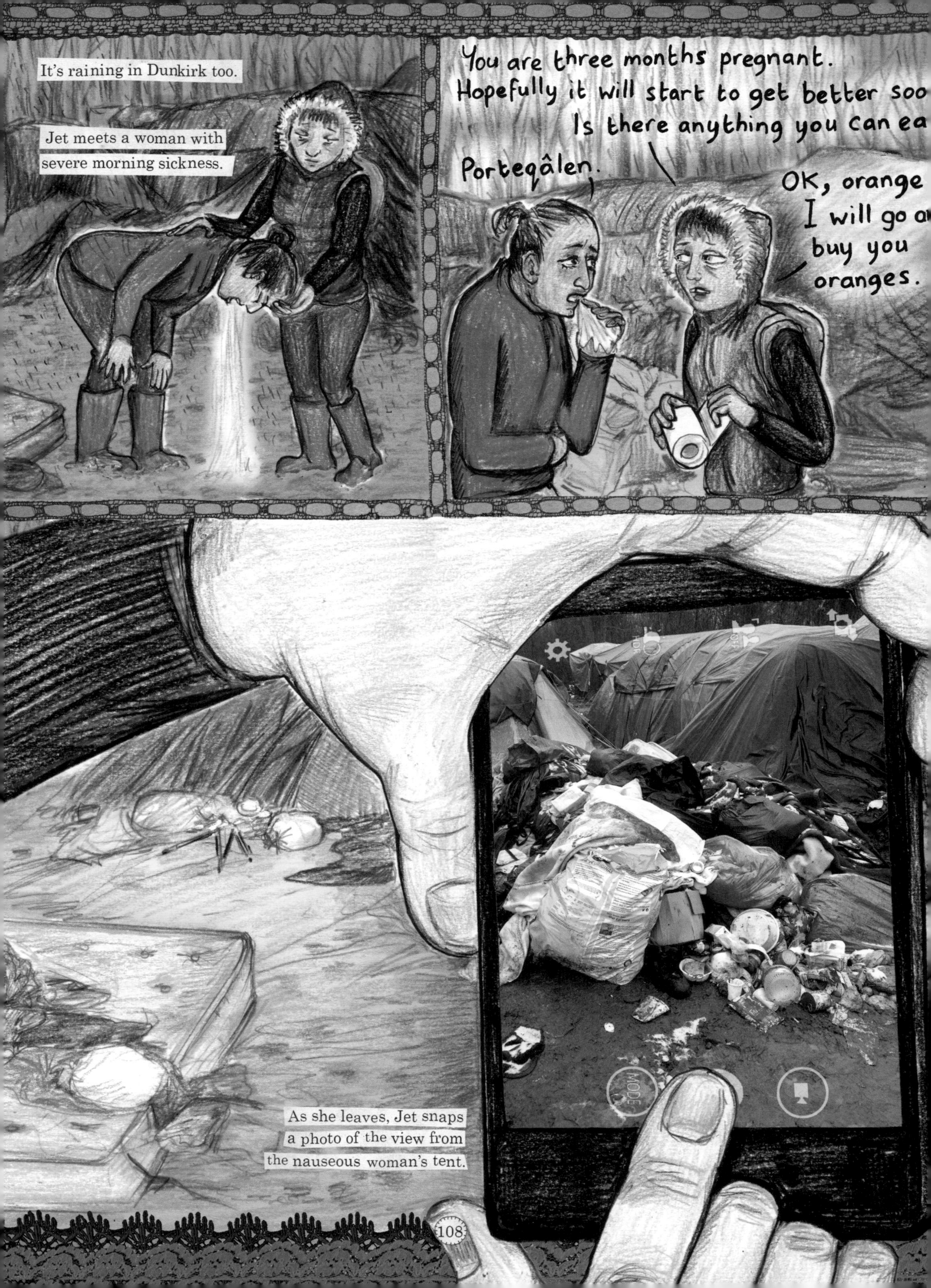

It's raining in Dunkirk too.
Jet meets a woman with severe morning sickness.
You are three months pregnant.
Hopefully it will start to get better soo
Is there anything you can ea
Porteqâlen.
OK, orange
I will go a
buy you
oranges.
MODE
As she leaves, Jet snaps a photo of the view from the nauseous woman's tent.

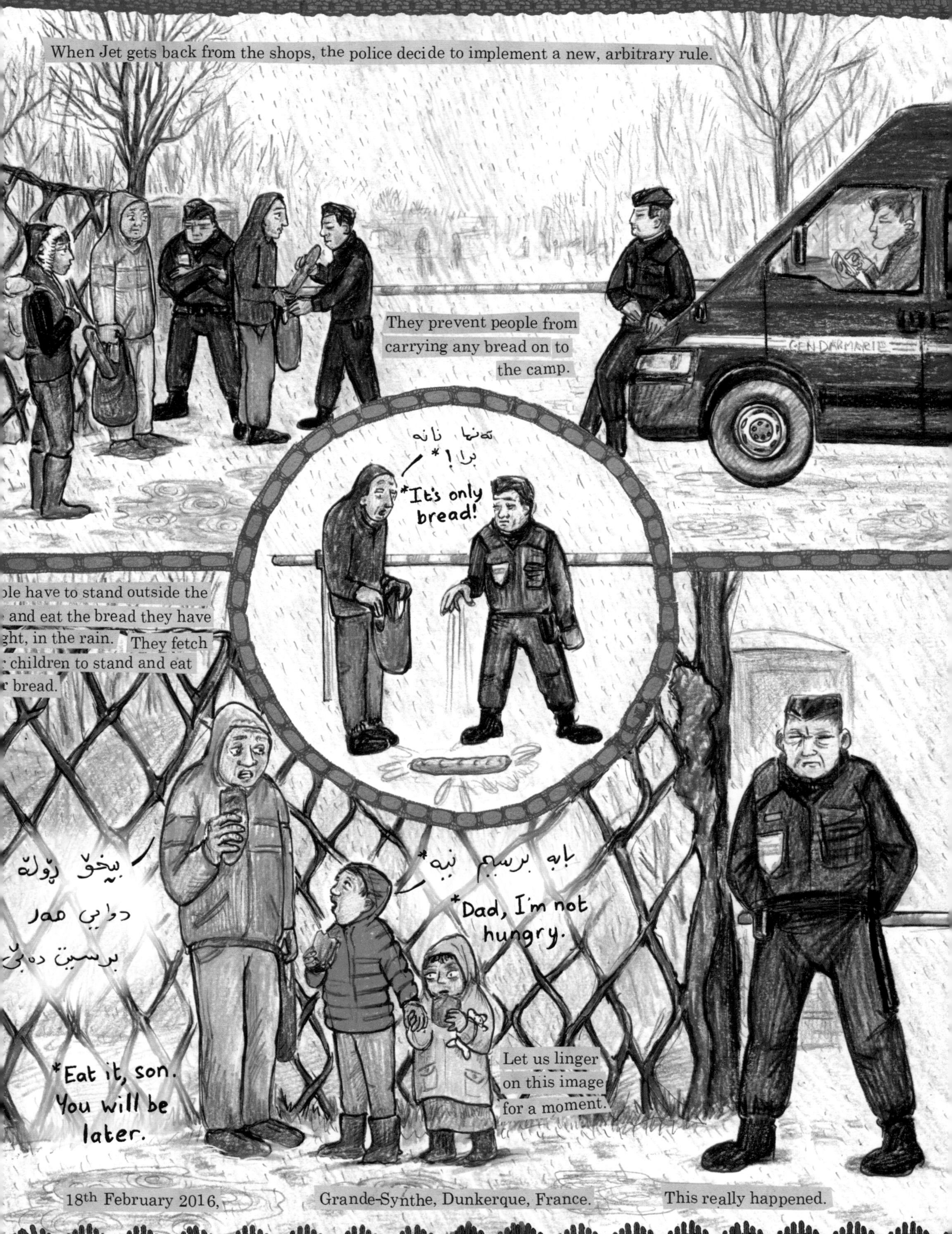
When Jet gets back from the shops, the police decide to implement a new, arbitrary rule.
They prevent people from carrying any bread on to the camp.
تەنها نانە برا! *
*It's only bread!
ple have to stand outside the
and eat the bread they have
ght, in the rain.
They fetch
children to stand and eat
bread.
بیخۆ ڕۆڵە دوایی هەر برسیت دەبێ
*Eat it, son. You will be later.
بابە برسیم نیە *
*Dad, I'm not hungry.
Let us linger on this image for a moment.
18th February 2016,
Grande-Synthe, Dunkerque, France.
This really happened.
GENDARMARIE

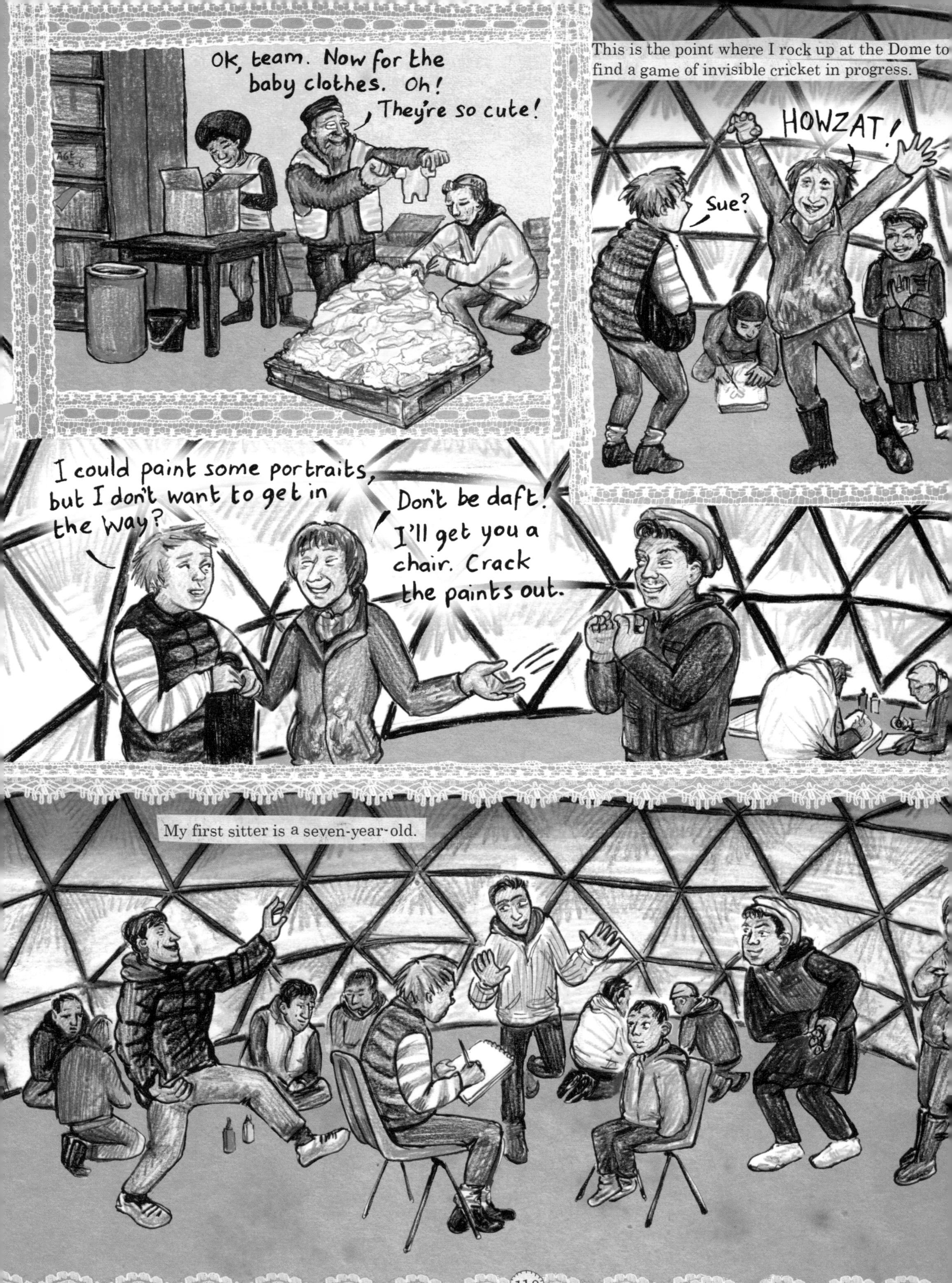
Ok, team. Now for the baby clothes. Oh!
They're so cute!
This is the point where I rock up at the Dome to find a game of invisible cricket in progress.
HOWZAT!
Sue?
I could paint some portraits, but I don't want to get in the way?
Don't be daft! I'll get you a chair. Crack the paints out.
My first sitter is a seven-year-old.

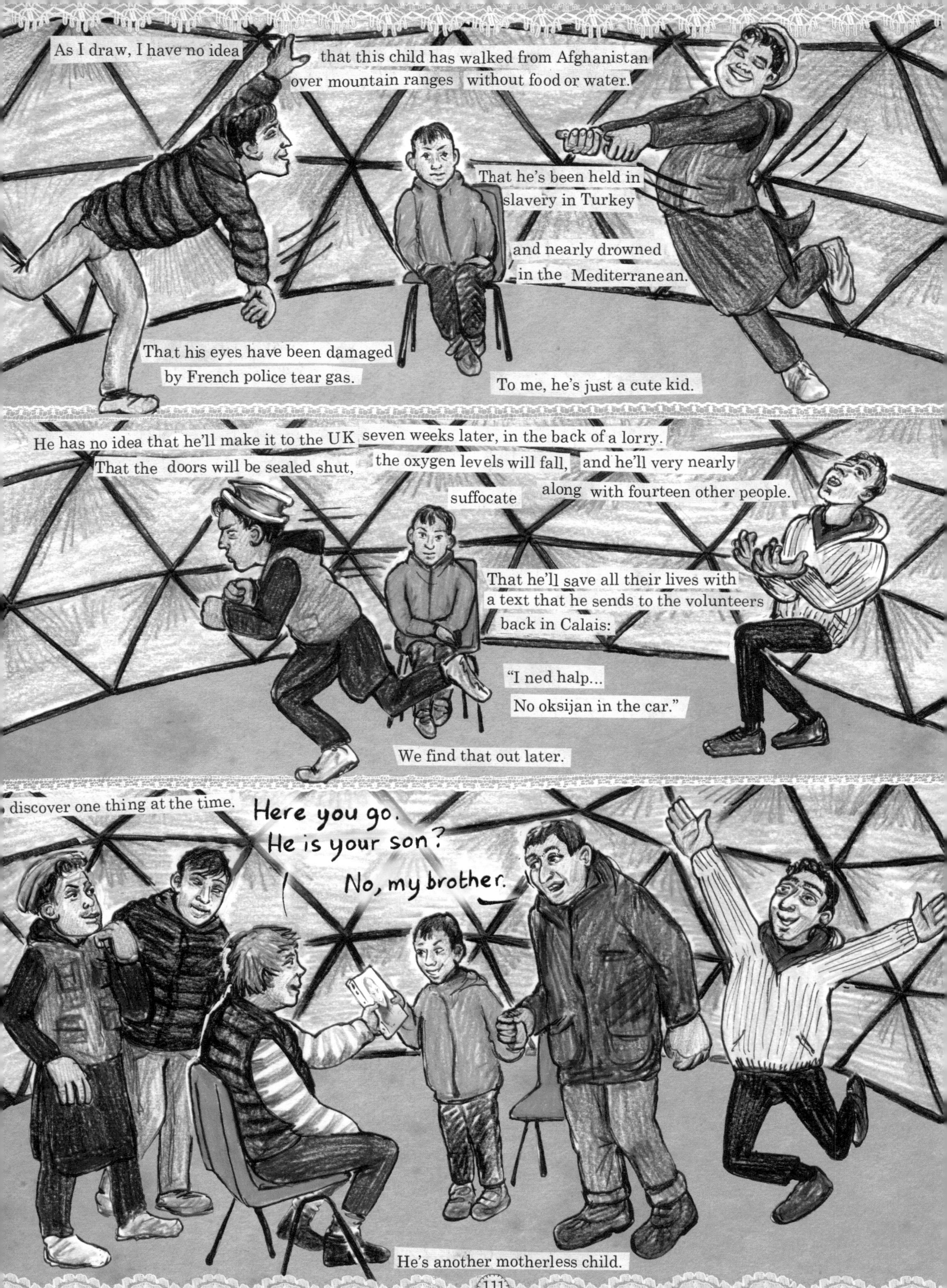
As I draw, I have no idea
that this child has walked from Afghanistan
over mountain ranges without food or water.
That he's been held in slavery in Turkey
and nearly drowned in the Mediterranean.
That his eyes have been damaged by French police tear gas.
To me, he's just a cute kid.
He has no idea that he'll make it to the UK seven weeks later, in the back of a lorry.
That the doors will be sealed shut, the oxygen levels will fall, and he'll very nearly suffocate along with fourteen other people.
That he'll save all their lives with a text that he sends to the volunteers back in Calais:
"I ned halp...
No oksijan in the car."
We find that out later.
discover one thing at the time.
Here you go.
He is your son?
No, my brother.
He's another motherless child.

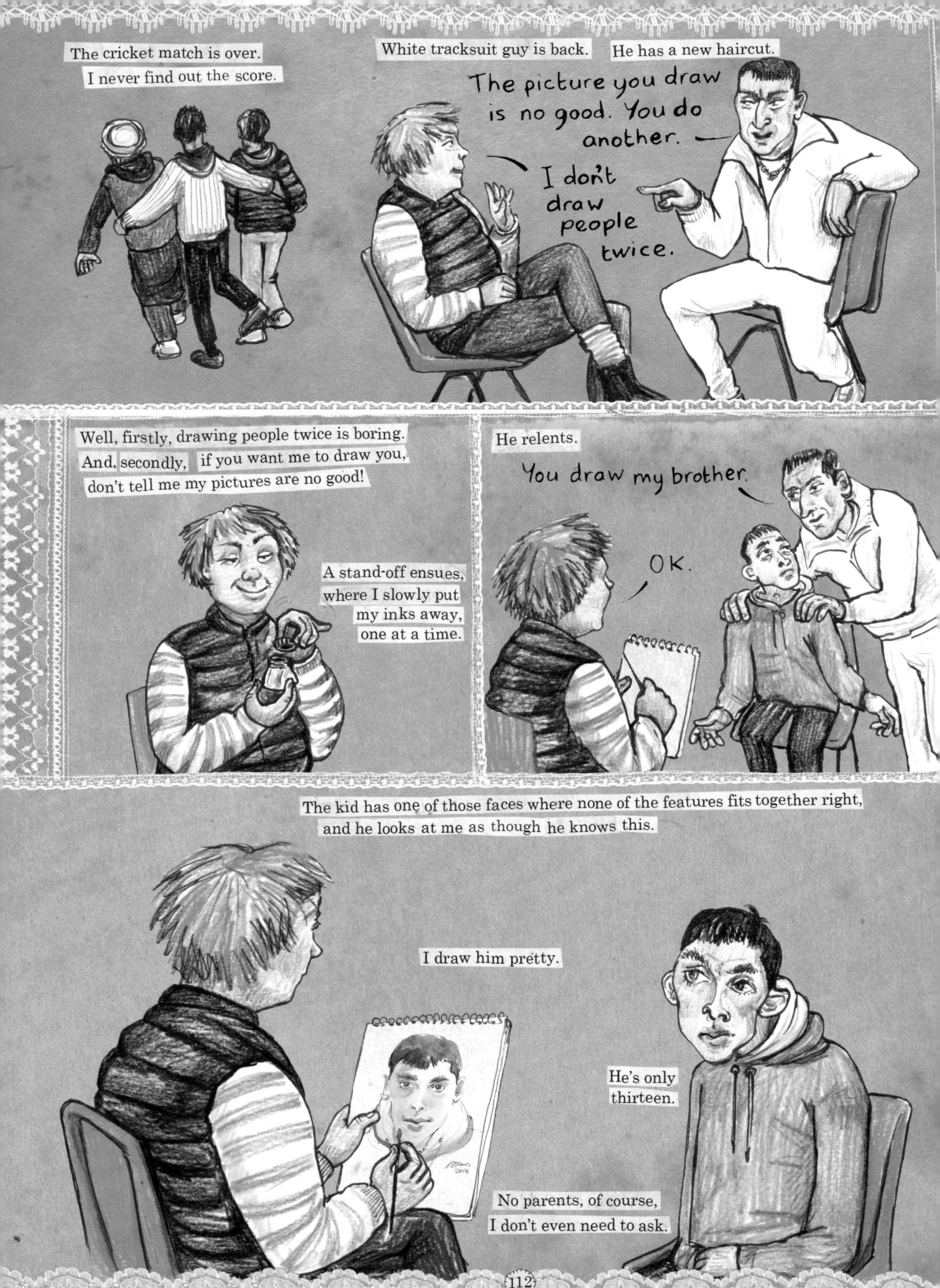
The cricket match is over.
I never find out the score.
White tracksuit guy is back.
He has a new haircut.
The picture you draw is no good. You do another.
I don't draw people twice.
Well, firstly, drawing people twice is boring.
And, secondly, if you want me to draw you, don't tell me my pictures are no good!
A stand-off ensues, where I slowly put my inks away, one at a time.
He relents.
You draw my brother.
OK.
The kid has one of those faces where none of the features fits together right, and he looks at me as though he knows this.
I draw him pretty.
He's only thirteen.
No parents, of course, I don't even need to ask.

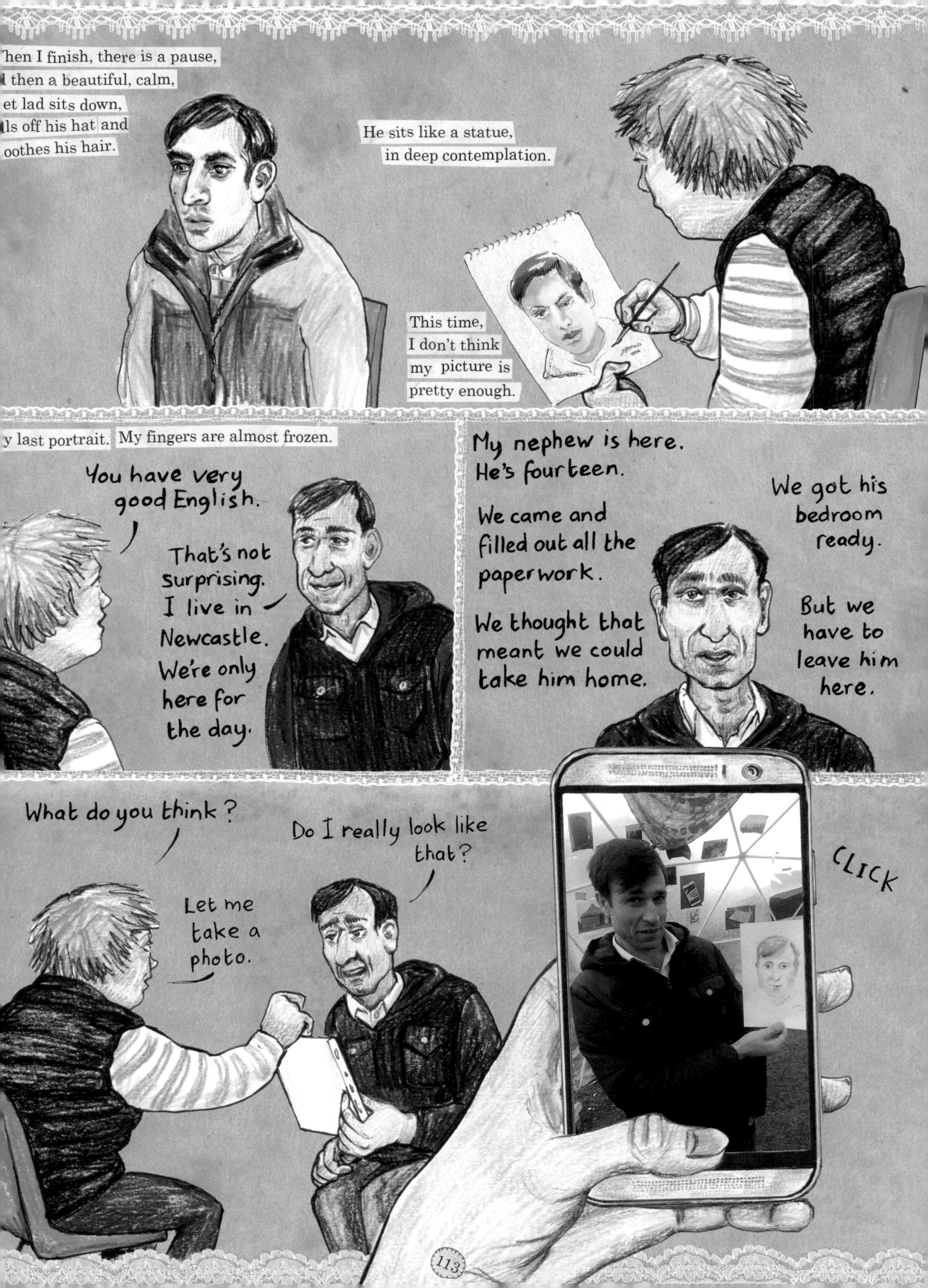
hen I finish, there is a pause,
l then a beautiful, calm,
et lad sits down,
lls off his hat and
oothes his hair.
He sits like a statue,
in deep contemplation.
This time,
I don't think
my picture is
pretty enough.
y last portrait.
My fingers are almost frozen.
You have very good English.
That's not surprising. I live in Newcastle. We're only here for the day.
My nephew is here. He's fourteen.
We came and filled out all the paperwork.
We thought that meant we could take him home.
We got his bedroom ready.
But we have to leave him here.
What do you think?
Do I really look like that?
Let me take a photo.
CLICK

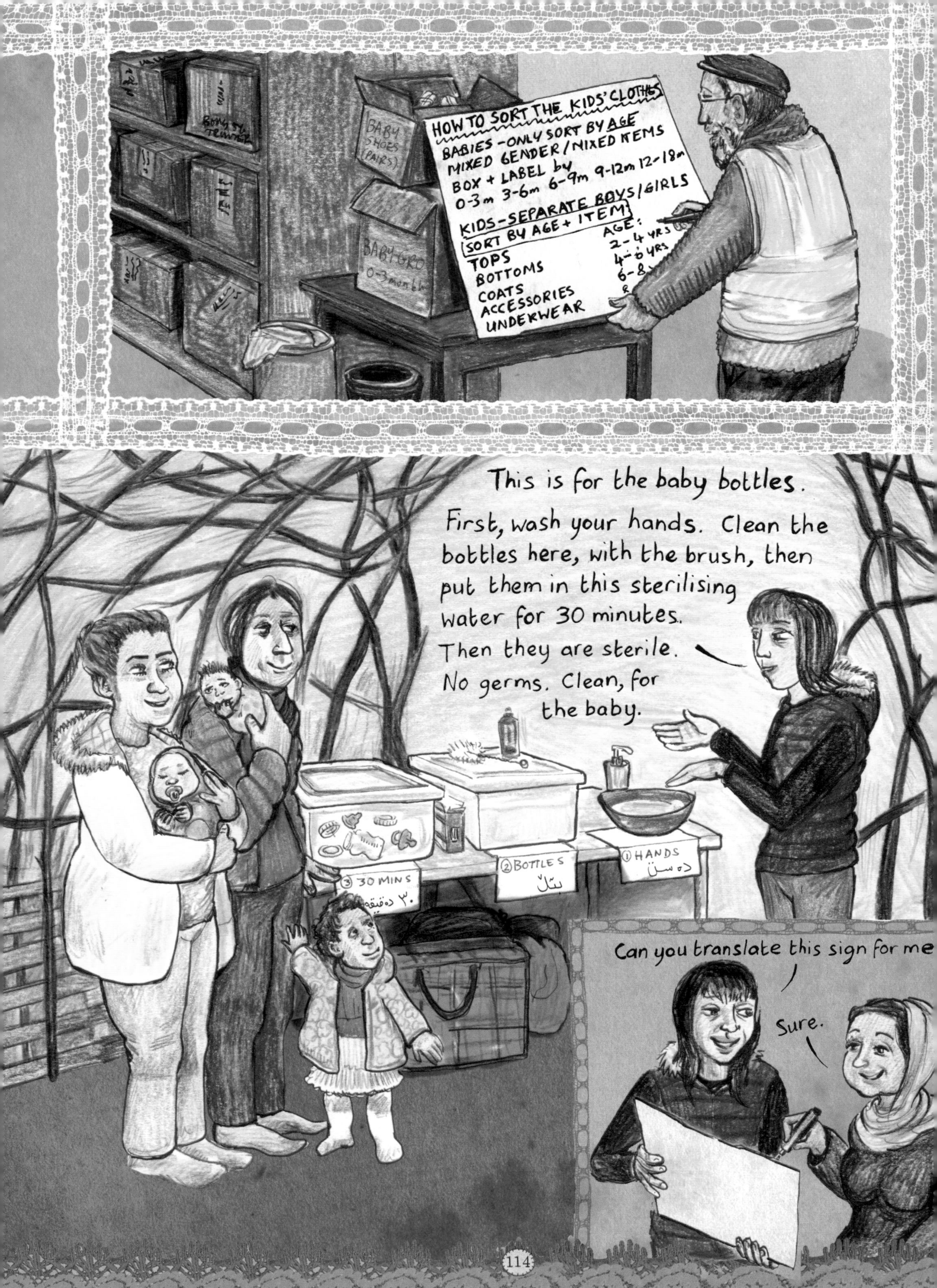
HOW TO SORT THE KIDS' CLOTHES
BABIES - ONLY SORT BY AGE
MIXED GENDER / MIXED ITEMS
BOX + LABEL by
0-3m 3-6m 6-9m 9-12m 12-18m
KIDS - SEPARATE BOYS/GIRLS
SORT BY AGE + ITEM
AGE:
2-4 YRS
4-6 YRS
TOPS
BOTTOMS
COATS
ACCESSORIES
UNDERWEAR
BABY SHOES (PAIRS)
This is for the baby bottles.
First, wash your hands. Clean the bottles here, with the brush, then put them in this sterilising water for 30 minutes. Then they are sterile. No germs. Clean, for the baby.
① HANDS
② BOTTLES
③ 30 MINS
Can you translate this sign for me
Sure.

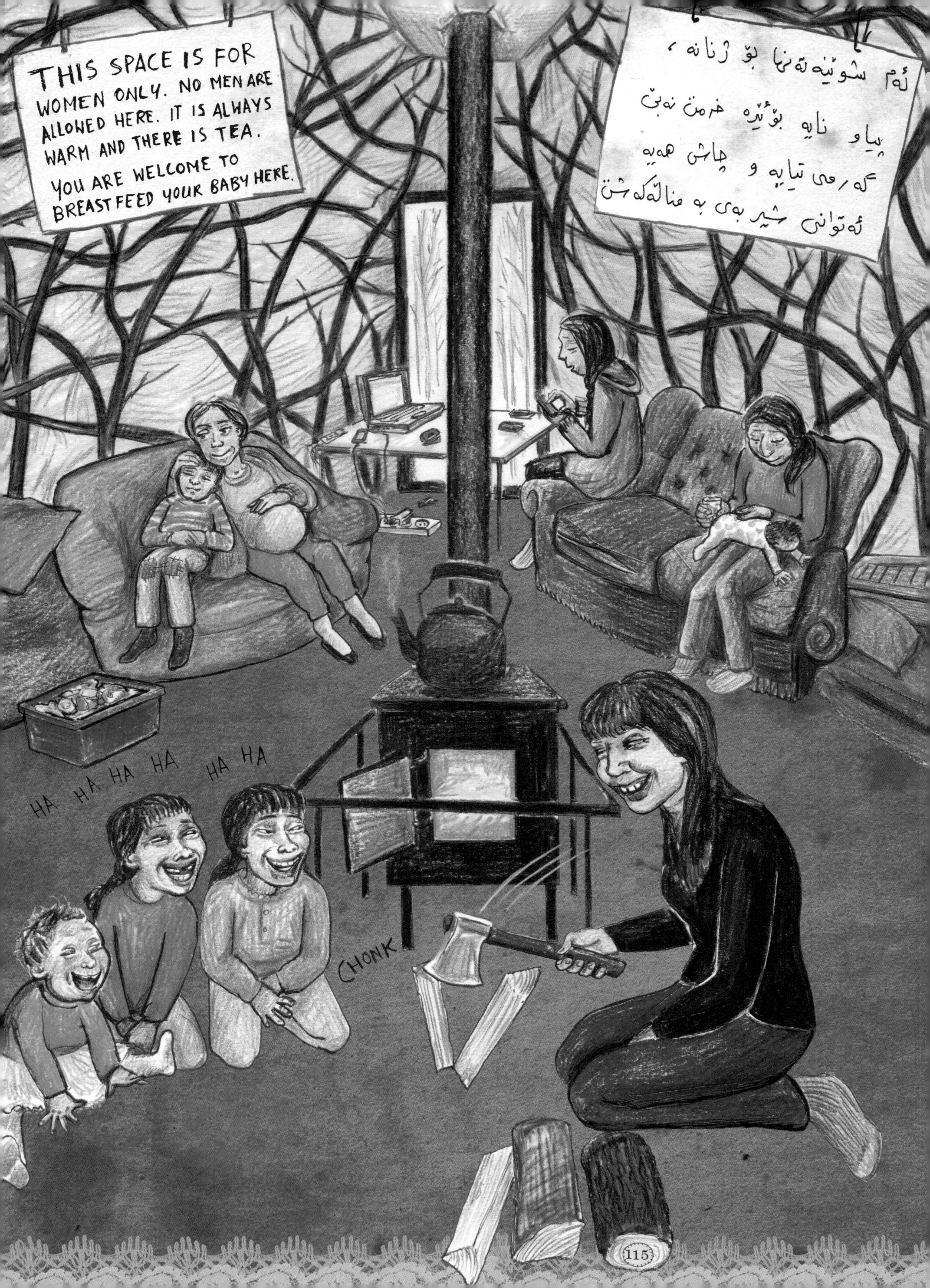
THIS SPACE IS FOR WOMEN ONLY. NO MEN ARE ALLOWED HERE. IT IS ALWAYS WARM AND THERE IS TEA. YOU ARE WELCOME TO BREASTFEED YOUR BABY HERE.
ئەم شوێنە تەنها بۆ ژنانە،
پیاو نایە بۆئێرە خەمت نەبێ
گەرمی تیایە و چاش هەیە
ئەتوانی شیر بەی بە منالەکەشت
HA HA HA HA HA HA
CHONK

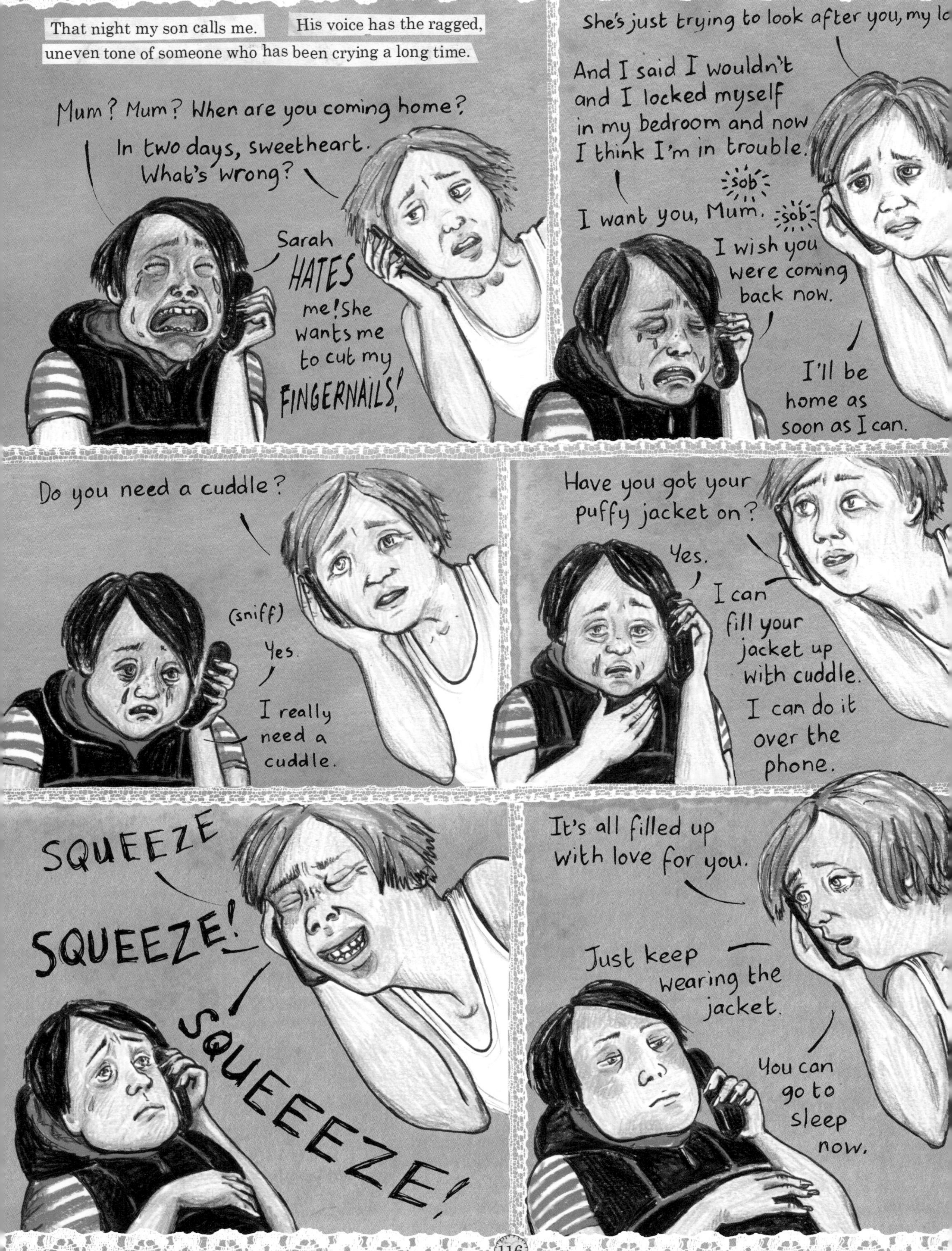

That night my son calls me. His voice has the ragged, uneven tone of someone who has been crying a long time.
Mum? Mum? When are you coming home?
In two days, sweetheart. What's wrong?
Sarah HATES me! She wants me to cut my FINGERNAILS!
She's just trying to look after you, my lo
And I said I wouldn't and I locked myself in my bedroom and now I think I'm in trouble.
sob
I want you, Mum.
sob
I wish you were coming back now.
I'll be home as soon as I can.
Do you need a cuddle?
(sniff)
Yes.
I really need a cuddle.
Have you got your puffy jacket on?
Yes.
I can fill your jacket up with cuddle. I can do it over the phone.
SQUEEZE
SQUEEZE!
SQUEEEEZE!
It's all filled up with love for you.
Just keep wearing the jacket.
You can go to sleep now.

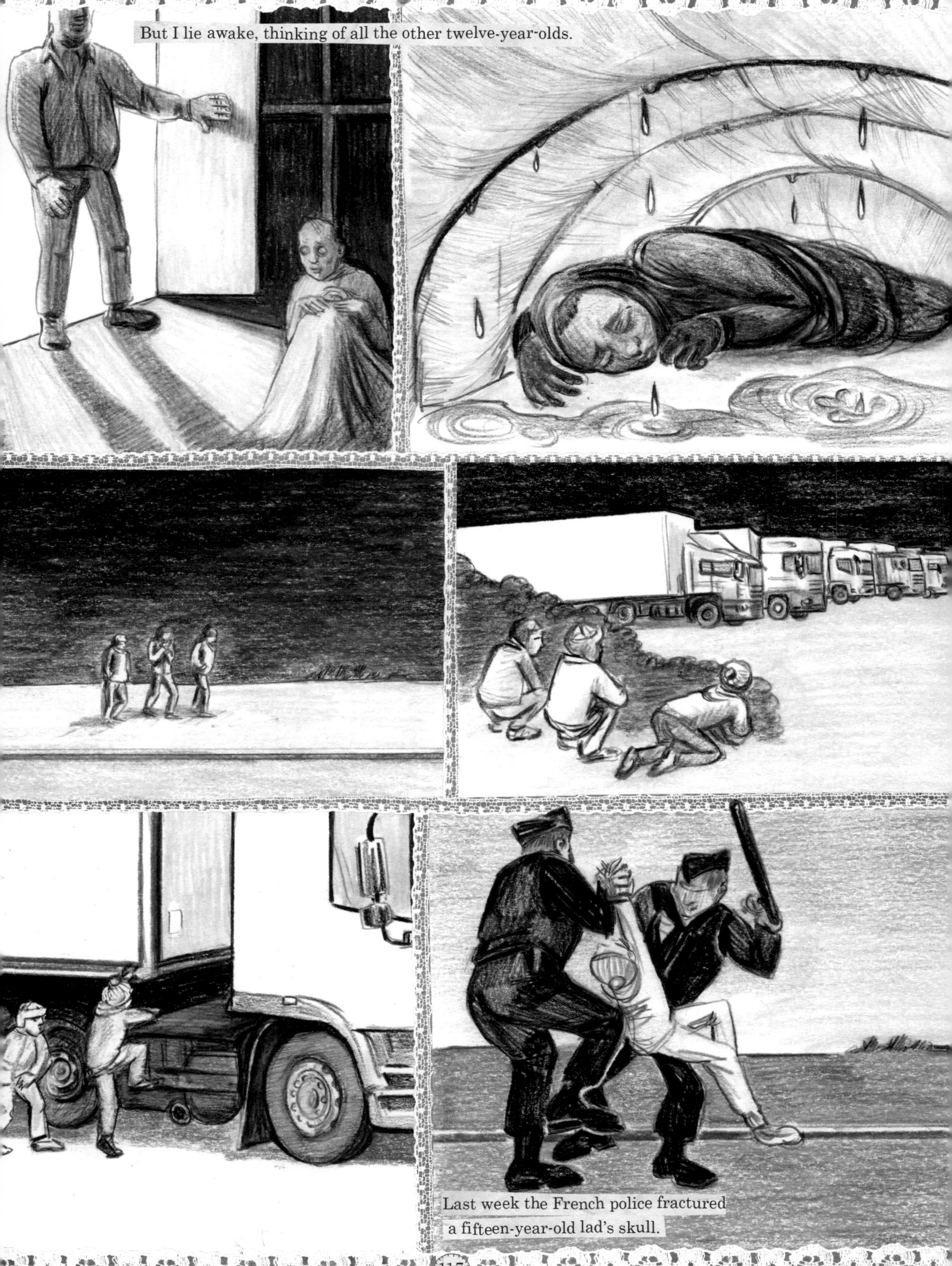
But I lie awake, thinking of all the other twelve-year-olds.
Last week the French police fractured a fifteen-year-old lad's skull.

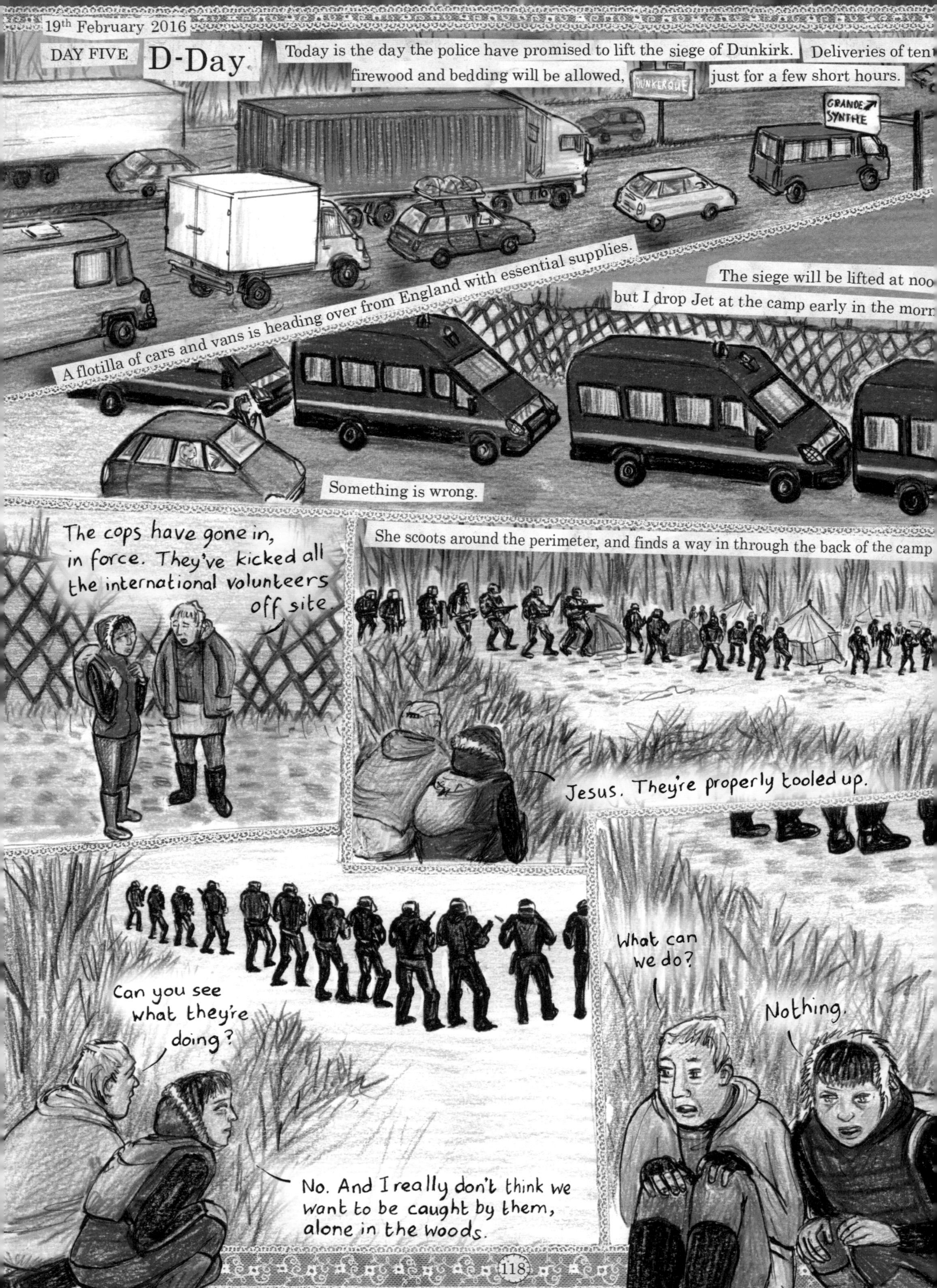
19th February 2016
DAY FIVE
D-Day
Today is the day the police have promised to lift the siege of Dunkirk.
Deliveries of ten
firewood and bedding will be allowed,
DUNKERQUE
just for a few short hours.
GRANDE SYNTHE
A flotilla of cars and vans is heading over from England with essential supplies.
The siege will be lifted at noo
but I drop Jet at the camp early in the morn
Something is wrong.
The cops have gone in, in force. They've kicked all the international volunteers off site.
She scoots around the perimeter, and finds a way in through the back of the camp
Jesus. They're properly tooled up.
Can you see what they're doing?
No. And I really don't think we want to be caught by them, alone in the woods.
What can we do?
Nothing.

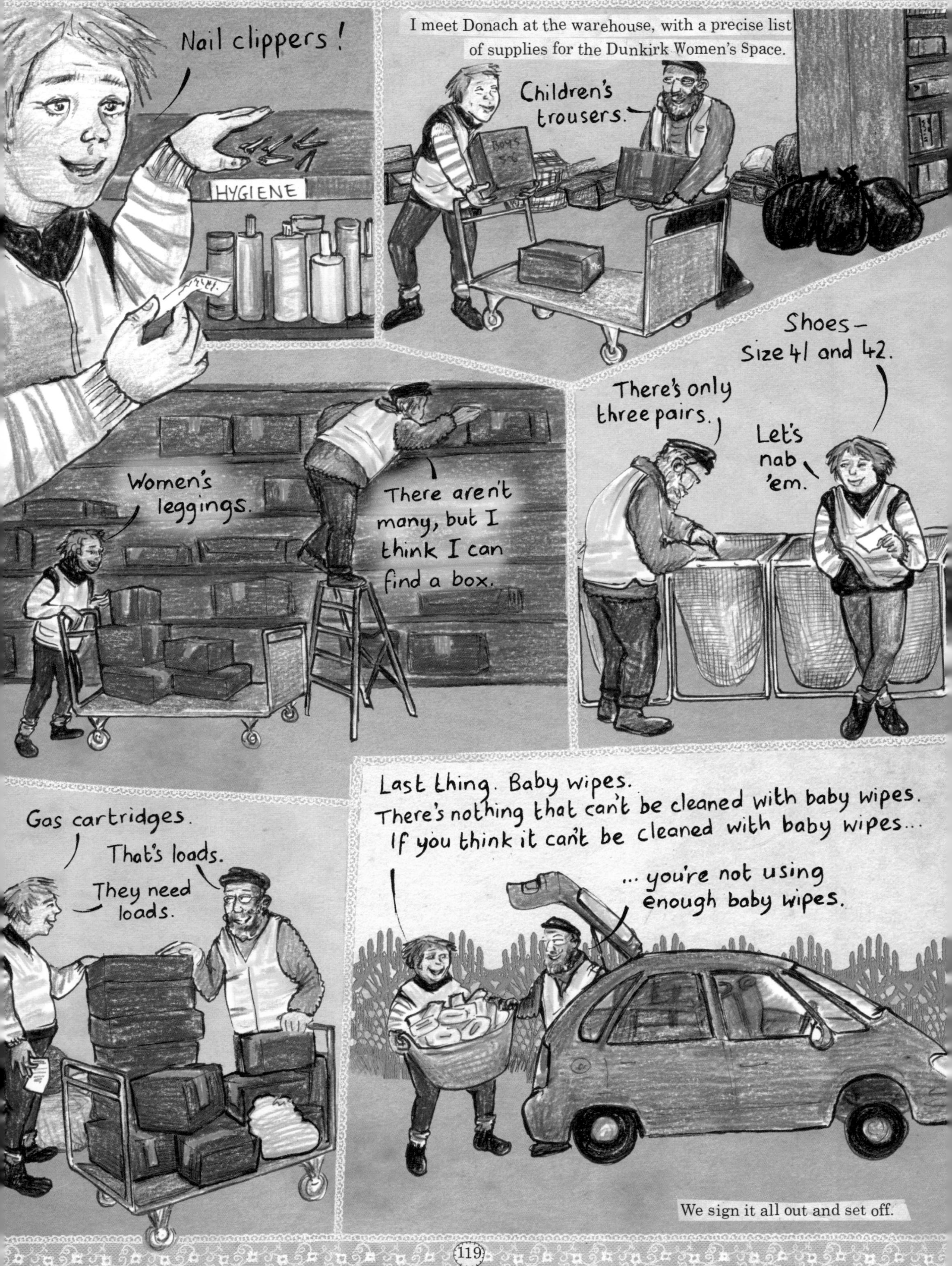

Nail clippers!
HYGIENE
I meet Donach at the warehouse, with a precise list of supplies for the Dunkirk Women's Space.
Children's trousers.
BOYS 5-6
Women's leggings.
There aren't many, but I think I can find a box.
There's only three pairs.
Shoes– Size 41 and 42.
Let's nab 'em.
Gas cartridges.
That's loads.
They need loads.
Last thing. Baby wipes.
There's nothing that can't be cleaned with baby wipes.
If you think it can't be cleaned with baby wipes...
... you're not using enough baby wipes.
We sign it all out and set off.

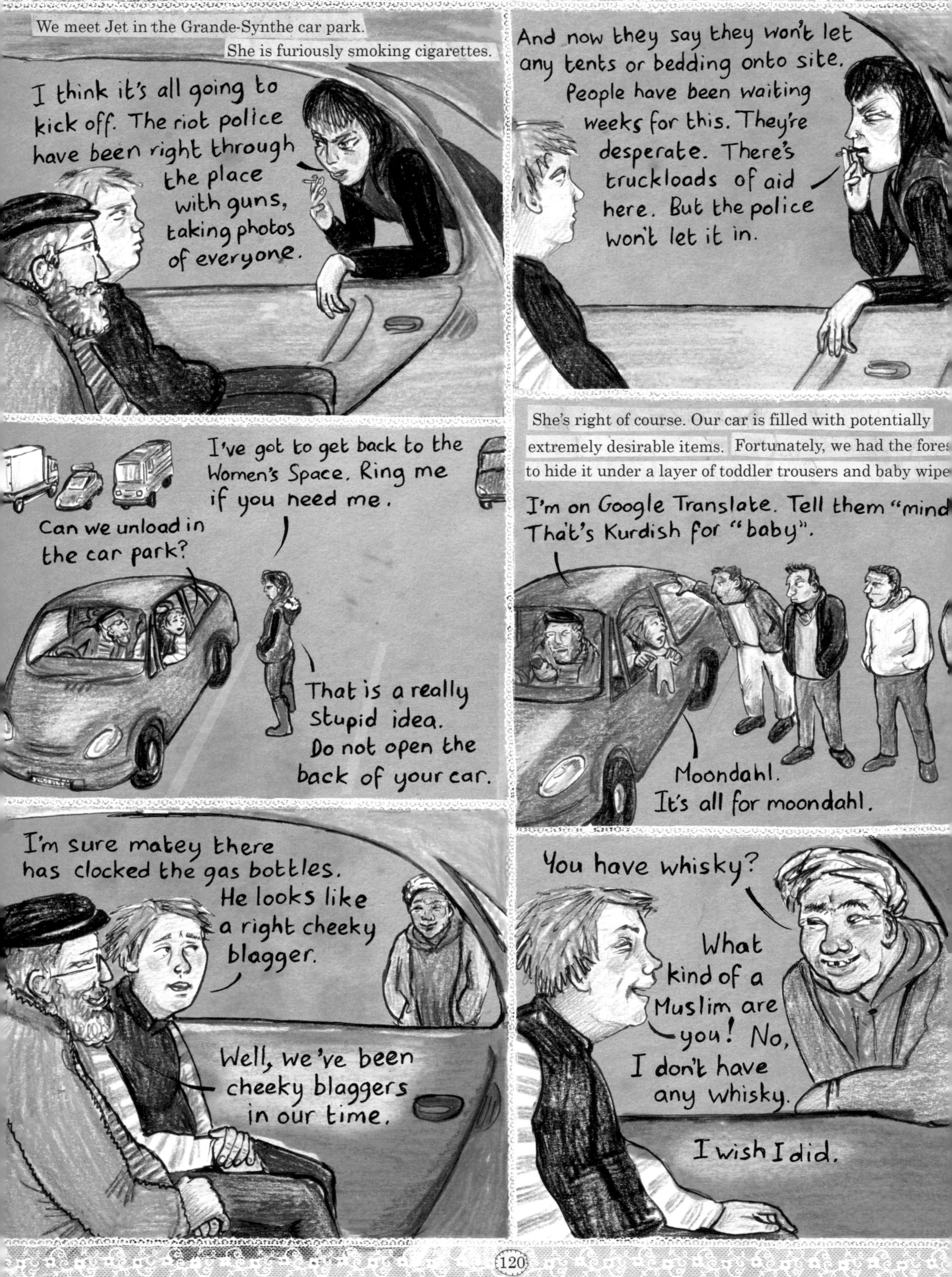
We meet Jet in the Grande-Synthe car park.
She is furiously smoking cigarettes.
I think it's all going to kick off. The riot police have been right through the place with guns, taking photos of everyone.
And now they say they won't let any tents or bedding onto site. People have been waiting weeks for this. They're desperate. There's truckloads of aid here. But the police won't let it in.
I've got to get back to the Women's Space. Ring me if you need me.
Can we unload in the car park?
That is a really stupid idea. Do not open the back of your car.
She's right of course. Our car is filled with potentially extremely desirable items. Fortunately, we had the fores
to hide it under a layer of toddler trousers and baby wipe
I'm on Google Translate. Tell them "mind That's Kurdish for "baby".
Moondahl. It's all for moondahl.
I'm sure matey there has clocked the gas bottles. He looks like a right cheeky blagger.
Well, we've been cheeky blaggers in our time.
You have whisky?
What kind of a Muslim are you! No, I don't have any whisky.
I wish I did.

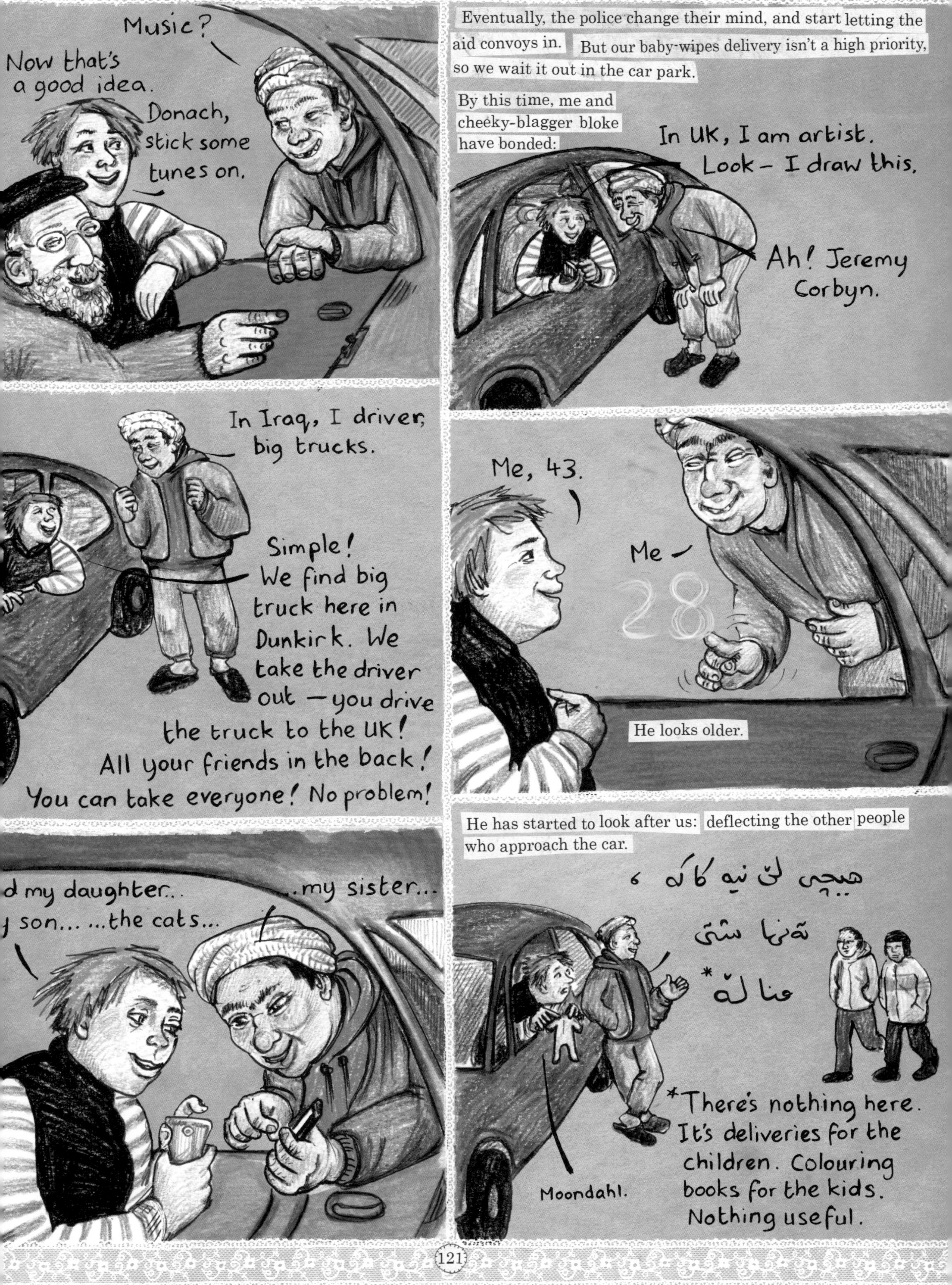
Music?
Now that's a good idea.
Donach, stick some tunes on.
Eventually, the police change their mind, and start letting the aid convoys in. But our baby-wipes delivery isn't a high priority, so we wait it out in the car park.
By this time, me and cheeky-blagger bloke have bonded:
In UK, I am artist. Look – I draw this.
Ah! Jeremy Corbyn.
In Iraq, I driver, big trucks.
Simple! We find big truck here in Dunkirk. We take the driver out – you drive the truck to the UK! All your friends in the back! You can take everyone! No problem!
Me, 43.
Me –
28
He looks older.
d my daughter..
son... ...the cats...
...my sister...
He has started to look after us: deflecting the other people who approach the car.
هیچی لێ نیە کاکە ،
تەنها شتی
منالە*
*There's nothing here. It's deliveries for the children. Colouring books for the kids. Nothing useful.
Moondahl.

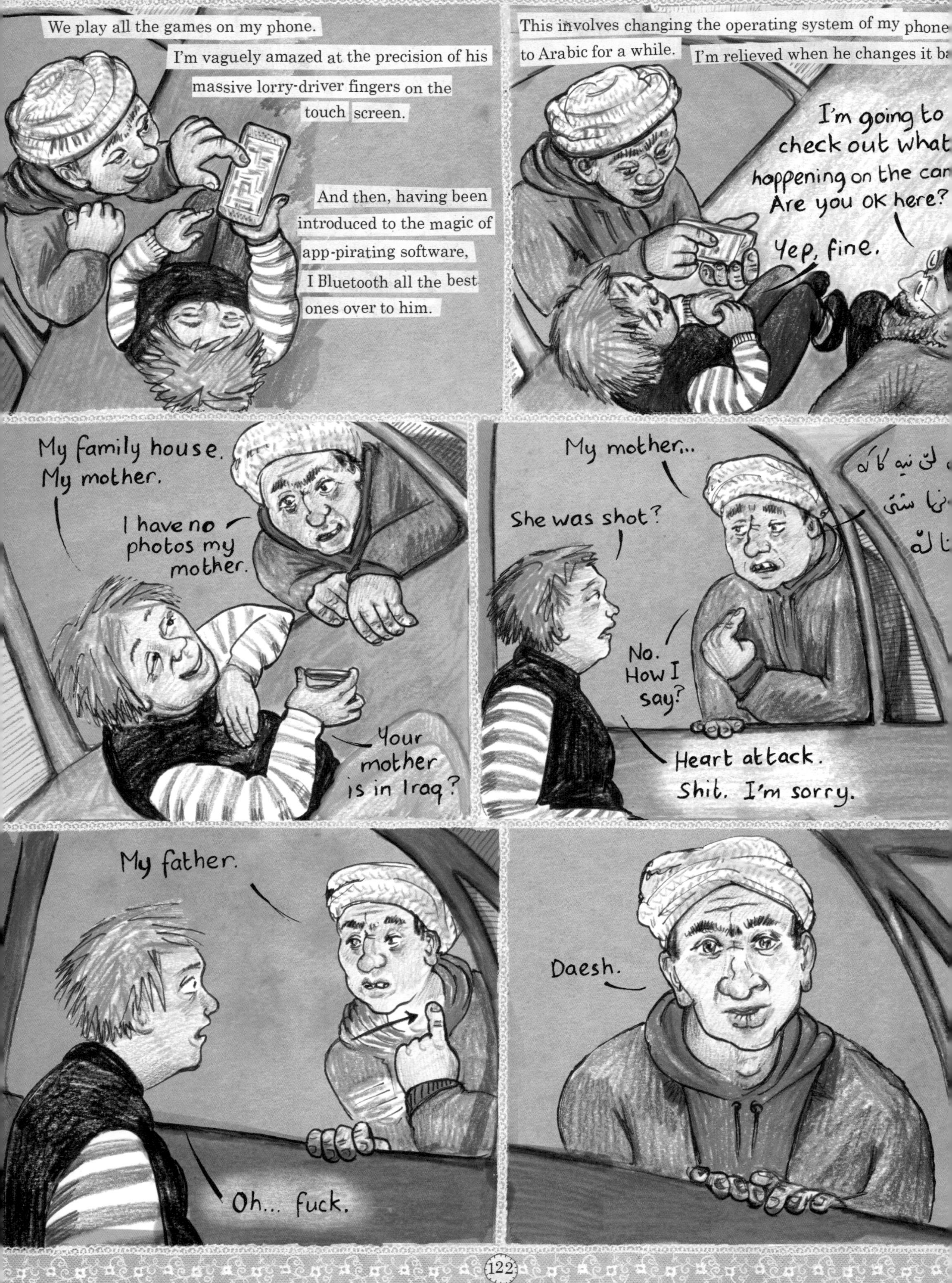
We play all the games on my phone.
I'm vaguely amazed at the precision of his massive lorry-driver fingers on the touch screen.
And then, having been introduced to the magic of app-pirating software, I Bluetooth all the best ones over to him.
This involves changing the operating system of my phone to Arabic for a while.
I'm relieved when he changes it ba
I'm going to check out what happening on the ca
Are you OK here?
Yep, fine.
My family house. My mother.
I have no photos my mother.
Your mother is in Iraq?
My mother...
She was shot?
No. How I say?
Heart attack.
Shit. I'm sorry.
My father.
Oh... fuck.
Daesh.

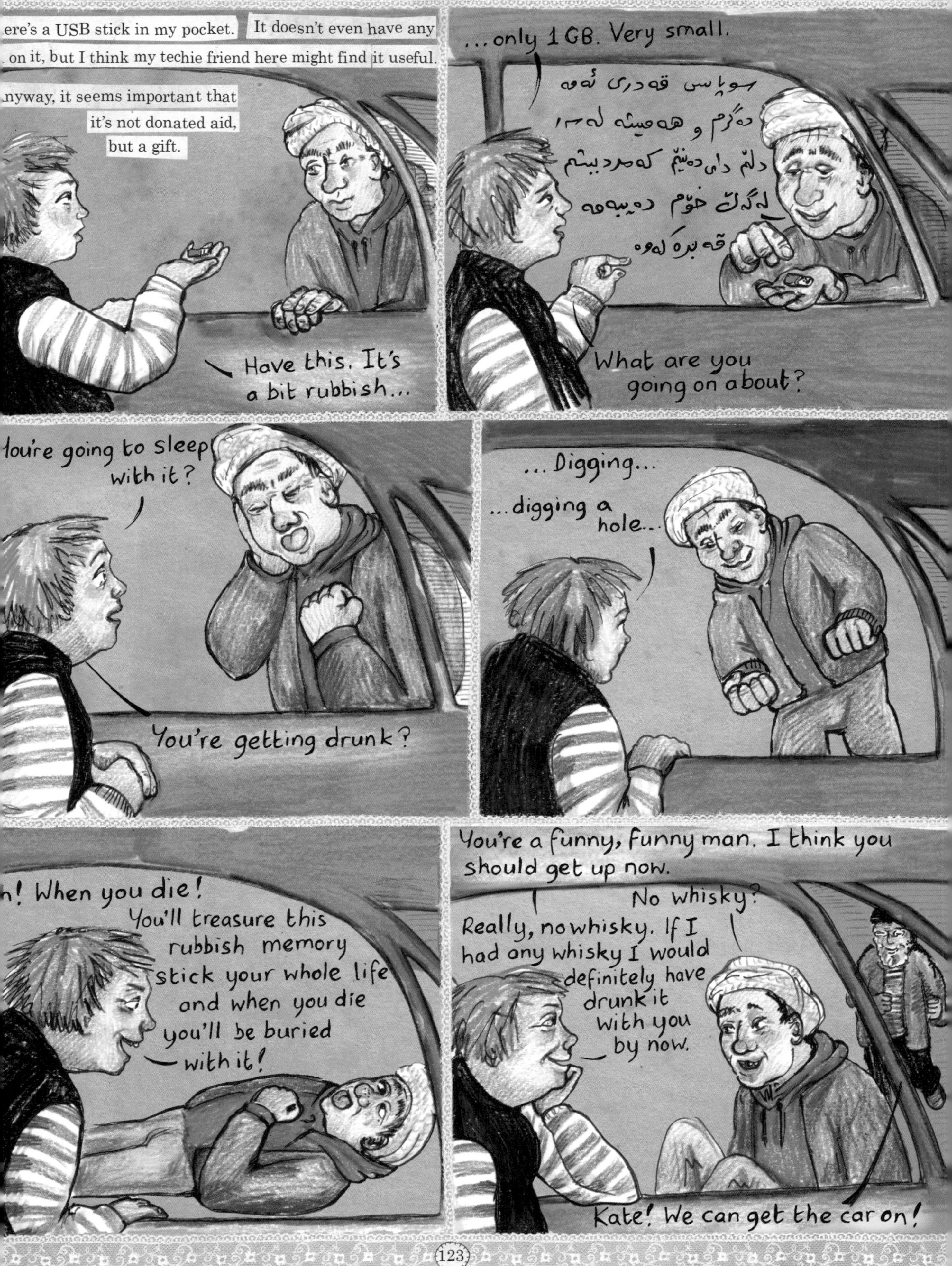
ere's a USB stick in my pocket. It doesn't even have any
on it, but I think my techie friend here might find it useful.
nyway, it seems important that it's not donated aid, but a gift.
Have this. It's a bit rubbish...
...only 1 GB. Very small.
سوپاس قەدری ئەوە دەگرم و هەمیشە لەسەر دڵم دای دەنێم کە مردبیشم لەگەڵ خۆم دەیبەمە قەبرەکەوە
What are you going on about?
You're going to sleep with it?
You're getting drunk?
... Digging...
...digging a hole...
h! When you die!
You'll treasure this rubbish memory stick your whole life and when you die you'll be buried with it!
You're a funny, funny man. I think you should get up now.
No whisky?
Really, no whisky. If I had any whisky I would definitely have drunk it with you by now.
Kate! We can get the car on!

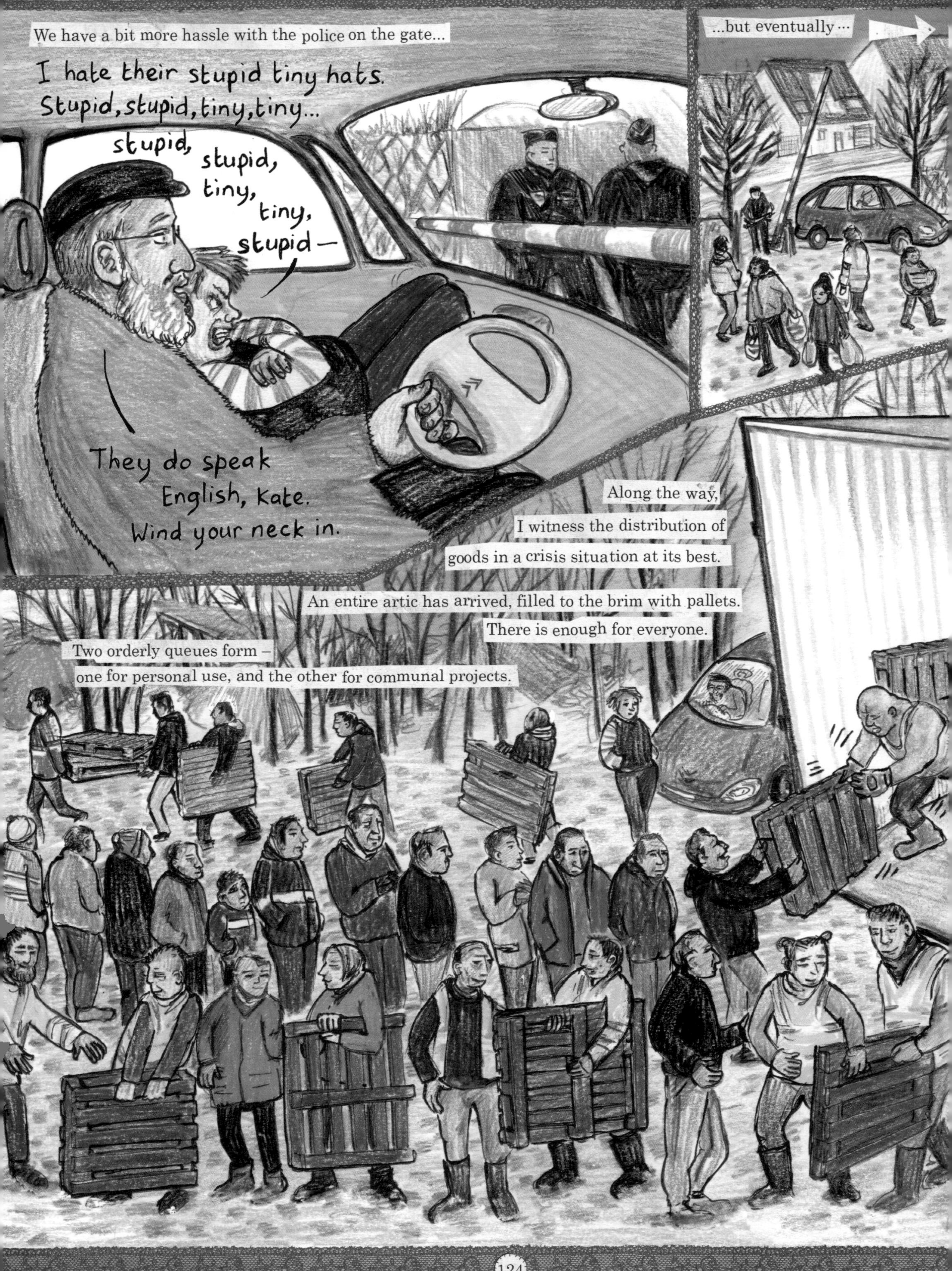

We have a bit more hassle with the police on the gate...
I hate their stupid tiny hats.
Stupid, stupid, tiny, tiny...
stupid, stupid, tiny, tiny, stupid —
They do speak English, Kate. Wind your neck in.
...but eventually...
Along the way, I witness the distribution of goods in a crisis situation at its best.
An entire artic has arrived, filled to the brim with pallets.
There is enough for everyone.
Two orderly queues form – one for personal use, and the other for communal projects.

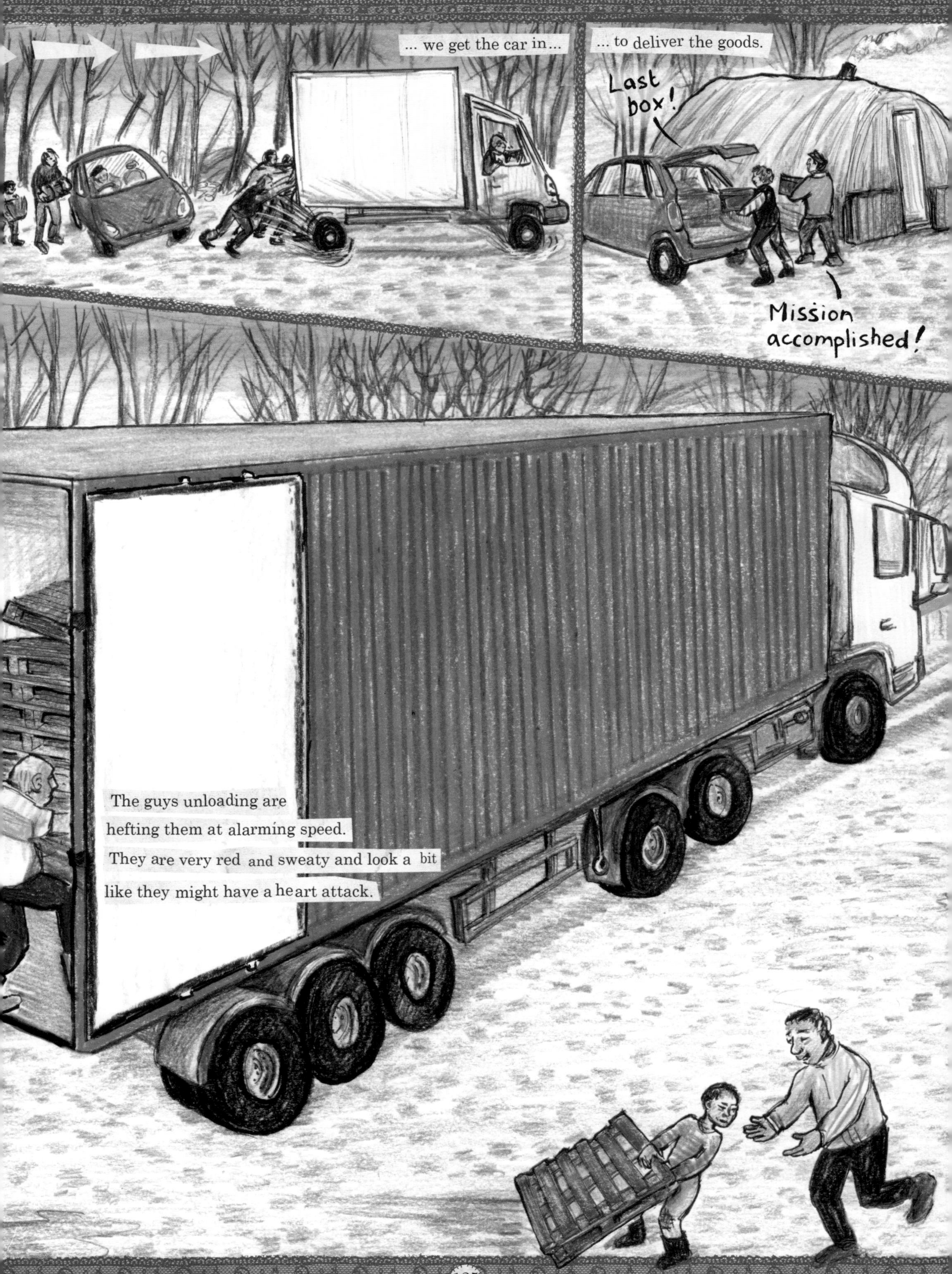
... we get the car in...
... to deliver the goods.
Last box!
Mission accomplished!
The guys unloading are hefting them at alarming speed. They are very red and sweaty and look a bit like they might have a heart attack.

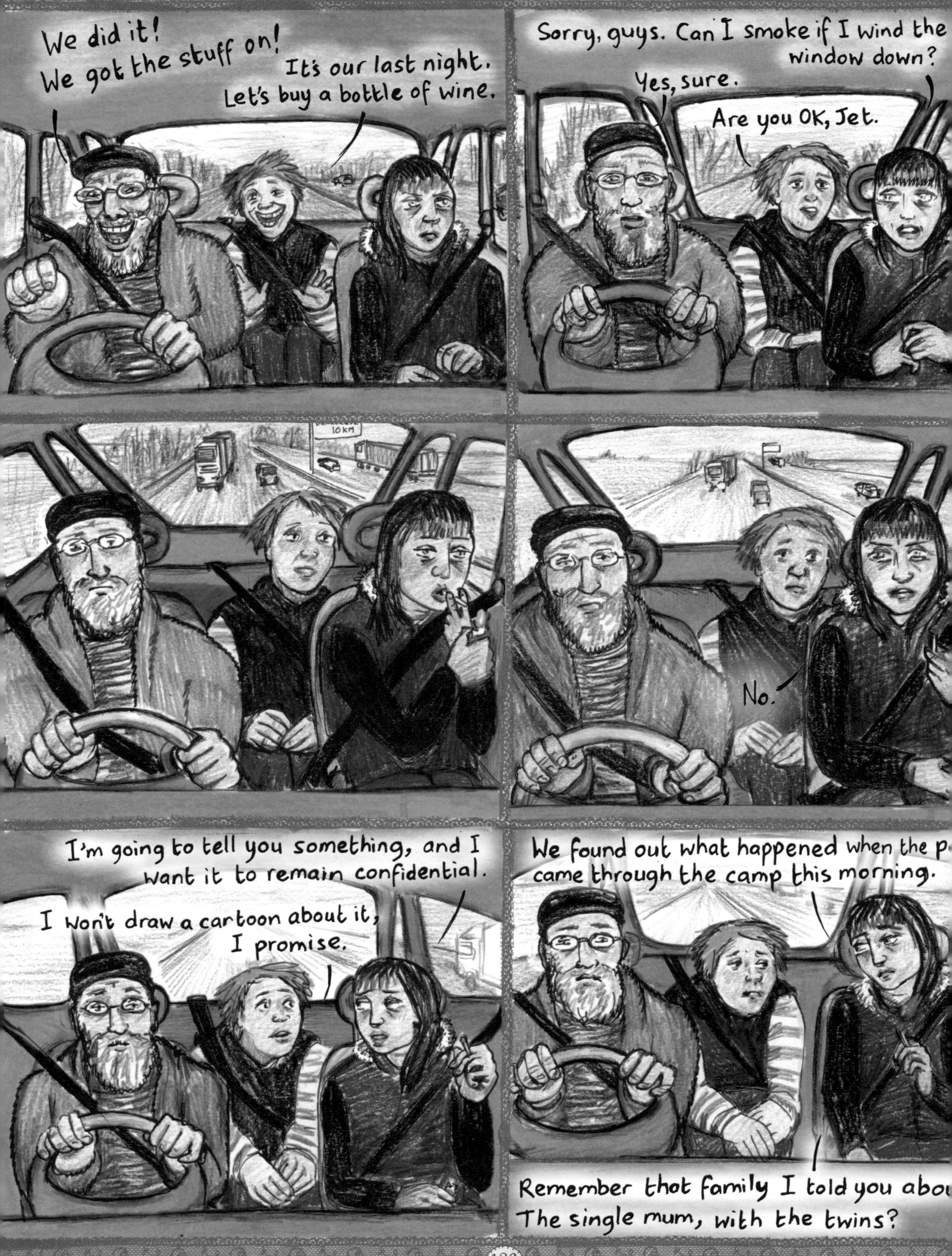
We did it!
We got the stuff on!
It's our last night.
Let's buy a bottle of wine.
Sorry, guys. Can I smoke if I wind the window down?
Yes, sure.
Are you OK, Jet.
10KM
No.
I'm going to tell you something, and I want it to remain confidential.
I won't draw a cartoon about it, I promise.
We found out what happened when the p
came through the camp this morning.
Remember thot family I told you abo
The single mum, with the twins?

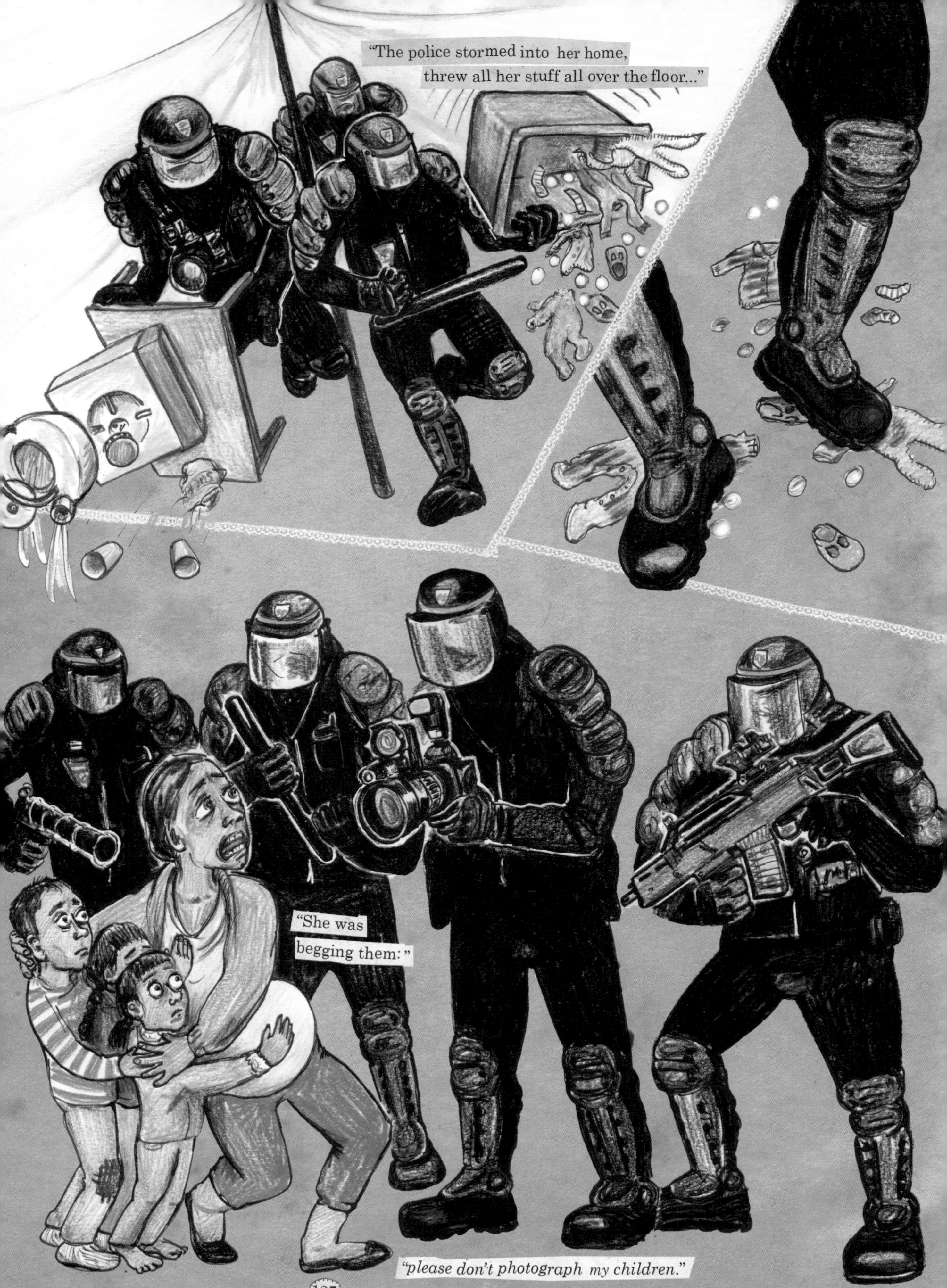
"The police stormed into her home,
threw all her stuff all over the floor..."
"She was
begging them:"
"please don't photograph my children."

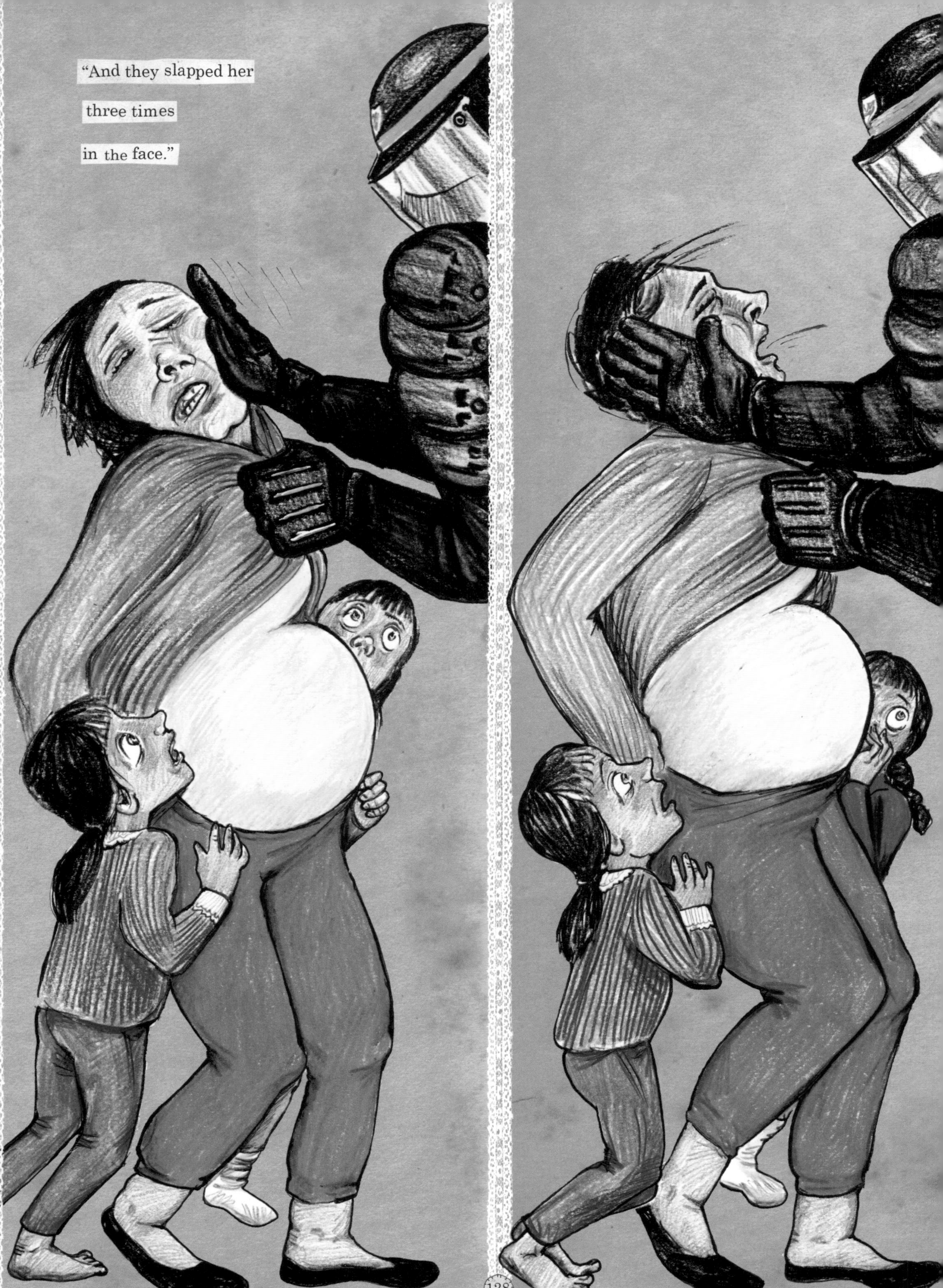
"And they slapped her
three times
in the face."

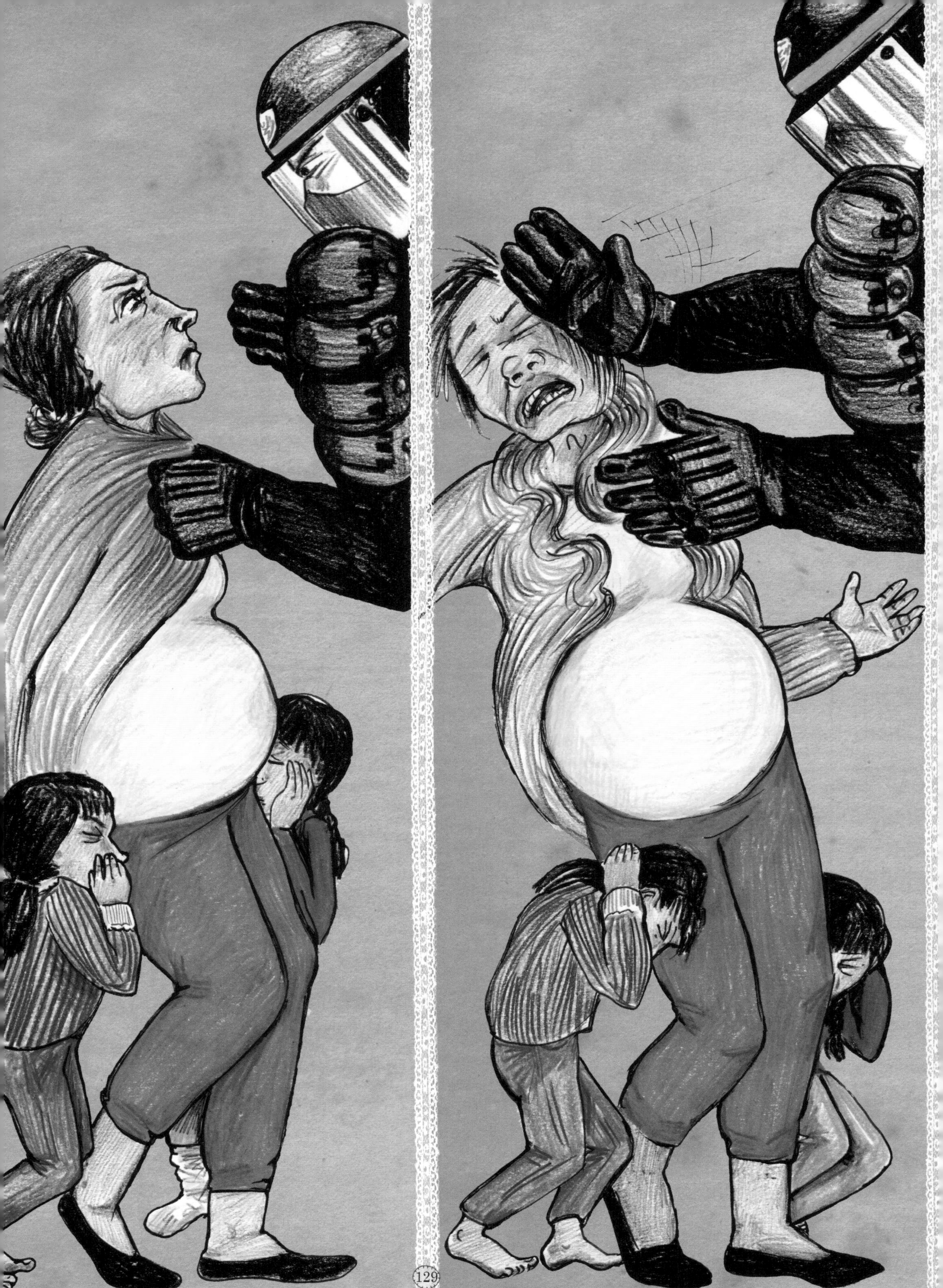

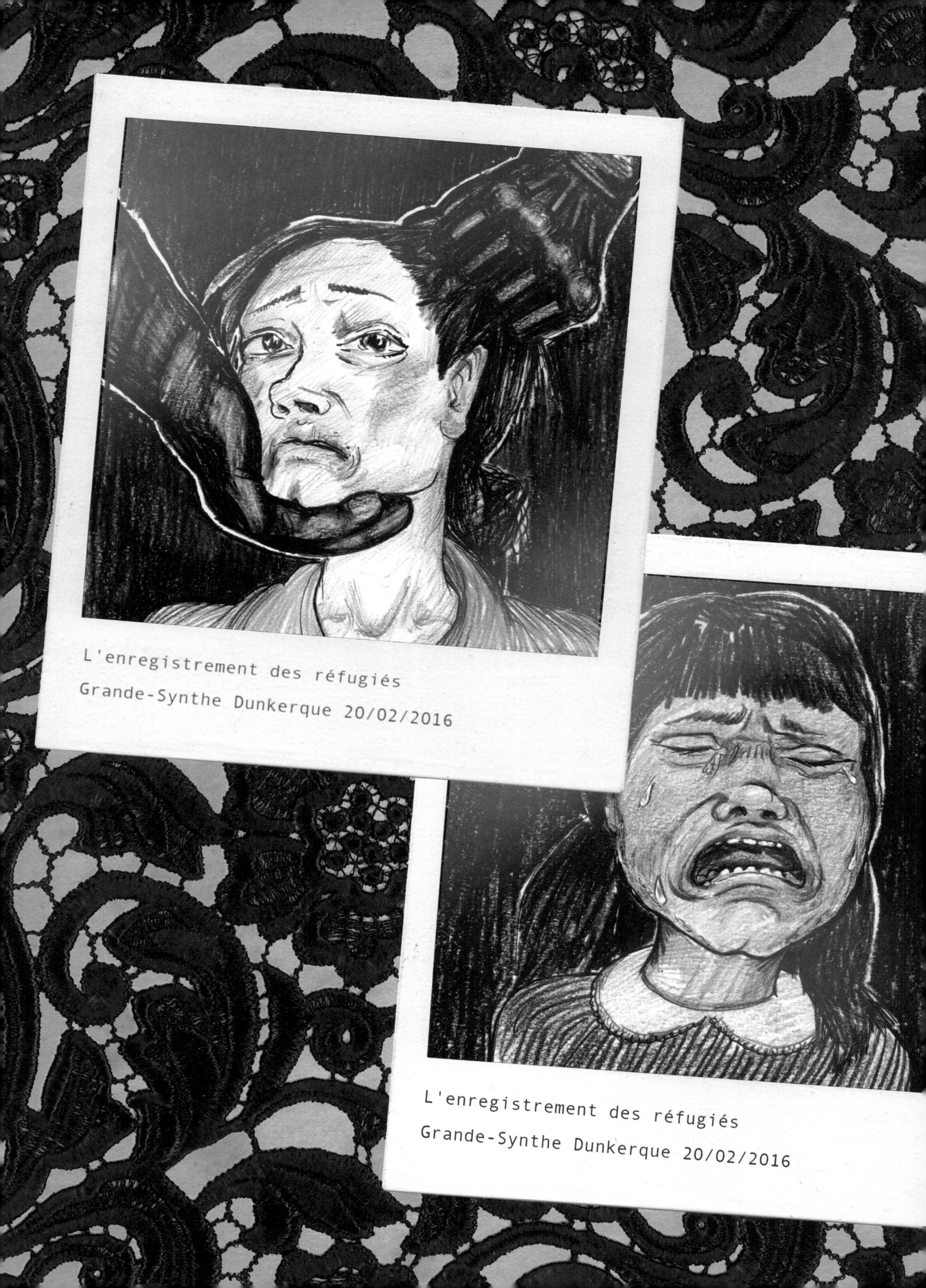
L'enregistrement des réfugiés
Grande-Synthe Dunkerque 20/02/2016
L'enregistrement des réfugiés
Grande-Synthe Dunkerque 20/02/2016

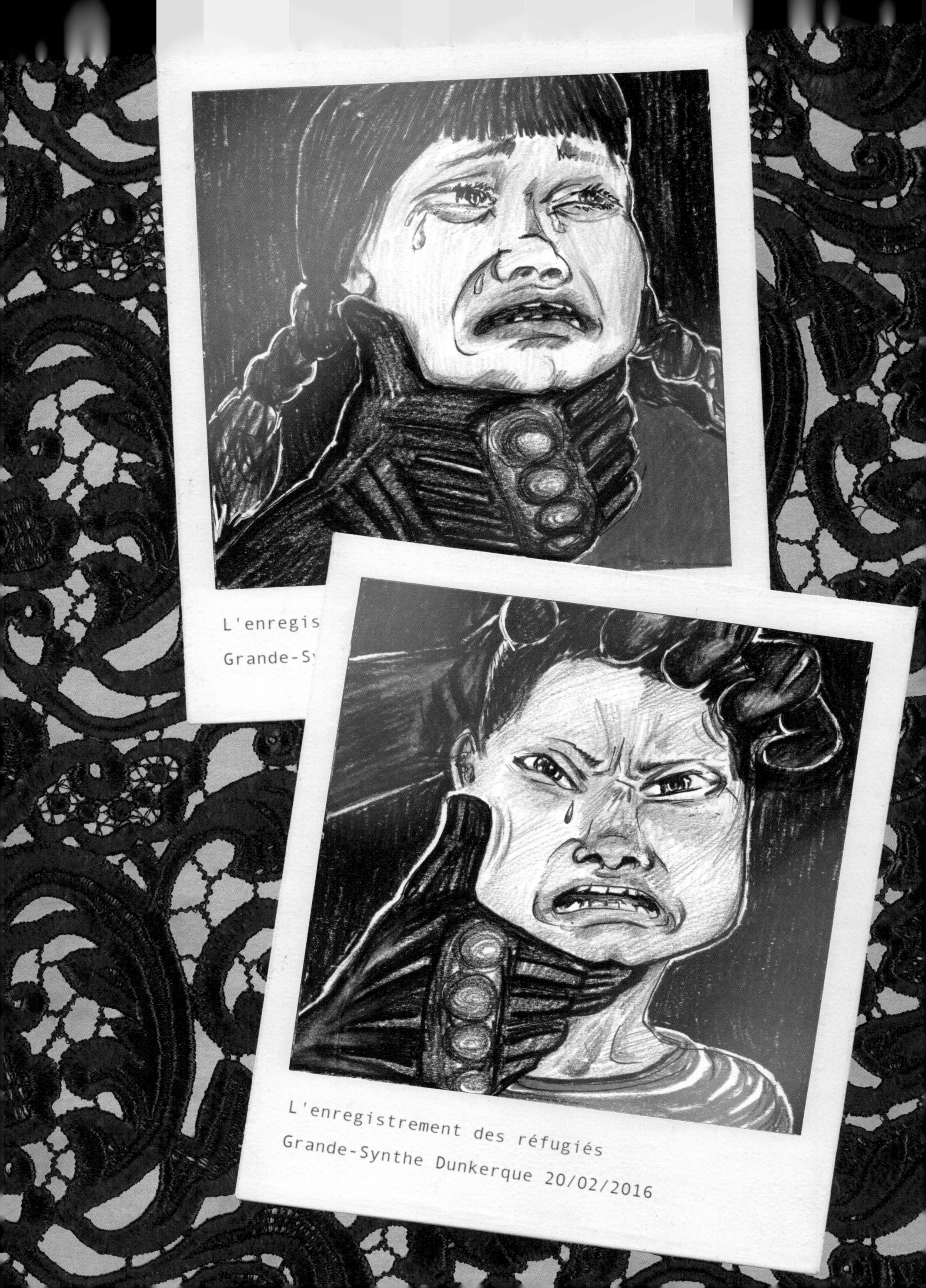
L'enregis
Grande-Sy
L'enregistrement des réfugiés
Grande-Synthe Dunkerque 20/02/2016

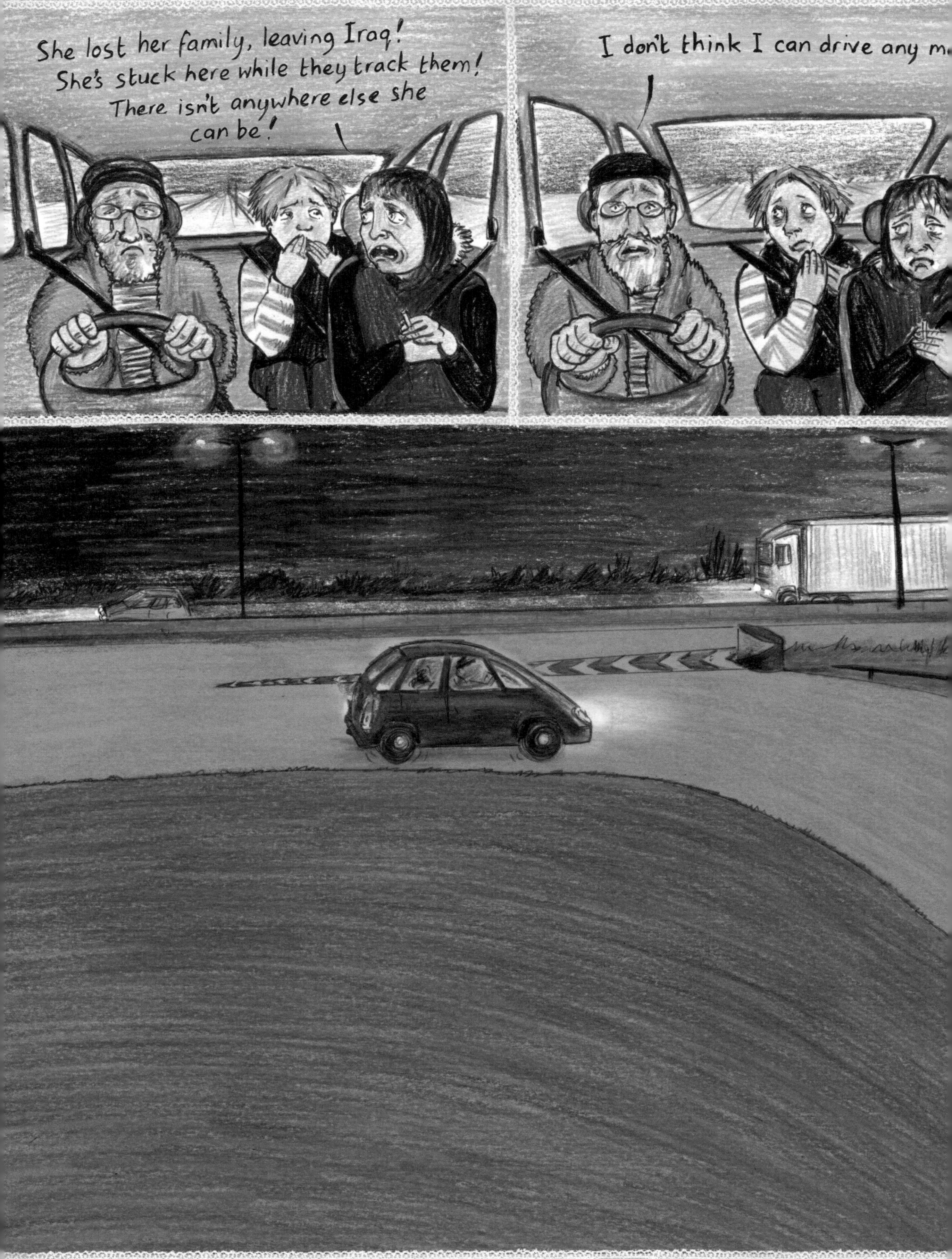
She lost her family, leaving Iraq! She's stuck here while they track them! There isn't anywhere else she can be!
I don't think I can drive any m

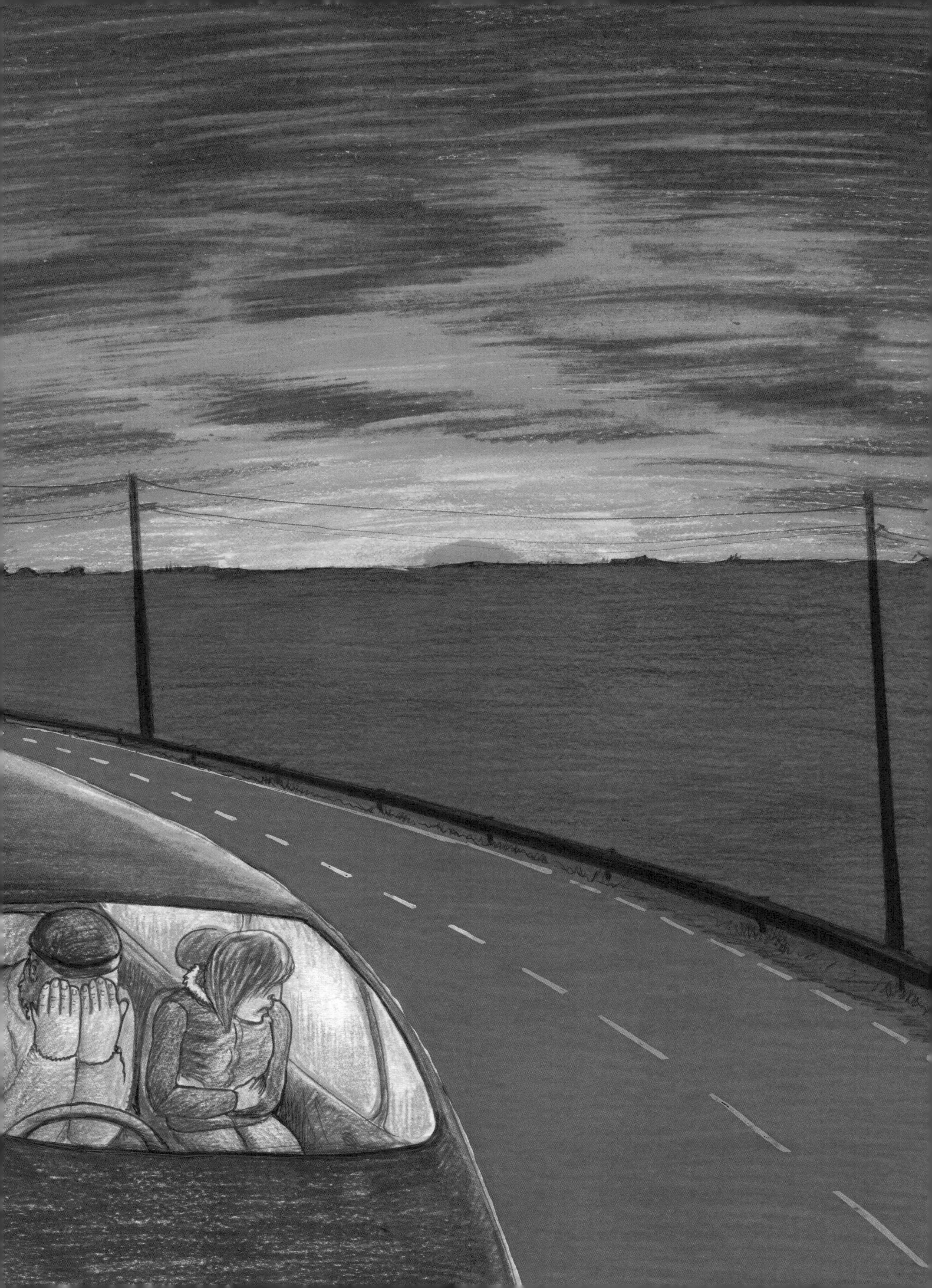

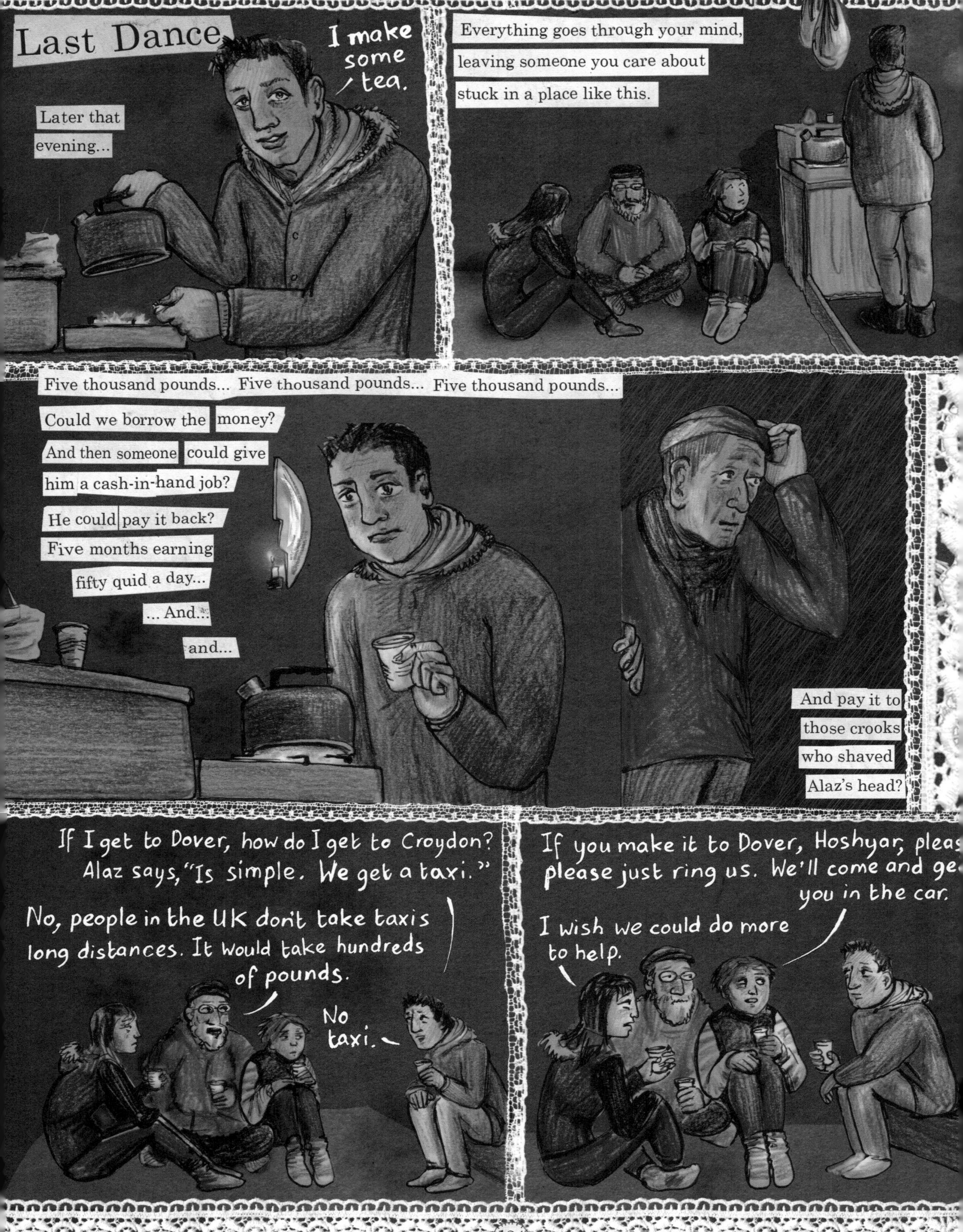
Last Dance
Later that evening...
I make some tea.
Everything goes through your mind, leaving someone you care about stuck in a place like this.
Five thousand pounds... Five thousand pounds... Five thousand pounds...
Could we borrow the money?
And then someone could give him a cash-in-hand job?
He could pay it back?
Five months earning fifty quid a day...
... And...
and...
And pay it to those crooks who shaved Alaz's head?
If I get to Dover, how do I get to Croydon? Alaz says, "Is simple. We get a taxi."
No, people in the UK don't take taxis long distances. It would take hundreds of pounds.
No taxi.
If you make it to Dover, Hoshyar, pleas please just ring us. We'll come and ge you in the car.
I wish we could do more to help.

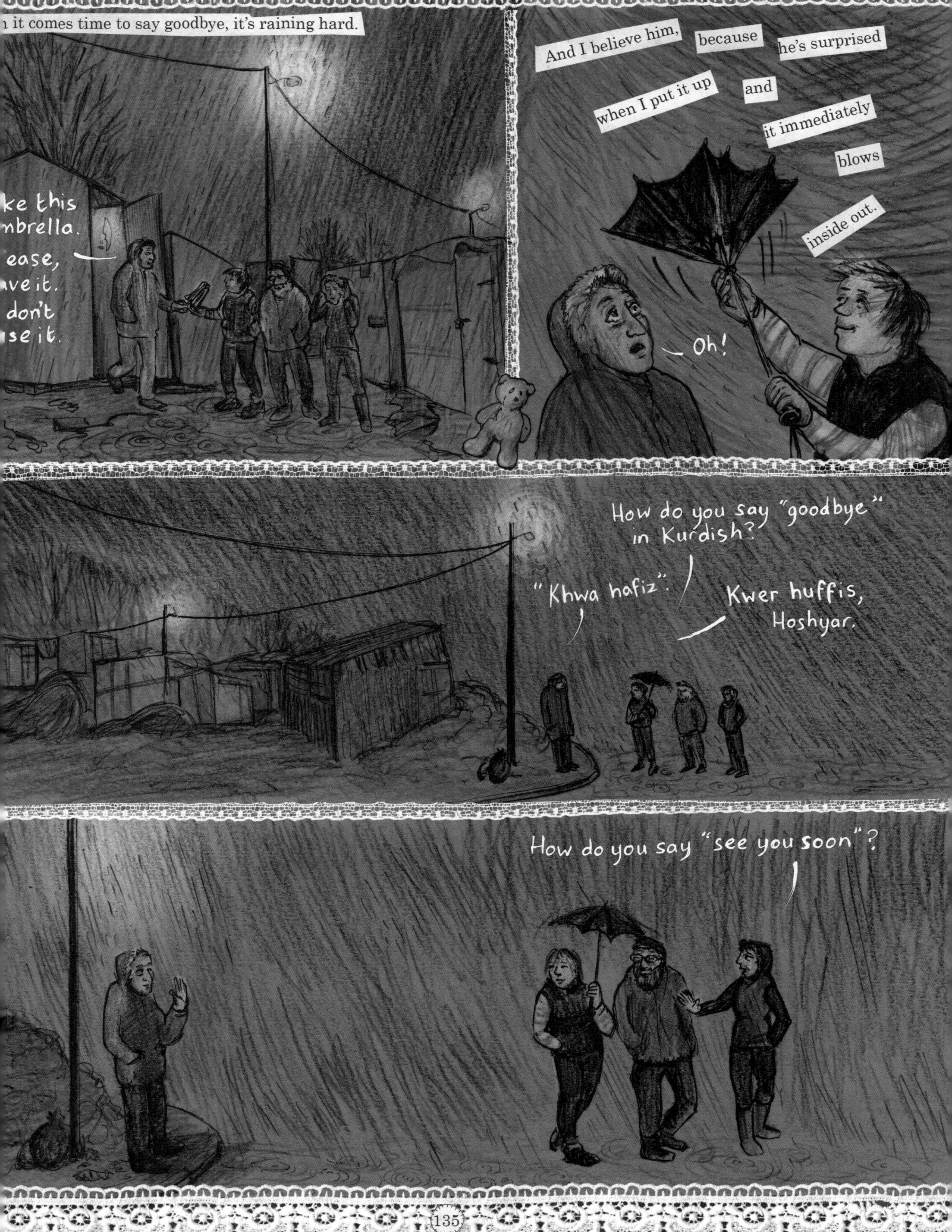

n it comes time to say goodbye, it's raining hard.
ke this
nbrella.
ease,
ve it.
don't
se it.
And I believe him, because he's surprised when I put it up and it immediately blows inside out.
Oh!
How do you say "goodbye" in Kurdish?
"Khwa hafiz".
Kwer huffis, Hoshyar.
How do you say "see you soon"?

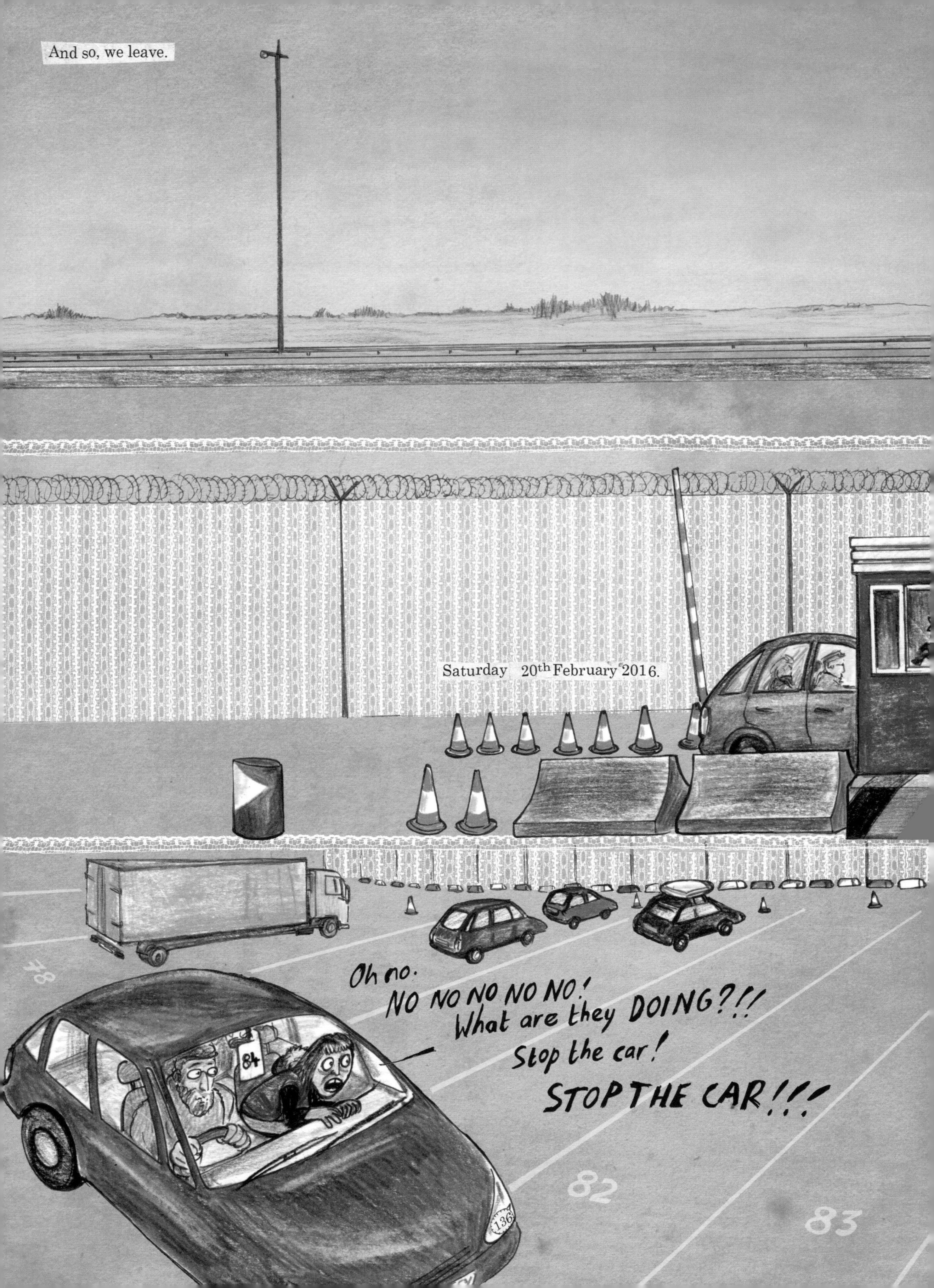
And so, we leave.
Saturday 20th February 2016.
Oh no.
NO NO NO NO NO!
What are they DOING?!!
Stop the car!
STOP THE CAR!!!

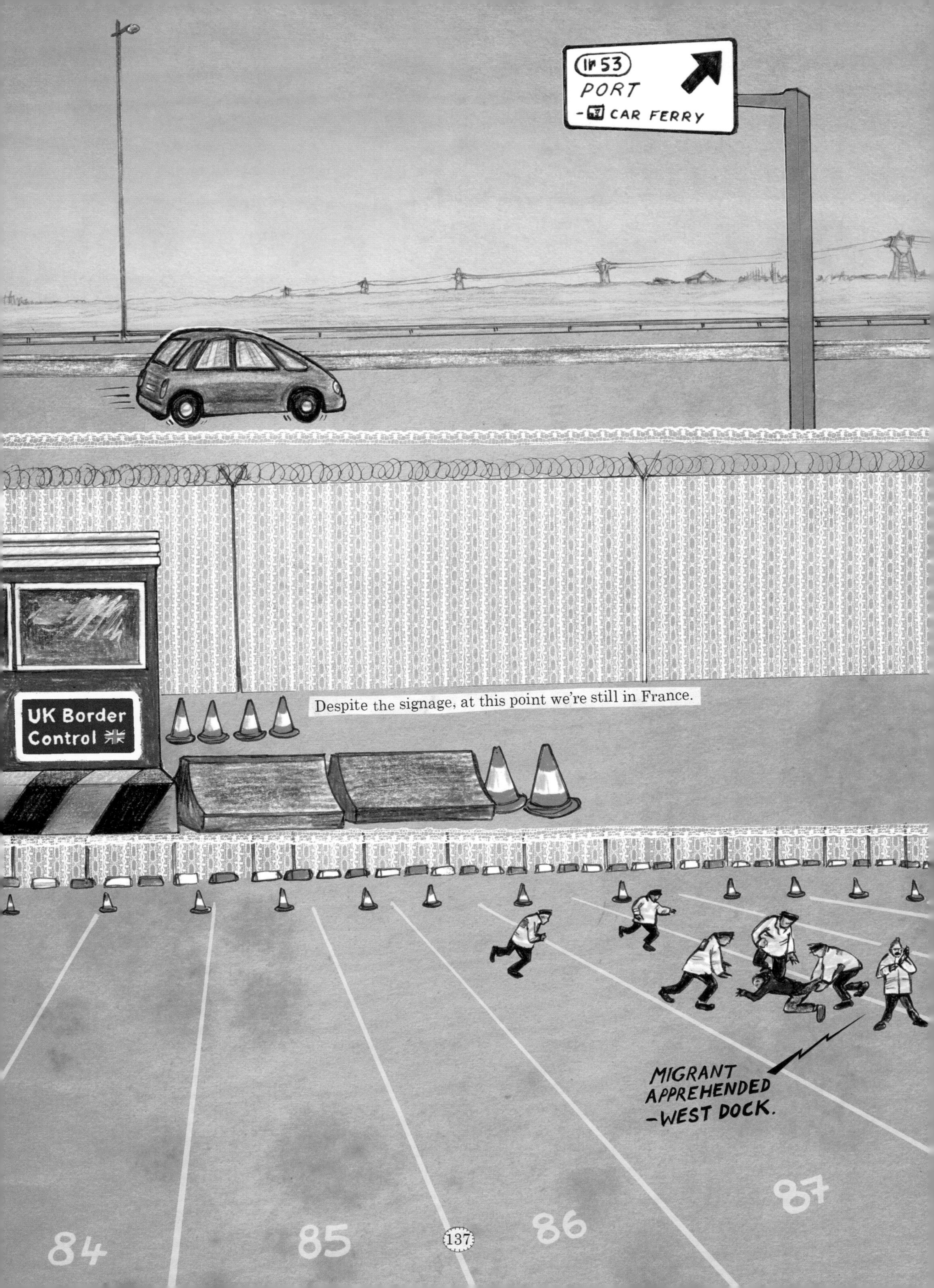
53
PORT
CAR FERRY
UK Border Control
Despite the signage, at this point we're still in France.
MIGRANT APPREHENDED -WEST DOCK.
84
85
86
87

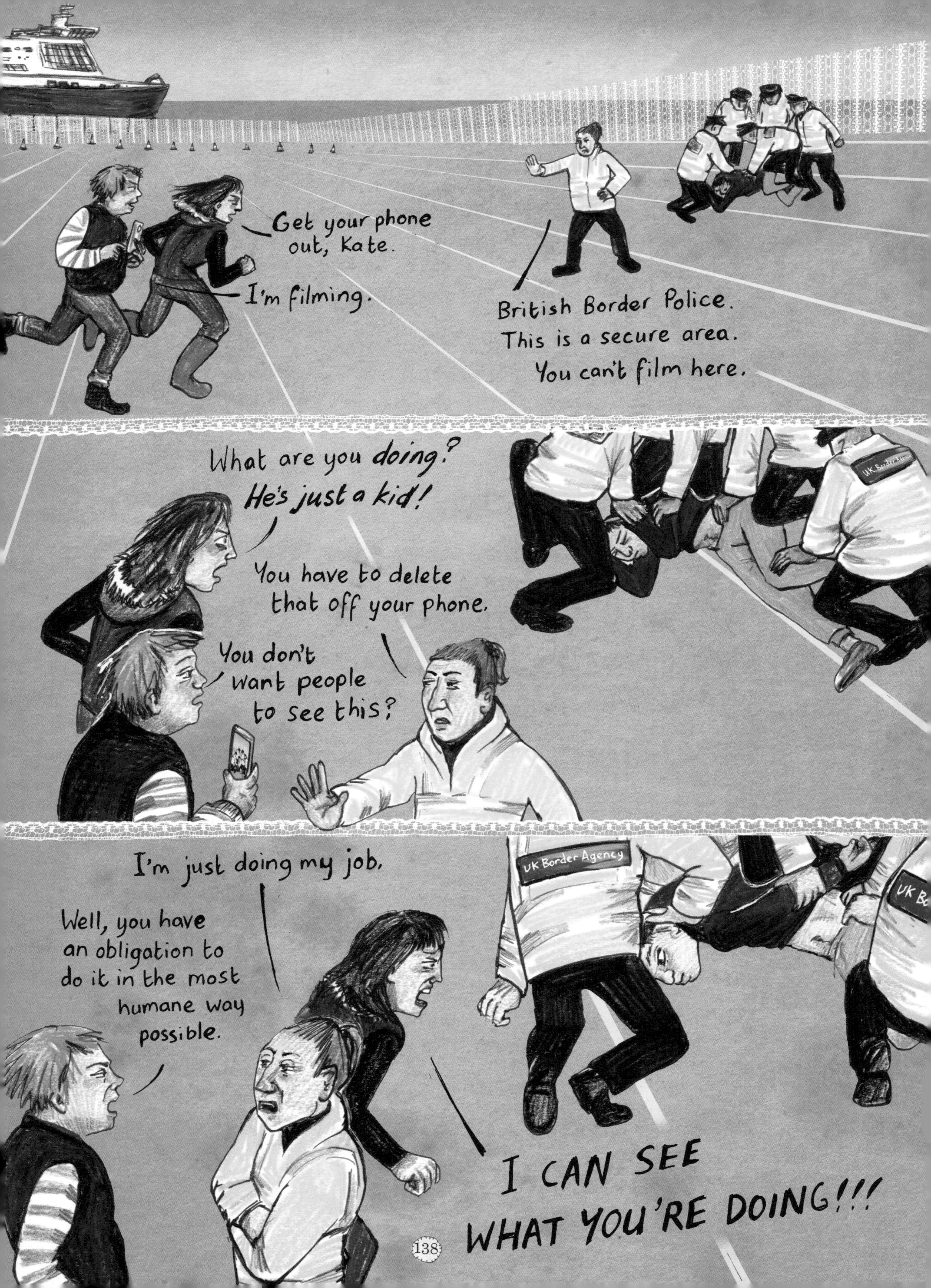
Get your phone out, Kate.
I'm filming.
British Border Police. This is a secure area. You can't film here.
What are you *doing*? *He's just a kid!*
You have to delete that off your phone.
You don't want people to see this?
UK Border Agency
I'm just doing my job.
Well, you have an obligation to do it in the most humane way possible.
UK Border Agency
I CAN SEE WHAT YOU'RE DOING!!!

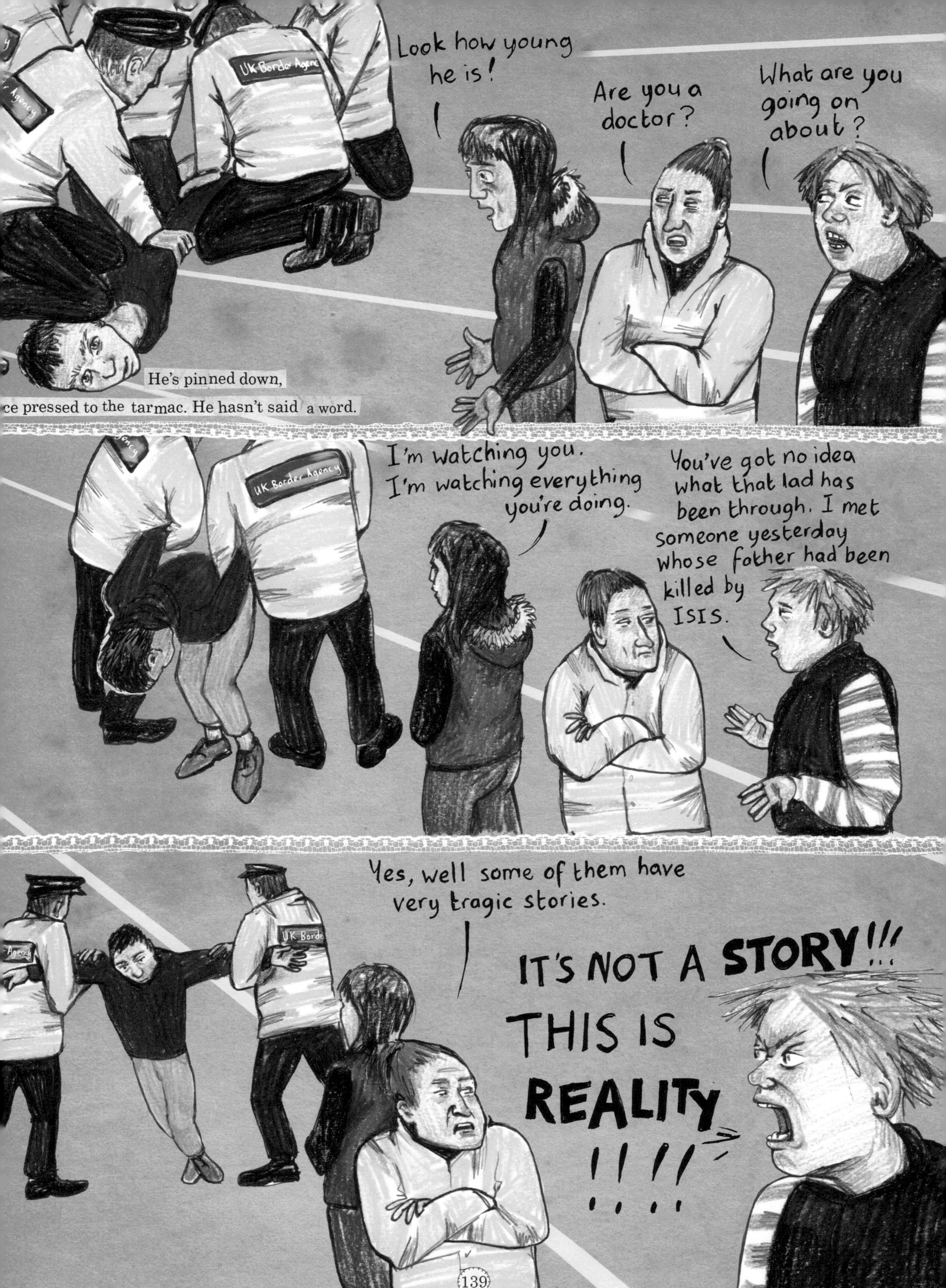
UK Border Agency
He's pinned down,
ce pressed to the tarmac. He hasn't said a word.
Look how young he is!
Are you a doctor?
What are you going on about?
UK Border Agency
I'm watching you. I'm watching everything you're doing.
You've got no idea what that lad has been through. I met someone yesterday whose father had been killed by ISIS.
Yes, well some of them have very tragic stories.
IT'S NOT A STORY!!! THIS IS REALITY !!!!

When the Americans came they gave my brother a job interpreting. One night we got a note saying he should stop working for the Americans or he will be killed. A few days later he disappeared and then we didn't see him. Then one morning his body was outside our door without his head.

My husband was beaten by the police in a detention centre until he died. His body was unrecognisable.

If our answers didn't satisfy the interrogator, they would pour boiling hot water on us.

The pain the chair caused was too extreme to feel any of the pain caused by the metal sticks and kicking. They burned me with cigarettes. I could feel nothing. I only smelt the burning of my own flesh.

They took turns at beating me until the shovel handle broke into pieces.

They held [my] shoulders and legs, took my testicles with the pliers, and pulled.

They gave me electricity with a stick, many times on the left leg, then on right leg, chest and belly. I was too weak, I couldn't resist and at that point they took both my hands and put them on the machine.

I thought that would be the last day of my life.

There is no hiding place for gay people like me in my country. People don't wait for the police to come, because they believe the police can just be bribed. So they will throw petrol on a tyre and set a gay person ablaze.

We heard gunfire and no one would go out onto the streets. My family and I stayed in our house for days because we were afraid. I cannot tell you the exact number of days. On the last day, we had no bread. We had nothing to eat.

The soldiers surrounded our house and pushed the door in by force. When they entered, they caught n husband. They tied his hands behind his back and took all my clothes off in front of my children. Then one of the soldiers stabbed him in the neck with a knife. I cried to them, "Please don't kill my husband! Please don't kill him!" They said if I didn't want my husband to be killed, I should just open my legs "and we will have sex with you".

A man bought me. For him, I was an object, or an animal, just a thing. He abused me so much. I was afraid, in the end, he would kill me.

As long as a girl has some breast, she is considered a woman and that entitles them to rape her. Some girls are as young as 10 and 11 years old.

One girl tried to run away and they shot her in the back of her head. Then we all had to walk over her body and you could see her brain showing.

There are nights I wake up more than one time wash my mouth as I remember what they did to and how they forced themselves on me.

I have no past and no future at the moment. I feel like I'm living like a bird with no fixed home. My heart is banging all the time and I'm always shaking not knowing what's going to happen next.

The day I left my country,
I was filled with sorrow.

To leave everything behind. To leave your loved ones and not know what is going to happen to them. I was lucky. I am grateful that I am alive, but I thought, "You know what? Why am I even alive? What is the point of being alone in the world anyway?"

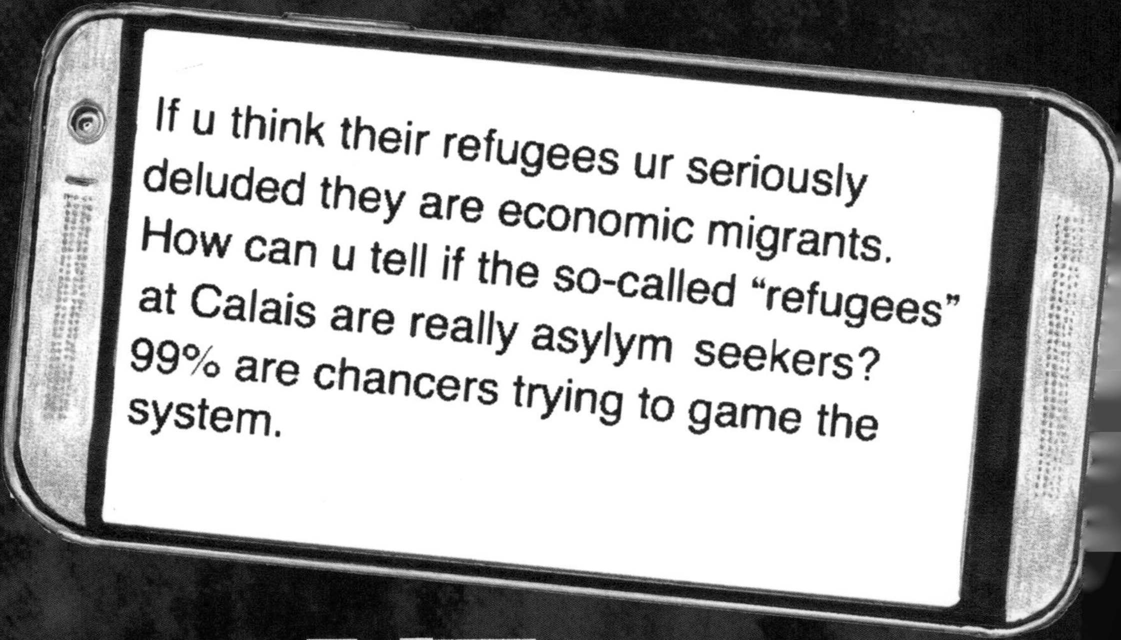
If u think their refugees ur seriously deluded they are economic migrants. How can u tell if the so-called "refugees" at Calais are really asylym seekers? 99% are chancers trying to game the system.

So? Reopen the
asylum-processing office
in Calais, and find out.

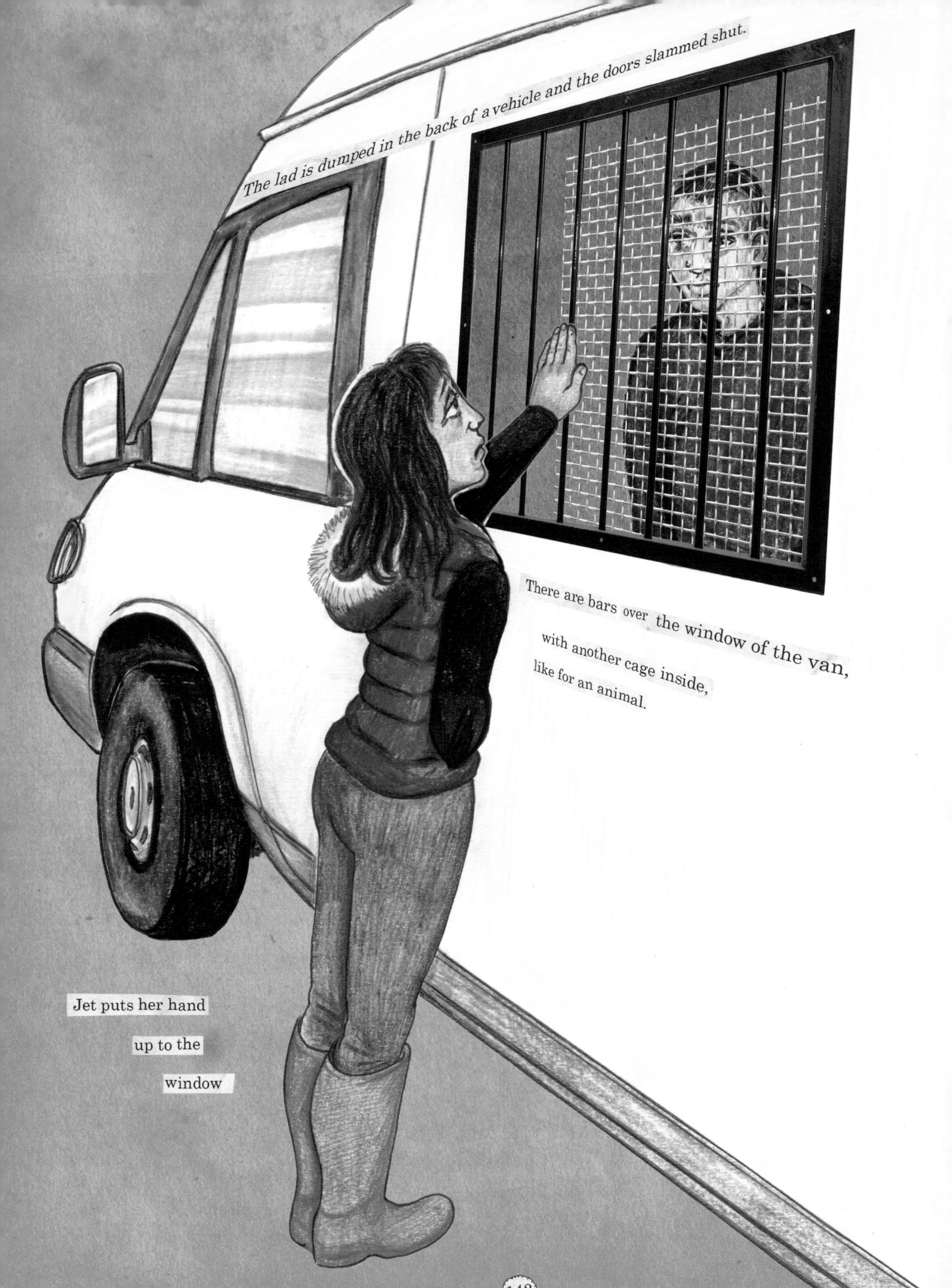
The lad is dumped in the back of a vehicle and the doors slammed shut.
There are bars over the window of the van,
with another cage inside,
like for an animal.
Jet puts her hand
up to the
window

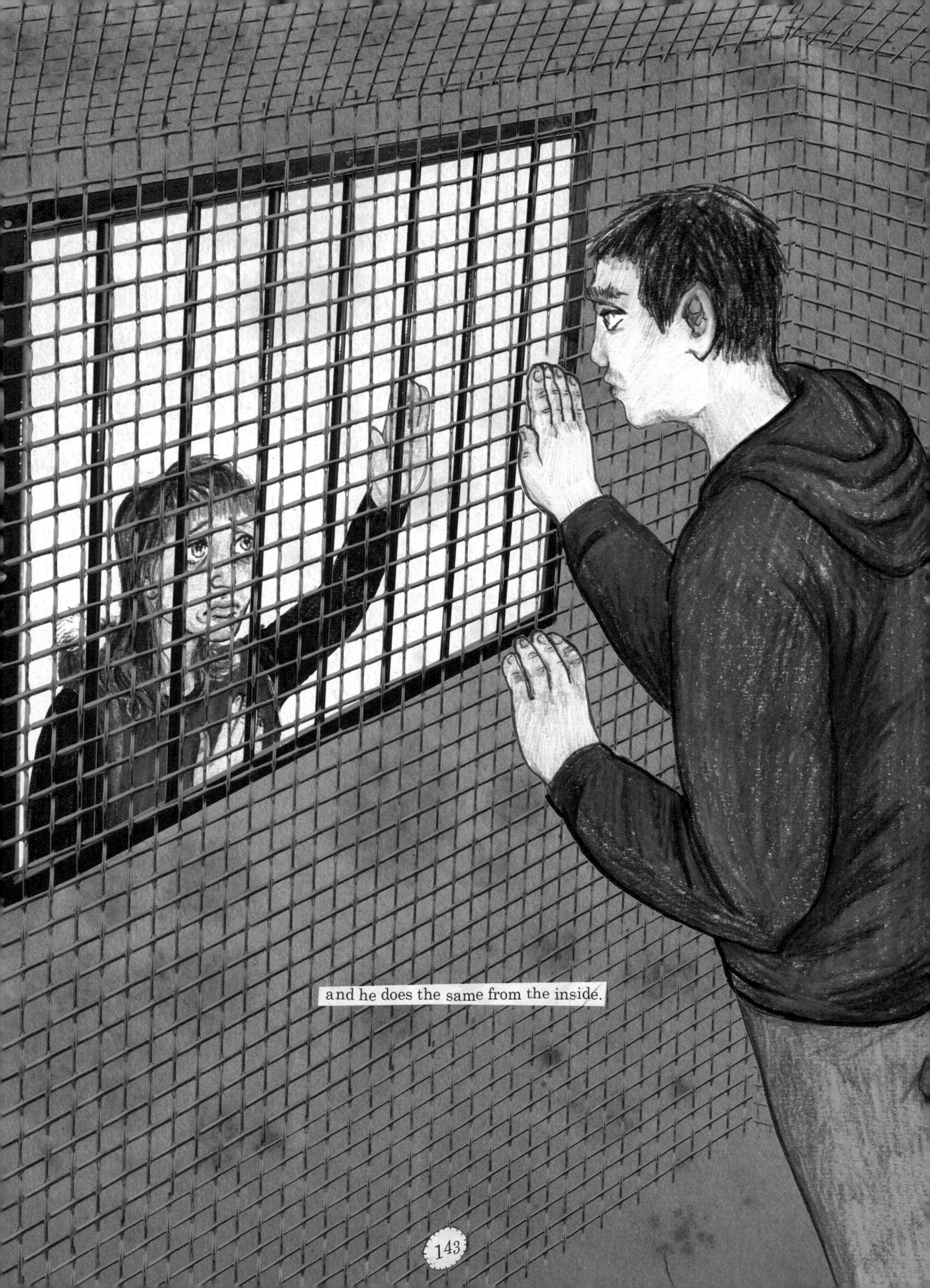
and he does the same from the inside.

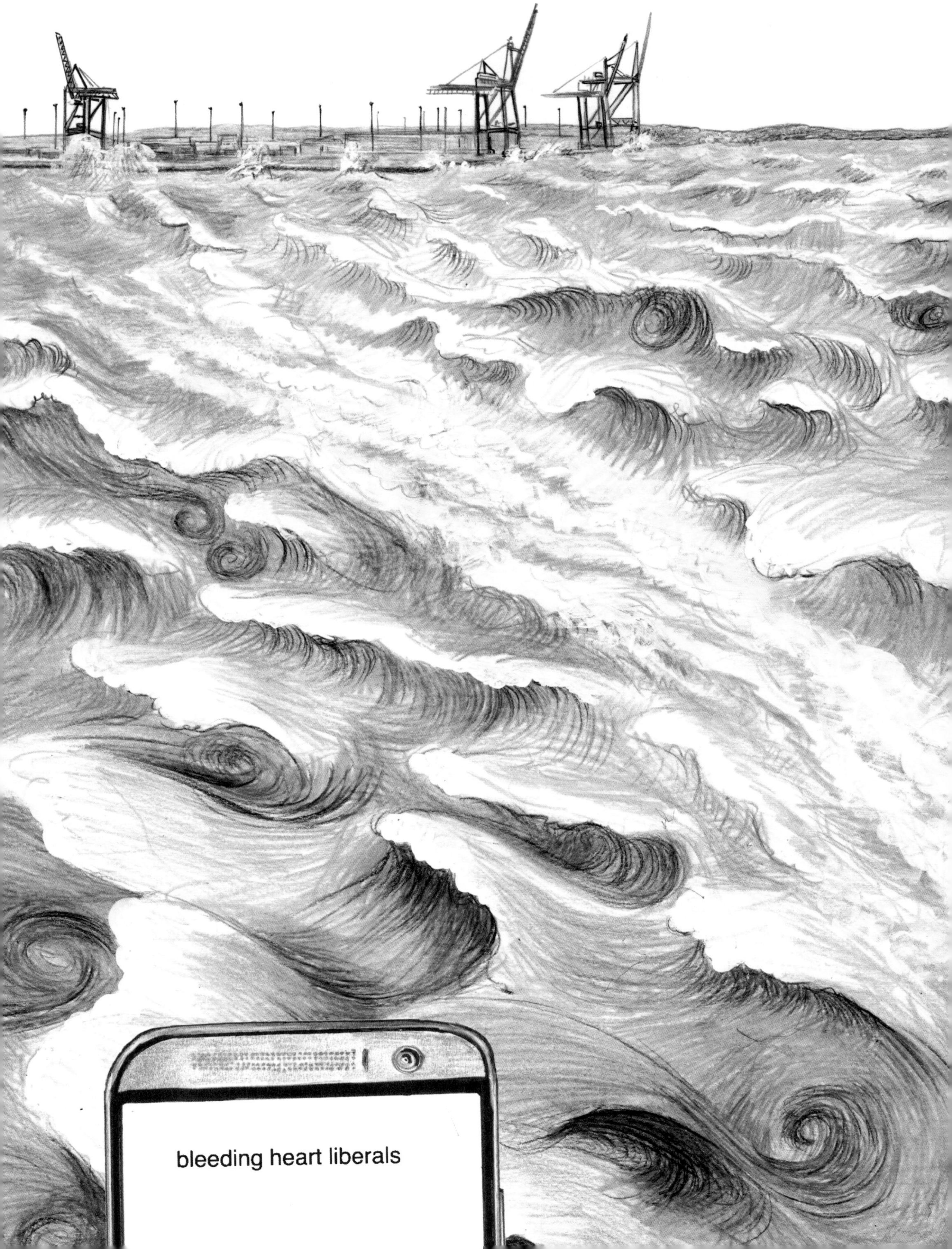
bleeding heart liberals

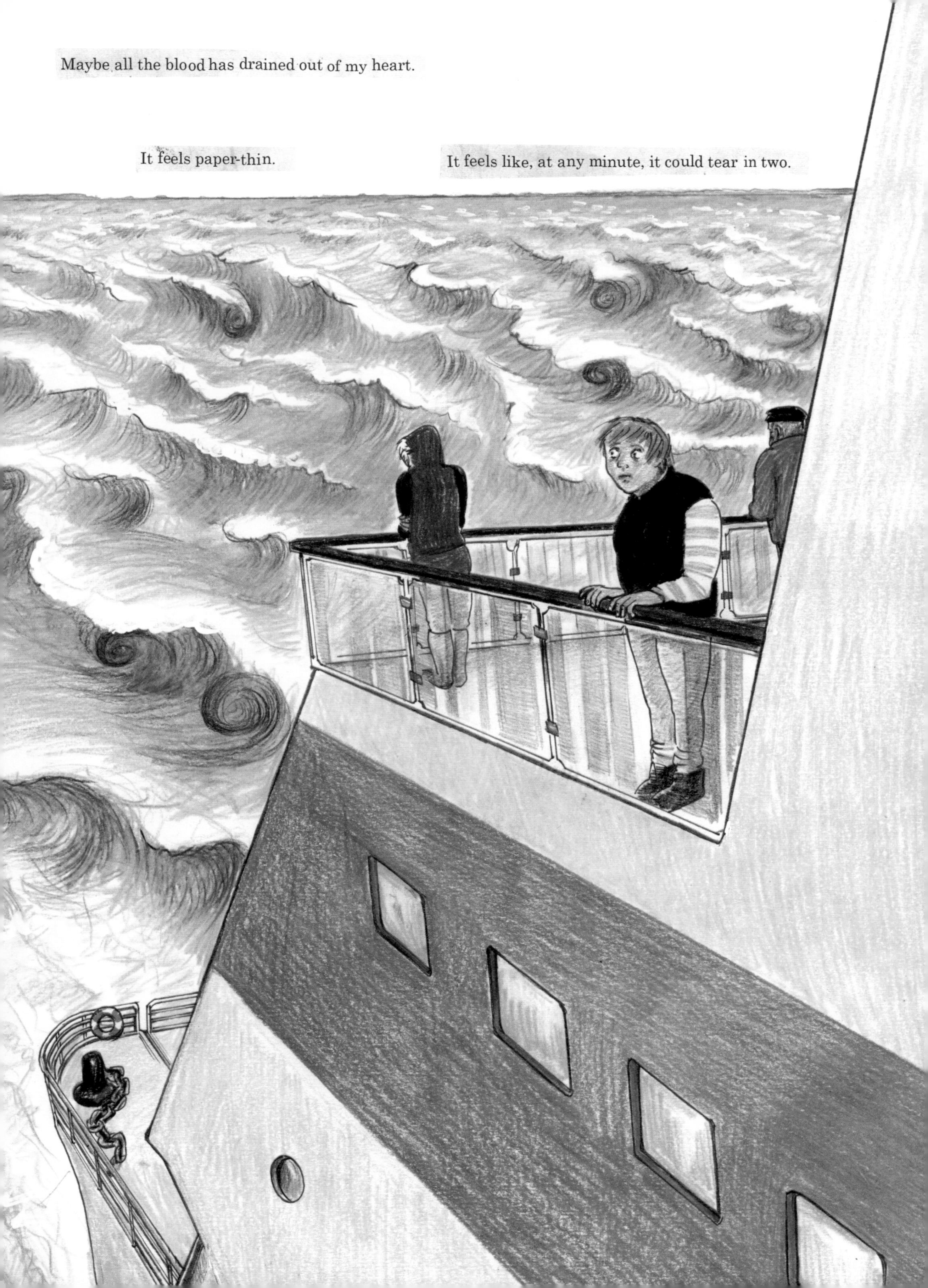
Maybe all the blood has drained out of my heart.
It feels paper-thin.
It feels like, at any minute, it could tear in two.

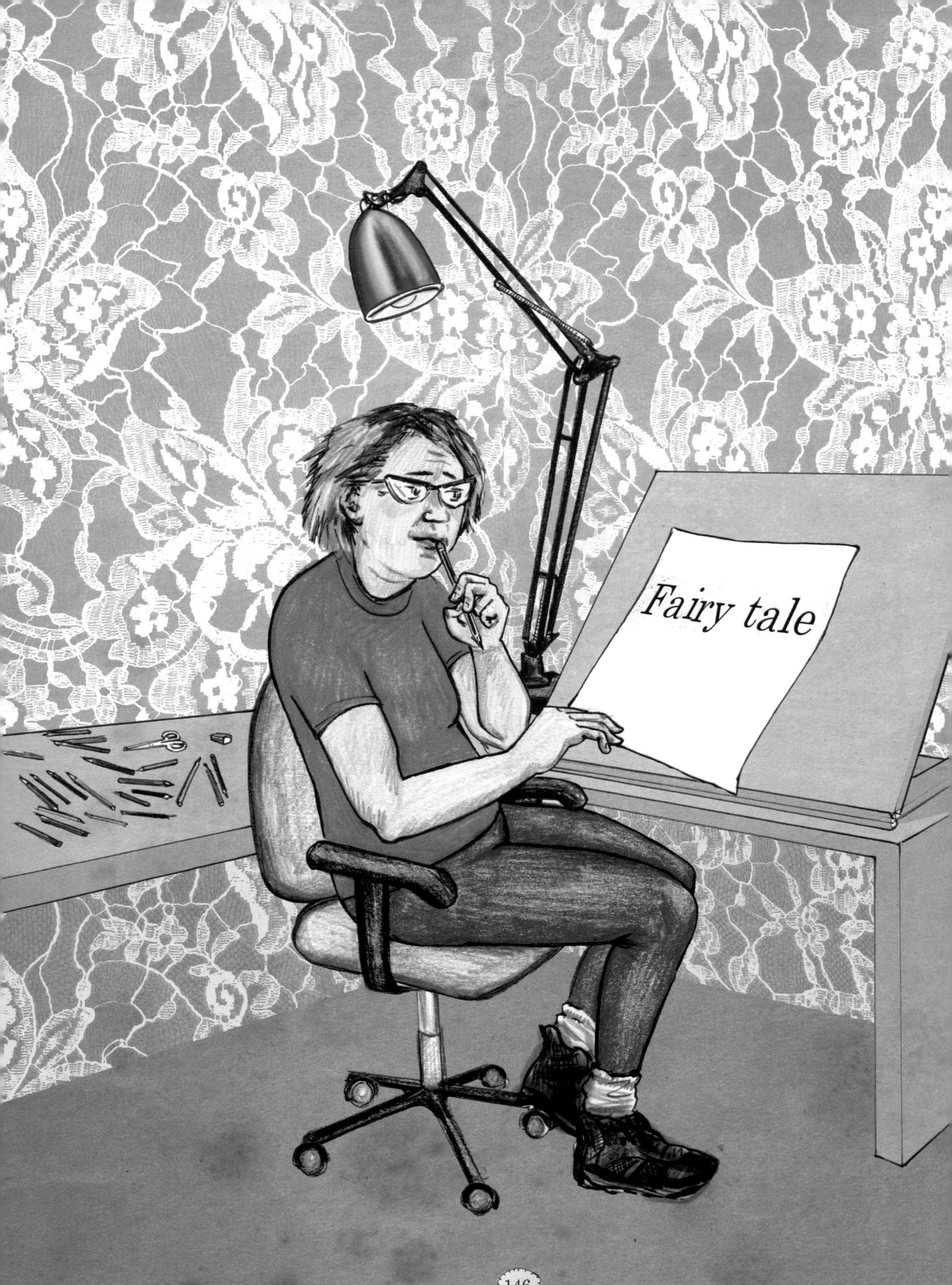
Fairy tale

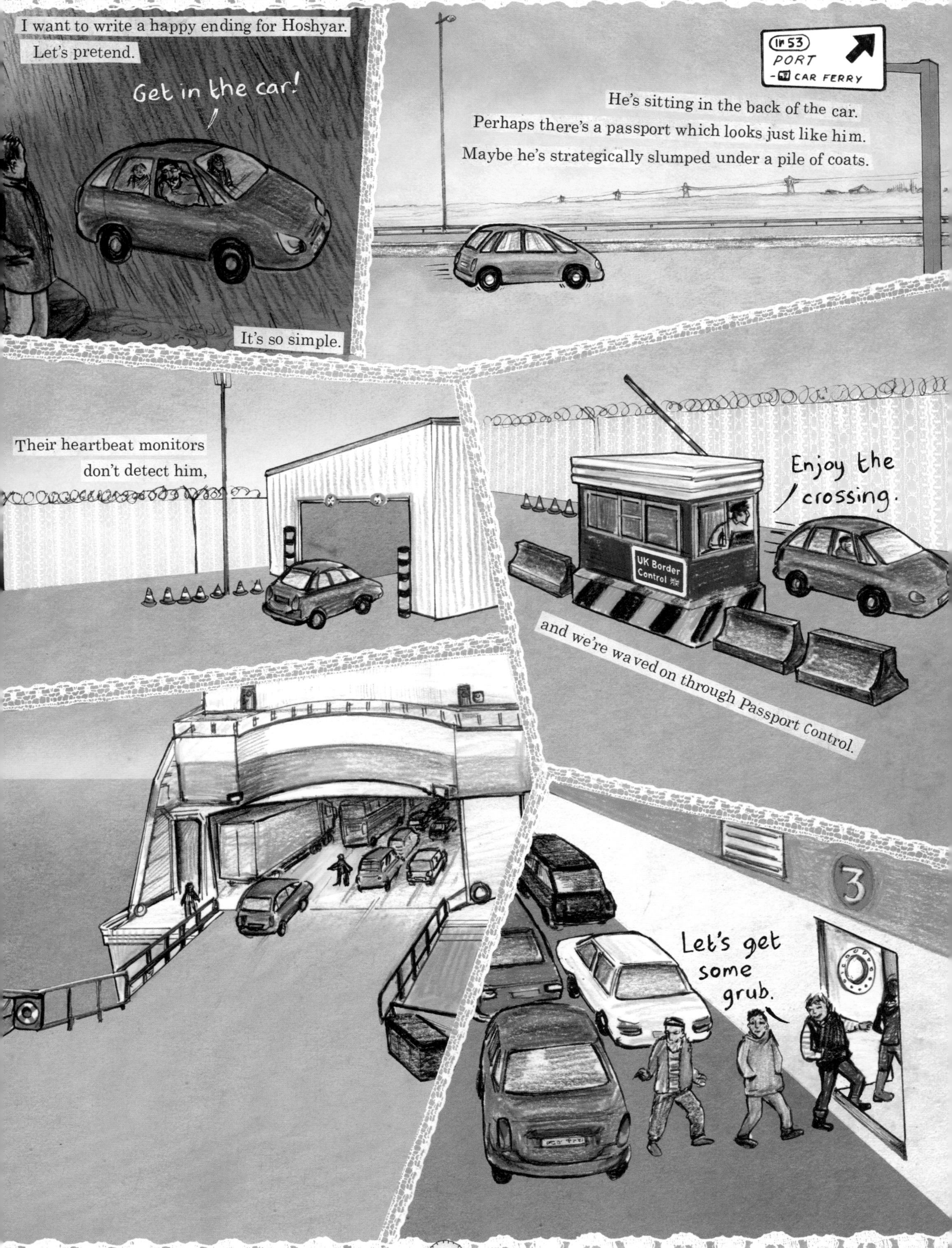
I want to write a happy ending for Hoshyar.
Let's pretend.
Get in the car!
It's so simple.
PORT
CAR FERRY
He's sitting in the back of the car.
Perhaps there's a passport which looks just like him.
Maybe he's strategically slumped under a pile of coats.
Their heartbeat monitors
don't detect him,
Enjoy the crossing.
UK Border Control
and we're waved on through Passport Control.
3
Let's get some grub.

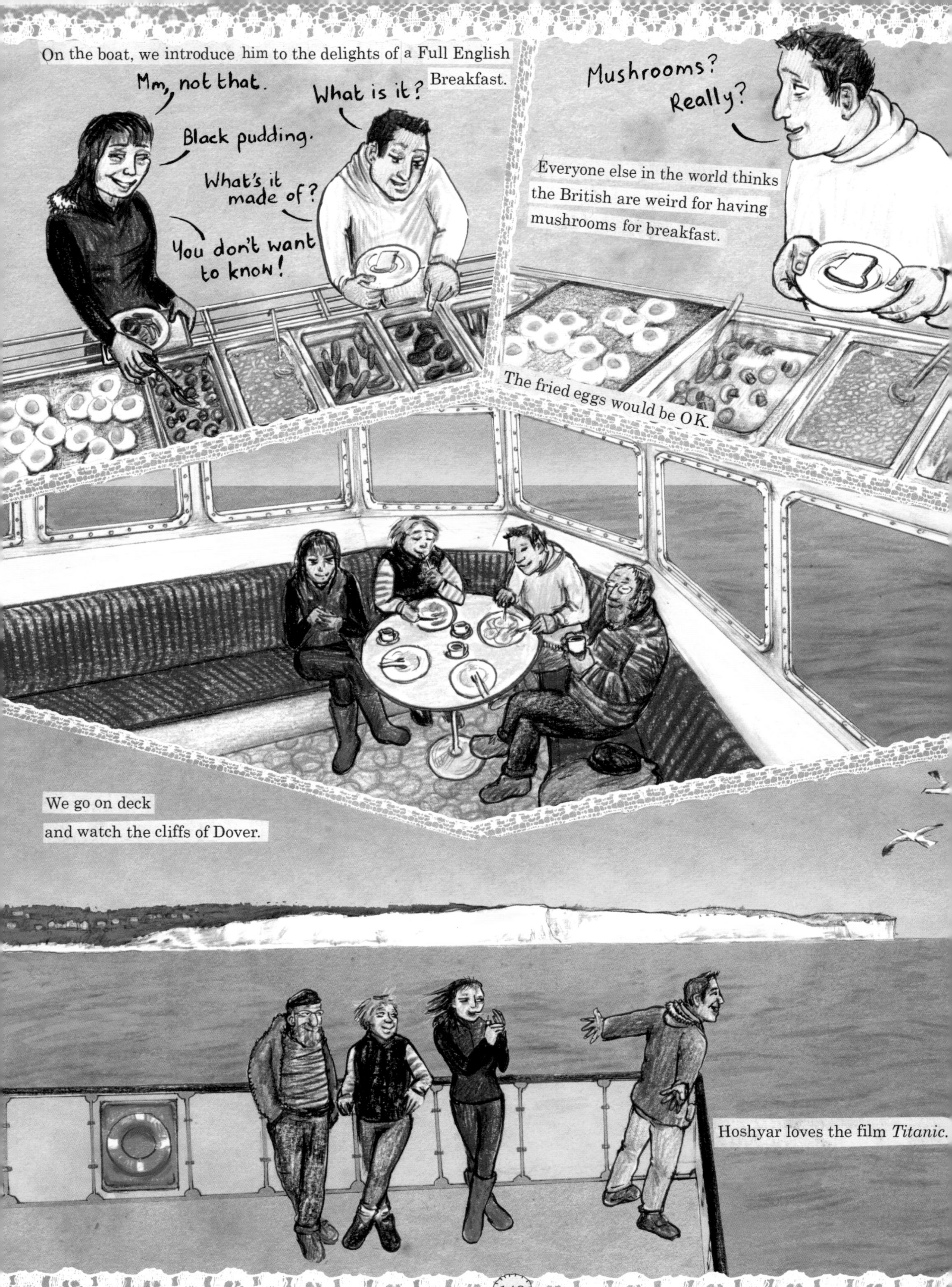
On the boat, we introduce him to the delights of a Full English Breakfast.
Mm, not that.
What is it?
Black pudding.
What's it made of?
You don't want to know!
Mushrooms? Really?
Everyone else in the world thinks the British are weird for having mushrooms for breakfast.
The fried eggs would be OK.
We go on deck
and watch the cliffs of Dover.
Hoshyar loves the film *Titanic*.

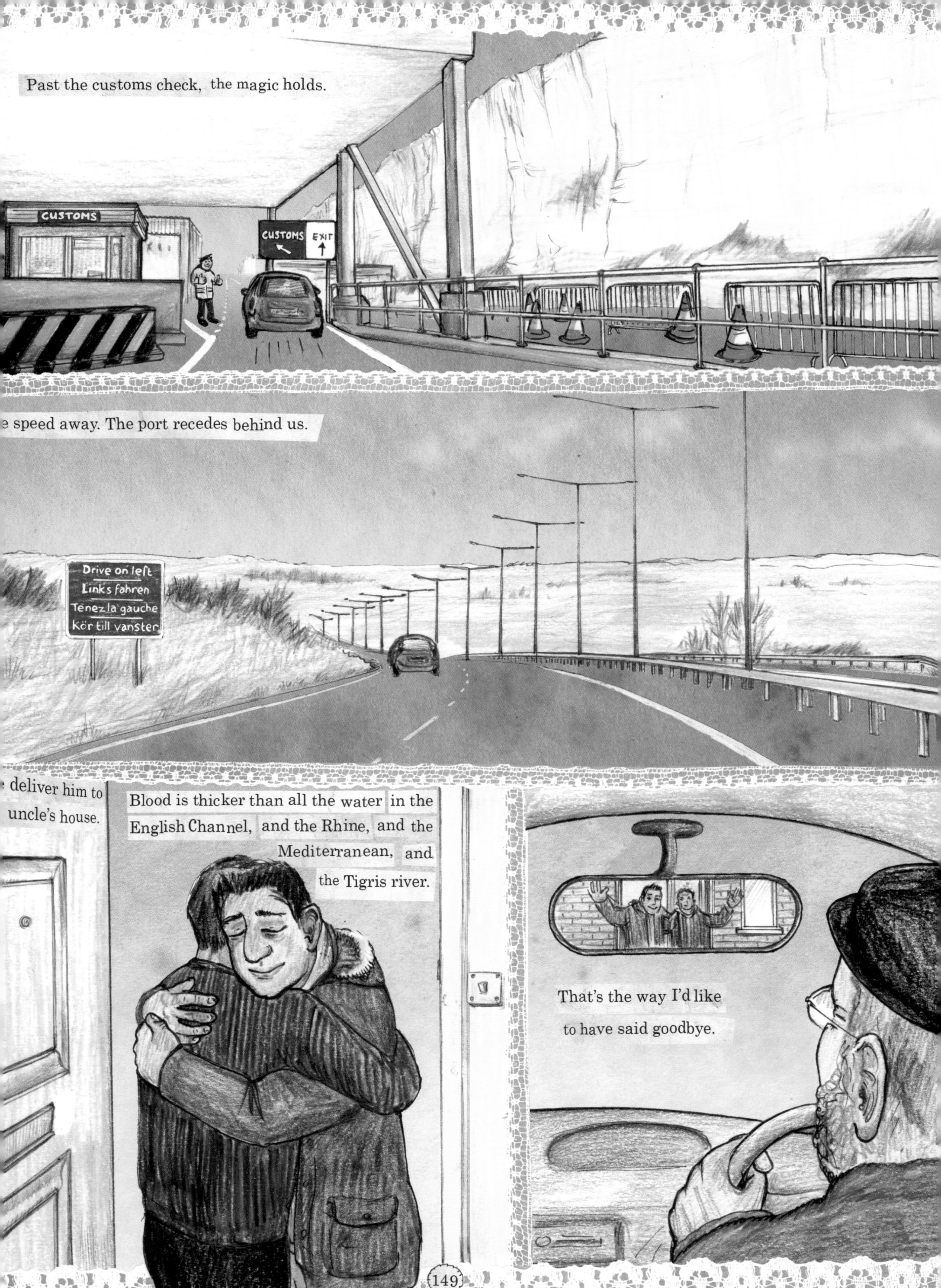
Past the customs check, the magic holds.
CUSTOMS
CUSTOMS
EXIT
e speed away. The port recedes behind us.
Drive on left
Links fahren
Tenez la gauche
Kör till vanster
e deliver him to uncle's house.
Blood is thicker than all the water in the English Channel, and the Rhine, and the Mediterranean, and the Tigris river.
That's the way I'd like to have said goodbye.

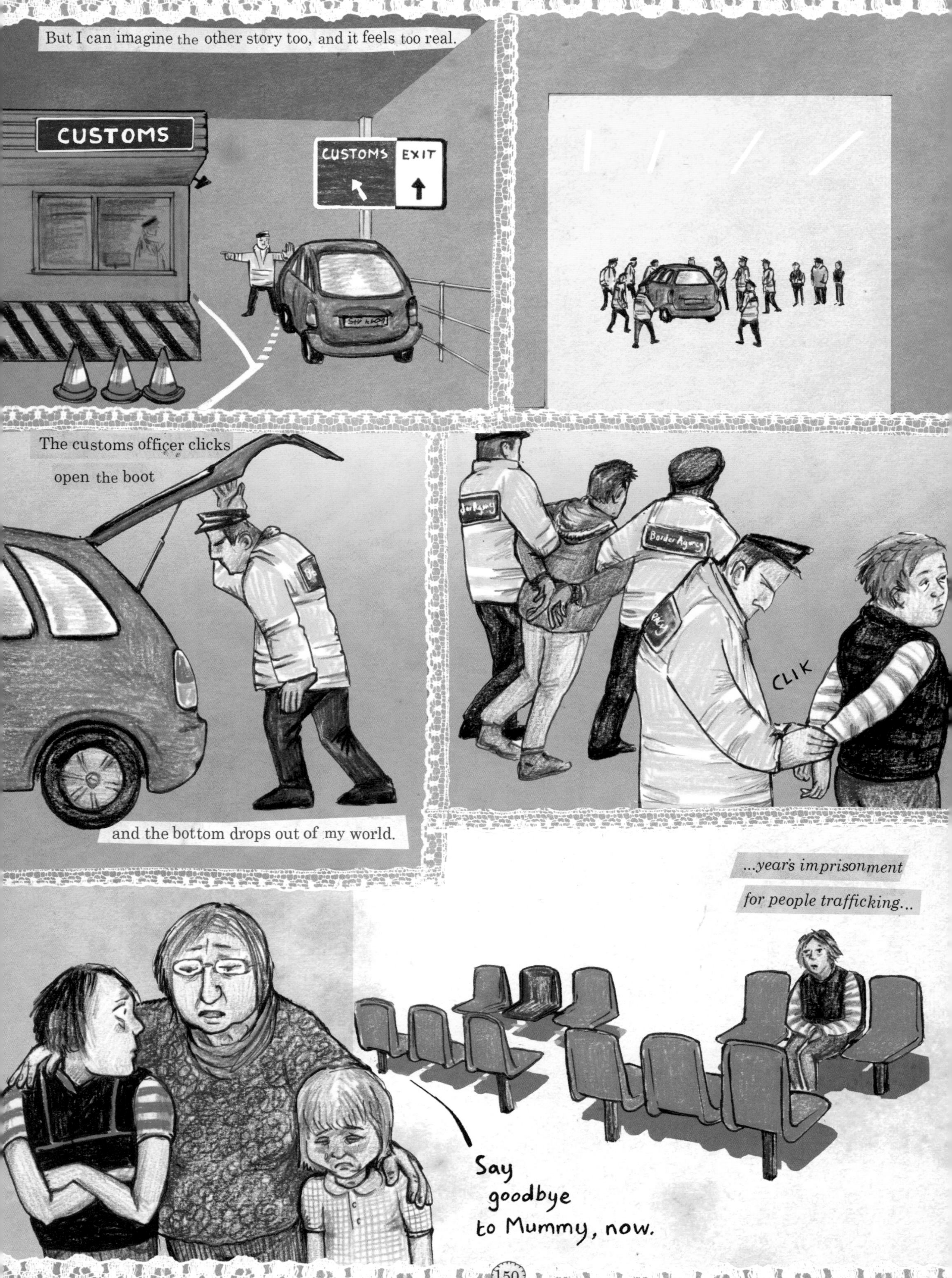
But I can imagine the other story too, and it feels too real.
CUSTOMS
CUSTOMS
EXIT
The customs officer clicks
open the boot
and the bottom drops out of my world.
Border Agency
CLIK
...year's imprisonment
for people trafficking...
Say
goodbye
to Mummy, now.

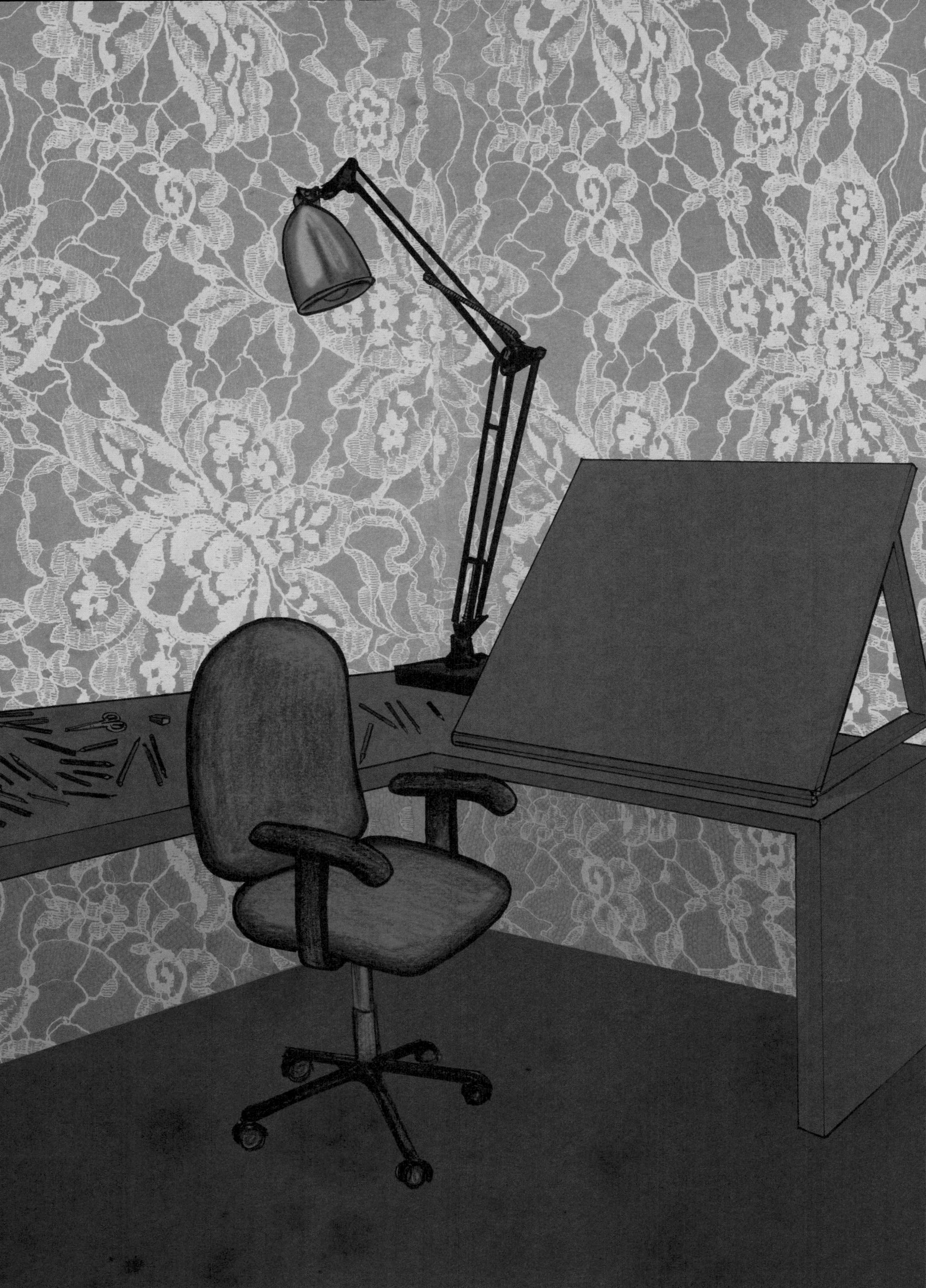

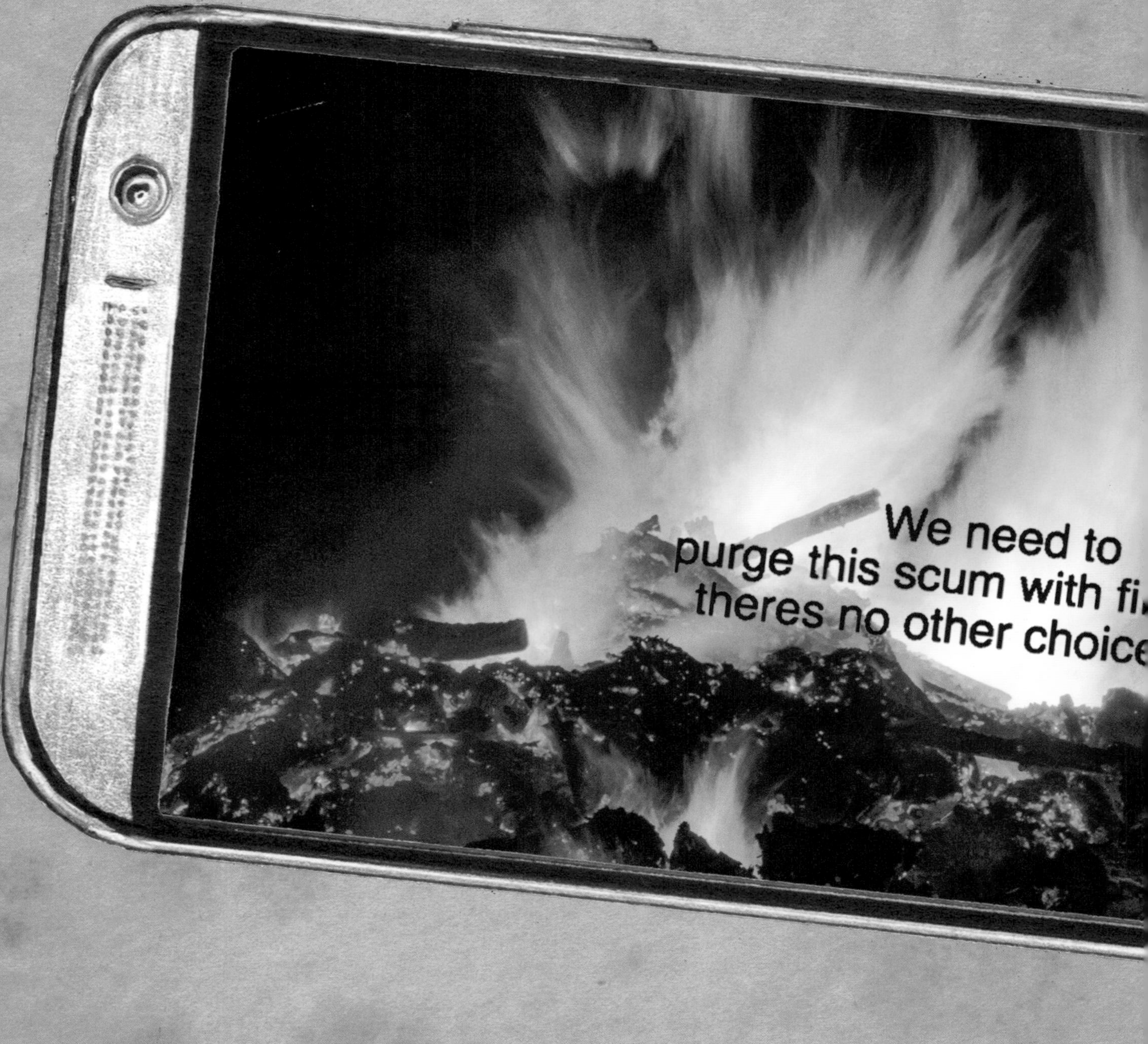
We need to
purge this scum with fi
theres no other choice

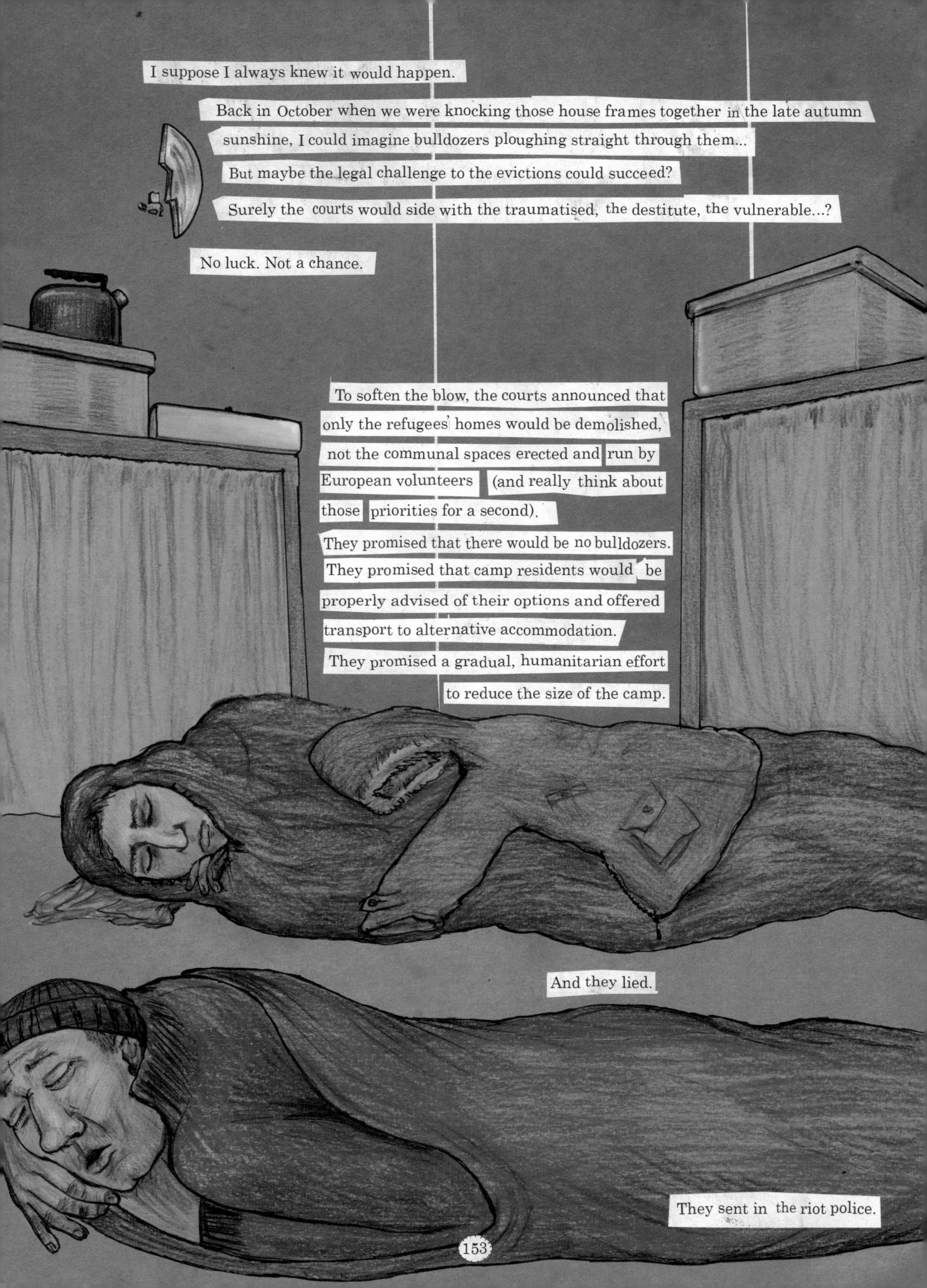
I suppose I always knew it would happen.
Back in October when we were knocking those house frames together in the late autumn sunshine, I could imagine bulldozers ploughing straight through them...
But maybe the legal challenge to the evictions could succeed?
Surely the courts would side with the traumatised, the destitute, the vulnerable...?
No luck. Not a chance.
To soften the blow, the courts announced that only the refugees' homes would be demolished, not the communal spaces erected and run by European volunteers (and really think about those priorities for a second).
They promised that there would be no bulldozers.
They promised that camp residents would be properly advised of their options and offered transport to alternative accommodation.
They promised a gradual, humanitarian effort to reduce the size of the camp.
And they lied.
They sent in the riot police.

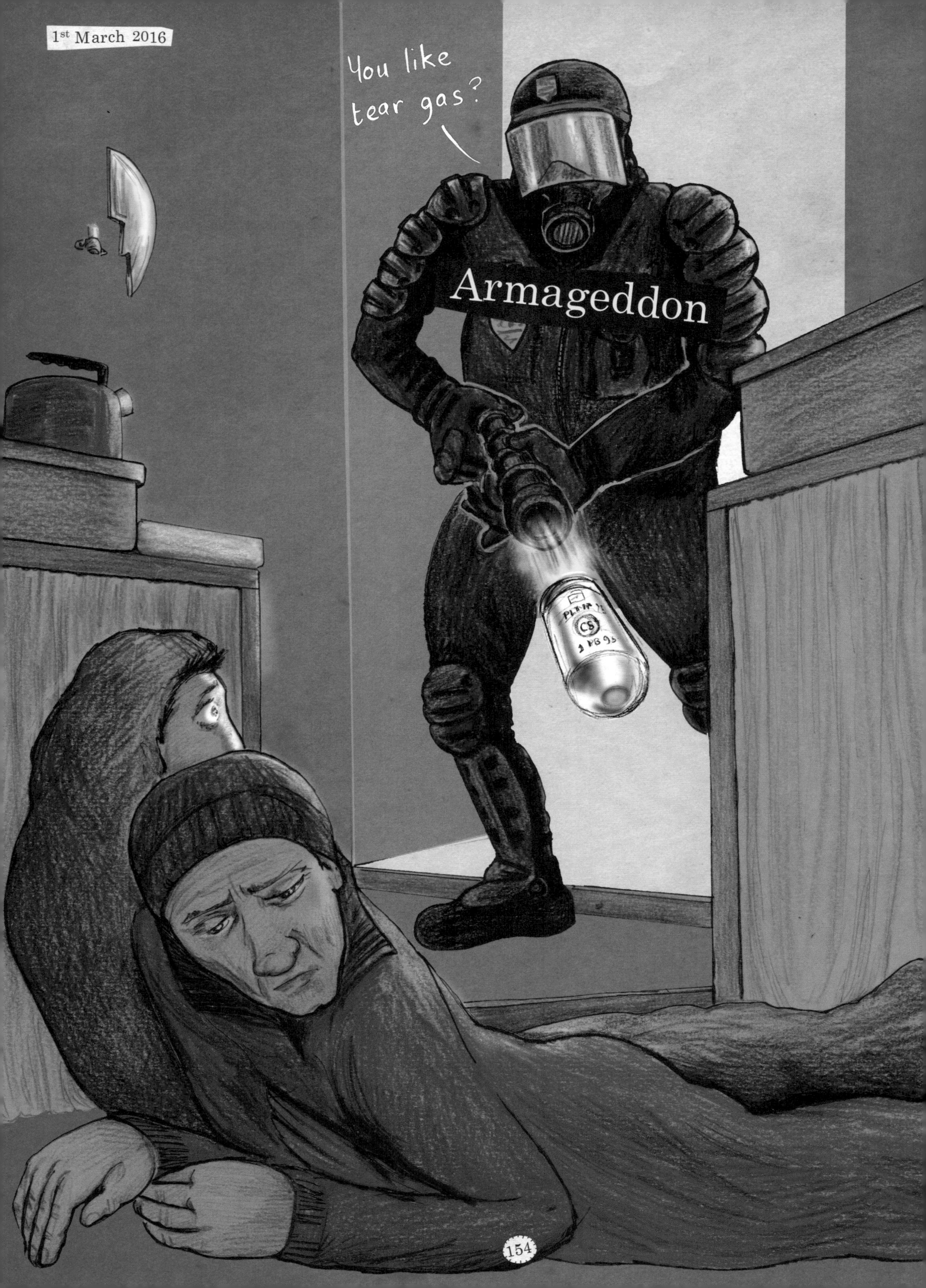
1st March 2016
You like tear gas?
Armageddon
CS

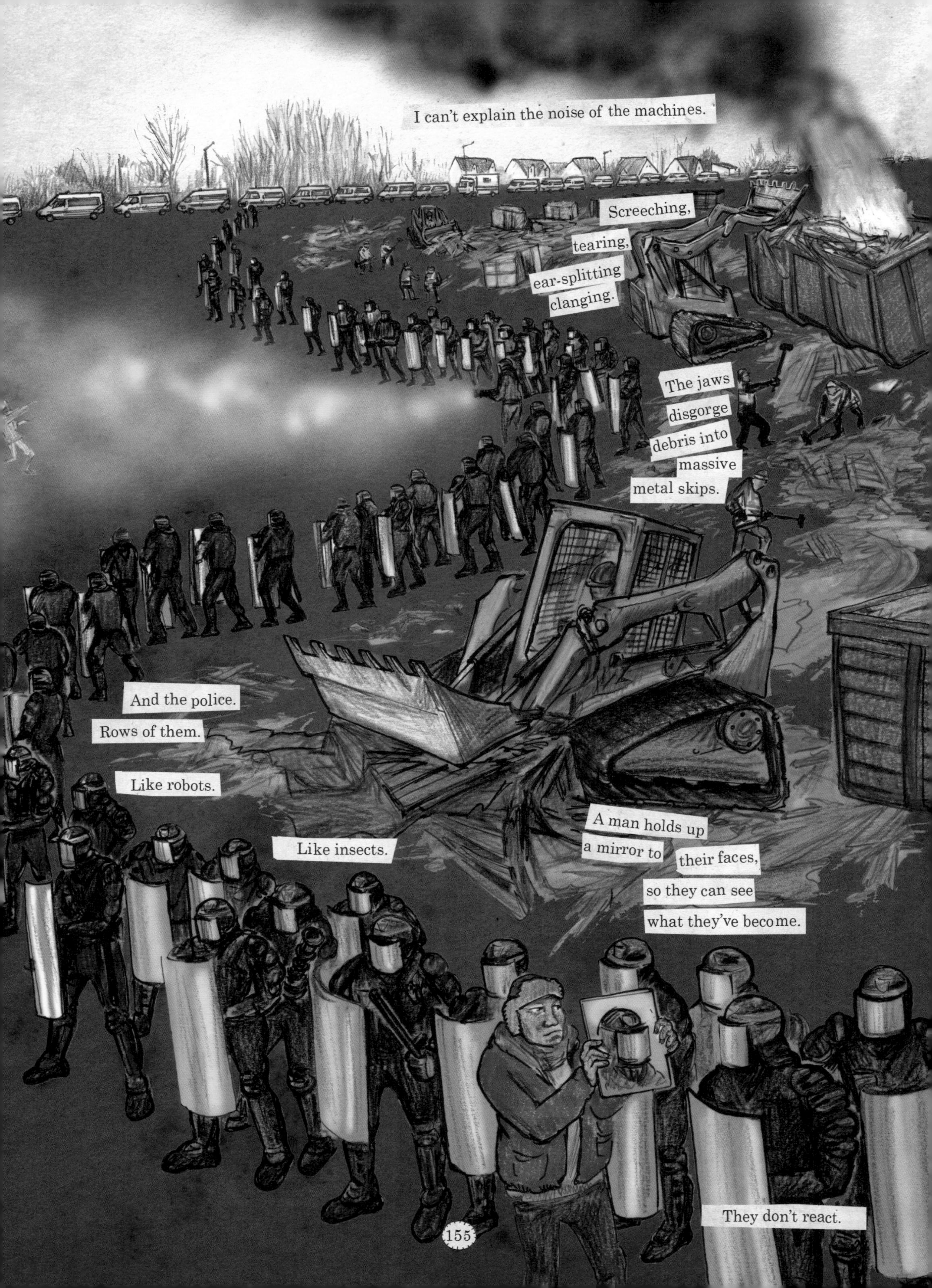
I can't explain the noise of the machines.
Screeching,
tearing,
ear-splitting
clanging.
The jaws
disgorge
debris into
massive
metal skips.
And the police.
Rows of them.
Like robots.
Like insects.
A man holds up
a mirror to
their faces,
so they can see
what they've become.
They don't react.

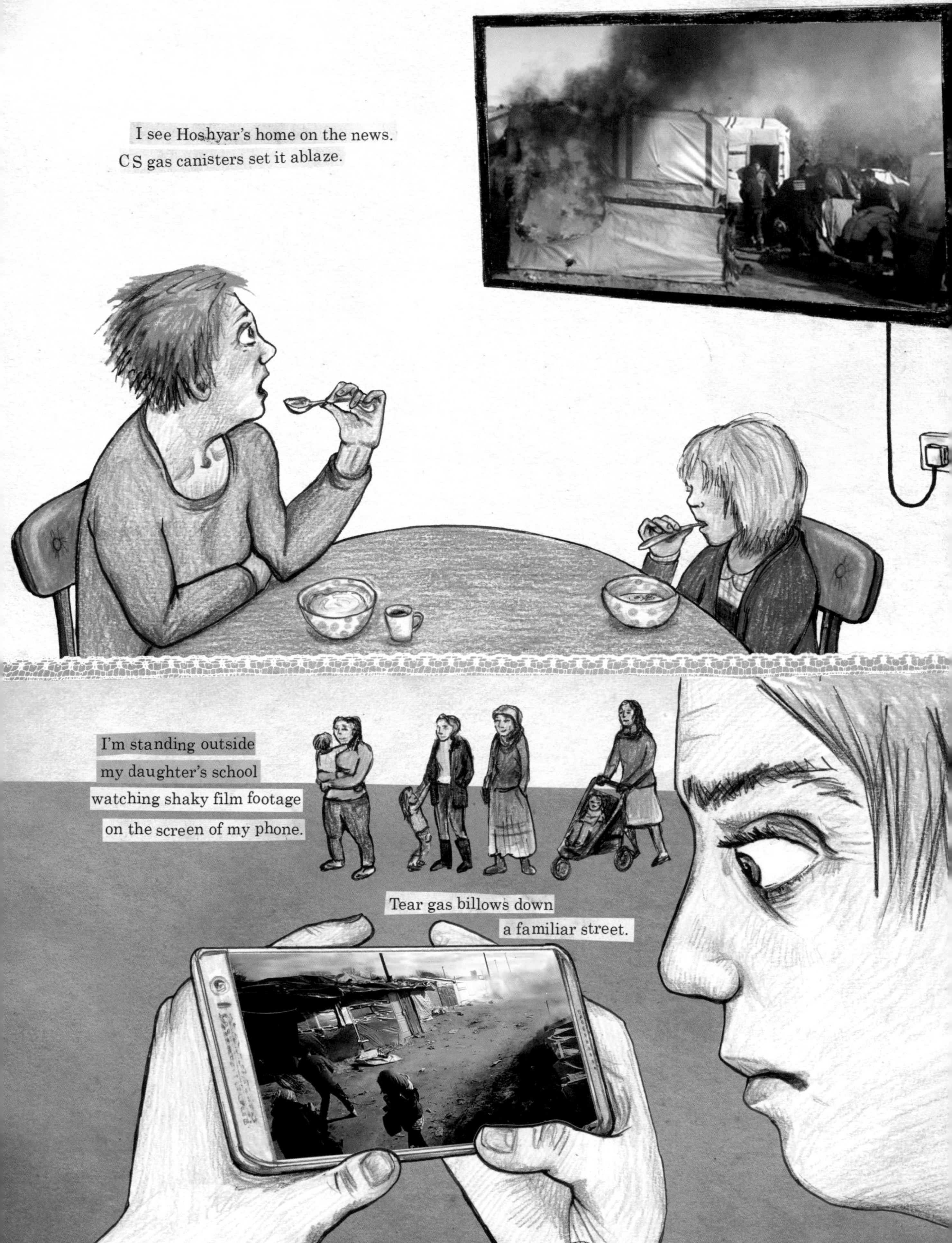
I see Hoshyar's home on the news.
CS gas canisters set it ablaze.
I'm standing outside
my daughter's school
watching shaky film footage
on the screen of my phone.
Tear gas billows down
a familiar street.

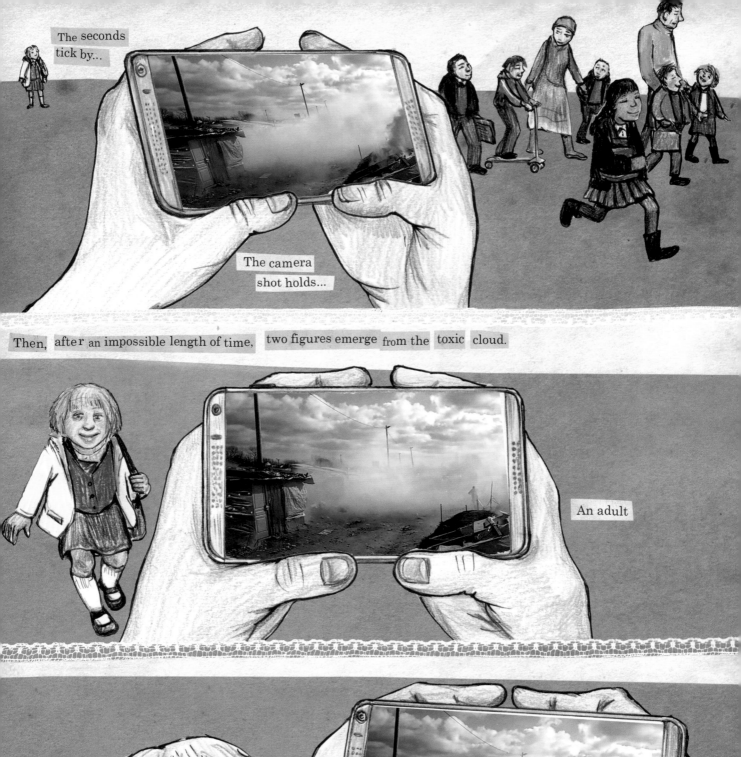

The seconds tick by...

The camera shot holds...

Then, after an impossible length of time, two figures emerge from the toxic cloud.

An adult

and a child.

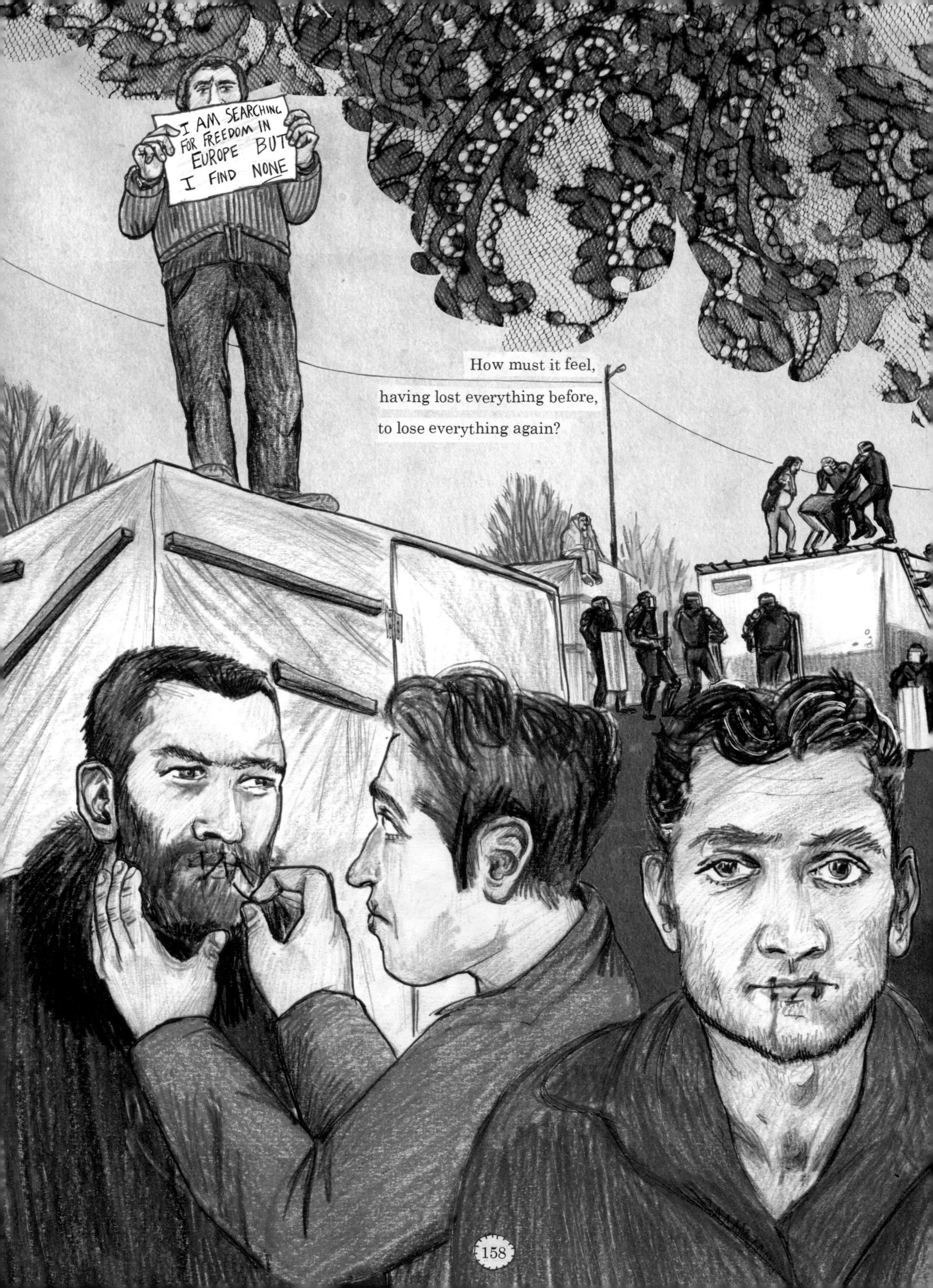
I AM SEARCHING FOR FREEDOM IN EUROPE BUT I FIND NONE
How must it feel,
having lost everything before,
to lose everything again?

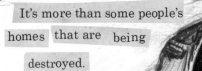

You might spiral past being able to feel.

It's more than some people's homes that are being destroyed.

It's their minds.

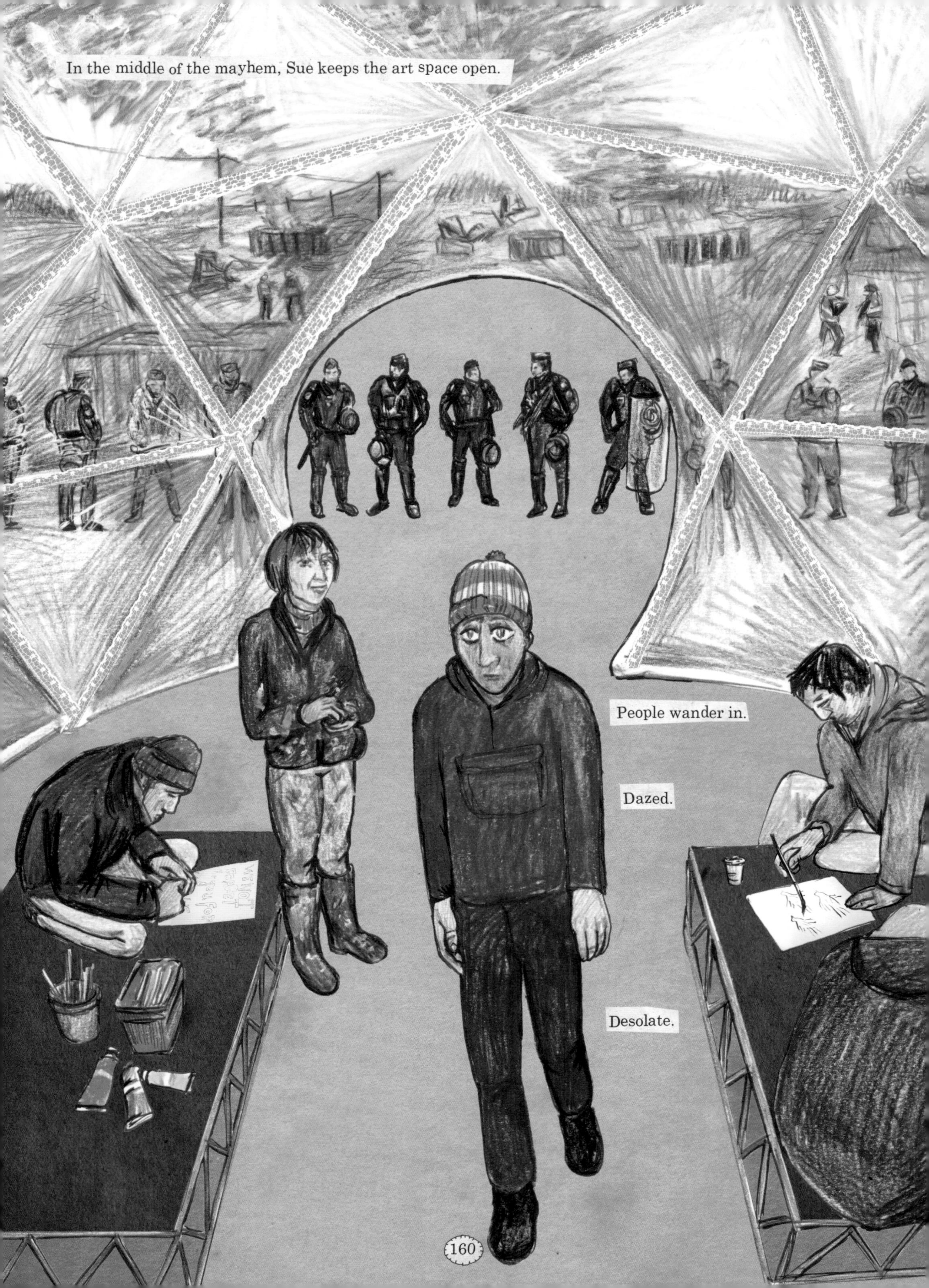
In the middle of the mayhem, Sue keeps the art space open.
People wander in.
Dazed.
Desolate.

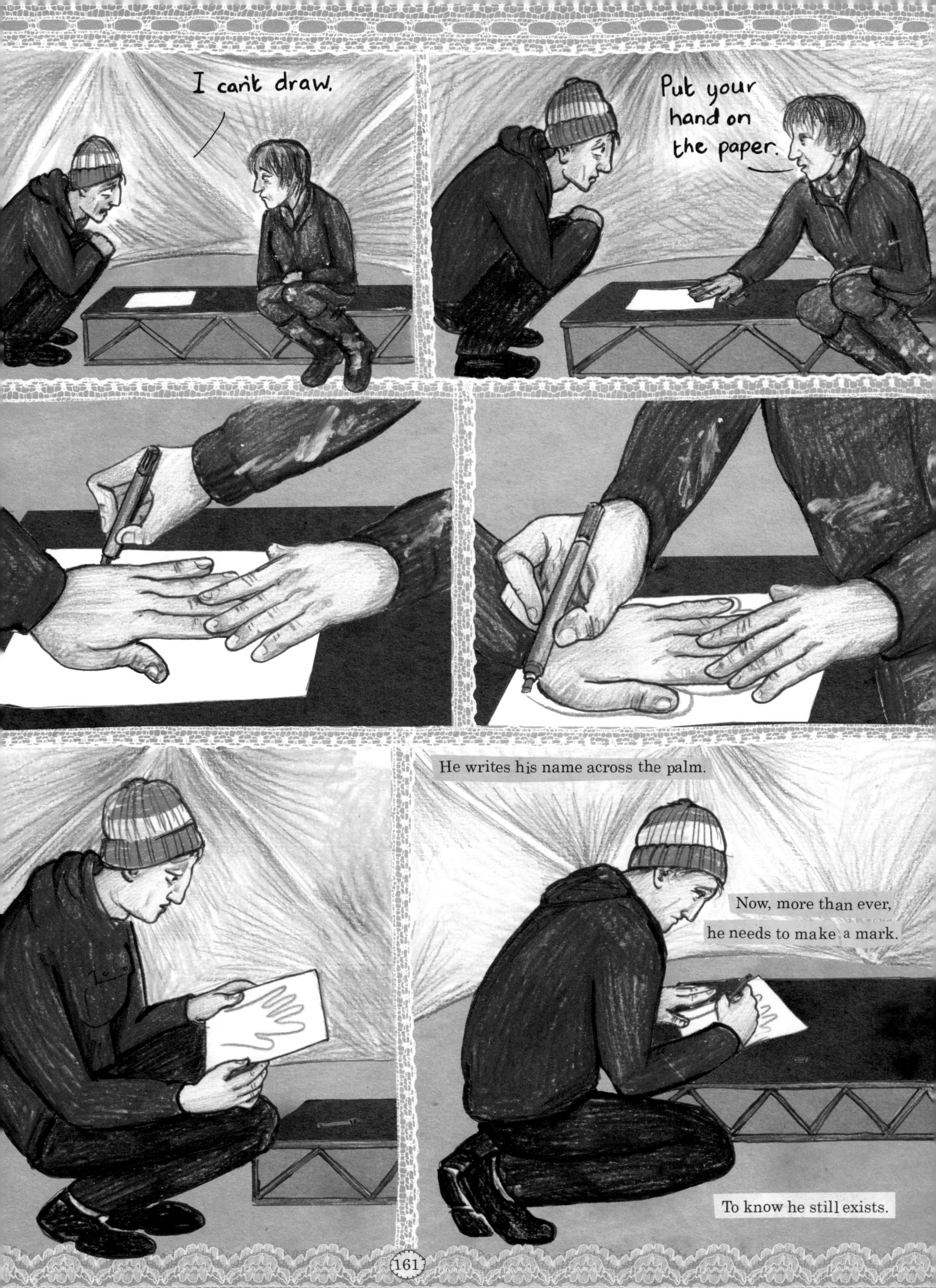

I can't draw.
Put your hand on the paper.
He writes his name across the palm.
Now, more than ever,
he needs to make a mark.
To know he still exists.

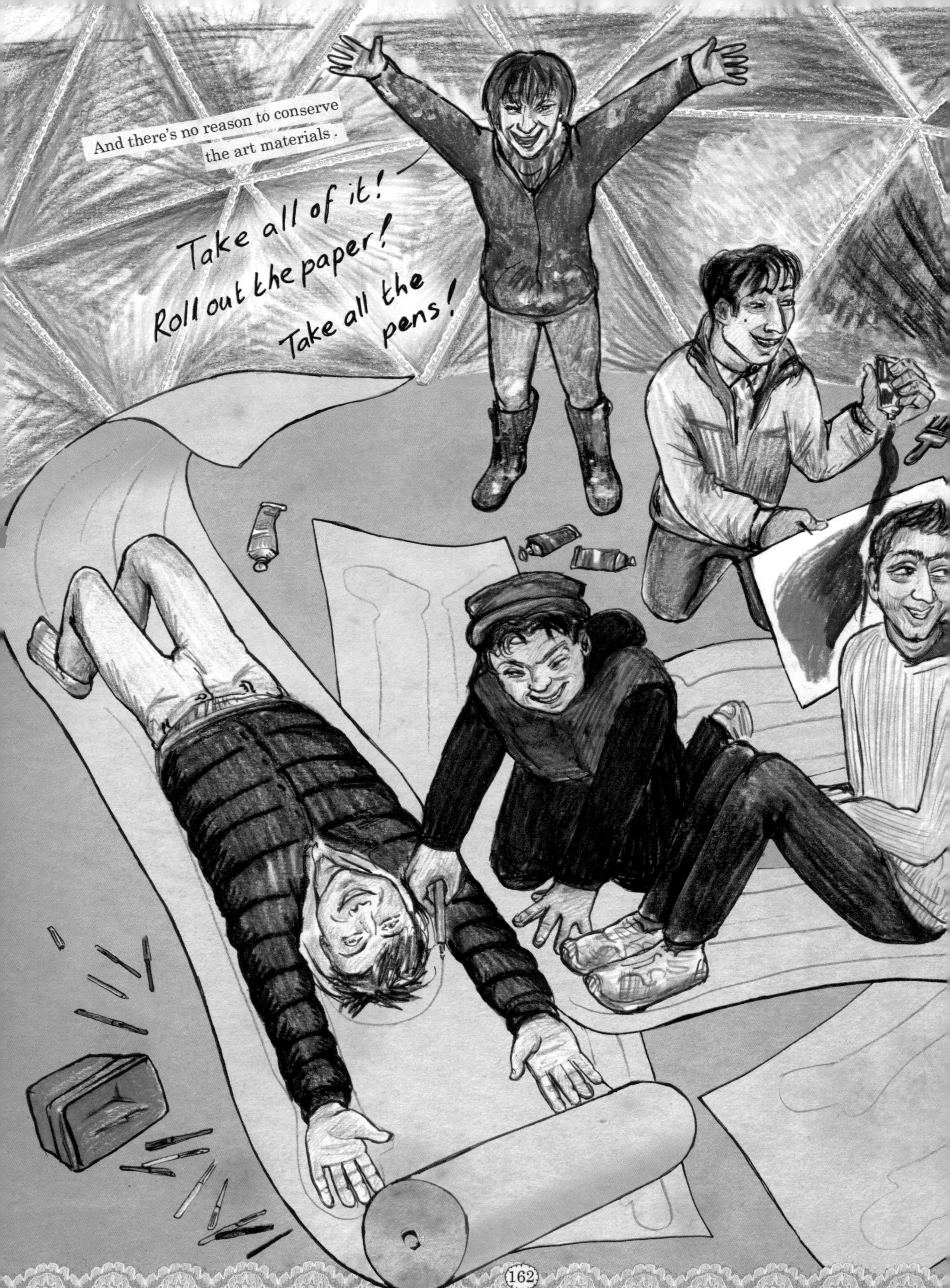
And there's no reason to conserve the art materials.
Take all of it!
Roll out the paper!
Take all the pens!

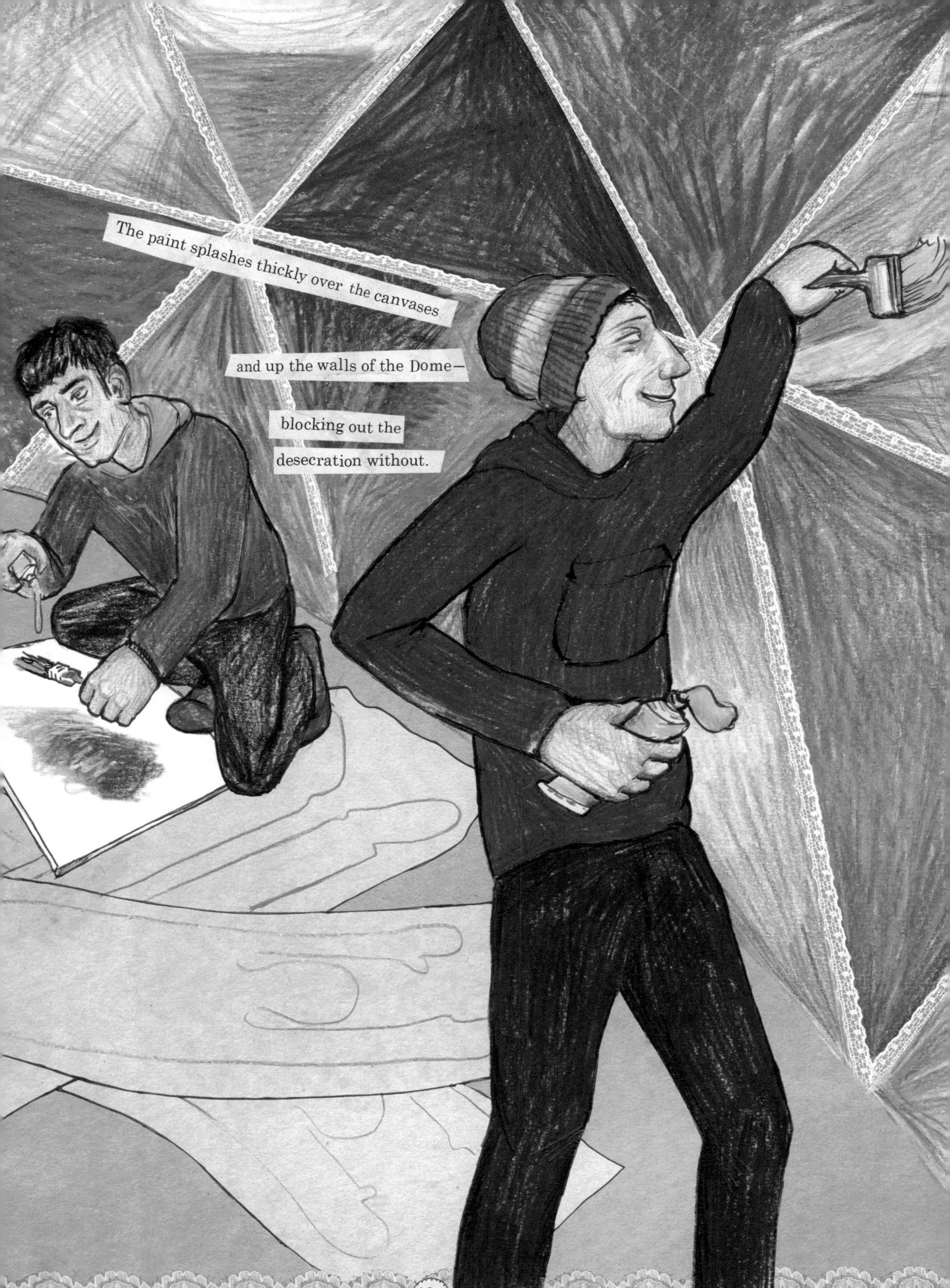
The paint splashes thickly over the canvases
and up the walls of the Dome—
blocking out the
desecration without.

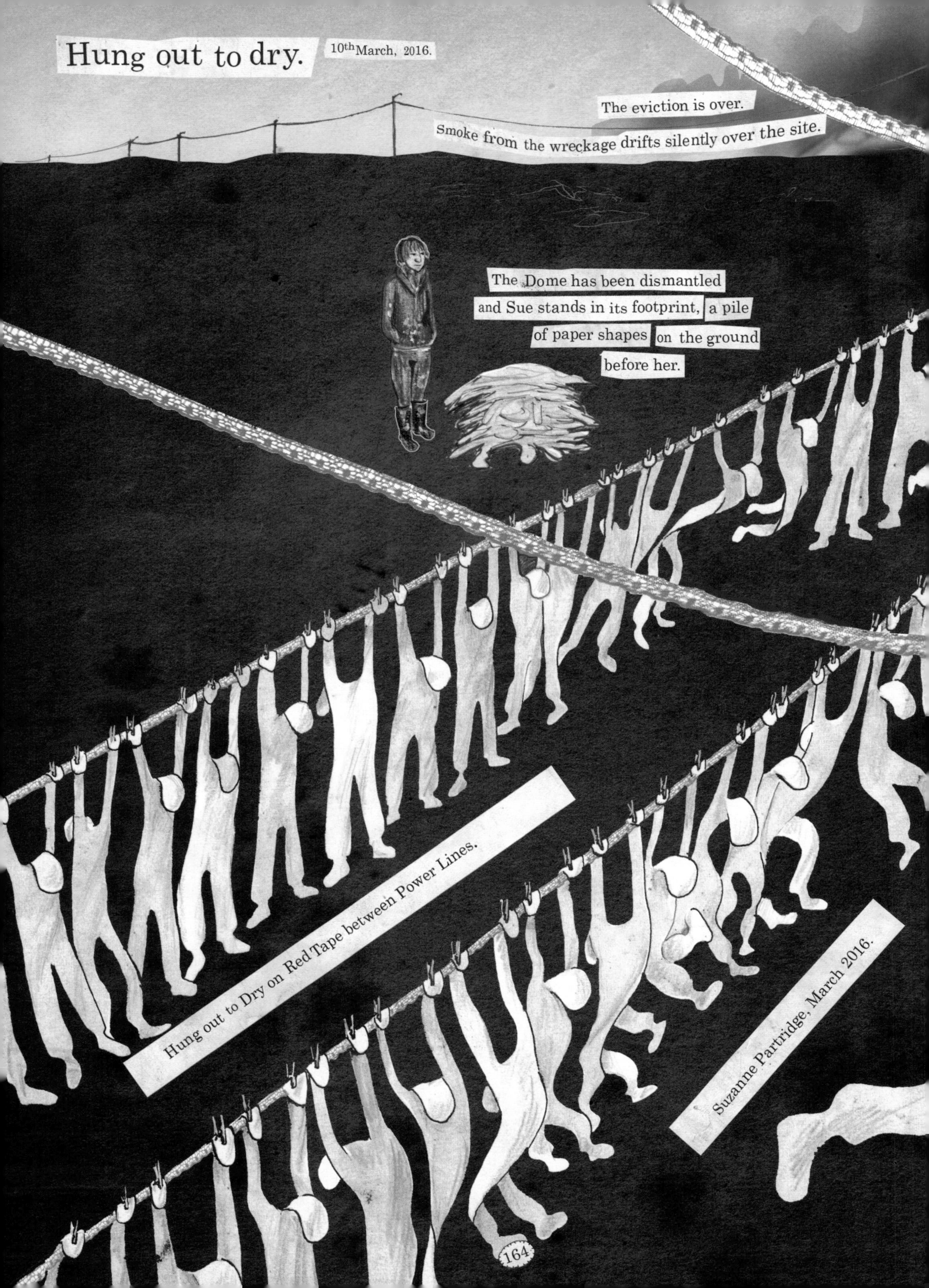
Hung out to dry.
10th March, 2016.
The eviction is over.
Smoke from the wreckage drifts silently over the site.
The Dome has been dismantled
and Sue stands in its footprint, a pile
of paper shapes on the ground
before her.
Hung out to Dry on Red Tape between Power Lines.
Suzanne Partridge, March 2016.

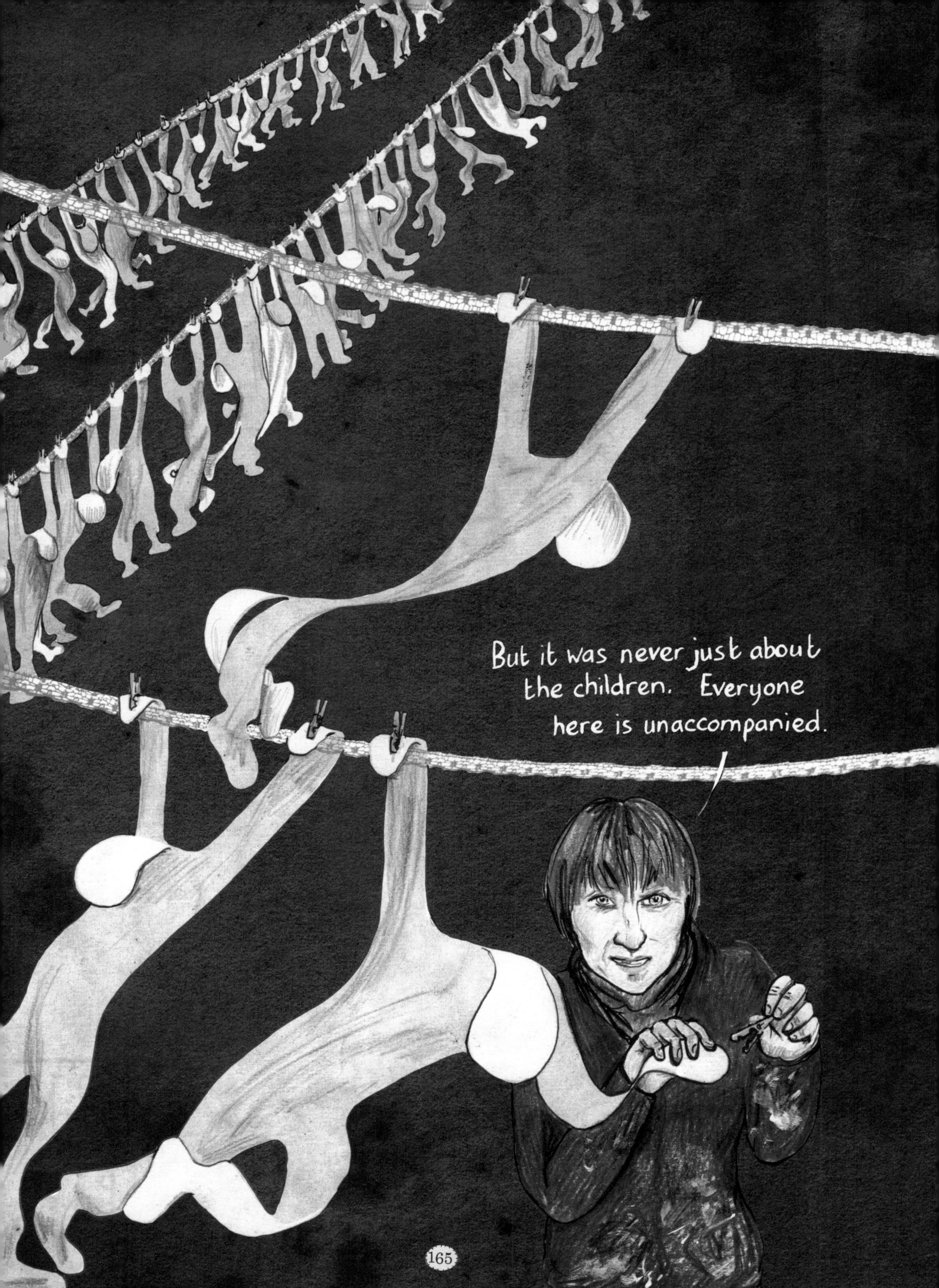
But it was never just about the children. Everyone here is unaccompanied.

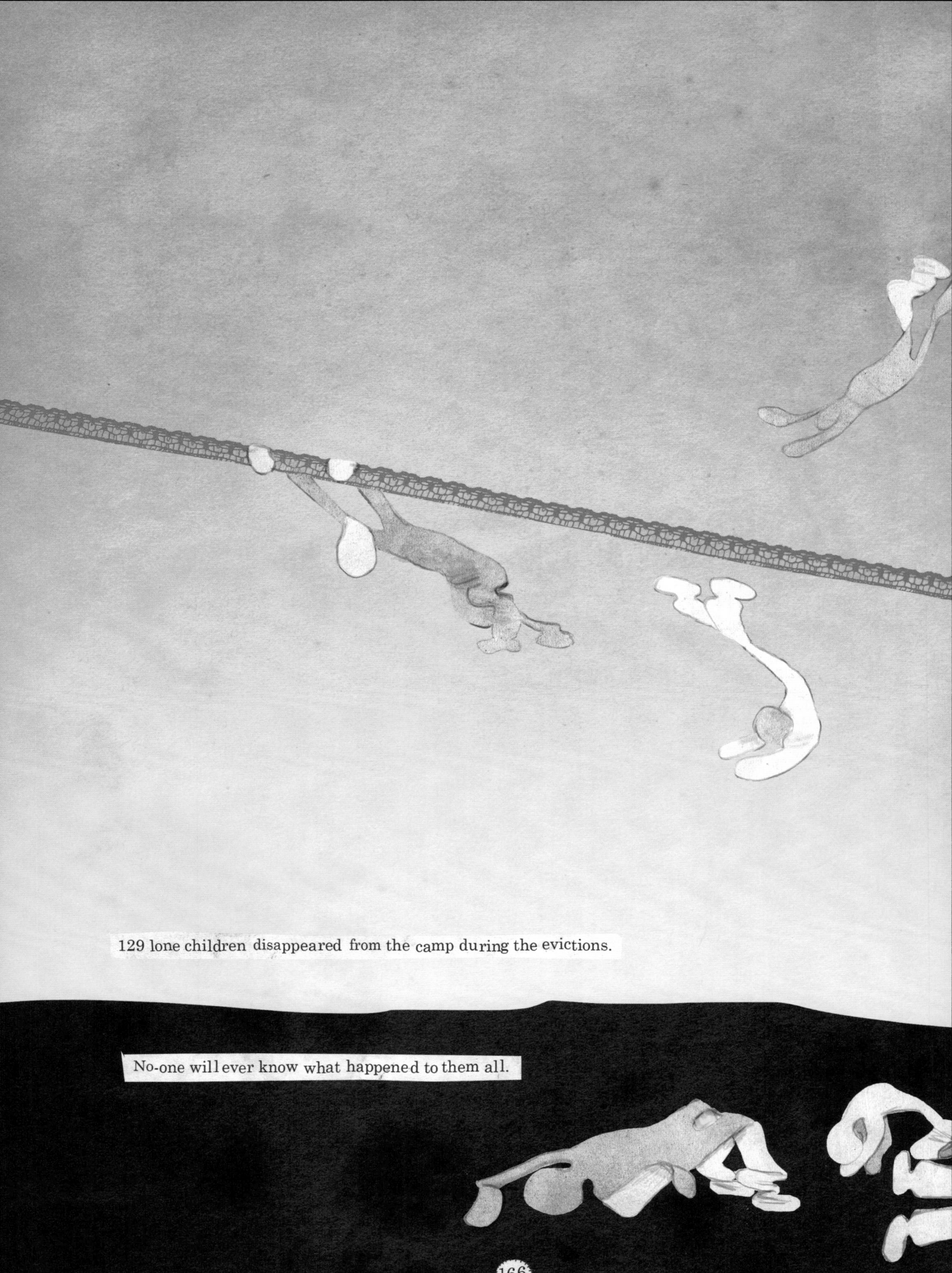
129 lone children disappeared from the camp during the evictions.
No-one will ever know what happened to them all.

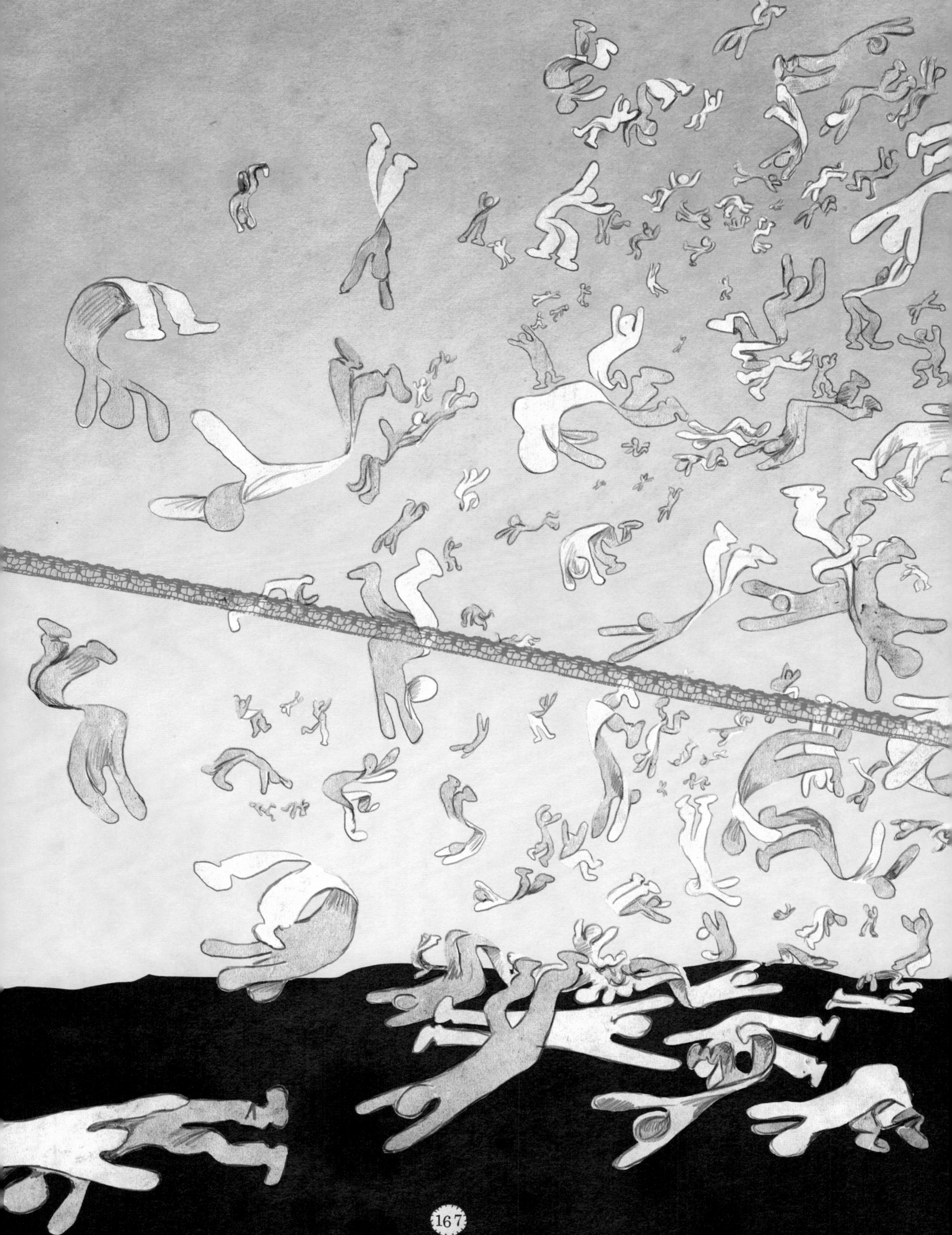

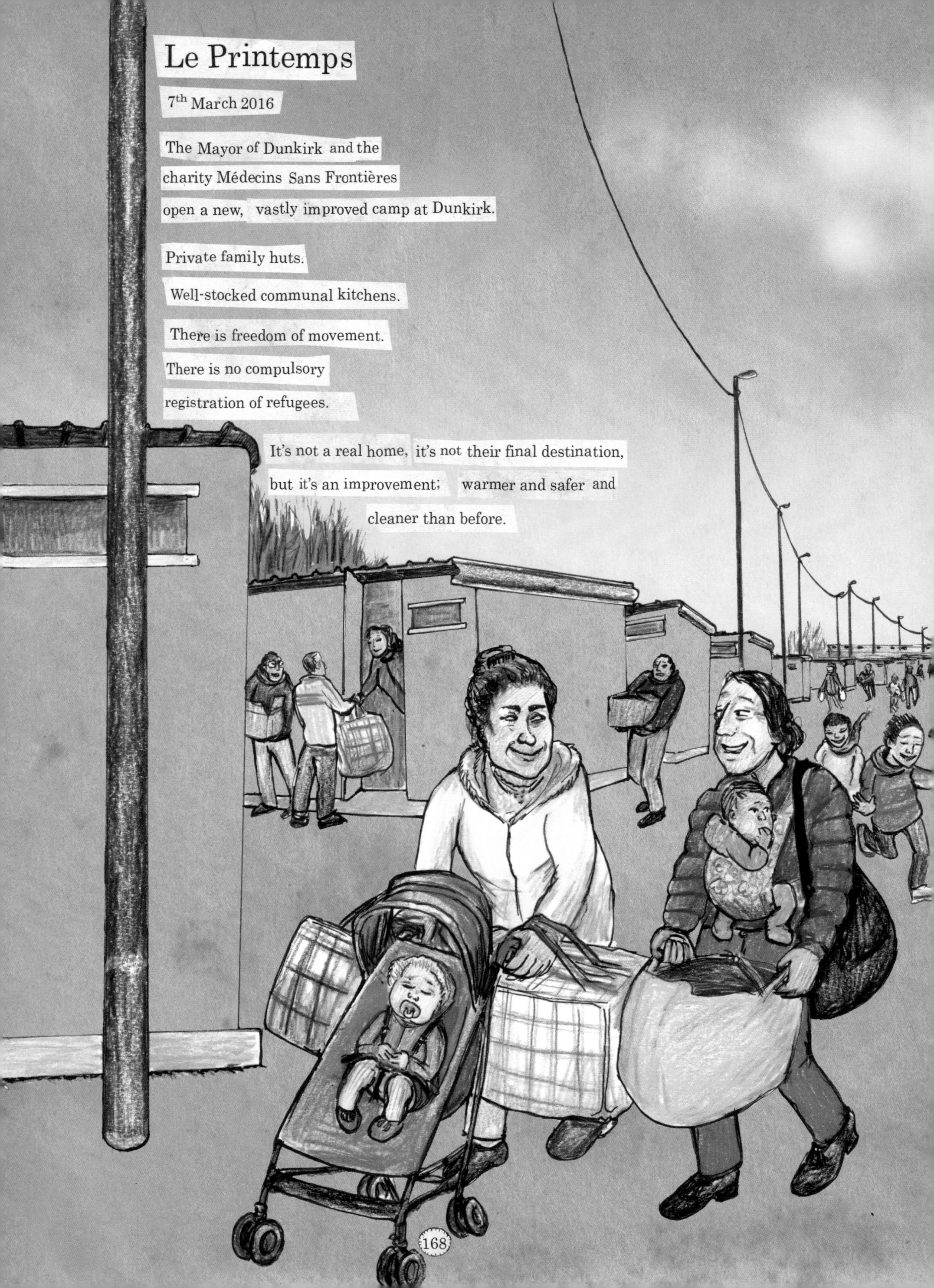
Le Printemps
7th March 2016
The Mayor of Dunkirk and the
charity Médecins Sans Frontières
open a new, vastly improved camp at Dunkirk.
Private family huts.
Well-stocked communal kitchens.
There is freedom of movement.
There is no compulsory
registration of refugees.
It's not a real home, it's not their final destination,
but it's an improvement; warmer and safer and
cleaner than before.

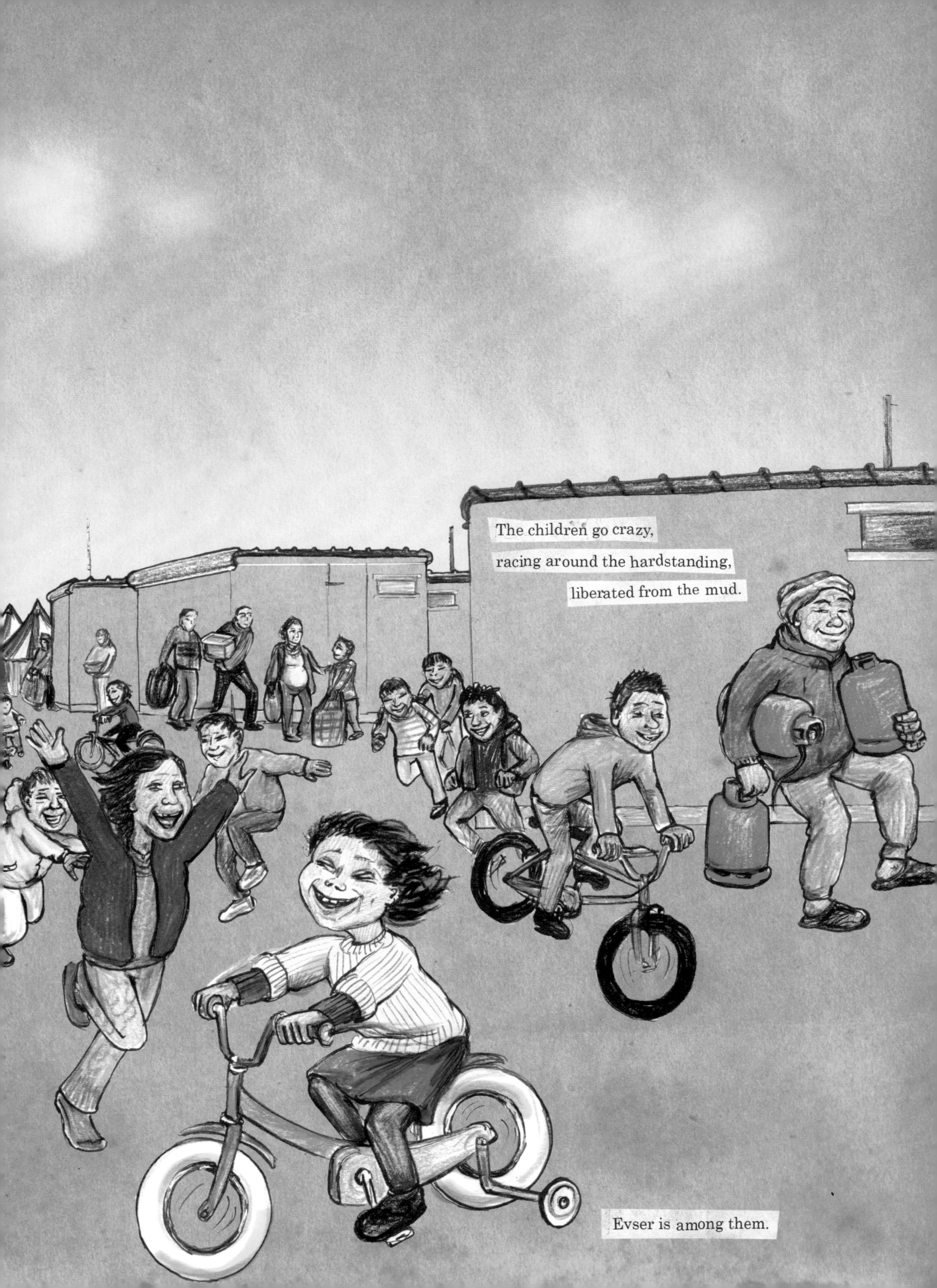
The children go crazy,
racing around the hardstanding,
liberated from the mud.
Evser is among them.

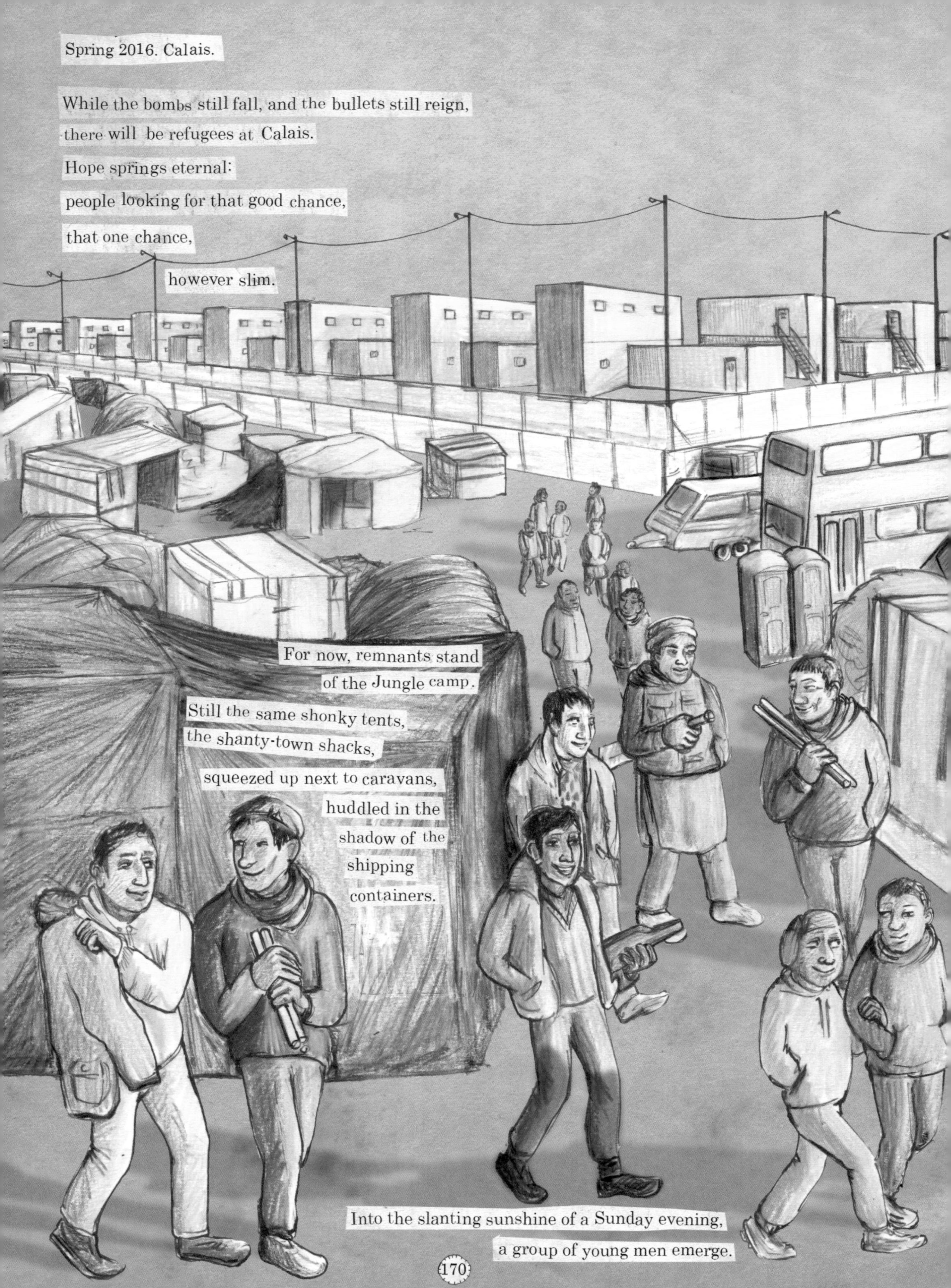
Spring 2016. Calais.
While the bombs still fall, and the bullets still reign,
there will be refugees at Calais.
Hope springs eternal:
people looking for that good chance,
that one chance,
however slim.
For now, remnants stand
of the Jungle camp.
Still the same shonky tents,
the shanty-town shacks,
squeezed up next to caravans,
huddled in the
shadow of the
shipping
containers.
Into the slanting sunshine of a Sunday evening,
a group of young men emerge.

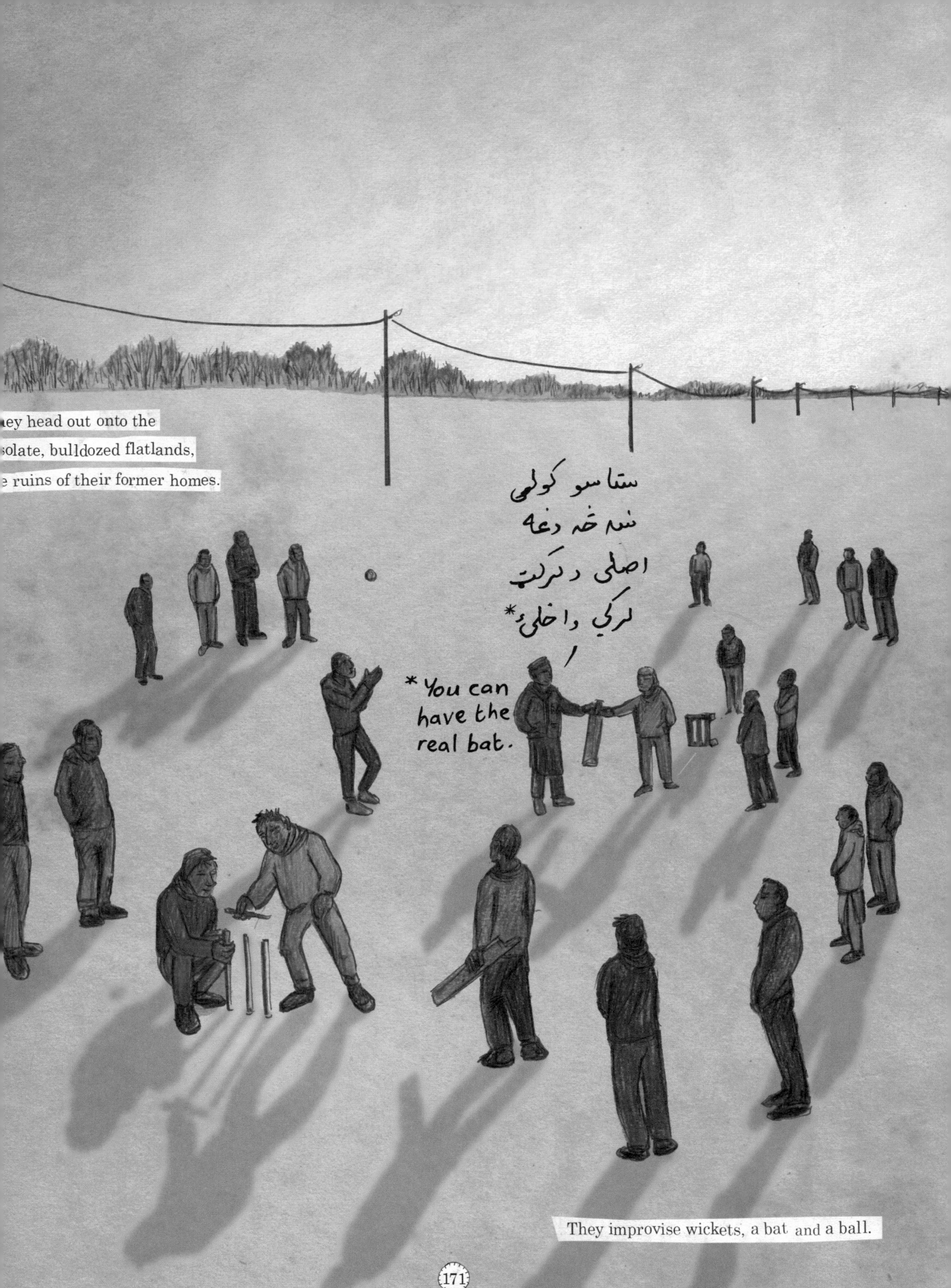
ey head out onto the
solate, bulldozed flatlands,
e ruins of their former homes.
ستاسو کولی
شئ دغه
اصلي د کرکټ
لرګي واخلئ*
* You can have the real bat.
They improvise wickets, a bat and a ball.

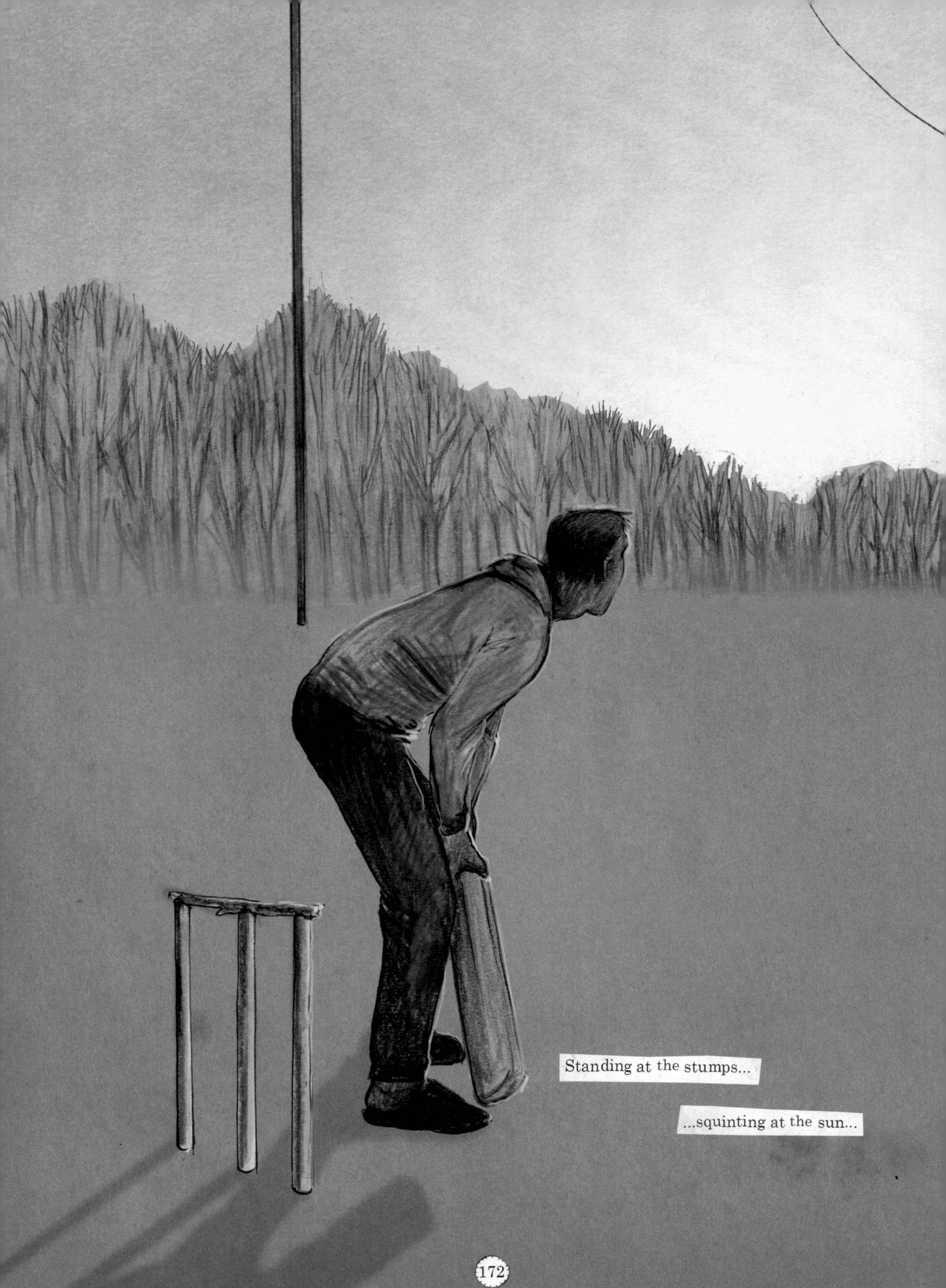
Standing at the stumps...
...squinting at the sun...

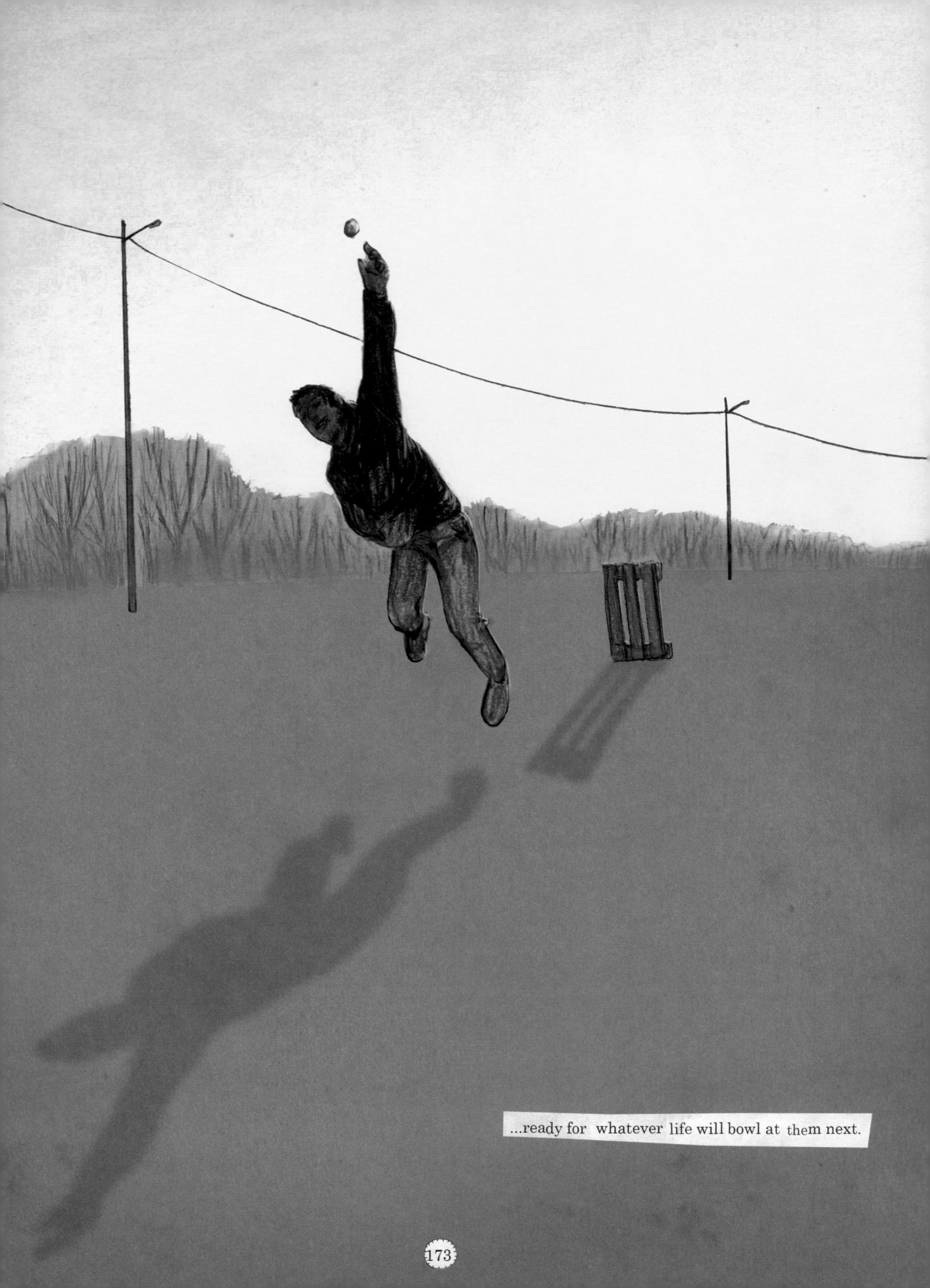
...ready for whatever life will bowl at them next.

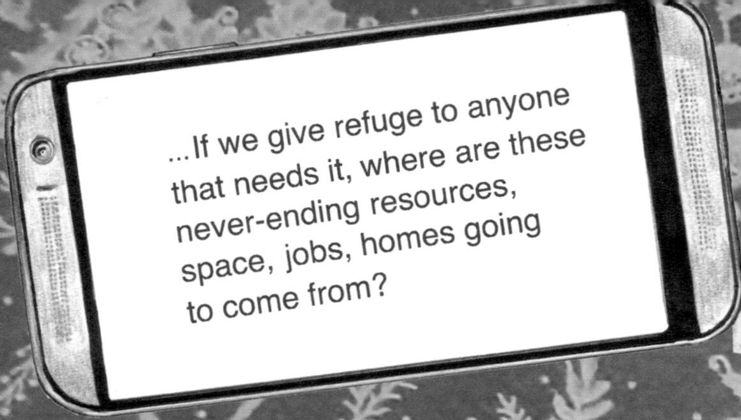
...If we give refuge to anyone that needs it, where are these never-ending resources, space, jobs, homes going to come from?

Hope

Immigrants didn't take your job. Immigrants create jobs. Immigration leads to economic growth. Immigrants are disproportionately young, motivated, and hard-working, and they are statistically less likely to claim state benefits than the native population. The UK population is ageing. We need immigrants in our country.

"The Fiscal Effects of Immigration to the UK", Dunstan and Frattini, November 2013,

Germany is accepting hundreds of thousands of refugees. This isn't a charitable act – it's happening because the German government can see it makes economic sense.

Of course, it makes no economic sense to trap refugees in poverty, to house them in the most deprived areas of the UK and prevent them from working, while subjecting them to a protracted, traumatic, bureaucratic asylum application process. That's not an economic decision, it's a political one.

Immigration is happening.

We can't prevent people from leaving their homelands if it's the only way to save their lives.

To prevent cheap immigrant labour from undermining British people's wages and working conditions, we need to legalise "illegal" immigrants, strengthen union representation and properly enforce a living wage for all.

When people move from where they cannot work productively to where they can, the whole world benefits. Mathematical modelling shows that removing all national barriers to migration would *double* global GDP. There isn't anything humans could do that would benefit the economy more.

"The New Economic Case for Migration Restrictions," Clemens and Pritchard

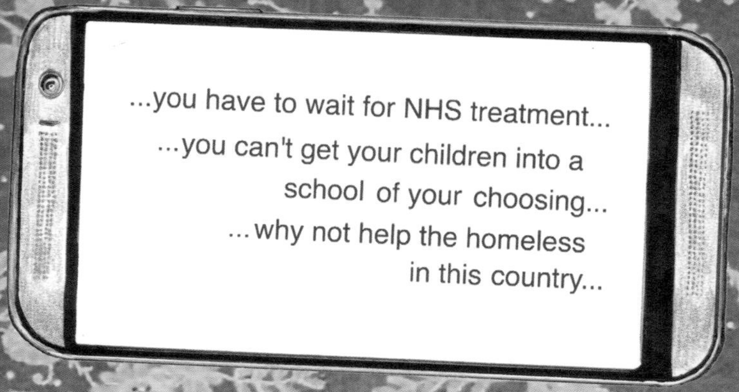
...you have to wait for NHS treatment...
...you can't get your children into a
school of your choosing...
...why not help the homeless
in this country...

Austerity is not a necessity. It's a political decision. This wholesale assault on public services is being conducted in the name of transferring wealth from the poor to the rich.

Inequality undermines our economy, weakens the fabric of our democracy and fuels the rise of the far right. Somehow it's so much easier to blame the poorest people in our society for our hardships than the richest.

Austerity doesn't prevent our government from directly subsidising the British arms industry.

We are the second-largest exporter of weapons in the world.

"Britain is now the second-biggest arms dealer in the world." Jon Stone, 5th September 2016, independent.co.uk.

The bombing raids we conduct over Iraq and Syria cost an estimated £1million each.

Money can be found to fund the causes of the refugee crisis, but not, it seems, to alleviate it.

"How much will airstrikes on IS cost taxpayer?" news.sky.com, accessed 24th September 2016.

"Inevitably in this century we will have open borders. We are seeing it in Europe already. The movement of peoples across the globe will mean that borders are... going to become irrelevant."

John McDonnell, Shadow Chancellor of the Exchequer,

Sunday, 31st January 2016.

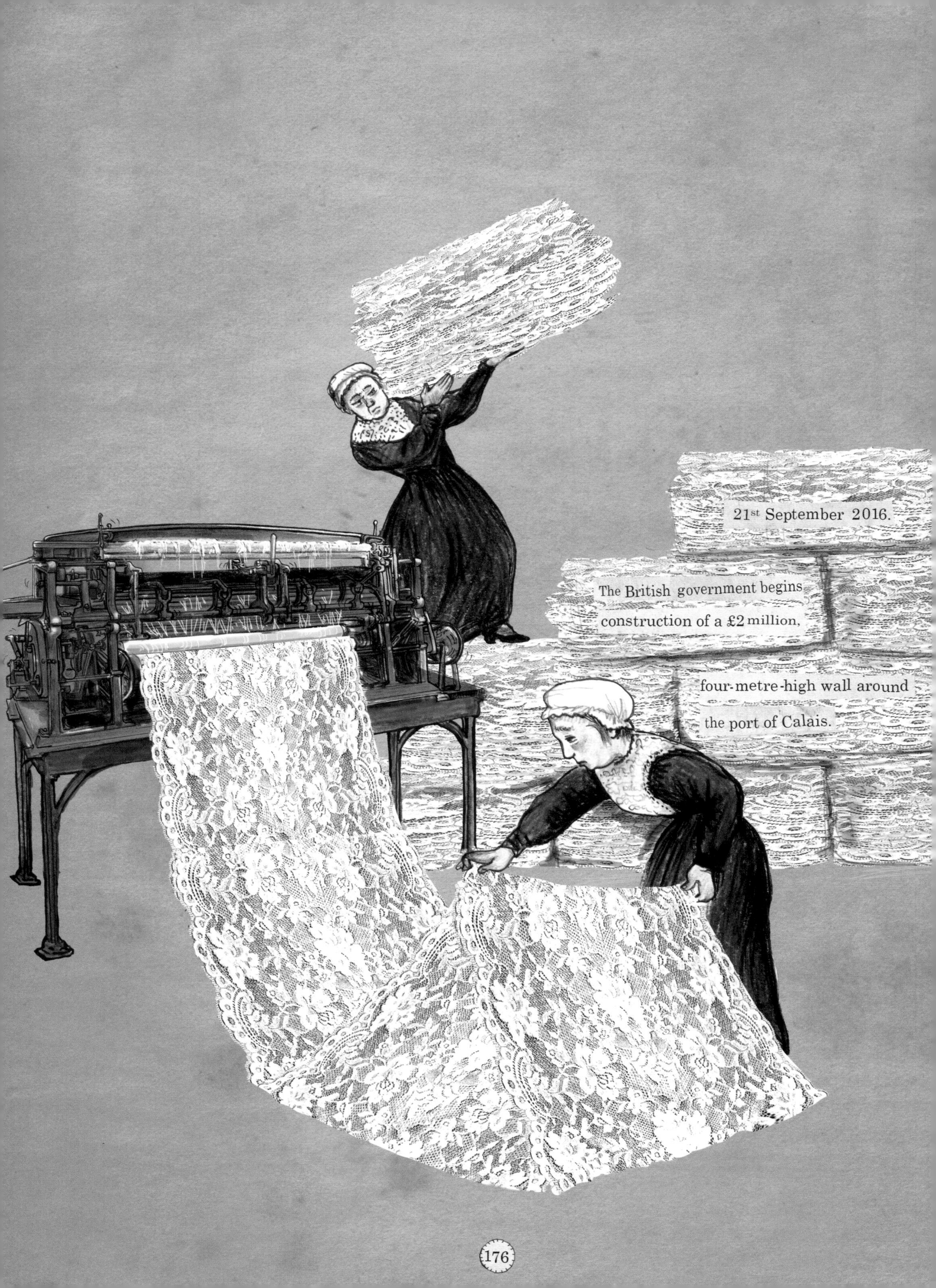
21st September 2016.
The British government begins construction of a £2 million,
four-metre-high wall around the port of Calais.

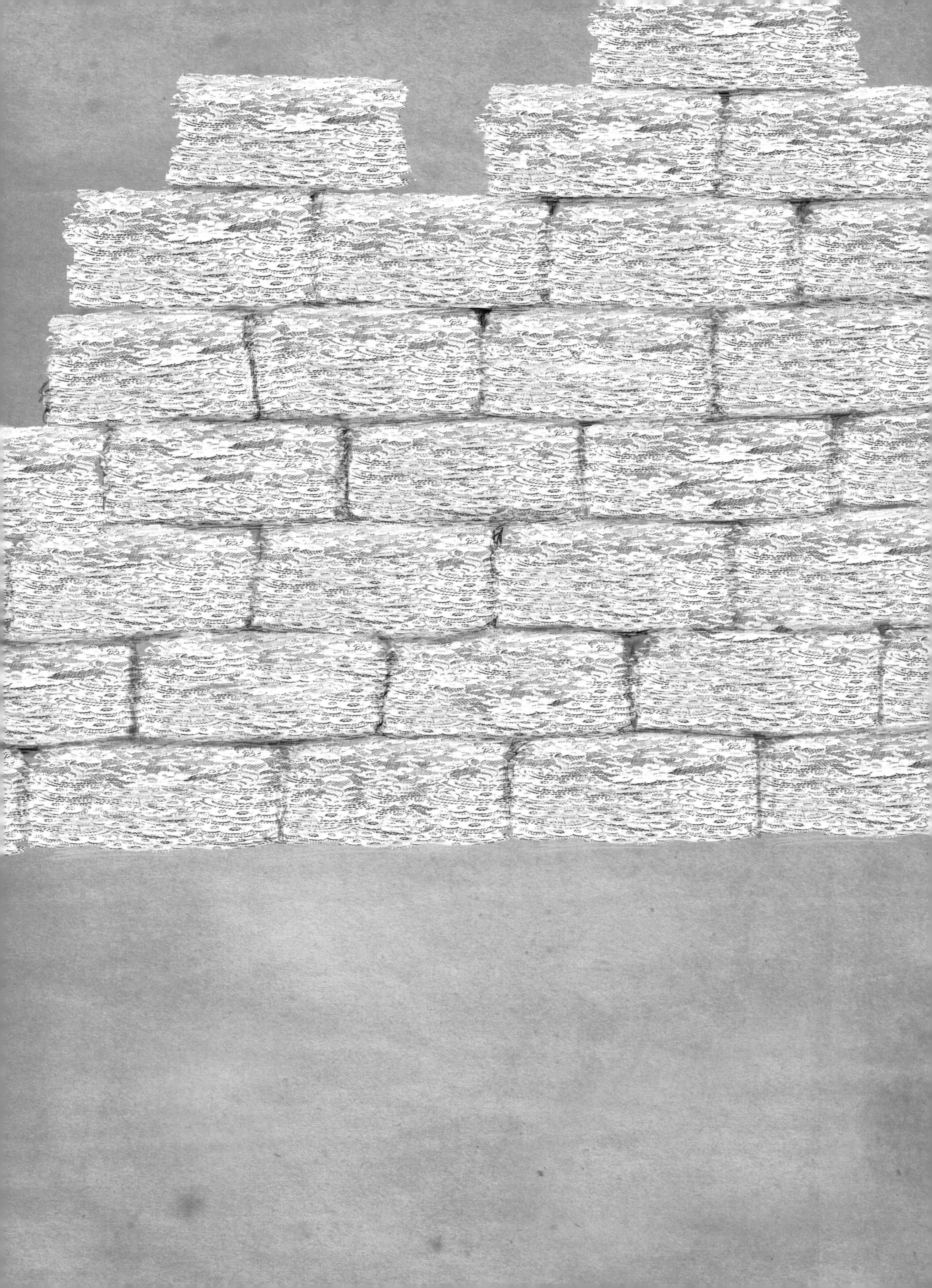